ACEH

The **Institute of Southeast Asian Studies (ISEAS)** was established as an autonomous organization in 1968. It is a regional centre dedicated to the study of socio-political, security and economic trends and developments in Southeast Asia and its wider geostrategic and economic environment. The Institute's research programmes are the Regional Economic Studies (RES, including ASEAN and APEC), Regional Strategic and Political Studies (RSPS), and Regional Social and Cultural Studies (RSCS).

ISEAS Publishing, an established academic press, has issued more than 2,000 books and journals. It is the largest scholarly publisher of research about Southeast Asia from within the region. ISEAS Publishing works with many other academic and trade publishers and distributors to disseminate important research and analyses from and about Southeast Asia to the rest of the world.

ACEH

History, Politics and Culture

EDITED BY
ARNDT GRAF
SUSANNE SCHRÖTER
EDWIN WIERINGA

INSTITUTE OF SOUTHEAST ASIAN STUDIES
Singapore

First published in Singapore in 2010 by
ISEAS Publishing
Institute of Southeast Asian Studies
30 Heng Mui Keng Terrace
Pasir Panjang
Singapore 119614

E-mail: publish@iseas.edu.sg
Website: <http://bookshop.iseas.edu.sg>

ISEAS Library Cataloguing-in-Publication Data

Aceh : history, politics and culture / edited by Arndt Graf, Susanne Schröter and Edwin Wieringa.
1. Aceh (Indonesia)—History.
2. Aceh (Indonesia)—Politics and government.
3. Aceh (Indonesia)—Economic conditions.
4. Religion and culture—Indonesia—Aceh.
I. Graf, Arndt.
II. Schröter, Susanne.
III. Wieringa, Edwin.
DS646.15 A1A175 2010

ISBN 978-981-4279-12-3 (soft cover)
ISBN 978-981-4279-13-0 (PDF)

Cover Design: Image of "Kasab" designed and embroidered by Hamidah Mouna Pirous Noor Muhammad, mother of A.D. Pirous in 1941. Photo courtesy of A.D. Pirous.

Typeset by Superskill Graphics Pte Ltd
Printed in Singapore by Utopia Press Pte Ltd

CONTENTS

PREFACE

The tsunami that struck on 26 December 2004 has caused tremendous long-lasting suffering in the coastal areas of Aceh and its surroundings. The process of post-tsunami recovery and reconstruction in this hard-hit region will take considerable time and not be easy. The task of trying to reshape Aceh's future, in every sense, is so enormous that help is not only required from the local, provincial, and national authorities, and from ordinary Indonesian citizens, but also from the international community. Foreigners already arrived immediately after the disaster, and numerous organizations have established long-term aid and reconstruction programmes.

However, comprehensive background information on Acehnese history, politics and culture, which would benefit expatriate aid workers in their dealings with the Acehnese people, is still difficult to find. This book is an attempt at providing such helpful knowledge. It is written by specialists in Indonesian and Acehnese studies from a number of countries, together with Acehnese scholars.

The task of collating this knowledge had its own difficulties. In certain areas of knowledge, publications are extremely rare and often even date back to the colonial era. Furthermore, it should be remembered that large parts of the region have not been accessible to foreign researchers for decades due to the civil war. Therefore, this book represents, in many aspects, a new, pioneering endeavour in Acehnese studies. Our hope is that, in the future, the cooperation between Acehnese and foreign scholars can be much closer than in the past, in order to enhance the international production and dissemination of academic knowledge on Aceh.

A lingering legacy of a tragic past is the collective trauma in Aceh of being colonized and occupied by outside forces. In particular, the Dutch colonial period, which featured the long and particularly cruel Aceh War (1873–1913), has left deep scars in Acehnese historical memory. In the pre-colonial period, much of Aceh was important and wealthy, and well integrated into the international trade routes between the Indian Ocean and the China Sea. However, that "golden era", as it is commemorated today, was ended by force, cutting Aceh off from its previous international partners and networks. The Japanese Occupation from 1942 to 1945 and the decades of civil war after Indonesian Independence also constitute important factors in the construction of modern Acehnese identity.

Islamic tradition in Aceh, initially spreading along the trading routes of the Indian Ocean, is among the oldest in insular Southeast Asia. It was in this region that one of the first Muslim sultanates in the archipelago once flourished. Building on the important historical role of Islam, it seems that the various traumas that Aceh has suffered since the colonial era have intensified the central role of religion and religiosity in Acehnese culture even more.

Another important factor in defining contemporary Aceh is, of course, its political framework. Hopefully, the Helsinki Peace Accord of 2005 may have laid the foundation for the successful further development of Aceh. Provided that the new political situation will promote peace and stability, the economic recovery of Aceh could exceed all expectations. The erstwhile "problem province" of Indonesia might then develop into one of the most booming parts of the archipelago. After having experienced all this trauma and suffering, there is at least a very strong motivation to finally improve the situation in Aceh in all areas. In the inner-Acehnese discussions, education plays a central role in helping the next generation of Acehnese to achieve a brighter future. There seems to be a strong will to improve not only the primary and secondary levels of education, but also the universities and other higher institutions of learning. The editors of and contributors to this volume hope that this strong emphasis on education might be supported at least in part by the present volume. In this sense, the main target groups of this book are (1) foreign aid and reconstruction workers in Aceh, (2) Acehnese who would like to look into international scholarly approaches to Aceh, and (3) international students who are interested in a scholarly introduction into a variety of aspects of Acehnese history, politics and culture.

The editors deliberately have invited authors who represent different academic schools of thought, from Germany and Switzerland, the Netherlands, the United States, Australia, and Singapore. The resulting volume, hence, contains a collection of highly varied chapters, thereby reflecting the current great heterogeneity of international studies on Aceh and Indonesia. That "a thousand flowers may bloom" is the spirit in which this "bunch of flowers" (*bunga rampai*) is offered; the editors hope that the present miscellany will encourage further studies on this fascinating region to delve into the multifaceted realities of Aceh.

Arndt Graf, Susanne Schröter, and Edwin Wieringa

ACKNOWLEDGEMENTS

The production of this volume would not have been possible without the support of a number of colleagues and institutions. In particular, the editors would like to thank those who volunteered to translate articles from Indonesian and German into English, namely Mercedes Chavez (Aceh), Anna Gade (Oberlin College), Jane Lindemann (Hamburg), ShawnaKim Lowey-Ball (New York), and Amanda K. Rath (Cornell University). Susanne Rodemeier (Frankfurt) and Rosemary Robson (Leiden) helped to edit several chapters, while Saiful Machdi (The Aceh Institute/Cornell University) and Bethany J. Collier (Cornell University) spent a lot of energy on the glossary.

The editors would also like to thank the Southeast Asia Program (SEAP) of Cornell University for permitting us to reprint the article by Kenneth George, which originally appeared in a volume published by the SEAP. Similar thanks go to the institutions in Singapore who gave us their permission to reprint the contribution by Anthony Reid, originally published on the National University of Singapore website.

THE CONTRIBUTORS

Agussabti was born in Alue Lhok (Eastern Aceh) in 1968 and received his Sarjana-1 degree (equivalent to B.A.) at the Faculty of Agriculture, Department of Social-Economic Agriculture, University Syiah Kuala in 1991 where he was appointed as lecturer in 1993. In 1997 he graduated from a Magister (= Master) programme in Development Studies at the Institute of Agriculture Bogor (IPB) where in 2002 he completed a Ph.D. programme in the same field. In addition to his activities as a lecturer, he also frequently conducts research with a number of off-campus institutions. One of these research products is "Leuser in the perception of the local population" that was published by the Unit Manajemen Leuser, Medan. In 2005, due to his research contribution to the state-funded project "A study of Seuneubok as system of regional management on the basis of Adat" he was honoured as the best Indonesian researcher in the social and economic fields. Currently, he is also working with DAI/USAID on a project on "Community Based Recovery-Initiative".

Hasan Basri studied at the Muhammadiyah University in Surabaya, East Java (graduating in 1987), at the State Islamic Institute IAIN Ar-Raniry Nanggroe Aceh Darussalam (B.A. degree in 1990), and in a Master programme at the University of Leiden (graduated in 1997). He visited several European countries (the Netherlands, Belgium, France, Germany and Switzerland) as well as Saudi Arabia. Currently, he is Professor of Qur'anic Exegesis and Islamic Thought, Faculty of Islamic Education, at the State Islamic Institute IAIN Ar-Raniry Nanggroe Aceh Darussalam, working at the same time on a Ph.D. dissertation at the State Islamic University (UIN) Jakarta and the State University Jakarta. His numerous publications on Qur'anic Exegesis include topics such as Islam and politics, mysticism (Sufism), Islamic approaches to science, and inter-religious studies.

Bethany J. Collier is Assistant Professor in the Department of Music at Bucknell University (Lewisburg, Pennsylvania, USA). She holds her Ph.D. in Musicology from Cornell University (2007), where she was awarded the Donald Grout Memorial Prize for her dissertation "The 'Chinese' in Contemporary Balinese Performing Arts: Stories, Objects, and Representations". In addition to her scholarly activities, she directs the Bucknell Gamelan Ensemble and is an active performing member of the New York City-based Gamelan Dharma Swara.

Kenneth M. George (Ph.D. Michigan, 1989) is Professor of Anthropology at the University of Wisconsin-Madison, and past editor of the *Journal of Asian Studies* (2005–08). Ken's early ethnographic work in South Sulawesi, Indonesia (1982–92) culminated in his first book, *Showing Signs of Violence: The Cultural Politics of a Twentieth Century Headhunting Ritual* (California 1996), which was awarded the 1998 Harry J. Benda Prize in Southeast Asian Studies. Since 1994, he has been collaborating with Indonesian painter A. D. Pirous and other artists in exploring the predicaments and possibilities for Islamic visual culture in national and transnational art publics, a project detailed in his most recent book, *Picturing Islam* (2010).

Arndt Graf (Ph.D. Hamburg, 1998; habilitation Hamburg, 2004) has been a Professor of Southeast Asian Studies at the Goethe-University Frankfurt, Germany, since October 2009. Previously, he served as Associate Professor (January 2007–July 2009) and Professor (August–September 2009) of Malay and Comparative Literature at the School of Humanities, Universiti Sains Malaysia, Penang (Malaysia) and as Assistant Professor (1999–2005) and Adjunct Professor (2004–06) of Southeast Asian Studies and Austronesian Languages and Cultures at the University of Hamburg. His teaching experience includes visiting lectureship at Cornell University, USA (1998–99), and visiting professorships at the State Islamic University Syarif Hidayatullah Jakarta, Indonesia (2004), and the Université de La Rochelle, France (2005–06). Arndt Graf's publications mostly cover aspects of rhetoric, media, and political communication in insular Southeast Asia.

Sher Banu A. L. Khan obtained her Ph.D. from Queen Mary, University of London and is now a Visiting Fellow at the Department of Malay Studies,

National University of Singapore. Her thesis is on the Sultanahs of Aceh in the second half of the seventeenth century. Her other research interests are female leadership in the Malay world, the world of Aceh in the seventeenth century and the general history of Southeast Asia in the pre-modern era. As a TANAP researcher she also focuses on VOC interaction and activities in Aceh and West Coast Sumatra during this period. Her other interests are research and practices in the pedagogy of history teaching at the secondary and higher education levels.

Damien Kingsbury is Director of the Masters program in International and Community Development at Deakin University, Victoria, Australia, and is author or editor of a number books on Indonesian politics, including *Violence in Between: Conflict and Security in Archipelagic Southeast Asia* (2005), *The Politics of Indonesia* (3rd ed., 2005), and *Power Politics and the Indonesian Military* (2003). In 2005 he was political adviser to the Free Aceh Movement in the Helsinki peace talks which ended twenty-eight years of conflict in Aceh.

Werner Kraus. After working as a civil engineer in Thailand and Indonesia he went back to university and did his doctorate in Southeast Asian Studies on "Islam in Nineteenth Century Minangkabau" at Heidelberg University (1983). In 1984 he was co-founder of the department of Southeast Asian Studies at University of Passau. He also worked at the Universities of Salzburg and Innsbruck. He is currently director of the private documentation Centre for Southeast Asian Art. His major research interests are Sufi Islam in Southeast Asia and Modern Art in Indonesia. He is writing a biography of the Javanese painter Raden Saleh.

Wolfgang Marschall is retired Full Professor of Cultural Anthropology (Berne University). He did field research on Nias in 1973–74 and several shorter visits to the island. His other areas of research include South Central Java, Bengkulu, Southeastern Sulawesi, and Central Flores.

Antje Missbach studied Southeast Asian Studies and European Ethnology at the Humboldt University in Berlin and wrote a Ph.D. thesis at the Australian National University in Canberra about "Long-distance politics in transition: Aceh's diaspora during and after the homeland conflict (1976–2009)".

Nazamuddin was born in Alue Raya (Western Aceh) in 1961. After his Sarjana-1 degree at the Faculty of Economics of the University Syiah Kuala in Banda Aceh, he completed a Master program at the School of Economics of the University of the Philippines (1987–89) and a Ph.D. programme at Colorado State University in America (1992–96). Apart from lecturing at the Faculty of Economics of the University Syiah Kuala since 1987, he has also been active in writing articles for academic journals as well as for the mass media, mostly concerning the economy of Aceh. Together with several colleagues, he co-founded the Center for Public Policy Studies for research on public policies. After the tsunami, he co-founded the Aceh Recovery Forum and the Aceh Institute.

Anthony Reid (Ph.D. Cambridge, 1965) was Founding Director of the Asia Research Institute at the National University of Singapore (2002–07), and before that taught at UCLA, the Australian National University (where he is now again based), and the University of Malaya. His books include *The Contest for North Sumatra: Atjeh, the Netherlands and Britain, 1858–1898* (1969); *The Indonesian National Revolution* (1974); *The Blood of the People: Revolution and the End of Traditional Rule in Northern Sumatra* (1979); *Southeast Asia in the Age of Commerce, 1450–1680.* (2 vols. 1988–93); and *Indonesian Frontier: Acehnese and Other Histories of Sumatra* (2004).

Manfred Rist was based in Singapore as the South East-Asia Correspondent for the Swiss daily *Neue Zürcher Zeitung* until July 2009. Before exploring tropical jungles and climbing semi-active volcanoes, he reported from crowded corridors about European Integration in Brussels where he was awarded the *Premio di Napoli* for journalism in 1999. He was the Chairman of the Swiss Business Association (Singapore) and the Vice-President of the Foreign Correspondents Association (FCA). Rist, a former consultant at Andersen Consulting, is a graduated economist from the University of Bern and holds a Master in Strategic Communication from Charles Sturt University (Australia).

Susanne Schröter was fomerly Professor for Southeast Asian Studies at the University of Passau, Germany, with a particular focus on Insular Southeast Asia. Since 2008 she has held the position of Professor for Anthropology of Colonial and Postcolonial Orders at the University of Frankfurt, Germany. She has published widely on indigenous modernities in Indonesia, gender, religion, globalization and local conflicts. She is head of a research group on the "Formation of Normative Orders in the Islamic World" at Frankfurt University, editor of the series "Southeast Asian Modernities" and board member of various academic organizations, among them the European Association for Southeast Asian Studies and the German Orient Institute.

Fritz Schulze (Ph.D. Cologne, 1990; Habilitation Frankfurt 2001) has been Adjunct Professor (*Privatdozent*) of Southeast Asian Studies at the University of Frankfurt since 2001. His previous positions include lectureships at the universities of Cologne, Jena, and Frankfurt. His main research areas are Islam in Southeast Asia (especially its intellectual history) and traditional Malay literature (esp. historiography).

Syamsuddin Mahmud was born in Lada (Pidie, Aceh) in 1935. After studying at the Faculty of Economics of the University of Indonesia in 1963, he continued his studies in Belgium where he obtained his Ph.D. in the field of monetary economics from the University of Ghent in 1975. In addition to his teaching obligations at the Faculty of Economics of the University Syiah (Ụnsyiah) Kuala Darussalam in Banda Aceh, he held the positions of Dean of that faculty (1977–81), Vice Rector for Academic Affairs of Unsyiah (1975–77), Head of the Regional Development Planning Institution for the Province and Special Region of Aceh (BAPPEDA, 1982–93), Governor of the Province and Special Region of Aceh (1993–2000), and member of the Special Advisory Council of President B.J. Habibie (1998–99).

Edwin Wieringa is Professor (Chair) of Indonesian Philology and Islamic Studies at the Department of Oriental Studies, University of Cologne. He is the author of numerous articles on Malay and Indonesian literatures. His most recent publications include "Acehnese", in *Encyclopedia of Arabic Language and Linguistics*, edited by Kees Versteegh (2006), pp. 5–12, and "Moral education through Islamic songs in twentieth-century Java", in *Religious perspectives in modern Muslim and Jewish literatures*, edited by Glenda Abramson and Hilary Kilpatrick (2006), pp. 90–111.

Patrick Ziegenhain is a senior research fellow ("Akademischer Rat") at the Department of Political Science at the University of Trier in Germany. He earned his Ph.D. from Albert Ludwigs University in Freiburg, Germany with a dissertation on the role of parliament in the Indonesian democratization process. His main research areas are systems of government, regime transitions, political parties and elections as well as political, social, and economic developments in Southeast Asia. As a freelance consultant, Dr Ziegenhain has worked for various German and international development agencies, mainly on good governance and decentralization in Southeast Asia.

PART I

History

1

THE SULTANAHS OF ACEH, 1641–99

Sher Banu A. L. Khan

INTRODUCTION

Aceh is perhaps best known as a staunchly Islamic kingdom in the north of the island of Sumatra and as a major trading centre for pepper. Pepper propelled Aceh's ascendancy in the sixteenth century and it became the main Muslim commercial centre, supplying pepper to the Mediterranean via the Red Sea, and rivalling the Portuguese (Reid 2005, p. 6).[1] The reign of Iskandar Muda (r. 1607–36) inaugurated a "golden age", when Aceh's influence expanded and reached as far south as Padang in Sumatra and Johor on the Malay Peninsula. During this period, in a little-known episode, four female monarchs in succession ruled this Muslim kingdom for over half a century from 1641 to 1699). Female rule seems a curious phenomenon in an Islamic state, yet these four queens were not only accepted by the majority of the *orangkaya* (aristocratic elite) and the *ulama* (religious leaders) but they were able to maintain Aceh's peace and prosperity in exceptionally challenging times. This was a time when indigenous polities suffered increasing interference and influence from Dutch and English companies. Most Malay and Muslim coastal polities in maritime Southeast Asia fell into European intruders' hands. Under its queens, Aceh was by far the most effective in maintaining its own independence and its own trade networks, and in engaging and counteracting the influence of the Europeans.

The four queens were Sultanah Tajul Alam Safiatuddin Syah (r. 1641–75), Sultanah Nur Alam Naqiatuddin Syah (r. 1675–78), Sultanah Inayat

Zakiatuddin Syah (r. 1678–88) and Sultanah Kamalat Zainatuddin Syah (r. 1688–99).

WOMEN'S POSITION IN ACEH

Queens are rare in the wider Islamic world,[2] but not in Muslim Southeast Asia. One of the features which distinguishes Southeast Asia as a region is the comparatively high position of women within its societies (Reid 1988, p. 146). Besides Aceh, Patani — a Malay Muslim polity in what is now southern Thailand — was also ruled by four women in succession, from 1584 to 1688. There were several more instances of female rulers in the region: in Sukadana between 1608 and 1622, in Jambi between 1630 and 1655, and in Solor from 1650 to 1670 (Cheah 1993, pp. 1–2). It is also not surprising, that Sultanah Safiatuddin was far from being the first queen in Sumatra. A pair of gravestones — one written in Old Javanese and one in Arabic — was found in the village of Minye Tujoh in Aceh, inscribed with the dates of death 781 and 791 AH (AD 1380 and 1390) respectively (Stutterheim 1936, pp. 276–77). According to Ibrahim Alfian (1994*a*, p. 2, the stones mark the grave of a Queen Nur Ilah, with the appellation "Queen of the Faith … who has rights on Kadah [Kedah] and Pase [Pasai]."[3] In what is now the district of North Aceh, another gravestone made of marble with exquisite Arabic calligraphy and Quranic verses was found. The Arabic calligraphy reads (in English) as "this is the grave of a brilliant holy woman, a Queen respected by all … Nahrasiyah … who died on 17 Zulhijah 823 (1428)" (Ibrahim Alfian 1994*b*, p. 16). These inscriptions indicate that female rulers were not just an innovation of the seventeenth century. By the late seventeenth century, it appears that women rulers were not at all exceptional in Acehnese politics. In fact, Dampier remarked that a queen rather than a king had ruled Aceh for so long that the English residents there were of the opinion that a queen had ruled Aceh since the beginning. From the antiquity of the present constitution, it was believed that the Queen of Sheba had been a queen of this country (Dampier 1931, p. 99)![4]

Europeans who visited royal courts in the archipelago during the sixteenth and seventeenth centuries report that palace women served as emissaries, advisors and guards. John Davis, who visited Aceh in 1599, claimed that Sultan Ala al-Din Riayat Shah al-Mukammil's (r. 1589–1604) "chiefest counsellers" were women (Markham 1880, p. 150). The women guards used "bowes, arrows, javelings and swords as their weapons." Al-Mukammil also had a woman *laksamana* (admiral) since "hee will trust no men" (Markham 1880, p. 150). Even the great Iskandar Muda (father of Sultanah Tajul Alam

Safiatuddin Syah) relied on female guards for his protection (Beaulieu 1764, p. 744).

POLITICAL ASPECTS

Having a tradition of strong women in positions of power aside, the question still remains as to why there was the decision to place *four* women consecutively on the throne at such a dangerous time? A variety of reasons and interpretations have arisen in response to this question. Reid argued that the reign of Iskandar Muda from 1607 to 1637 saw the height of royal absolutism in Aceh. Iskandar Muda exterminated the old powerful nobility and created new ones entirely dependent on him. A complex administrative and judicial hierarchy developed under his authority where even the slightest hint of disloyalty was punished with exemplary cruelty (Reid and Ito 1985, p. 12). After his death, the nobility no longer wanted to have to endure such a reign of terror again. Thus, female rule was one of the few devices available to a commercially oriented aristocracy to limit the despotic powers of kings and to make the state safe for international commerce (Reid 1988, p. 641). Reid concluded that having experimented with the female alternative, these aristocrats sought to perpetuate it. Marsden (1986, pp. 447, 454) saw female rule in Aceh as something strange and an aberration, believing that these female rulers were weak and did not have the power to appoint or dismiss officials without the presence and consent of the other nobles who formed the state council. Veth, on the other hand, saw female rule not as an aberration, nor as an experiment conducted by the elite, but as a normal part of the indigenous practices of Southeast Asian states (Veth 1870, pp. 362–65). He cited other examples of *vrouwenregeeringen* (government by women) in Patani, Borneo, Palembang and Celebes. He argued that the necessity for numerous discussions with the state council and finally the agreement of the council members did not illustrate weakness and was not unique to female rule but was part of the Malay political institution practised even under a male sovereign — the sultan. Mohammad Said, an indigenous writer, argued too that female rule in Aceh was not an aberration. A few centuries ago, Aceh had a female admiral, *laksamana* Keumala Hayati, and this was acceptable in the Acehnese custom since women could be as powerful and as capable as men (Mohammad Said 1961, p. 379).[5]

An examination of primary sources, both European and indigenous, and of reports by European travellers, the *ulama* and the VOC's (Dutch East Indies Company) and the EIC's (English East Indies Company) officials in Aceh during the reign of the queens seems to illustrate that they were not favoured for their weakness. Most Europeans found them impressive, especially Sultanah Safiatuddin who ruled for thirty-five years and not merely as a figurehead. Nor did they draw from the idea that the *orangkaya* had placed a female on the throne the inference that the queen did not rule in her own right. The *orangkaya* in the Acehnese court were not a unified and homogeneous group. There were several factions with different political leanings and commercial interests, and they were very jealous of each other. The court of Aceh was filled with political intrigue in their efforts to out-manoeuvre each other. The Dutch factors who were present at the court observed that these jealousies were kept hidden and the queen was successful in maintaining peace and authority by becoming the final arbiter (Chijs et al., *Dagh Register 1641–42*, pp. 96, 123). This suggests that the queen was not a mere figurehead, restrained by obligations to the nobility. The queen's presence, on the contrary, it could be argued, was crucial to prevent these jealousies and factions among the nobility from degenerating into civil wars that could have consigned Aceh to the fate of other polities in the region. In a private confession to a Dutch factor, one of the *orangkaya* admitted that he would not have been able to last for even an hour without the queen, since he had so many enemies.[6]

Towards the last decade of the seventeenth century, the kingdom of Aceh had evolved from being an absolute monarchy to one characterized by power-sharing and consensus-gathering. Jacob de Roy, a Dutch private trader who resided in Aceh at that time, went to the extent of even describing the kingdom as a "republic". Though the term "republic" might be an exaggeration, Sultanah Kamalat, he said, "is a queen that presumes an unlimited power and authority and convenes the Assembly but she is obliged to wait for a favourable resolution from the majority of her courtiers."[7] A few years earlier, Thomas Bowrey observed that Aceh had for such a considerable amount of time been governed by a queen that the very title of "king" proved to be nauseous to them. The men who served under her office were all very submissive and respectful to her, not daring to do anything until they had thoroughly acquainted her with the matter at hand (Bowrey 1905, p. 299).

There was, however, a conflict of opinion among European observers. William Dampier observed that though her subjects respected and revered her, the queen had little power or authority and was more of a figurehead, with power resting in the hands of the *orangkaya* (Dampier 1931, p. 100). Whatever their position at home, it was evident that the queens found it hard to maintain the regional power wielded by Iskandar Muda. Bowrey noted that the kings of Jambee, Androgeero and Pryaman, vassals of the kingdom of Aceh, were much more independent and paid less homage to the crown of Aceh than they had done previously (Bowrey 1905, p. 295). De Roy commented on the lack of fortifications in Aceh, and concluded that the VOC could capture and subdue Aceh easily and with little expense.[8]

This evidence led many modern historians to observe that Aceh had been seriously weakened under these female rulers by the end of the seventeenth century. Mohammad Said (1961, p. 377), Ilyas Sutan Pamenan (1959, pp. 35–36), Anthony Reid (1988, p. 641), and M.C. Ricklefs (1993, p. 36) are just some of those who have held this view. Reid argued that the "reduced skill and authority of the rulers" who succeeded Iskandar Muda and the growing power of the Dutch led to the decline of royal power (Reid 1975, p. 52). Aceh, pressured by a Dutch blockade from 1647 to 1650, could not prevent the VOC from gaining control of the dependencies that produced the pepper and tin on which its prosperity had been based (Reid 1993, p. 266). Kathirithamby-Wells, who had briefly studied relations between Aceh, the VOC and West Coast Sumatra up to the 1660s, examined the gradual loss of Aceh's pepper-rich dependencies in West Coast Sumatra (Kathirithamby-Wells 1969, pp. 453–79). The Treaty of Painan in March 1663 and another treaty signed in April 1668 placed a number of these states under the protection of the Dutch (ibid., pp. 473, 478).[9] She concluded that "the decline of Aceh's authority over the area from the mid-century onwards was conditioned by external commercial forces connected with Dutch ascendance in the Straits, by the capture of Melaka and its consequent effects on the Sultanate's power and prestige" (ibid., p. 479).

In reviewing the reigns of queens in Aceh, with the above in mind, the most important question is perhaps the one asked by de Roy. He described how, from time to time, around three to four thousand men from the hinterland would come to the palace demanding a king instead of a queen from the ministers, but, despite this, he wondered why this demand was never met.[10] Despite the so-called decline of Aceh and opposition from some *orangkaya*, why did female rule still survive?

The best approach to an answer lies through an examination of the very features of female rule that have traditionally been identified as weak. During the "golden age" of absolutism, expansion and militarization of society under Iskandar Muda, success and strength were defined in terms of the monopoly of power by a king and control of territories and resources through military means. By comparison, the queens' subtler, more collaborative exercise of power and reluctance to resort to war have been viewed as weakness and the fall of Aceh from its "golden era". However, one could argue that the devolution of power, an emphasis on a rule of law rather than military might, wariness of increasingly powerful external enemies, and an economical use of state resources provide for a different form of government but not necessarily a weaker one. In fact, a more accommodative and consensual approach based on the law and the ability to keep foreign diplomats and merchants happy could well have been the answer to Aceh's continued peace, prosperity and survival as an independent kingdom.

THE REIGN OF SULTANAH TAJUL ALAM SAFIATUDDIN SYAH

Female rule was indeed collaborative — designed to keep factions in balance, subjects in obedience, and courtiers occupied. It was often inventive, and by no means hidebound by traditional structures of power. Sultanah Safiatuddin ruled with the help of four principal *orangkaya* — the Lebai Kita Callij, the Maharadja Sri Maharadja, the Eunuch Raja Adonna Lilla and the Laksamana Paduka Tuan — in addition to numerous other officials, like the Shahbandar. Pieter Sourij commented that the government of the Queen was a good-natured but awe-inspiring one, and she could not perform her duties without the advice of the principal *orangkaya*.[11] According to Pieter Willemszoon, her court also had representation from *Groote Vrouwen* (great/noble women) who could make representations and recommendations in their own right.[12] According to Rusdi Sufi, the Acehnese manuscript *Qanun Meukuta Alam*, listed the names of some ladies who represented their own district areas in court (Rusdi Sufi 1994, p. 51).

De Roy offered an answer to his earlier question by noting that none of the *orangkaya* dared to be bold enough to seize power for themselves because the balance of power was such that none of them were powerful enough to do so. This observation is corroborated by reports from VOC officials who not only led delegations to Aceh but stayed in Aceh for three to four months at a time and had a good vantage point from which to observe court politics through their negotiations with the elite and their presence during court audiences and proceedings. It appears that Sultanah Safiatuddin proved herself to be a very adept ruler by keeping her ministers satisfied, by keeping herself above the factions and intrigues, and by treating each faction equally. She also allowed them to pursue their own commercial interests but, as we shall see, ensured that her royal revenue and wealth were safeguarded.

From the arsenal of absolutism, Safiatuddin wielded the display of anger and withdrawal of favour expertly. Any misbehaviour by the elite that might possibly threaten her position was punished, as a clear deterrent to the others. However, this punishment was not so harsh or cruel that it would alienate them to the extent that they would come together to conspire to overthrow her. One occasion perhaps demonstrates this strategy most clearly. In order to regain control over some lands in her dependency, in Pidie, Sultanah

Safiatuddin decreed that those lands distributed by her late husband, Sultan Iskandar Thani (r. 1637–41), would be repossessed by her. When she sent her trusted eunuchs to investigate the situation, they discovered that one of the principal *orangkaya*, Maharadja Sri Maharadja, had hoarded the best lands for himself and left the poorest ones for the Sultanah. At court, in front of all the important ministers, foreign merchants and diplomats, the Maharadja was questioned and scolded. While crying, he asked for forgiveness and stood for two hours with both his hands on his head as a sign of submission to the Sultanah.[13] This act of humiliation to the *orangkaya* seemed to work more effectively than the spilling of blood.

Safiatuddin's methods were something of a template for her female successors. Royal proceedings and grand court ceremonies, as in the Ottoman and Mughal courts, seem to have been quite consistent from the time of Sultanah Tajul Alam Safiatuddin Syah to that of Sultanah Kamalat Syah. Although continuing the traditions set by her husband and father in practices such as the reception of letters from foreign powers, the presentation of gifts and the sending down of the royal seal to newly arrived vessels, Tajul Alam's reign was noted for her impeccable hospitality, which was consistently reported throughout the second half of the seventeenth century. The VOC's envoys, like Pieter Sourij and Vlamingh, reported that they were treated royally by Sultanah Safiatuddin. In the *balieuw* (audience hall), they were treated to seven to nine-course banquets served on silver and gold dishes. At the palace courtyard in front of the Queen's lodgings, officials from foreign missions and local guests would be seated on fine carpets, entertained and served fruits and areca nuts. As they were seated, a big golden box of betel leaves was placed before them. The whole ceremony continued with more feasting and dining. To sweeten the palate, sweetmeats, delicacies and all sorts of excellent fruits were served. Entertainment for the guests was just as varied as the foods and drinks served. Officials from foreign missions were treated to elephant and tiger fights in the palace yard.[14] The presents brought by the foreign ambassadors were placed on golden vessels or trays and carried by the Sultanah's eunuchs. These eunuchs were flanked and protected by gilded pavilions that were carried over them. If there was an official letter from any of the foreign representatives, it would be accorded an even more dignified reception. The letter would be carried separately with great stately ceremony and royally attended by the Queen's favourites. The letter would be placed on a silver plate and covered with yellow silk cloth.[15] The foreign official who had brought the letter would be presented with gifts and the commander of the mission would be given a suit of silk and a turban. On taking their leave, at the palace yard, awaiting the commander would be a stately elephant richly decorated to transport him back to his dwelling or factory. He would be accompanied by the *orangkaya* and other important men of the court. This procession was a grand one with accompanying music from pipes and drums, and flags carried by footmen (Bowrey 1905, p. 308). The procession was accorded such respect and importance that, according to Thomas Bowrey, if any native was in their way and did not move after being told to do so by the footmen, he would be lanced. As the grand procession passed by the city, many other merchants would sprinkle rosewater on them as a mark of honour and respect. When the parade finally ended at the house or factory of the foreign diplomat, they alighted from the elephants and exchanged ceremonial complements and good wishes before the *orangkaya* took their leave.

Besides court protocol, the reigns of these queens were peppered with many festivities and amusements. Sultanah Safiatuddin, who ascended the throne as a young widow of only twenty-nine, was fond of entertaining guests, organizing outings and hunting.[16] During these outings and festivities, not only were the *orangkaya* of Aceh invited but also all the foreign envoys and important merchants. Sourij, who was invited to join a fishing trip organized by the Sultanah, described the merry ceremony where lots of dancing and feasting took place, and where he noted that he was served with fish caught by Her Majesty's ladies-in-waiting,[17] whilst Vlamingh reported that on yet another of the Queen's fishing trips, he was served with fish caught by Her Majesty herself![18] Being young, the Queen proved to be, at times, cheeky. One occasion illustrates this well. After a long series of negotiations with the Dutch representatives, the Sultanah finally agreed to accept and pay for some of the jewels previously ordered by her late husband. She had previously refused to do so on account of the fact that these jewels had not been ordered by her and that some of these were of no use to her since they were meant to adorn a man's dress and her husband was already dead. After making the first payment, the Sultanah joked that the Dutch should now be happy and insisted that they show their joy by dancing together with the Acehnese. The funny sight of the Dutch representatives hopping to Acehnese music drove everyone to peals of laughter. Jokes aside, these relaxed occasions, numerous under female rule, provided excellent opportunities for the Acehnese elite to forge friendships and alliances with these foreign representatives and merchants.

One festival described by Bowrey illustrates the grandeur of the Acehnese court during the reign of Sultanah Nur Alam Naqiatuddin Syah (r. 1675–78). He witnessed a royal procession down the river, "the like I believe was never paralleled in the universe," which took place shortly after Nur Alam became queen (Bowrey 1905, p. 325). Nur Alam, whom Bowrey estimated to be at least sixty years of age,

> went downe in a most stately barge most bravely carved and gilded from one end thereof to the other, with a very stately summer (or pleasure) house in the midst thereof, the which was covered with Massy Gold of incredible Substance and Value, and surrounded with very Stately Pillars, covered with the richest cloth of Gold hangings. Others, but a very great deal inferiour to this, attended, yet very rich ones, in their proper stations, vizt. One right ahead, one upon each quarter, all rowed by women, and seemed to doe it both with great reverence and rejoyceings, with Varieties of musick, and delicate Voices, that Sange to the great Honor and Majestie of their great Virgin-Princess. These were to admiration adorned with Flaggs and Pendants and fine tapestrie, with 500 of the Queene's most warlike Elephants (rigged in the greatest State) followed the barges very close (and in the water), for which reason they rowed the Easier. Above 100 of the riders, yea those that kept near the Queene's barge (or that wherein it was said the Queene was) were Eunuchs of her own household. Each of them wore his Turban after the Arabian mode of beaten pure Gold, and very large Shakels of beaten Gold quite up their arms and leggs, and bore each of them a lance of beaten Gold of 7 or 8 foot longe, and proportionately thick. The other riders were said to be Lords and Gentlemen of the Citty, and very richly attired in Cloth of Gold, and armed with creest[19] and lance. And upon the banks of the River on each side went 500 or more of the delicatest horses in the Kingdome; their Saddles, Stirrops, bits and buckles were of pure gold, their Saddle cloths and bridles and Crupors richly beset with many Diamonds, Rubies, Pearle and Saphir ... (ibid., pp. 325–26)

Bowrey also described the grandeur of the Sultanah's court when he wrote that she was attended by one hundred eunuchs and one thousand of the most beautiful women in the kingdom whose skin, according to the observant Bowrey, was fairer than that of common women (ibid., p. 310).

If the queens were competent governors, whose methods were canny rather than weak, it would be surprising to find evidence of absolute decline in the state. Indeed, contrary to more recent assessments, earlier accounts given by both Dutch and English free traders and travellers appear to paint a picture of abiding effectiveness in the late seventeenth century. Aceh was a metropolitan city — very pleasant, healthy and populous — with good laws and government (ibid., pp. 285–88; Dampier 1931, pp. 84–89). The laws were very strict; offenders were punished swiftly and, if needed, with great severity (Dampier 1931, p. 96). If a thief was apprehended, he would be taken to the palace with great speed and brought in front of the *orangkaya* to be tried. If he had stolen anything up to the value of four *maces* (about five ounces of gold), both his hands were cut off at the joints. For a subsequent theft, his feet would be chopped off and if he was incorrigible, his head would go too. Those thieves who escaped the death sentence were exiled to a neighbouring island called Pulau Wei (on the northern tip of Aceh). This was done to serve as an example to the others. However, a thief would be given the death sentence immediately if he stole (even for the first time) a cow, buffalo or horse or something to the value of these since they were not only prized possessions but also symbols of power (Bowrey 1905, p. 315). Under the rule of the queens, some exceptionally cruel acts of punishment, like pouring molten lead down criminals' throats, submerging their hands in a pot of boiling rice or oil, or making them lick hot iron were no longer meted out. The representative of the Dutch East India Company in Aceh noted in 1644 that "everything here was in order and peace, and governed in a peaceful way by the Queen, without people hearing anything of murder and death, though in former times occurred here almost daily [*sic*]."[20] The Queen reserved the right to punish her own subjects when a misdeed had been committed to a foreigner regardless of the subject's wealth or rank. For example, one of her messengers (*bujang*) who mistreated a sick Dutch soldier had his hands and feet amputated.[21] The foreign communities, however, reserved the right to punish their own employees if the crimes were committed to one of their own kind.

This positive view of life in Aceh at that time is corroborated by indigenous literature, which, almost irrespective of its source of patronage, tends to evaluate the queens highly. *Bustan al-Salatin* (garden of Kings) written by the famous seventeenth-century *alim* (scholar) Nuruddin ar-Raniri, revealed that Aceh was prosperous and peaceful under Sultanah Tajul Alam Safiatuddin Syah. Ar-Raniri was a Gujarati *alim* who was appointed by the late Sultanah's husband, Sultan Iskandar Thani, to be his most trusted advisor. Though the *Bustan* is seen as a historical-religious text, the *Bustan* is a court chronicle and it was commissioned by Sultan Iskandar Thani. It is understandable, therefore, that the descriptions of rulers' exploits tends to be at times formulaic and that it meant to put the sovereign in a good light. Nevertheless, what is noteworthy is that the praise accorded to a female ruler was as high as that of her male counterparts. This is in contrast to mainstream Islamic contemporary writings which tended to hold derisive views on women's involvement in politics.[22] More significantly, Sultanah Safiatuddin was not only accepted as a legitimate ruler but also as an exemplary Muslim. When she came to the throne, the *Bustan* related that:

> The port of Aceh was never quiet, being very busy where ships, junks and boats from many other lands came to trade throughout the year. Bandar Darus Salam was very prosperous and food was very cheap and every person lived in peace and obeyed all her instructions. She was fair in all matters of the law and had firm conviction (*tawakal*) in everything she did... (T. Iskandar, ed. 1966, p. 59)[23]

Sultanah Safiatuddin was represented as the provider of all good things, and ar-Raniri stated that with her ascension to the throne, the metaphorical "umbrella" of her rule was erected, under which her subjects would receive her protection and blessings. He recounted the happiness of people whilst she was on the throne — the happiness being likened to how plants and flowers received the soothing coolness of rain during a hot spell. The rain allowed the flowers to blossom and spread their sweet scent and the trees were brought to fruition in all parts of the kingdom. The wind of happiness blowed and the sun shone in all its grandeur as proof of her sovereignty. Her just (*adil*) rule and exemplary behaviour were famed in the other kingdoms (Siti Hawa Salleh, ed. 1992, pp. 42–43).

Her character determined the material prosperity of the country and its subjects because she was patient (*sabar*) in most matters, yet very strict and firm in eschewing evil. Her greatness (*haibat*) could be seen in all that she took, and her wisdom (*kebijaksanaan*) and wittiness was illustrated in all her speeches. She was very graceful and well-mannered (*halim*) and loving towards her subjects (*ra'yat*). She was also very caring and charitable to the poor. She was very respectful and loved all the *ulama* and all the descendents of the prophet who visited Aceh. She was generous in her rewards and gifts of wealth and elephants to all her advisors (*wazir*) and soldiers (*hulubalang*) who sought an audience with her. She was just as generous to her subjects, whether male or female who came to see her. She loved her subjects as a mother would her children (ibid., pp. 43–44).

She was, in addition, the upholder of religious authority:

> Her royal highness our lord Seri Sultan Tajul Alam Iafiyyat al-Din Shah Berdaulat the shadow of Allah on earth was possessed of many praiseworthy and virtuous traits, as well as being fearful of Allah and always praying five times a day and reading the Quran aloud, repeating the name of Allah and always reading the book of Allah, and commanding people to perform good deeds and forbidding them to commit bad deeds, as was sent down by Allah to our Prophet Muhammad, and was extremely just in the matter of examining and sentencing all the servants of Allah. On account of the blessing of the royal power and good fortune of *Yang Maha Mulia*, there

> were many of the servants of Allah who were faithful believers and prayed five times a day and pursued knowledge (ibid., p. 62).

The text implies that it was her personal piety and her virtuousness which made Aceh peaceful and prosperous. Thus, being a good Muslim was a more important and valued attribute for a ruler than sex. The third sultanah, Inayat Zakiatuddin Syah, was another example of a good Muslim. In 1683, she welcomed the delegation from Mecca headed by the representative of King Syarif Barakat, El Hajj Yusuf E. Qodri, with great ceremony. When the envoys returned to Mecca, they were laden with gifts of gold, sandalwood, camphor and money to be donated to the poor in Mecca (Snouck Hurgronje 1888, pp. 553–54).

Their ability to inspire praise and manipulate propaganda is, indeed, a measure of the queens' success. To establish their legitimacy was one of the main tasks they faced; it could by no means be taken for granted. Indigenous writings, such as the *Taj-Us-Salatin* (Khalid M. Hussain, ed. 1992), limited the legality of female rule to the absence of a male heir. The *Sulalat-Us-Salatin* (Muhammad Haji Salleh, ed. 1997) described several powerful aristocratic women behind the throne during the Melakan sultanate and illustrated that, in some instances, their influence was positive (Cheah Boon Kheng, ed. 1998, p. 25). In chapter five of the *Taj-Us-Salatin,* under the section on *kerajaan* (state of having a king or kingdom) and the *hukumat* (laws regarding the sultan), the writer, albeit reluctantly,[24] states that a woman could succeed a male king, but, only in special circumstances: in the event of the absence of a male heir in the royal family and to prevent chaos in the country (Khalid M. Hussain, ed. 1992, p. 60).

Certainly, when it came to defending their legitimacy, the facts were in the queens' favour; but the facts alone were not sufficient to be the deciding factor without a good deal of debate and persuasion. In February 1641, Aceh found itself in the exact set of special circumstances defined by the *Taj-Us-Salatin.* Sultan Iskandar Thani died suddenly at the age of thirty-five, leaving his young widow childless. Sultan Iskandar Muda, the previous king, did not leave any legitimate male heir, having killed his only legitimate son just a few months before his death. In the absence of a male heir, and with the rather ominous presence of the Dutch, who had just conquered Melaka from the Portuguese in January 1641, the court of Aceh was thrown into a state of confusion. After some debate in the council, the principal elites finally decided to appoint Iskandar Thani's widow, who was the legitimate daughter of Iskandar Muda, as queen of Aceh (Hoesein Djadjadiningrat 1911, p. 188). Such an excellent political pedigree might not at first guarantee the succession since there was still the issue of whether female leadership was legal in a Muslim state.[25] In this context, the elites of Aceh could have used the *Taj* in reference to the issue of the legality of female leadership in Islam. Whether or not the *ulama* referred to the Taj was uncertain but it appeared from the writings of both ar-Raniri and al-Singkil that the sex of the ruler was not as critical as the moral right of the ruler to rule. Ar-Raniri wrote in the *Bustan* that Sultanah Safiatuddin's rule was accepted and justified because she was generous, caring and pious (T. Iskandar, ed. 1966, p. 73). To al-Singkil, a female could be regarded as a leader of an Islamic community and be accepted as God's *khalifah* (deputy) in implementing God's laws and the community should offer its loyalty in return. In his *Mirat-al-Tullab*, commissioned by Sultanah Safiatuddin and completed in 1663, he wrote that this *kitab* was in honour of her and professed his loyalty to her (Amirul Hadi 2004, pp. 85–86).

The proliferation of Islamic learning and literature that took place during the reign of the queens, representing a golden age of Islamic and Malay cultural renaissance, has remained unrivalled till today, and this was testament to the effective collaboration between the sultanahs and the *ulama*. Ar-Raniri wrote at least seven well-known books pertaining not only to religious knowledge but also history, literature and law during the time of Sultanah Safiatuddin. Some examples include *Shiratul Mustaqim* (The Straight Path), *Syaiful-Qutub* (Medicine for the Heart) and *Bustanul Salathin fi Dzikril-awwalin wal-Akhirin* (The Garden of Sultans Concerning Biographies of People in the Past and Future). The Sultanah also commissioned Abdul Rauf to write a book on *fiqh* (laws pertaining to ritual obligations), the result of which was the *Mir'at al Tullab,* the first book on canon law written in Malay (Rusdi Sufi 1994, pp. 47–49). Sultanah Inayat Zakiatuddin also commissioned Abdul Rauf to write his commentary on forty *Hadiths* (oral traditions relating to the words and deeds of prophet Muhammad) (Amirul Hadi 2004, p. 74).

ECONOMIC ASPECTS

As far as we can tell from the present state of research, Aceh did not appear to be a kingdom in decline. As late as the third quarter of the seventeenth century, the Acehnese port-polity was noted for its great traffic of peoples and commerce. Merchants and ships from all nations and races could be found in the harbour, which was touted to be fine and deep, and always littered with hundreds of ships from many nations. With these ships came numerous traders and craftsmen of many nationalities, such as the English, Dutch, Danes,

Portuguese, Chinese, Malabarese, Bengalese, Gujaratis, Javanese, Malays, Makassarese and so on (Bowrey 1905, p. 286). The main commodities brought in were white and blue baftas, cotton and cotton yarn, course paintings, quilts and carpets from Surat, rice, butter, oil, long cloth, chintz and slaves from the Coromandel coast, fine chintz from Masulipatam, and broadcloths, knives, scissors and Spanish dollars from England (ibid., pp. 288–89). From Bengala, there came rice, wheat, oil, butter, sugar, and slave boys and girls.[26] Rice came from Java and Pegu, and tin from Tanassarrim, Junk Ceylon, Kedah and Perak. From Siam came tin, copper, china wares and rice (Bowrey 1905, p. 290). Striped and flowered silks, steel pots and pans, copper and porcelain were brought from China. From Java Major, sugar, rice, slaves and diamonds arrived and sapphire came from Borneo and Makassar. From the west coast of Sumatra, gum, benjamin, camphor, sandalwood, brimstone, pepper, rattan, damar and bezoar stones arrived (ibid., p. 242).

Aceh's main exports were the goods obtained from its dependencies of Sumatra West Coast and the Malay Peninsula, especially tin and pepper. Aceh's most valuable mineral resource, however, was gold. Gold was discovered in several mountains during the reign of Sultanah Safiatuddin (T. Iskandar 1966, p. 73) and was mined with the utmost care, so that no foreigner would know where it was or set foot there. De Roy attested that as late as the 1690s, gold was still exported in very large quantities from three excellent goldmines.[27] Acehnese coins (*mas*) were minted and the queen had the right to coin money without any interference from her ministers. Each of the sultanahs had their own coins minted and inscribed with their titles on the face of the coins and their names on the reverse side (Ibrahim Alfian 1979, p. 45). The Acehnese themselves were reputed to be richer than most because of these goldmines and the frequent trade with foreigners. In 1696, the largest of ships carrying merchandise to Aceh would be emptied in the course of just three months due to the high level of consumption — every article being sold promptly and paid in ready money or gold dust.[28]

Trade was by far the most important source of revenue for the Acehnese polity. The section in the *Adat Aceh* (Customs of Aceh) on *Balai Fardah* (Court dealing with commercial law) sets out the taxes and levies that were imposed on trade and visiting ships into Aceh.[29] The ruler and court officials were to be given various "gifts" by merchants in exchange for the right to anchor and trade goods. The VOC factors faithfully recorded in detail all the "gifts" given and the total value of these "gifts" to the queen and her *orangkaya*, complaining that these were expensive but without these, they could not achieve anything since the officials must be kept happy. In addition, merchants had to pay taxes of 5 per cent of the price of the goods traded.

Foreign traders were required to obtain a licence to trade in areas controlled by Aceh in West Coast Sumatra and the Malay Peninsula. The licence could be obtained from the court for a fee. Royal wealth depended almost exclusively on trade. The queens were not unaware of this and facilitated the provision of security for goods and property for all their subjects and foreigners alike. Whereas, according to Beaulieu, the surest ways for the *orangkaya* to court death during Iskandar Muda's reign was to be notable for "the good reputation they have among the people, and secondly their wealth" (Beaulieu 1744, p. 257), such predatory behaviour was not manifest during the reigns of the queens. The *orangkaya* were free to make profit in peace. VOC officials such as Pieter Sourij, Peter Willemszoon and de Vlamingh reported on the numerous orders for gold thread and Japanese paper by the *orangkaya* in exchange for the pepper that they were able to procure from these Acehnese court officials. To this end, the Acehnese seemed to have been concerned with facilitating trade and preventing capital flight. When the city was besieged by men from the hinterlands opposing the accession of another queen, Dampier writes, "the *Shabander* sent to the Foreigners, and desired them to keep in their own Houses in the night, and told them, that whatever might happen in the City by their own civil Broyls, yet no harm should come to them" (Dampier 1981, p. 15). The *orangkaya* and the queen also granted foreigners a considerable degree of freedom. Sultanah Safiatuddin had granted permission to the Franciscans to build a church and establish a mission in Aceh (Reid 1995, p. 52).

Even though keen to keep foreigners secure and happy to trade in Aceh, Sultanah Safiatuddin was careful to protect her own royal wealth. One of the highly lucrative products, besides pepper, coveted by European companies was tin. The VOC sent many missions to Aceh, from the first day of the Sultanah's accession to the throne, to ask for exclusive trading rights for pepper in Sumatra West Coast and tin in the Malay states of Perak and Kedah. While not refusing the Dutch outright, even by 1646, the governor of Melaka, de Vlamingh van Oudshoorn, wrote that "they were met with fine words and friendly countenance but no more than 10 *bahar* of tin in Perak." Yet, the Indian traders carried 488,000 pounds of tin in 1646 and 1,500 *bahar* of tin from Perak in 1647.[30] By 1680, far from monopolizing the trade, the Dutch still faced problems even procuring tin from Perak, and competition from English, Portuguese and Indian traders actually increased.

Another commodity highly prized by Sultanah Safiatuddin and her male predecessors was elephants since these were not only sources of great wealth but symbols of power and prestige. Truijtman reported that she so jealously guarded her prized elephants that she did not consent to let the VOC buy even one single animal. The Sultanah reasoned with Truijtman that the Dutch should be content with the generous privileges she had granted to them in Sumatra West Coast and Perak. She further added that she was following the customary practices of her predecessors and had no wish to reverse their policy. Truijtman however reported to the governor general in Batavia that he suspected the real reason was because the Sultanah and her *orangkaya* found this trade very profitable indeed since they could benefit from the high customs and excise duties imposed. They also did not want to jeopardize the age-old commercial links they had enjoyed with the Indian traders who were the main buyers of these elephants in exchange for their cloth.[31] Not only were the Dutch not able to gain a foothold in the elephant trade, but Aceh's trade in this commodity actually grew from the 1640s to the 1660s (Ito 1984, p. 415).

By the mid-1660s, it appears that the power of the kingdom of Aceh relative to the VOC was reduced. The influence of Aceh over her dependencies in Sumatra West Coast and Minangkabau hinterlands had diminished. In contrast, the Dutch seemed successful in making inroads into these areas and they took these minor *rajas* under the company's protection. This new status, however, did not necessarily translate into political and economic realities. The company's power and control here were nominal and the company was not able to maintain peace for periods long enough to establish full control over economic resources. On the other hand, although Aceh's political domination in these territories declined, the kingdom still benefited commercially through economic links. Even though Aceh lost the revenue it used to derive from a percentage of the customs duties collected by her *panglima* (governor) there, the kingdom continued to receive supplies of pepper and gold brought in directly by Minangkabau traders. Similarly, Aceh's former vassals of Asahan and Deli continued to supply rice to Aceh despite the company's attempts to disrupt this trade (L. Andaya 2004, pp. 74–75). Aceh's international trade might have decreased by the end of the seventeenth century, but Aceh showed itself to be a resilient regional port with Muslim and non-Muslim traders skill frequenting its harbour.

EXTERNAL RELATIONS

At first glance, it appears that female rule was not able to withstand the pressures imposed by European companies. This may be well true as Aceh lost her vassals and Aceh's influence was reduced to the area known as *Aceh Rayeuk* (Great Aceh) or *Aceh Inti* (Aceh Proper). In the first few years of her reign, Sultanah Safiatuddin conceded some trading concessions to the

Dutch. When Joost Schouten arrived in Aceh in March 1641, he acquired a letter of privilege where the VOC was awarded the exemption from toll for one ship, *de Grol,* trading in Tiku, Priaman, Indrapura and Padang annually (Van der Chijs et al. *Dagh-Register 1640–1641*, p. 221). Furthermore, she granted to the VOC exclusive trading rights in these places — a privilege that had proved elusive to the VOC during the reign of her predecessors.[32] This contract was renewed in 1649 and again in 1659. She also appeared to be more accommodative to Aceh's age-old enemy, Johor, and finally negotiated peace with them, with the mediation of the Dutch in Batavia (Van der Chijs et al. *Dagh-Register 1640–1641*, p. 424). In 1659, the VOC succeeded in pressuring the queen of Aceh to agree to share the tin in Perak equally between Aceh and the VOC (Iljas Sutan Pamenan 1959, p. 61).

However, a more accommodative, peaceful foreign policy need not necessarily mean a yielding of control and power or a failure to withstand external foreign demands. In this context, it is noteworthy that the kingdom of Aceh, despite the loss of her dependencies,. remained politically and economically autonomous. Some of the concessions granted remained on paper since other nations continued to trade in Sumatra West Coast and the VOC failed to achieve its aim of monopolizing trade. Although it is true that by the second half of the seventeenth century, Aceh's military was a shadow of its former self, partly owing to the decades of incessant warfare to oust the Portuguese from Melaka, it appears that the decision to eschew military means as an instrument of foreign policy was a deliberate one. Under female leadership, the non-belligerent policy of peaceful coexistence adopted in the foreign sphere seemed to be an extension of internal governance based on consensus and power sharing. This change illustrates a conscious response to re-orientate Acehnese diplomacy from one concerned with power and control based on military might to one based on negotiation and treaties. It was also a tactic to meet the new political realities in the Straits of Melaka.

After 15 January 1641, Aceh had to face an entirely new and radically different balance of power in the region. With the Portuguese ousted, the VOC was now the new master of Melaka. Johor, a former vassal of Aceh, had broken free from the Acehnese yoke by finding itself a new protector by allying itself with the Dutch to conquer Melaka. After 1641, Johor was now strengthened by virtue of the backing and protection they were entitled to receive from the assistance they had rendered to the Dutch and was set to challenge Aceh's pre-eminent position as the strongest and wealthiest Malay polity in the region. Aceh then had two choices: to continue with Iskandar Thani's and Iskandar Muda's traditional methods of "diplomacy", i.e., to try and maintain Aceh's pre-eminent position by trying to oust the new master of Melaka and to reassert Aceh's position in the Malay world by attacking and subjugating Johor, or to face the new political realities and to reorientate their world view and concepts regarding traditional Malay diplomacy.

The new constellation of power had rendered traditional diplomacy almost redundant. Aceh realized that in its present situation, the military option was no longer viable. With the military option closed because of its weakened military might, Aceh had to pursue peace by other means. Thus, in contrast to Iskandar Thani, his widow adopted a *volte-face* of the Acehnese stance and approach to the Western powers. Aceh's desire to establish a friendship with the new Western powers was clear. Not only had Aceh to abandon its preoccupation with power and status and the desire to be lord of the Straits of Melaka, as was the norm under the previous male kings, but the new leadership had decided to make use of the treaty system in order to effect a new kind of relationship which was different from the traditional use of aggression to maintain power. Aceh's interests would now have to be pursued and safeguarded by using new instruments of diplomacy, where relations were based on mutual interests. The Acehnese realized that in the context of the new realities facing them, supernatural and sacrosanct powers of legitimacy, royal lineage, ties of kinship, and even military might were in themselves insufficient to regulate interstate relations (Sher Banu Khan, unpublished Ph.D. thesis, p. 97).[33] A new basis for legitimacy, peace and order was needed to regulate international relations and to conduct trade.

On the part of the VOC, the company preferred to treat Aceh with caution and use persuasion rather than force to get their way lest too much pressure backfire and the Acehnese retaliate by making it difficult for the Dutch to gain access to pepper in Sumatra West Coast. Readings of VOC records also reveal that the VOC was in favour of female rule. When Sultanah Safiatuddin succeeded to the throne after the death of her husband, the company hoped that the Queen would remain as the ruler and safeguard their privileges (Van der Chijs et al. *Dagh Register 1640–1641*, p. 483). The Dutch reported that she was a better ruler than her predecessor — her husband, Iskandar Thani — since she was able to maintain the peace and prevent outright rivalry amongst her *orangkaya* (Van der Chijs et al. *Dagh Register 1640–1641*, p. 123). This perception is not really surprising since a reading of the VOC's documents reveal that when she came to power she was much more accommodative to the demands of the VOC.[34] In contrast, the VOC's officials did not have a good impression of Iskandar Thani, describing him as whimsical and unreliable. According to Schouten's report, after the king's death, "all was taken care of". He wrote that he was well-received by the Queen. Aceh's *volte-face* in its foreign policy was very much evident when the Queen sent her envoys, Siry Bidia Indra and Mottaber Khan, to

Batavia bearing gifts and a letter to the Dutch governor general, Antonio van Diemen. She informed him that when Iskandar Thani died, she had succeeded him by the choice of Almighty God and as the crowned Queen, she hoped to continue their friendship and union with the Dutch."[35] As an act of honour to Antonio van Diemen, she claimed in her letter "to know the value of the goodness of his sincere heart and to her estimate, Aceh and Batavia are nothing else but similar to each other…"[36]

Though the Acehnese elite were careful to forge friendly relations with the Dutch to ensure that there would be no excuse for the company to attack them, there were some instances that gave cause for worry. The company's persistent demands and sometimes high-handed approach brought some sharp responses. For example, when the Dutch signed an agreement with the government in Surat in 1649 stating that ships from Surat and Bengal were not allowed to enter Aceh's port, Sultanah Safiatuddin ignored this and continued to encourage Indian traders to trade their cloth in Aceh and to obtain tin from Perak. Also, in retaliation to Dutch interference in Perak in 1650 to 1651, the Sultanah stopped Dutch ships from trading in Sumatra West Coast and allowed English ships to enter ports in Minangkabau. When the Dutch stepped up their efforts in wooing the areas around Minangkabau away from Aceh's control in the 1660s, the Acehnese were anxious to counteract the influence of the Dutch by actively courting other powers. The English had sent missions to Aceh since the 1640s but had withdrawn in the 1650s to 1660s due to interference in their trade by the Dutch, only to renew this interest in the early 1680s. With the loss of Bantam to the Dutch in 1682, the English needed another port in Sumatra for trade. In 1684, the third queen of Aceh, Sultanah Inayat Zakiatuddin Syah, received the English delegation led by Ralph Ord and William Cawley (Marsden 1811, pp. 449–50)[37] in an effort to counterbalance the Dutch.[38] Though nothing came of this, since the Sultanah was not willing to allow the English to build a factory in stone for fear that this might be turned into a fortified garrison, the English managed to obtain a toe hold further south in Bengkulu instead (ibid., p. 451). Besides the English, the Sultanah also sent an invitation to the king of Siam to renew an "ancient connexion" and tried to unite in league with the Siamese to deter the Dutch (ibid., p. 453).

CONCLUSION

In 1699, the last queen of Aceh, Sultanah Kamalat Syah, was deposed, for reasons still intriguingly unclear. According to Veth, the weapon that managed to remove the Sultanah from her throne was a writing from a certain Kadhi Malik al-Adil from Mecca. Armed with this letter (which later writers described as *fatwa* (religious decree), the group who opposed the Sultanah went to the people of Aceh to inform them that the exercise of highest authority by a woman was against Islam (Veth 1870, pp. 368–69). But since the *ulama* in Aceh had always accepted female rule, the use of this purported letter to depose Sultanah Kamalat Syah may well be due to the changed internal political situation in Aceh, such as the death of the moderate *ulama* Abdul Rauf in 1693. This ended a unique phase in Aceh's political history. Never again was Aceh ruled by a woman.

The history of Aceh under the four sultanahs does not bear out traditional and recent analyses, with their insistence on the decline of the state and the culpability of the queens. Rather, the evidences illustrate key features of J.C. van Leur's famous thesis:[39] the importance of continuity, the survival of indigenous forms of government, and their ingenuity in absorbing and adapting to new influences. Female rule could well be one such ingenuity. Contrary to belief that Aceh declined during this period because it was not led by a strong hand (Iljas Sutan Pamenan 1959, pp. 35–36),[40] Aceh was able to withstand Western pressures because it was ruled with a softer, more flexible hand. The queens could never escape gendered perceptions, especially the mistake of associating such commonly assumed feminine characteristics as gentleness with weakness, and flexibility with fickleness. However, but even these assumptions could be exploited and turned to the kingdom's advantage. Perhaps one occasion best illustrates this, and one of the *orangkaya* himself was not too abashed at using this to his advantage. From 1641 to 1645, the Acehnese elite were heavily involved in intense, sometimes difficult, discussions over the issue of the acceptance of some very expensive jewels that had been ordered by the first Queen's late husband.[41] The Sultanah and the *orangkaya* refused to accept the jewels because they were too expensive and they had not been ordered by them. However, when the Dutch representatives, Sourij and later de Vlamingh, pressed them for payment incessantly, the Maharadja Sri Maharadja, in an effort to placate the Dutch and perhaps at the same time to stop the Dutch from pestering him, said that this decision was up to the Queen herself. However, considering a woman's inconsistency (*ongestadich*), he said it would be very difficult to judge what her final decision would be. Nevertheless, knowing Her Majesty's great discretion, he was very confident that this affair would turn out to the satisfaction of the Dutch![42]

Notes

1. See also Charles Boxer (1969).
2. Female rulers were also rare in Christendom until the sixteenth century. However,

the neglect, and sometimes silence, in Islamic discourse on women heads of state perhaps reflects the insignificant numbers of these women rulers in Islamic history. The few women rulers who have been recognized and recorded in history include, in India, Sultanah Radiyya, who ruled Delhi in 1236. Others were Mongol queens such as Tindu, who ruled the Jallarid Dynasty from 814 to 822, Kutlugh Khatun who reigned from 1257 to 1282, her daughter, Padishah Khatun, who ruled from 1282 to 1295, her niece, Absh Khatun, who ruled the Atabek Dynasty from 1263 to 1287, and Sati Bek who became Head of State in 1339. The Fatimid Dynasty, who established their own Ismai'li Shi'i caliphate in Yemen to rival the Sunni Abbasids, placed two queens on the throne, Malika Asma and Arwa, who held power from 1019 to 1038. In the Maldives, three queens — Sultanah Khadijah, Sultanah Myriam and Sultanah Fatima — ruled from 1347 to 1388. The very fact that the number of such politically active and prominent women is very small, even though Islam has been an established religion for the past fourteen centuries, shows that women holding high positions in the world of politics is an exception rather than the rule. It is also worthy of note that these women leaders were not found in the heartland of Islam in the Middle East but in remote regions peripheral to mainstream Islam, which generally is taken to comprise orthodox Sunnis. See Mernissi (1993), pp. 90, 107–108).

3. Translated from Old Javanese by C. Hooykaas. Quoted in Ibrahim Alfian (1994*a*), p. 3.
4. Dampier resided in Aceh for six months in 1689.
5. This was the very same female admiral mentioned by John Davis in 1599.
6. Dagh-Register of Pieter Sourij, 15 Mei–18 August 1642, VOC 1143, ff.559V-560R.
7. "Voyage made by Jacob Janssen de Roy to Borneo and Atcheen, 1691. Completed in 1698 in Batavia at the order of William van Oudtshoorn, Governor-General of Netherlands East Indies. Translated from Dutch into English in 1816." (East India Office, MSS Eur/Mack 1822/25, p. 366).
8. "Voyage made..." (1822/25, p. 369).
9. In 1661, the delegation led by Raja Panjang who represented the Minangkabau *rajas* of Silida, Painan, Batang, Kapas, Kambang and Lakitan went to Batavia to place themselves under Dutch protection. They were followed by the *rajas* of Dua-belas kota, Padang, Inderpoura and Ticou. In April 1668, another treaty was signed between the VOC and the Minangkabau ruler, which recognized the independence of the Minangkabau territories. The area from Baros to Manjuta acknowledged Minangkabau authority under the protection of the company.
10. "Voyage made..." (1822/25, p. 367).
11. Dagh-Register of Pieter Sourij, 1642 VOC 1143, f.565V.
12. Dagh-Register of Pieter Williamsz, 1642 VOC 1143, f.527R. Also, see Dagh-Register of Arnold de Vlamingh van Oudtshoorn, 1644 VOC 1157, f.606R.

13. Dagh-Register of Pieter Williamsz, 1642, VOC 1143, f.527R.
14. Dagh-Register of Arnold de Vlamingh, 1644, VOC 1157, ff.598R-598V.
15. Dagh-Register of Arnold de Vlamingh, 1644, VOC 1157, f.578R.
16. Dagh-Register of Pieter Sourij, 1642, VOC 1143, f.680R.
17. Dagh-Register of Pieter Sourij, 1642, VOC 1143, ff.568V-569R.
18. Dagh-Register of Arnold Vlamingh, 1644, VOC 1157, ff.604V-605R.
19. *Kris* (Malay dagger).
20. Dagh-Register of Arnold de Vlamingh, 1644, VOC 1157, f.570V.
21. 1652, VOC 1191, f.750v. Report by Johan Truijtman.
22. During the latter period, especially from the seventeenth century onwards, women's involvement in politics was viewed derisively and women were seen as a factor contributing to the decline of the Ottomans and other Islamic dynasties such as the Safavids and Mughals. See Hambly (1999), p. 9. Virtually all historians of the Ottoman Empire, whether local or Western, have concurred that the influence of the harem, or to quote the phrase coined by the twentieth-century historian, Ahmad Refik, "the sultanate of women", contributed to Ottoman decline. Interestingly enough, during this period in Islamic history, the event of Aishah leading the Battle of the Camel was used to argue in favour of the exclusion of women from public life. This battle has been seen by most as disastrous because it resulted in the major schism that split the Muslim community into the Sunni and Shi'ite sects.
23. The *Bustan al-Salatin* was written by Nuruddin ar-Raniri during the reign of Iskandar Thani (r. 1636–1641).
24. The reason why I suggest that Al-Jauhari reluctantly agrees to female rule is because, in his explication of the ten prerequisites to good leadership, he advises kings to spend less time with women because to him they lack good deeds. He also states that a king by right should be male because a king is also an *imam* and a woman can never be an *imam* (Khalid M. Hussain 1992, p. 60). The concept of *imam* is open to various interpretations amongst the Islamic jurists depending on their cultural and political affiliations. A general definition of *imam*, however, is someone who is a religious leader and leads congregational prayers in mosques. A woman may lead her own kind in prayers but is forbidden to lead men, thus, debarring her from taking this position.
25. This issue arose due to a difference in opinion among the court elite, where one faction proclaimed that a woman as head of a kingdom contravened Islamic law since a woman cannot even become an *imam* (leader of prayer) or *wali* (witness legally responsible for a bride). Cf. Rusdi Sufi (1994, p. 43).
26. Voyage made..." (1822/25, p. 358).
27. See Dampier (1931, pp. 84–89) and "Voyage made..." (1822/25, p. 356).
28. Voyage made..." (1822/25, p. 361).
29. Ramli Harun and Tjut Rahmah, translit, *Adat Aceh* (Jakarta: Apartment Pudidikan dan Kebudayaan, 1985), pp. 75–101.
30. A *bahar* was a measure of weight in Malaya. The value of a *bahar* varied from

place to place but remained fairly constant throughout the Peninsula at between 360 to 370 pounds per *bahar*.

31. Origineel Rapport van den Oppercoopman Johan Truijtman in dato 13 Januarij, 1651, VOC 1175, ff.309R-310R, ff.323V–324R.
32. See "Treaty CXXXVI-Atjeh-Sumatra West Coast, February-Maart, 1641", in Heeres (1907–1938), pp. 423–25.
33. In her thesis, the author examines the concepts of traditional diplomacy in Aceh, where the ideas of status and hierarchy, honour and might were important determinants of inter-state relations.
34. The delegation, led by Joost Schouten, was granted the privilege of exemption from toll for one ship, *de Grol*, trading in Priaman, Ticou, Padangh and Indrapoura annually. The VOC was especially pleased with the concession granting them trade in the above-mentioned places to the exclusion of other traders such as the Danes, English and French. In contrast, her husband had side-stepped the issue (Heeres 1907–38, 1, pp. 345–46). This same contract was mentioned in Van der Chijs et al. *Dagh Register 1640–1641*, pp. 423–25.
35. Letter from Queen Safiatuddin Syah to Governor-General Antonio van Diemen, 1641 VOC 1141, ff.146R–149R, f.146R.
36. See Letter from Queen Safiatuddin Syah, VOC 1141. Ibid.
37. See also A. Farrington (1999), p. 20.
38. The English had just lost their factory in Bantam in 1682 and had looked towards Aceh as an alternative source of pepper. Although unsuccessful in their request to build a factory in Aceh, the English gave the Dutch some headaches in Priaman, Indrapura and Batang-Kapas but finally prevailed only in Bengkalau in 1686, Silebar in 1691, and Triamong in 1695. See Marsden (1811), pp. 451–52.
39. Van Leur (1955). In this thesis, van Leur advocated the writing of autonomous history where the focus of enquiry shifts to the natives instead of the Europeans. In contrast to other Euro centric writers, he saw the importance of local agents and internal forces in stimulating change and development where Asians themselves shaped their own destiny.
40. Pamenan argues that female rule was not appropriate especially since Aceh was not economically secure at that time. He contends that Aceh needed a strong hand to earn the respect of foreigners and a woman would not be able to carry out such heavy and important responsibilities.
41. Sher Banu A.L. Khan, "The Jewel Affair: The Sultanah, Her *orangkaya* and the Dutch Foreign Envoy". Presented at the First International Conference on Aceh and Indian Ocean Studies. Banda Aceh, Sumatra, 24–26 February 2007.
42. "Dagh-Register of Arnold Vlamingh", f.599V.

2

ACEH AND THE TURKISH CONNECTION[1]

Anthony Reid

For Southeast Asian Muslims, the faraway Ottoman Dynasty in Turkey represented a dream: a longing for Islamic power at a time of Islamic political decline. However, there were important moments when that dream had immediate political effects.

When the last fully independent Muslim state in Southeast Asia, Aceh, was attacked by the Dutch in 1873, it appealed to all the great powers of the time to come to its aid — Britain, France, United States, and Italy. As fellow colonial powers, all refused to break ranks with Holland. Only Ottoman Turkey took up the cause with the capitals of the world, going so far as to issue a formal offer of mediation to bring about peace in Sumatra, which was of course rejected by the Dutch. The most striking feature of this mediation offer was the grounds on which Turkey presumed to intrude into an area where the big powers were desperately discouraging intervention. Turkey claimed to have been the suzerain — the overlord — of Aceh since the sixteenth century, when the Ottoman sultans had accepted the tribute offered by Aceh in return for military protection. This overlordship had been renewed on both sides as recently as 1850, as the letter pointed out in its highly diplomatic language. Wrangled over between diplomatic chanceries for months before it was finally issued, the letter offering mediation hearked back to a time when the Ottomans conquered the area around the Red Sea in the 1520s.

> The Acehnese sent a deputation to the feet of the conqueror, recognized the supremacy of the powers inherent in his title of Caliph, made an act of

> submission into the hands of the famous Sinan Pasha, raised the Ottoman flag in their ports and on their vessels, declared themselves vassals of Sultan Selim and asked in return for his high protection. Sultan Selim received these offers favourably. By his orders the Vezir Sinan Pasha sent to the vassal Sultan the cannons and swords of honour which are still to be seen in Aceh (Woltring 1962, p. 612).

RAJA RUM

In many Southeast Asian traditions of the fifteenth to nineteenth centuries, "Rum" features as a mysterious amalgam of powers in the West, conflating Rome, Constantinople, and Alexander the Great. Mythologies of the Peninsula and Sumatra associate *Raja Rum*, the great king of the West, with *Raja Cina* (China), the great king of the East. According to one origin myth of Johor, Iskandar Dzul Karnain (Alexander the Great) had three sons by the daughter of the King of the Ocean. After a contest between the three brothers in the Singapore Straits, the eldest went to the West to become *Raja Rum*, the second East to become *Raja Cina*, while the third remained in Johor, to begin the later Minangkabau Dynasty (Marsden 1811). In the eighteenth century, rulers of Minangkabau styled themselves younger brothers of the rulers of *Rum* and *Cina* (ibid., pp. 338–41).

One Gayo origin myth also goes back to a shipwrecked child of *Raja Rum*. Among Bataks, his name was still so mythically powerful in 1890 that the Italian traveller Elio Modigliani, having admitted he came from Rome, found himself acquiring followers as the word spread that he was an envoy, or perhaps incarnation, of the magically powerful *Raja Rum*.[2]

However, in the sixteenth century it became clear to Muslim Southeast Asian leaders, at least, that the Ottoman sultans were this *Raja Rum* of shadowy memory. Paradoxically, it was the Portuguese invasion of the Indian Ocean in 1498 that put Aceh directly into contact with Turkey. In the fifteenth century, Sumatra's pepper had mostly gone to China, and what westward trade there was from Southeast Asia to the Mediterranean — in cloves, nutmeg and other luxury tropical products — was broken up into separate stages. Sumatrans had then been in direct contact only with South India, while the onward stage to the Red Sea and Persian Gulf ports was in the hands of Arabs and Gujaratis.

PEPPER

The Portuguese disrupted Islamic shipping in the years after 1500, and in particular attacked ships travelling from India to the Red Sea (heading for

Mecca or Cairo). They also conquered Melaka (in 1511), and greatly interfered with the activities of the pepper-producing sultanates on the north coast of Sumatra.

The Muslim traders regrouped around states strong and willing enough to protect them, notably Aceh in Southeast Asia, Calicut in South India, and Turkey, which expanded its control to the Red Sea ports in the reign of Selim I (r. 1512–20). It became dangerous even for Muslim shippers of Indian pepper from Kerala to defy the Portuguese predators to try to reach the Red Sea and from there, Cairo, Alexandria and Venice. Hence, an alternative Muslim pepper supply route developed, whereby Gujarati, Arab, Turkish and Acehnese traders shipped Southeast Asian pepper and other spices directly from Aceh to the Red Sea, without having to go near areas of Portuguese naval strength in India. The earliest European reports of such shipments reaching the Red Sea date from around 1530. By the 1560s, as much pepper was being shipped that way to Europe as was being hauled by the Portuguese around the Cape to Lisbon. Aceh and Turkey shared an economic as well as a religious motive to resist and, if possible, crush their Portuguese rivals in the pepper trade.

The strongest of the Ottomans, Sultan Suleiman "the Magnificent" (r. 1520–66), was the first to extend Ottoman power into the Indian Ocean. In 1537, he instructed his governor of Egypt, Suleiman Pasha, to equip a powerful fleet to demolish Portuguese naval power in the Indian Ocean. This fleet reached Gujarat, and besieged the Portuguese in Diu for a few months in 1538, but achieved nothing militarily. Nevertheless, there seem to have been soldiers of this fleet who reached Southeast Asia, since Mendez Pinto referred to them as greatly strengthening Aceh in its wars against the Bataks and Portuguese, and also helping Demak in similar wars in Java (Reid 2004, pp. 74–78).

In the 1560s, the pepper link was at its peak, and we have Venetian, Turkish and Acehnese sources all mentioning the envoys who travelled from Aceh to the Red Sea with the pepper ships. The first well-documented Acehnese mission to Istanbul occurred round 1561–62. In response to this appeal, Turkish gunners were sent to Aceh at least by 1564, and were gratefully acknowledged by the Acehnese in a letter recently rediscovered in the Ottoman archives.

Another mission, led by an envoy called Husain, which probably covered the years 1566 to 1568, came close to achieving more spectacular success. He carried an appeal for help, in January 1566, from the Acehnese sultan, Ala'ud-din al-Kahar, to the Caliph, protector of all Muslims, which is also preserved in the Ottoman archives. The Aceh ruler acknowledged the safe arrival of eight Turkish gunners sent in response to an earlier request. He appealed repeatedly to the Turkish sultan to come to the aid of Muslim pilgrims and merchants being attacked by the "infidel" Portuguese as they travelled to the Holy Land. "If Your Majesty's aid is not forthcoming, the wretched unbelievers will continue to massacre the innocent Muslims." (Farooqi 1986, pp. 267–68).

After a delay caused by the death of Suleiman the Magnificent in 1566, his successor, Selim II, energetically took up the project of extending Turkish power into the Indian Ocean. In a series of decrees in 1567, he not only ordered a fleet of fifteen galleys and two barques to be sent to assist Aceh, but also instructed the governor of Egypt to construct a canal at Suez so that his warships could go back and forth to the Indian Ocean on a regular basis. However, a serious revolt in Yemen interrupted these plans and the designated fleet was diverted to suppressing it, and only a few guns and gunsmiths appear to have reached Aceh (Reid 2004, pp. 79–87; Reid 1993, pp. 146–47).

Nevertheless, these contacts made a big impression in Southeast Asia, and especially in Aceh. In the years following this initiative, a pan-Islamic sense of solidarity against the infidels was probably stronger than at any time before the modern era. Aceh used its Turkish arms to attack Portuguese Melaka in 1568, and again in 1570 and 1573; the second time apparently coordinating with the four South Indian Muslim sultans — Bijapur, Golconda, Bidar and Ahmadnagar — who briefly buried their differences to attack Portuguese Goa (Smith 1958, pp. 298–99; Eaton 1978, pp. 83–85). In Maluku at the same time, Sultan Baab Ullah of Ternate (r. 1570–83) threw out the Portuguese and launched a crusade against them in the spice islands.

MEMORY

The strong direct connection between Turkey and Aceh lasted less than a century. The Dutch and English ships that began making the journey around Africa in 1600 were far more numerous and efficient than the Portuguese, and by 1630, the Muslim-Venetian pepper route, from Aceh to the Mediterranean, was no more. Even Istanbul needed to get its pepper from the Dutch and English after that. The most prominent pilgrims to Mecca in the rest of the seventeenth century went on Dutch or British ships as far as Surat (Gujarat), and then took Indian ships to the Red Sea.

Nevertheless, the memory remained, especially in Aceh, where it was kept alive by the presence of the Turkish flag, adopted as Aceh's, by the enormous cannons which remained at the capital, and by the popular mythologies that formed around these items. The chroniclers of Aceh, including the famous Nurud-din ar-Raniry, attempted to record the history behind these items:

> He [Sultan Alau'd-Din Ri'ayat Shah al-Kahar] it was who created the system of government of Aceh Daru's-Salam and sent a mission to Sultan Rum, to the state of Istanbul, in order to strengthen the Muslim religion. The Sultan Rum sent various craftsmen and experts who knew how to make guns. It was at that time that the large guns were cast. It was also he who first built a fort at Aceh Daru's-Salam, and he who first fought all unbelievers, to the extent of going to attack Melaka in person.[3]

However, more colourful stories were more popular. The largest of the cannons was popularly known as *lada secupak* (a measure of pepper), because of a story that the Aceh envoys took shiploads of pepper as their tribute to the Caliph, but that the journey was so arduous that only one (bamboo) measure remained to be offered as tribute. (Figure 2.1 shows these Turkish cannons as Dutch war trophies three centuries later.)

NINETEENTH CENTURY

Contacts between Aceh and the Ottoman Empire were revived in the 1840s, as both felt the winds of modernization and nationalism and the common threat from the ever more powerful West. The emigration of thousands of Arabs from Hadhramaut to Southeast Asia provided a further link, for they could consider themselves Turkish subjects when it suited them. In the 1840s, the pepper trade of Aceh was again flourishing, though increasingly it was shipped to the world via the entrepôt of Penang. Sultan Ibrahim of Aceh took advantage of the pilgrimage to Mecca of a wealthy Acehnese pepper trader, Muhammad Ghauth, in 1849, to entrust him with royal letters both to France, which had just sent an impressive state letter to Aceh, and more importantly to Turkey. Once in Cairo, Ghauth obtained surprising encouragement from the local representatives of both powers. He was able to send one of his followers to Paris as the guest of the French government for a few months, while he himself was feted in Istanbul as a symbol of Turkey's lost greatness (Reid 2004, pp. 171–74).

Sultan Abdul Mejid of Turkey issued two decrees (*firman*) in 1850: one renewing Turkish protection over Aceh, and the other confirming Ibrahim as a vassal ruler.[4] Ghauth was sent back to Aceh in style, with a recommendation to the viceroy (*Khedive*) in Egypt, and instructions to the Turkish governor of Yemen to send the envoy safely home. The Turkish connection returned to the centre of Acehnese thinking. When the Crimean War began in 1853, Ibrahim

FIGURE 2.1
Trophies of war: Turkish and Acehnese guns on their way to Dutch museums after the Dutch conquest of the Aceh capital in 1874 (Illustrated London News)

GUNS BROUGHT FROM THE KRATON DOWN TO THE RIVER BANK TO BE SENT TO EUROPE

sent a contribution of 10,000 Spanish dollars to his Ottoman counterpart to show his loyalty and solidarity against the Russians. He received in return confirmation of the right to fly the Turkish flag, and an imperial decoration (the *Mejidie*), which he made a point of wearing when receiving the Dutch envoys in 1855 (Reid 1969, p. 84; Woltring 1962, pp. 612–13; de Klerek 1912, pp. 216–17). The Crimean War, generously covered in the Straits press, aroused considerable pro-Turkish enthusiasm in Aceh and the Malay world, as evidenced by a number of surviving poetic celebrations (Voorhoeve 1994, pp. 54–59).

This brings us back to Aceh's most desperate appeal to its erstwhile overlord, when the Dutch threat became real in 1873. An extremely persuasive Hadhrami

Sayyid, Habib Aburrahman az-Zahir, prime minister of Aceh before the war, made Istanbul his chief target once it became clear the British would do nothing to help Aceh, despite much support to do so in Penang. For most of 1873, the Habib was in the Turkish capital, drumming up support among reformists and pan-Islamists alike. He and his Turkish sympathizers located in the Turkish archives evidence of Ottoman suzerainty over Aceh from both the sixteenth and mid-nineteenth centuries. The Dutch pulled out all stops to prevent a painfully weak Turkey from doing anything that would stir up Acehnese and Southeast Asian resistance, and in the end, only a polite diplomatic offer of mediation was forthcoming; equally politely declined by the Dutch. Rumours circulated of Turkish help for the Acehnese, or for other potential rebels in restive parts of Indonesia, but it was nothing as frightening as the Dutch had feared.

Palembang and Jambi were also sites of resistance to Dutch advances in the mid-nineteenth century — a resistance which became more religious as it became more desperate. A new sultan of Jambi, Taha Safi'ud-din, neglected to declare his allegiance when he ascended the throne in 1855, and resisted Dutch attempts two years later to negotiate a more binding treaty with him. While envoys from Batavia were trying to win him round, Taha appealed to the Ottoman sultan for a document declaring Jambi to be Turkish territory in which foreigners had no right to interfere. Taha entrusted this letter to his connections in Singapore, one of whom was provided with 30,000 Spanish dollars to undertake the journey to Constantinople. The emissary, Sharif Ali, apparently travelled only as far as Mecca, where he acquired forged letters from the Caliph authorizing the expulsion of the Dutch from Southeast Asia. Taha's letter did, however, reach its destination. The Turkish grand vezir asked the Dutch ambassador whether Jambi was independent, and when assured that it was part of Netherlands Indies, he promised to give no reply.

In November 1858, a Dutch expedition occupied Taha's capital and installed a new sultan. Taha escaped, and after the withdrawal of the Dutch troops, he remained the de facto ruler of Jambi for almost half a century. For several years, he continued his attempts to have Jambi recognized as Turkish territory, backed by his agents in Singapore, who were reported to be raising money and arms for him there. One Arab who had been active in his cause in Singapore went to Mecca in 1861, possibly with another appeal to the Caliph.[5]

PAN-ISLAM, JIHADISM AND THE OTTOMANS

A mindset which we might today call "jihadist" or Islamist, and attribute to the global projection of struggles in Palestine and Iraq, does in fact have a long history in Southeast Asia. The twentieth-century rise of nationalism not only marginalized such thinking, which colonial writers labelled "pan-Islamic", but made it seem quixotic; its importance exaggerated by colonial paranoia. A century later, with nationalism again vigorously challenged by concepts of solidarity with a global Muslim community (*umma*), the situation looks very different. This current must be seen as a continuing one within the Islamic world, emerging with far greater salience at some periods, such as the present, than at others.

The period between 1870 and 1918 was another such time of Muslim frustration, when the solidarity of the *umma* loomed particularly large in the region, with some very specific consequences. At the point of their terminal decline, paradoxically, the Ottoman sultans were a central part of this mindset. Especially during the reign of the last Ottoman sultan, Abdul Hamid II (r. 1876–1908), the movement for a universal and effective caliphate received consistent encouragement from the top. After the disastrous Russo-Turkish War of 1877–78, Abdul Hamid turned his back on the West and suspended the liberal constitution of 1876. Encouraged by the sympathy he received from all over the Muslim world, including Southeast Asia, he hoped to make up in Asia for the influence he had lost in Europe. The Sultan made clear that he wished to be regarded as a sort of pope and protector for Sunni Muslims everywhere, and the Turkish press reflected this change in mood (Arnold 1924, pp. 173–77; Snouck Hurgronje 1915, pp. 23–27).

Pan-Islamic hopes were more than ever focussed on Turkey in this period, as the only Islamic power, the claimant to the caliphate, and also the nominal overlord of Mecca and of most Arabs. Southeast Asian Arabs would readily claim to be Turkish subjects when it seemed likely to benefit them. The Arabs of Singapore, in particular the most prominent Alsagoff and al-Junied families, as well as their close confidant Sultan Abu Bakar of Johor, not only travelled to the Middle East and made the pilgrimage to Mecca but also visited Istanbul, and took a substantial interest in Turkish affairs. They also sympathized with the Acehnese and other Indonesian Muslims that they thought were being oppressed by the Dutch. The actions of Turkey in Asia, however symbolic, assumed greater importance through the mediation of such men, and their counterparts throughout the archipelago.

TURKISH CONSULATES

Neither Britain nor the Netherlands liked the idea of Turkish consuls in their colonies, because of their fear that they would become the focus for pan-Islamic agitations. However, since both London and The Hague wanted the right to appoint consuls in places like Alexandria, Tunis, Aleppo and Damascus, they had to make some concessions in their own empires.

When Britain allowed Turkey to have its first consul in Singapore in 1864, the Dutch were particularly alarmed. He was the wealthy Hadhrami merchant Sayyid Abdallah al-Junied. As they feared, the Indonesian pilgrims to Mecca who travelled via Singapore, as well as other prominent Muslims, tended to regard him as the spiritual and political representative of the Caliph. At his death in 1865, therefore, the Dutch requested that London forbid the appointment of another Muslim as consul, because the British and Dutch had a common interest, they argued, to guard against "the smouldering and easily inflammable element of fanaticism" among Southeast Asian Muslims.[6]

Istanbul had apparently intended to appoint Abdallah's brother, Sayyid Junied al-Junied, to the vacant office, but when Britain deferred to Dutch pressure, Turkey agreed to leave the position vacant. Nevertheless, Sayyid Junied was regarded locally as the honorary consul or, as the Dutch complained, as "a sort of acting consul for Turkey" for several years thereafter.[7] In other words, Britain supported the Dutch to the extent of not officially recognizing Junied's consular status, but not to the point of preventing him from acting in Turkey's interests. Sayyid Muhammad Alsagoff, the most influential of Singapore's Muslims in the 1880s and 1890s, assumed the same role at that time (Reid 2004, pp. 232–33, 267–72).

Dutch agents and spies in Singapore reported a great deal of Turkish meddling in Southeast Asia in this period, perhaps partly because they were paid to do so by the Dutch consulate. In 1881, two prominent *imams* from Mecca sailed to Singapore with what the British and Dutch thought was some kind of political mission to Java and Palembang. It may have been intended mostly to gain support for Turkish causes, but undoubtedly had the effect of raising the hopes of Muslims in Sumatra for help in their own struggles.[8] The *imams* were prevented from sailing to Palembang, but two Turkish ex-army officers did apparently get there, and allegedly inspired a group of thirty Palembang conspirators, including several members of the former royal dynasty, to plan the murder of all the Europeans in the town. All were rounded up by the Dutch before anything of the sort could happen.[9] Under interrogation, some of them revealed their understanding that Javanese Muslims were being roused for the same cause, and that visits to Java by Muhammad Alsagoff and the Sultan of Johor in 1881 were meant to have similar incendiary effects. Dutch Consul General W.H. Read also harboured deep suspicions of Muhammad Alsagoff, whom he claimed had offered hospitality to several of those involved in the Palembang conspiracy.[10]

In 1890, a Turkish warship on a visit to Japan created great excitement in Singapore, and the local Muslim community passed news of its arrival to Sumatra. The hopes of the Acehnese of help from that quarter revived, and an Aceh envoy was sent to Singapore with letters requesting that both the Turkish warship's commander and Sayyid Muhammad Alsagoff bring Aceh's plight to the attention of the Caliph. The Turkish warship had long departed by the time the letters arrived, but Alsagoff received the letters, and raised Acehnese expectations by leaving soon after on a tour of Europe. On his return to Singapore in 1892, Alsagoff sent a personal envoy to Aceh, after attempting to quieten Dutch alarm by telling their consul that he was simply passing on Turkish advice that Aceh should submit to Dutch rule. The mission apparently had the opposite effect, however, and indeed, the website of the current Alsagoff family in Singapore remembers with pride that their famous forebear "helped the Acheh people to fight against the Dutch".[11] At any event, preparations were soon made for an Acehnese diplomatic mission to Constantinople. The envoy, Teuku Laota, was equipped with a Turkish sword and decoration as tokens of Turkey's earlier recognition of Aceh's status as a Turkish protectorate.[12]

Laota appears to have travelled no further than Singapore, where he may have been discouraged in his efforts by more realistic Muslims.[13] Instead, the Acehnese sultan wrote directly to Constantinople at the end of 1893. His letter fell into Dutch instead of Turkish hands (Gobée and Adriaanse 1957–59, pp. 153–57), and there is no record of further attempts in this direction.

Britain's patience with Dutch sensitivity about allowing an official Turkish consul in Singapore had worn particularly thin once they saw a Turkish consul in Batavia. In July 1901, therefore, they allowed a Turkish official, Haji Attaullah Effendi, to take up the job. In 1903, this consul received an appeal from Sultan Taha of Jambi, who had been defying the Dutch in the interior for nearly fifty years. He must have forwarded it to his government, since Turkey made representations on Taha's behalf to The Hague shortly thereafter (Gobée and Adriaanse 1957–59, p. 1662; Smit 1957, pp. 271–74, 328–29, 364–66, 443–45). The Dutch were sufficiently aroused by the dangers such involvement represented to pursue and kill Taha the following year. A few months thereafter most of the Jambi nobility was again in revolt, apparently incited to action by a Hungarian officer in the Turkish army, who claimed to have a special commission from the Caliph to assist in the defence of Jambi. He was quickly arrested, nineteen chiefs were captured and exiled, and Jambi was again gradually subdued during the following two years.[14] Britain did not again allow an Ottoman consul in Singapore.

Meanwhile, the Netherlands Indies government had allowed a Turkish consul general in Batavia since the 1880s, on the grounds that they could better control any pan-Islamic activity on their own territory than that which operated out of Singapore.

This assumption went somewhat awry, however, with Muhammad Kiamil Bey, the consul general in Batavia from 1897 to 1899. He was far more zealous than his predecessors, notably in encouraging Arabs in the Indies to regard themselves as Turkish subjects and to bring their grievances to him. He sent eleven young Arabs for schooling in Constantinople between 1898 and 1904, and they came back with Turkish passports which they claimed entitled them to "European" status (which had been given to the Japanese a few years earlier) (Gobée and Adriaanse 1957–59, pp. 1617, 1619–20, 1737–38). The Dutch finally threw him out when they caught him offering assistance to Indonesian rulers, including the Acehnese sultan who had just submitted to the Dutch (ibid., p. 1662). Turkey transferred him to Singapore, but Britain refused to give him an exequatur. Besides his excessive enthusiasm in colonial eyes, he was said to have offended some of the Johor royal family by marrying Abu Bakar's widow.

The most important result of Kiamil Bey's sojourn in Batavia was to foster closer links between Southeast Asian Arabs and the Middle Eastern press. Towards the end of 1897, the Arabic *al-Malumat* of Constantinople, the *Thamarat al-funun* of Beirut, and several Egyptian newspapers had all acquired correspondents in Batavia or Singapore, who regularly complained about the injustices to which Muslims in general, but Arabs in particular, were subjected by the Dutch. This press campaign aroused high hopes that Turkey would intervene to push the Dutch to give "European" status to Netherlands Indies Arabs. The campaign alarmed Batavia for a time, but faded somewhat when The Hague mobilized diplomatic pressure on Istanbul (Reid 2004, pp. 243–45).

THE CALIPH AND THE GREAT WAR

The First World War, which pitted Turkey for the first time against the colonial powers — Britain, France and Russia — was potentially the most dangerous moment for European colonial rule over Asia's Muslims. Although there were some, largely German-inspired, attempts to use the idea of a holy war on behalf of the Caliph, it was not pursued with much commitment or imagination by the Turks themselves. The Young Turks were in the process of redefining themselves as the most secular of nationalists, and would succeed in ending the absolute monarchy in 1918.

Many of their erstwhile Arab subjects, meanwhile, turned nationalist and anti-Turkish at British urging.

Nevertheless the idea of the Ottomans as the hope of Muslims had enormous and often fatal attraction. In the Singapore mutiny of February 1915, the most sanguinary anti-colonial act in Singapore history, there was again a Turkish theme. On 15 February 1915, only three months after Turkey entered the war, 815 Indian troops and 100 Malays of the Malay States Guides rebelled, tried to release 300 imprisoned Germans, largely from the capture of the *Emden*, and killed 33 British military men and 18 European civilians before reinforcements arrived in the city to combat them. The governor's letter analysing the events noted the unruliness within largely Muslim units, "at a time when Great Britain was at war with Turkey, whose ruler is looked up to as the spiritual head of the Mohammedan religion, was without doubt the principal cause of the mutiny."[15] A Singapore Gujarati merchant, Kassim Ali Mansoor, one of the few Singapore civilians executed over the mutiny, had sought to provide a link between Turkey and the Malay States Guides, who in December 1914 refused orders to proceed to East Africa. His letter to his son in Rangoon had been intercepted that same December. It proved to contain an appeal, meant to be forwarded to the man thought to be the Turkish consul there (though the consulate had ceased to exist with Turkey's entry into the war), to send a warship to Singapore, to take the Malay soldiers to somewhere where they could fight for the Turks instead of against them (Kuwajima 1988, p. 83; Harper and Miller 1984, pp. 204–06; Sareen 1995, p. 11).

Needless to say, the dream of a strong, progressive Muslim power has continued to inspire Muslims everywhere who feel themselves weak and dominated. The Ottomans were at the heart of that dream for 400 years.

Notes

1. An earlier version of this paper was composed as a lecture for the Asian Civilisations Museum in Singapore, on 3 November 2004, in connection with its exhibition "The Ottomans", and published as Working Paper Number 36 of the Asia Research Institute, National University of Singapore <http://www.ari.nus.edu.sg/pub/wps2005.htm>.
2. A translation of the relevant section of Elio Modigliani's *Fra I Battachi Indipendenti* (1892) is in Reid (1995), pp. 199–209.
3. Ia-lah yang meng'adahan segala isti'adat kerajaan Aceh Daru's-Salam dan menyuroh utusan kapada Sultan Rum, ka-negeri Istanbul, kerana menegohkan ugama Islam. Maka di-kirim Sultan Rum daripada jenis utus dan pandai yang tahu menuang bedil. Maka pada zaman itu-lah di-tuang orang meriam yang

besar-besar. Dan ia-lah yang pertama-tama berbuat kota di-negeri Aceh Daru's-Salam, dan ia-lah yang pertama2 ghazi dengan segala kafir, hingga sendiri-nya berangkat menyerang Melaka. (T. Iskandar, ed., 1966, pp. 31–22).

4. Heldewier to Gericke, June 19 and 26, 1873, Buitenlandse Zaken Dossier Atjeh.
5. Note by Bureau A: "Turksche bemoeijing in den N.I. Archipel," n.d. (1864), Algemene Rijksarchief [henceforth ARA] Kol.Kab.H 10, Dossier 5970. Rochusscn to Van Goltstein, Sept-4, 1858; Van Zuylen van Nyeveldt to Goltstein, Sept. 30, 1858; ARA, Buitenlandse Zaken [henceforth B.Z.] Dossier 3076. Locher-Scholten (1994), pp. 121–22; Tideman (1938), pp. 31–33.
6. Van de Putte to Cremers, Jan. 4, 1866; also Read to Cremers, July 31, 1865; ARA, B.Z. Dossier 3076.
7. Read to Loudon, June 23, 1873, copy Koloniën to B.Z., Sept. 6, 1873, Buitenlandse Zaken Dossier Atjeh.
8. Weld to Kimberley, May 18 and 28, 1881, C.O. 273/l08.
9. Weld to Kimberley, Aug. 27, 1881, C.O. 273/109.
10. Weld to 's-Jacob, Oct. 4, 1881 (most confidential), private Singapore letterbook III, Singapore Museum.
11. http://kukupnet.tripod.com/alsa.htm
12. Sultan Daud to Alsagoff, 18 Ragab 1307H (Mar. 10, 1890), trans. Governor-General to Koloniën, Sept. 12, 1890; Van Assen to Van Teijn, Sept. 13, 1890, copy G-G. to Koloniën, Sept. 26, 1890; A.R.A., Kol.Kab. H16, Dossier 6198.
13. Deijkerhoff to Pijnacker Hordijk, Mar. 17, 1893, copy G-G. to Koloniën, Mar- 30, 1893, A.R.A., Kol.Kab. N8, Dossier 6219. Enclosures in Smith to Meade, May 30, 1892 (private), and Smith to Ripon, Oct. 19, 1892, C.O. 273/180 and 273/183.
14. Koloniaal Verslag 1905, p. 43. Locher-Scholten (1994), pp. 243–65. At the same period four Turkish instructors were reported to be assisting in the defense of Boni (Celebes) against the Dutch. Gobée and Adriaanse, eds. (1957–1959), II, p. 1743.
15. Governor of Straits Settlements to Secretary of State for Colonies, 19 August 1915, in Sareen, ed. (1995), p. 709.

3

THE ACEH WAR (1873–1913) AND THE INFLUENCE OF CHRISTIAAN SNOUCK HURGRONJE

Antje Missbach

With the Netherlands Indies government's territorial incorporation of Aceh, the appropriation of Indonesia — in its basic form as it existed until the declaration of independence — was formally completed. The conquest of Aceh and the guerrilla warfare that lasted almost forty years between the troops of the Royal Netherlands Indies Army (Koninklijk Nederlands-Indisch Leger, KNIL) and their elite troops, respectively on the one hand, and the Acehnese guerrillas and religious leaders on the other hand, certainly belongs to one of the cruellest chapters of Dutch colonial history. While the Acehnese were fighting to defend their homeland, the actions of the colonial government and their subordinates were shaped primarily by their imperial aims, which served to consolidate Dutch spheres of influence and power within Southeast Asia.

The military and political strategies that were to be applied to pacify Aceh as rapidly as possible had to be changed several times during the course of the war. A crucial watershed marked the appearance of Christiaan Snouck Hurgronje in the political arena. As a councillor of the colonial government, he provided recommendations which helped to split the resistance movement, to slowly finish the armed resistance and to start administrative cooperation. He could not have predicted the long-lived consequences of his advice and the implications that the war has had until even now. He was awarded for his scholarly success and his methodologies during his lifetime and beyond.

Since the 1970s and with the beginning of a more critical discourse in the Netherlands on its colonial past, Snouck has started to be criticized more harshly (Wertheim 1973).[1] Even though Snouck cannot be called solely to account for the colonial government's Aceh policy — since he is ideologically seen as, of course, a 'child of his times' (Benda 1983, pp. 20–21) — a critical debate about him as a person, scholar and representative of Ethical Policy[2] is still required.

ACEH'S PRE-WAR SITUATION

Contacts with European powers, who arrived in greater numbers in Southeast Asia at the end of the fifteenth century to acquire profitable goods (such as pepper, betel nuts, camphor, gold and tin), reach back several decades before Aceh's real pre-colonial heyday. Attracted by the spice trade, first, it was the Portuguese and later, the Dutch who tried to gain ground in the region. The Portuguese conquest of Melaka (in 1511) turned out to be profitable for the sultanates of both Aceh and Johor because they were able to develop into significant transhipment centres within the maritime trading network between China and India. Before that, there had been several autonomous and competing harbour trading cities on the north coast of Sumatra that controlled the spice trade. Under the reign of Sultan Ali Mughayat Syah (reigned 1496–1528) the whole coast was conquered and the inner areas were incorporated into a territorial entity under one central ruler. The core centre, Aceh Besar, was not a business zone itself, but it remained essential to control the harbour trading cities (Reid 1975, p. 46).

Under the rule of Iskandar Muda (r. 1607–36) Aceh reached its heyday of power due to its economic and territorial expansion. By means of despotic rule and arbitrariness, not only trading monopolies could be kept, but also the basic elements for a centralized administration and a kind of juridical system for monitoring trade regulations could be established. Such regulations were mainly based on Islamic law. Last but not least, it was due to Islam's egalitarian juridical commitments that Islam spread relatively quickly and non-violently along the Southeast Asian trading routes, even if pre-Islamic elements and religious influences from India were never replaced completely, but often only superposed.[3] After the death of Iskandar Muda, the territorial control of the sultans vanished and was restricted mainly to the west and north of Sumatra; none of his male or female successors[4] ever gained as much power as he. Nevertheless, Aceh could assert itself as an important Islamic trading centre with far-reaching contacts stretching to India and even Turkey (see Chapter 2 in this volume).

Similarly attracted by the profitable pepper trade, Dutch interests aimed at repelling the direct trading control of the sultan within the pepper business. With the Treaty of Painan[5] (in 1663), a legal basis was created to gradually reduce the influence of the Acehnese sultanate and to broaden the power of the Dutch United East-Indian Company (Vereenigte Oostindische Compagnie, VOC). By conquering Melaka (in 1641), the VOC had already succeeded in becoming the dominant power in the western part of the Malay Archipelago, where Aceh's political power was concentrated — much to her disadvantage. Not only the VOC but also other European and Asian traders tried to bypass the sultan's taxes — one of his most important tools for power — by trading directly with the *uleebalang*.[6] These quasi-feudal heads, also called the "pepper kings", controlled the harbours and collected taxes. Their relationship to the sultan was more or less latent: they did not execute territorial power; they were primarily coordinators of trade. In order to ensure their trustworthiness, the sultan certified letters of loyalty (*sarakata*). Siegel concluded:

> There is an inconsistency in the relationship between the *uleebalang* and the sultan. On the one hand, there is the great honor the *uleebalang* paid him; on the other, there is the complete flouting of his authority. (Siegel 1969, p. 47)

With the dissolution of the VOC (in 1800), all possessions within the Indonesian Archipelago were passed to the Dutch crown. As a consequence of the political transfer of power in Europe after the Napoleonic Wars and the associated assimilation of the Netherlands into French territories, as well as the grave financial and administrative burden of maintaining the Netherlands Indies, the Dutch were not sufficiently able to strike back with greater force against the offensives of the British in Southeast Asia. The British interim government (1811–16) lasted only a few years, but created far-reaching political and economic changes. After the defeat of Napoleon, the Dutch king, William V, was rehabilitated and the Netherlands became a monarchy. According to the London Convention (1814), its former possessions were returned, although in practice the return was delayed for two years. While the Netherlands had not been playing an important economic role globally yet, the colonial seizures, the utilization of all the many trading advantages and the exploitation of Indonesian natural resources were about to grant a voice to that small country on an international level.

Despite the conventions that regulated international diplomacy, the principle clashes of interest between the two monarchies continued to remain strong and even intensified due to various strategic offensive measures that took place over the years. Against the political manoeuvring of the British between Sumatra and Borneo stood the intensified Dutch policy of expansion towards the north of Sumatra. Forthcoming confrontations within the until-recently-autonomous Aceh — in contrast to other regions, the Acehnese sultans had not abandoned their power through formal treaties either with the British or the Dutch[7] — seemed therefore almost inescapable.[8]

Since both powers had a profound interest in a peaceful solution, they agreed on a compromise. In 1824, both governments signed the London Treaty. This substantial agreement regulated the distribution of spheres of interest along the Straits of Melaka: the Netherlands set aside its colonial possessions on the Malay Peninsula (e.g. Perak and Selangor) and accepted the use of the free-trade harbour in Singapore, which had been founded in 1819 by Sir Thomas Stamford Raffles, while Great Britain ceded its rights in Indonesia, including its last military bases in Bengkulu, to the Dutch. In order to avoid conflicts within the border areas, Aceh was left as a neutral buffer state.

However, despite this contractual agreement, conflicts occurred and existing areas of potential conflict between the two colonial powers emerged. Traders, especially from Penang and Singapore, feared for their commercial freedom[9] since they were worried about the irresistible expansion of the Dutch in Sumatra. As the Dutch wanted to prevent military confrontation in Sumatra, they restricted their territorial expansion during the 1840s mainly to other regions in Bali, Kalimantan, Sulawesi and Nusa Tenggara.

CAUSES OF THE WAR

In order to achieve their trading interests better, both the Netherlands and Great Britain felt obliged to give up their policy of non-intervention by and by. The long-term goal of the Netherlands was to bind as many parts of the archipelago to the mother country as possible, as well as to administer and exploit them. However, the proto-nationalist resistance against the Dutch, which occurred around the turn of the century in areas such as Bali, Sulawesi and Aceh, was not only defeated by military means, but also with the help of a widely ramified contractual system which coerced local power holders into transferring their suzerainty. *Korte Verklaringen* (short declarations) was the name of these treaties (since 1898), that included massive restrictions to local power holders' rights, such as the right to conduct sovereign foreign relations.

The sultanate of Aceh, which still existed as an independent state due to the contractual arrangements with Great Britain in 1824, was a thorn in the Netherlands' flesh, and not only because of its wealth, resulting from the profitable global pepper trade. Aceh participated actively in the China-India trade route along the Straits of Melaka and flourished even more with the opening of the Suez Canal in 1869. Even more decisive than its agricultural potential and the discovery of oil resources[10] at the end of the nineteenth century was the strategic location of Aceh in the Straits of Melaka — one of the most important thoroughfares within Southeast Asia and beyond.

As it did not belong to the Dutch colonial empire, Aceh was a "power vacuum" that could be easily filled by the other Western powers whose interest in Southeast Asia arose at the same time. Snouck Hurgronje noticed in 1896:

> Our aim was clear from the very beginning: Our political prevalence has to be felt energetically in Atjeh, in order to prevent the settlement of foreign powers on Sumatra, to repress the Atjehnese piracy and slave trading with more vehemence, and to guarantee more security to the trade with that country. (Snouck Hurgronje 1924*a*, p. 316).

The risk of potential offensives by other colonial powers threatened the Dutch enormously. After it became known that Sultan Mansur Shah (Ibrahim) had already, in 1869, contacted the Ottomans in Turkey to ask for assistance in case of Dutch-initiated armed hostilities, they perceived a revision of the London Treaty as unavoidable. The British were also interested in a reorganization of Dutch-British relations before a third great power, such as the French or the Americans, was successful in gaining ground in the archipelago (Lee 1995). The colonial race was under way.

As a result of recurring disturbances in trade, the governments of Great Britain and the Netherlands agreed in 1871 on the Sumatra treaty.[11] The Netherlands abandoned the Gold Coast in Africa in favour of the British, and therefore gained permission to export Indonesian contract labourers to Surinam. Concerning Aceh, there was nothing left from the British side that could hinder the Dutch from their aspirations of expansion, because the British had received fixed trading guarantees within the Netherlands Indies in exchange for their cooperation. Furthermore, the importance of mutually fighting the piracy[12] that took place in the Straits of Melaka was agreed upon.[13] Basically, that treaty was a public declaration of war towards Aceh: the Sultan had been neither contacted for consultation by anyone of the competing powers nor had he been involved in the diplomatic negotiation process in any way. The beginning of the war was just a question of time. At that moment, however, no one would have guessed that the war to come would be such a drain on the Dutch government's money and resources.

THE DEVOLUTION OF THE WAR

The course of the Aceh War is usually divided in three phases. The first phase (1873–93) includes the two so-called Aceh Expeditions and the construction of the "concentration line" (*Geconcentreerde Linie*). In the second (until 1903) and the third phases (until 1913), counter-guerrilla warfare formed the main action against the insurgents (Schulten 1988, pp. 60–62). There are divergent opinions about the official ending date of the war, because views of what constitutes the end differ.

In 1871, the Dutch colonial government sent a pre-war expedition to Aceh to study the prevailing conditions. This encroachment into Acehnese territory raised distrust among the people there because they feared that the Dutch might intervene in a local conflict following their principal conviction of *divide et impera* — this time between the regions of Simpang Ulim and Idi. As usual, the Dutch had long before prepared a contract for the regional ruler to sign to "voluntarily" accept Dutch authority. The Dutch hoped the Sultan would sign the treaty after receiving their support in the local conflict between the two rival parties in Aceh, but he did not.

The ultimate *casus belli* was discovered in a rumour that the United States — hoping for extra-territorial trading advantages — would offer the Acehnese a helping hand and grant them support. At the beginning of 1873, an Acehnese mission had contacted the American consul in Singapore to talk about a possible American-Acehnese treaty. Although the United States had shelved their plans, the Dutch insisted on sending in an already prepared armed expedition (Reid 1969, pp. 91–93). On his part, Sultan Mansur Shah (Ibrahim) had asked for support from the British, French, Italian and Turkish diplomatic representations, though the Turks[14] were the only ones to answer positively, offering to negotiate a peaceful solution — an offer that was refused by the Dutch (Ricklefs 1993, pp. 144–45).[15] The viewpoint of the war's main proponent appears very clearly in the following excerpt of a letter:

> An end must come to the equivocal policy of Atjeh towards the Netherlands Government. The state remains our weak point as far as Sumatra is concerned. As long as it does not recognise our sovereignty foreign intervention will continue to threaten us like the sword of Damocles.... Without this military expedition it is almost certain that Atjeh will keep the matter hanging, in expectation of foreign intervention.... Holland can no longer allow its existence in, and peaceful possession of, Sumatra to be dependent on the whim of a state hostile to us there. Atjeh has cast the die.[16]

Aceh was confronted by a choice between voluntary submission and war. On 26 March 1873, four battalions of infantry landed on Aceh's coast under the instructions of Major General J. H. R. Kohler. This date therefore marks the official beginning of the war; previously, there had already been an announcement of war in Europe itself. Two weeks later, about 3,000 soldiers arrived in Aceh, and immediately commenced a bombardment of the palace of Sultan Mahmud Syah (r. 1870–74) in Kutaraja. Assuming that the palace (*kraton*) was not only a domicile but also the administrative centre, the Dutch thought that the war would be easily won by just assaulting the palace, because the subordinate regions would then give up and submit themselves to Dutch power immediately after the defeat of the capital. Lacking enough indigenous knowledge, the Dutch did not recognize the weakness of the *kraton*. They had overestimated the Sultan's power. The Acehnese sultanate was no nation-state conforming to Western beliefs. It was much more of a loose confederation with a symbolic head of state. There was no national identity in this spirit yet, but it started to develop gradually later on (Bakker 1993, pp. 56–57).

Although the Acehnese were left to fight with only their own resources, the Dutch suffered severe setbacks due to the fierce resistance they faced — costing Major General Kohler his life — at a level that they had never experienced before. After a few weeks, at the end of April, they had to abandon the field and retreated — now under the official command of Colonel E.C. van Daalen (Schulten 1988, p. 62).

The continuation of military intervention had to be deferred due to the start of the South-West monsoon. The Acehnese therefore gained time to improve the organization of their resistance and their equipment. The most often used weapons were machetes (*klewang*) and daggers (*rencang*); most of their firearms were purchased from Malay traders (Schulten 1988, p. 60). Since Aceh's power rested on maritime trade, the Dutch decided in June 1873 in favour of sea blockades as instruments of warfare. By doing this, they committed a breach of their agreements with and defied the interests of Chinese and British traders. The British had pledged their neutrality and declared that they would not deliver firearms to Aceh (Reid 1969, pp. 104–105).

At the time of the second military expedition, under the instructions of General J. van Swieten, the Dutch troops numbered about 8,500 soldiers and 4,300 servants and coolies, as well as 1,500 soldiers in reserve (Reid 1969, p. 110).[17] On 24 December 1873, the KNIL soldiers again attacked the capital city, Kutaraja. After succeeding in conquering the main mosque on 6 January 1874, they captured the *kraton* within a few days. Like most of the inhabitants, Sultan Mahmud Syah had already fled to the mountains where he passed away shortly due to cholera. The power of his successor

Muhammad Daud Syah (r. 1875–1907, with interruption) was more of a symbolic kind and only later did he manage to gather sufficient forces to form a resistance against the colonial intruders.[18]

After that alleged victory, General van Swieten declared that the war had ended. On 31 January 1874, he announced Aceh's inclusion in the Netherlands Indies state territories, which was welcomed in the Netherlands Indies as well as in the Netherlands itself with great enthusiasm, despite the large numbers of deaths, which continued to rise due to the outbreak of a cholera epidemic. Henceforth, the Dutch colonial government took over the role of the sultan; officially, the sultanate was even abandoned. Major General J. L. J. J. Pel was appointed commander of Aceh.

After the end of the second Aceh Expedition, it was assumed by the Dutch that Aceh would submit to permanent occupation and that blockades and sieges would break down the last remnants of resistance. However, the Acehnese did not for a long time feel defeated. Apart from concerns about security at its armed posts, the Dutch continued to fear native aggression. The resistance of the Acehnese villagers was not only organized along lines of kinship, but also religious affiliation, and this continued to be the main factor of coherence between different groups (Bakker 1993, p. 57).

While van Swieten tried to avoid military conflicts in the inner parts of Aceh, his successor Major General K. van der Heijden acted more aggressively. In 1876, there was the first military expedition into the inner parts, where resistance was most intensive. It was followed by a second one a year later. In April 1877, there were Dutch flags flying all over the west coast (Reid 1969, p. 182). However, it can still be assumed that even those occupied areas did not feel completely defeated, but instead started supporting the resistance in other parts both financially and morally. Prosperous pepper traders in the coastal areas made concessions to the Dutch in order to escape trade restrictions. However, at the same time, they supported the guerrillas in the inner parts financially (Ricklefs 1993, p. 145).

Up to 1877, the Aceh War had cost the Netherlands about 70 million guilders, but gradually the Dutch government refused to pay for the ambitious military offensive of the particular commanders in charge. In order to gain a better understanding of the situation in general, van Landsberge, the governor general, undertook a survey of the territory, after which he claimed, full of optimism, that total territorial occupation would be achieved within a very short period of time.

In the meantime, the Dutch were confronted with a loss of face abroad because they seemed incapable of permanently resolving the conflict. At the same time, there was opposition to be found within the Netherlands itself about the way the war was being conducted in Aceh. Levinius Keuchenius only spoke out what was thought by probably many in private, when he said, in 1880, that the war was "one of the most horrible and unjustifiable, ever undertaken in the Indies" (quoted in Reid 1969, p. 202). In 1881 the end of the war was declared yet again, but new fighting reoccurred only shortly after. The guerrillas received broad support among the population because the fight was increasingly led under the banner of *jihad* against intruding infidels (*kafir*).

Between 1882 and 1883, there was hardly a single week without fatal attacks on Dutch security posts or their lines of supply. The new governor in Aceh, Laging Tobias, sought political changes but, at the same time, also asked for more troops. In 1883, there was a conference in Kutaraja to discuss the proceedings further. The most important results were, among others, the restoration of the sultanate and the instalment of more severe measures for controlling trade. In May, Laging Tobias introduced the so-called shipping regulation (*Scheepvaartregeling*), which meant that only seven pre-chosen harbours under Dutch control were allowed to be visited by trading ships. It was expected to hamper the arms supply to the Acehnese. About one million guilders were needed each month in order to effectively control these harbours. This was much too expensive and therefore, just five months after the blockade started in April 1885, the *Scheepvaartregeling* stopped in September of the same year. Due to financial cuts it was also decided to dismiss some hard-won security outposts. Aceh's trade became more unrestricted than ever during those years after 1873.

After dismissing most of the outposts, the occupied area was limited to just twenty square kilometres in the area around Kutaraja. This defensive line was provided with watchtowers, connected streets and even telegraph wires.[19] Within this "concentration system" (*Concentratiestelsel*), the Dutch awaited the coming developments more or less defensively. Soldiers were not allowed to fight the guerrillas outside that protected area anymore (Reid 1969, p. 244ff.).

For the following five years, bloodshed continued on both sides. Teungku Cik di Tiro, who was known for leading several guerrilla groups from the end of the 1870s onwards, collected *zakat*[20] in order to purchase arms and ammunition, recruited further Acehnese with the help of *jihad* homilies, and attacked the Dutch-occupied area four times in 1886 alone. Also, in the following year, the guerrillas broke through the concentration line, arguing that they were going to pray at the tomb of the seventeenth-century saint Sheikh Abdurrauf of Singkel which was within the Dutch area. In 1888, Teungku Cik di Tiro led different acts of sabotage against the concentration line, demolishing telegraph masts, block houses and railways.

Teungku Cik di Tiro had received the Sultan's trust. The Sultan had even given him the royal seal (*cap sikureueng*) as a *signum* for important verdicts shortly before he passed away. Because he had the Sultan's trust, di Tiro was seen as a legitimate authority for religious matters in Aceh (Reid 1969, pp. 251–52).[21] After Teungku Cik di Tiro died in 1891, the attacks on the Dutch decreased because his descendants were not as capable of inspiring the Acehnese resistance.

In the course of time, it became more and more clear to the Dutch that they would not gain lasting success if they continued with the same war strategies. They were confronted with a choice between final retreat or complete occupation. In 1893, the "concentration system" was ultimately abandoned and more aggressive tactics were put into operation (Schulten 1988, p. 63). During the third and final phase, there were two dominant strategies. One, the co-option of local leaders had been tried since the middle of the 1890s. The most well-known case is certainly that of Teuku Umar who was equipped with modern arms and adequate amounts of ammunition by the Dutch in order to fight the Acehnese resistance, together with about 1,000 adherents. However, this measure proved to be a total disaster, because Teuku Umar changed sides again and fought the Netherlands Indies army until his death in 1899. On the other hand, there was a fairly effective measure applied under the command of General J. B. van Heutsz: *Korps Marechaussee*[22] (anti-guerrilla units). These small groups of troops — consisting of about fifteen soldiers and only equipped with small arms (since artillery and cavalry had proved to be useless in the mountainous environment) — roamed Aceh, fighting native guerrillas. Further operations followed under the command of Lieutenant Colonel L. L. E. van Daalen, mainly against the Acehnese minorities (the Gayo and Alas) and killing more than 3,000 people (Bakker 1993, p. 58).

> Coercive measures dealing with Achehnese trade and shipping failed to be effective not only because they were not pushed on with sufficient energy, but still more because it is always possible for an Achehnese to supply himself with his own limited requirements even without the aid of foreign trade, so long as he is left (as the "concentration scheme" left him) in undisturbed possession of the whole land. (Snouck Hurgronje 1906, p. xi)

The ideas for the coming strategic paradigm shift were derived first and foremost from Snouck Hurgronje's research findings about Acehnese society, their internal structure, their alliances and rivalries. Snouck himself was not a "belligerent man" like General van Heutsz (Bakker 1993, p. 67); Hurgronje thought of war more as a necessary evil. He was convinced of the rightness of his paternalistic ideas and of the inevitability of the *divide-et-impera* model in order to grant the Acehnese the benefits of the Ethical Policy.

Before going more into details of the third phase and the ending of the war, Snouck Hurgronje's life, his ideas and his efforts will be briefly sketched.

CHRISTIAAN SNOUCK HURGRONJE AND HIS INFLUENCE ON THE COURSE OF THE WAR

Many colonial officers who came to the Netherlands Indies did not have a deep anthropological or sociological understanding of the religious and cultural conditions there. Most notably concerning Islam, many of their beliefs emanated from mistaken presumptions. It was widely presumed, for instance, that Islam was a tightly organized religion governed by a hierarchy similar to that of the Roman Catholic Church. It was also believed that the Turkish sultan still exercised his influence over most of the parts within the archipelago. Generally, the Dutch feared Islam as an international political threat since they were concerned about the possibility of alliances being formed with other Muslim states outside of the Netherlands Indies. From the very beginning, the Dutch policy focussed on cooperating with the secular holders of power, such as regional aristocrats and *adaptable* leaders (Benda 1983, p. 19). Many of the mistaken assumptions were to be changed and corrected by the writings and appeals of Christiaan Snouck Hurgronje (1857–1936).

Snouck Hurgronje, born the son of a Reformed Church pastor in Oosterhout, initially studied theology at Leiden, but later addressed himself mainly to studies about Islam and Arabic. He also earned his doctorate in this field, writing his dissertation on the origin of the pilgrimage to Mecca. After his graduation, he got a position at the Indische Instelling (institute for the training of colonial civil servants) and taught Arabic there from 1881 to 1889. His postdoctoral research included primarily the study of Islamic law. In addition, he carried out an expedition to Mecca (Freitag 2003, pp. 40–41).

Snouck was one of the first Western scholars who were able to enter the Holy City at the time. Altogether, he stayed there for about five months[23] in 1885, under the Islamic name of Abd al-Ghaffar, in order to study the role of the pilgrimage among Indonesian Muslims and its influence on their anti-colonial endeavours. In order to conduct his research properly, he not only needed informants, but also a credible appearance. To what extent his conversion to Islam was only a pretense, or has to be seen as "cultural mimesis" (Freitag 2003, p. 49), is still open to debate.[24] For his scholarly intents and purposes, the stay proved to be very productive. After his sojourn,

Snouck published two volumes: a history of Islamic conquests and a history of Mecca.

During his stay in Mecca, Snouck had also met pilgrims from Aceh. These contacts steered his interest towards local peculiarities of Acehnese Islam and he wanted to study these on location (Pedersen 1957, pp. 22–24). His first attempt to travel incognito from Penang to Aceh in 1889 failed, because his plans had become known within official circles.

In May 1889, Snouck Hurgronje went to Batavia and took up an official position as adviser on Islamic affairs for the colonial government. His duties included research on Islam in Java. He was obliged to find out more about Islam's role within the rebellion in Banten in 1888. His research lasted for two years (Bakker 1993, p. 70). His assignment was not primarily the analysis of existing causes of discontent within the local population, but rather the development of operational instructions for the colonial government to react more adequately in case of future religiously-motivated uprisings (Wertheim 1973, pp. 90–91). In 1893, he handed in his report to the colonial government.

Two years earlier, in 1891, Snouck had already received an offer from the University of Leiden to take up a position there, which he did not accept due to his happiness with his current occupation as colonial adviser. Holding such a function enabled him finally to travel to Aceh; his entry could no longer be rejected. From July 1891 until February 1892, he stayed in Kutaraja for the first time and studied the Acehnese language, customs and institutions. He himself described his duty as follows:

> In order to get at the very foundations of a knowledge of the influence of Islam upon the political, social and domestic life of the Achehnese.... (Snouck Hurgonje 1906, p. v)

Snouck Hurgronje was known to the Acehnese as *Toean Beusa Seunot to Waleeta Peureudan* (Sir Snouck of Weltevreden) and as *doeli Chol Charoenja* (His Majesty Hurgronje) (Damsté 1947, pp. 252–53).

In order to understand Snouck's involvement better, some central points of his findings have to be outlined. Snouck exposed the non-existence of a religious umbrella organization, meaning that the Acehnese were not subordinates of Constantinople, but regarded the sultan only as a symbolic figure. In Snouck's words:

> Fortunately, we need not worry with regard to our Dutch-Indian Mohammedan population. They adopted Islam when the Turkish Empire had already come into existence, but without Turkey's noticing it; and they

> have never had any contact with the Crescent. The Sultan of Rum, as they call the Great Lord of Constantinople, has remained a legendary creature for them. To be sure, the panislamistic idea has penetrated into the East-Indian Archipelago, but is has found little favourable ground. The large mass of the lower classes remains untouched, and the majority of the higher classes is entirely immune against this politico-religious mixture of deceit and nonsense. And we have good reason to believe that this immunity will constantly spread. (Snouck Hurgronje 1923, p. 282)

The Turks were not able to pursue their pan-Islamic ambitions in any way. Snouck realized that there was no feeling of unity among the Indonesian Muslims and that there were major differences and shades concerning their "radicalness". Not all Muslims had been influenced by reformist ideas from the Middle East or had turned consequently into "fanatics". Furthermore, Snouck exposed the fact that most of the religious leaders were subordinate to secular leaders. Generally, Islam in Indonesia was characterized by these syncretistic elements. Although Islamic law influenced certain juridical domains like marriage and family law, in other domains it was *adat* or custom that regulated communal cooperation and adjudication. Unconditional adherence towards Islam and its authorities could not be postulated offhand. Snouck distinguished between the political and religious domains of Islam and, therefore, concluded that Islam should not be fought as a religion — meaning the banning of rituals, celebrations and customs — but advised taking action against its political power claims (Benda 1983, pp. 19–21; Benda 1985, p. 63).

His report about the social life of the Acehnese, that mainly stressed the elementary distinction between more commercially-orientated trading chiefs (*uleebalang*) and the religious scholars (*ulama*)[25] and their conflicting interrelationships, was handed in to the colonial government in 1893. The charismatic leadership of some *ulama* had attracted Snouck Hurgronje's attention, because they proved to be able to mobilize a large number of adherents who followed their "fanatic" aspirations during this time of hardship. The political strengthening of the *ulama* at the cost of the *uleebalang* during wartime had especially caught his interest, next to the *uleebalang's* fading economic power and their weakening financial strength due to the Dutch trading restrictions. Snouck regarded the *uleebalang* as traditional representatives of Acehnese society, whereas he perceived the *ulama* as less authentic.

Many Acehnese turned to the more radical *ulama* because they were disappointed by the quick surrender of some *uleebalang* after the death of Sultan Mahmud Syah, and also by their attitude of give and take towards the Dutch. Basically, the *ulama* strived for a purification of Islam, including the abolition of habitual pleasures such as cock fighting, gambling, and the consumption of alcohol and opium (Siegel 1969, p. 9). Their efforts were further promoted by the destitution caused by the war, leaving many parts of Acehnese society open to religious promises of a better life. The reorientation of Acehnese society towards the leadership of the *ulama* can also be explained by the existence of a common goal: the resistance against the Dutch unbelievers.

The *ulama* ensured that they would rank highly within the resistance movement by protecting certain areas of the population. Some of them, like Teungku Cik di Tiro and Teungku Kutakarang, knew perfectly well how to encourage the population with the help of poetic narratives on the holy war (*hikayat perang sabil*).[26] It was promised that every martyr would enter heaven directly, which greatly encouraged the people's perseverance and their readiness to sacrifice.

> The blessings of God are unlimited for those who serve, who fight the prang sabil. To those He gives paradise full of light, seventy heavenly princesses. More than can be counted He gives. (quoted in Siegel 1969, p. 75)

In contrast to these heavenly rewards, cowards would suffer agonies (Christie 1996, p. 144; Siegel 1969, pp. 75–77).

Snouck Hurgronje's advice for the strategies to follow resulted from his precise analyses. Concerning purely religious (ritual) fields, he recommended neutrality and non-interference. He, for instance, advised bringing to an end the restrictions imposed on pilgrims headed for Mecca, since not every pilgrim returned as a fanatic or attached himself to the insurgents. However, concerning the war in Aceh, Snouck demanded more aggressive methods because, in his opinion, neither the costly maritime blockades nor the expensive defensive line could serve to quell the resistance and to pacify Aceh permanently. In a letter addressed to the German scholar Theodor Nöldeke in June 1898, Snouck noted:

> I dare to say, although many mistakes were made within our undertakings in Atjeh during that quarter of a century and we have been sitting around fainthearted — no other power could have succeeded faster. The Acehnese are masters of guerrilla warfare and kept learning more and more in order to escape from our troops and to exhaust them. Therefore, sometimes huge cleansings are needed in this swathe of land and furthermore restless counter-guerrilla actions. (Snouck Hurgronje 1985, p. 65, my translation)

Snouck Hurgronje advocated, on the one hand, military action to totally repel the insurgents in Aceh under the leadership of the *ulama*, and on the other hand, he promoted cooperation with the *uleebalang* and their inclusion into the colonial government.

In 1899, Snouck was designated as Adviser for Native and Arabic Affairs. His recommendations could no longer be ignored by the colonial government, since the problems the Dutch were facing in Aceh could also no longer be hidden from the European public, especially since the conflict threatened to cross the border into neighbouring areas. In the first half of 1893, Acehnese guerrillas, under the command of Cut Nyak Din,[27] infiltrated Sumatra's eastern coast and made the plantations there a dangerous place not only for the Dutch, but also for the British, the Americans and other investors.

In contrast to its predecessor, the new liberal government in The Hague, having held office since 1891, was more understanding towards the financial demands from the colony to quell the war in Aceh.[28] The new governor general, C. H. A. van der Wijck, who took possession of his office at the end of 1893, ordered Colonel Deijkerhoff to employ the renegade Teuku Umar[29] for their purposes. Umar was equipped with weaponry and ammunition in order to fight his own people. Although he produced some remarkable results in the beginning due to his flexibility, his knowledge of the terrain and his tactics, he changed his mind before long. He entered into a coalition with Teungku Kutakarang and, furthermore, he succeeded in convincing more influential *ulama* and even some uncompromising *uleebalang* of all the advantages they would enjoy when they also simulated loyalty to the Dutch in order to receive more weapons to support the guerrillas secretly.

On 28 March 1896, Teuku Umar changed sides for the very last time and used $18,000 and 880 rifles to attack the majority of the Dutch security posts instead of the guerrillas' shelters (Reid 1969, p. 274). Deijkerhoff, who had trusted Teuku Umar so much, was immediately dismissed from office after the scandal become public. He was replaced by General J. A. Vetter.

> What ever might have been possible and advisable earlier, as history now once has proceeded, it is certain that we in Atjeh cannot have any considerable and durable impact other than to take the reins of these matters in our own hands and to keep them. (Snouck Hurgronje 1924*a*, p. 318, my translation)

Snouck's advice was to continue military efforts to deprive the resistance fighters of any possible places to fall back. Major General J. B. van Heutsz was charged with this mission. He had already been in close cooperation with Snouck Hurgronje since 1898.[30] In the course of the third phase of the war, van Heutsz was appointed the civil-military governor in Aceh and under his command, Snouck could come and stay in Aceh *ad libitum*. Snouck joined several operations.

The partnership between van Heutsz and Snouck operated under the following premises: he was not allowed to enter into relationships with family members of the Sultan or the *ulama*; Teuku Umar and the other guerrilla leaders had to be refused any fallback position; and the possession of arms and ammunition was to be declared illegal for Acehnese in general. If the Acehnese villagers or *uleebalang* refused to cooperate with the Dutch troops, fines had to be paid. Aside from the former security posts of the concentration line, there were now new permanent outposts built in order to more effectively pursue Teuku Umar and his adherents. He, as well as the supporters of the other two most important resistance leaders, Sultan Daud and Panglima Polem, was forced to move further towards the north-west coast to evade the Dutch. Van Heutsz followed them with a vengeance along the northern coastline into the mountainous regions outside Pidie. In order to expand into that pathless wilderness, van Heutsz operated with small groups of lightly armed troops (mainly recruited from Ambon) who were under the command of Dutch officers. In order to be better prepared for ambushes, the commander of each unit marched in the middle of two rows of native troops — a formation that was called the "duck order" (Schulten 1988, p. 65). In an essay which was published for the first time anonymously in 1908, Snouck remarked that:

> The great merit of van Heutsz was not due to that he denounced how the suppression of Atjeh had to take place, but hence, due to that this was ordered by the government, he hence knew how to make use of the available means in a way, like maybe nobody else had been able to do so at that time. (Snouck Hurgronje 1924*b*, p. 131, my translation)

In February 1899, Teuku Umar was trapped in an ambush and killed. Sultan Daud[31] surrendered in January and Panglima Polem in September 1903.[32] Until the end of that year, the Dutch managed to establish a steady administration in Aceh with the help of cooperating *uleebalang*.

After signing a *Korte Verklaring* (short decree), Aceh was henceforth to be governed as a directly-ruled colonial territory. The so-called *Atjeh school* initiated by van Heutsz, Snouck Hurgronje and their adherents seemed to confirm the assumption that offence was the best method of defence and that it was a great deal less complicated to be in charge of a united territory rather than of several single units. Under the government of the Calvinists in the Netherlands (1902–05), van Heutsz was appointed governor general of the Netherlands Indies in 1904, and Snouck Hurgronje, who kept on advising the officials, was also highly rewarded (Reid 1969, pp. 278–80). However, after a severe dispute with van Heutsz, Snouck Hurgronje turned away from Aceh. Three years later, he accepted Leiden University's offer of a professorship in Arabic studies and went back to the Netherlands. During the following years, van Heutsz's troops continued to expand Dutch colonial power throughout almost the whole of the Indonesian archipelago, which had been, until then, indirectly ruled.

Even in the decade to follow, after the formal defeat of organized native resistance, the perception was that Aceh had hardly been beaten into total submission. Although active resistance was continued only by a small number of *ulama,* all the following governors in Aceh — van der Wijck (1904–05), van Daalen (1905–08), and Swart (1908–18) — still had to cope partially with native unrest. Only between 1910 and 1912, after the *Korps Marechaussee* had been able to get hold of the most important descendants of Teungku Cik di Tiro, did the *ulama* finally stop their guerrilla warfare. The supply of weaponry and ammunition had also become very limited due to the continuing restrictions to trade. The last actions of protest and resistance were small-scale, individual actions which were called *Atjeh-moord* (Aceh murder); between the years 1910 and 1937, there were about 120 fatal assaults on colonial officials and time-servers (Siegel 1969, p. 83).

THE APPRAISAL OF SNOUCK HURGRONJE

> Snouck Hurgronje did more than influence the Islamic policy of the colonial government: in a very real sense he created it and, along with his successors, implemented it. (van Niel 1956/7, p. 592)

Although Snouck Hurgronje and his advice were very conducive concerning ending the war, some of his assessments and evaluations were, in essence, oversubscribed or even mistaken. Siegel disapproved of Snouck Hurgronje's over-evaluation of the conflict between *uleebalang* and *ulama* (Siegel 1969, p. 50).[33] Wertheim criticized Snouck because he had not recognized the progressive aims of the *ulama*, and had advised combating them. Instead, Snouck had proposed supporting and integrating the feudal chiefs — the *uleebalang* — into the administrative system. His decision was definitely influenced by the premise that secularization was necessary as a basic requirement for modernization, as seen by the Ethical (welfare) Policy. Understandably, the *uleebalang* were not interested in the dissolution of the quasi-feudal system from which they profited, and consequently, cooperation with them meant that there could not be any far-reaching efforts at modernization (Wertheim 1973, pp. 93ff.). Reid has also referred to the fact that nothing was done by the Dutch to dispel the resentments between the *ulama* and *uleebalang*; these were even strengthened in the course of time and left behind a deeply divided population. The consequences of that polarization appeared mainly after the Second World War, when the time-serving *uleebalang* were paid back most bloodily (Reid 1979, p. 7).

Apart from the political implications, Snouck Hurgronje's two volumes of *De Atjehers* (1893/4), translated as *The Acehnese* (1906), remain a classic study of colonial ethnography. His abilities to collect data, his keen perception and his powers of analysis were reckoned as exemplary by his students. Johannes Pedersen, a former student, rendered homage to his master on the occasion of Snouck Hurgronje's one hundredth birthday and called him his "highly esteemed master" (Pedersen 1957, p. 5) and a "full-grown scholar" (ibid., p. 8).

> His vast experience gave Snouck a deep knowledge of human nature and a great personal superiority. During his whole life he nourished an indomitable zeal for truth and justice. (Pedersen 1957, p. 29)

> The human sympathy that characterized Snouck also became evident in his intense disposition for friendship. (ibid., p. 30)

> At the same time, van Niel called Snouck a "*formateur* of Dutch colonial policy". Most Dutch scholars and many students of Indonesian affairs would readily agree that few men have had as intimate acquaintance with the Indonesian archipelago and its people and have had as wide a reputation as an expert on this part of the world as the late Snouck Hurgronje. (van Niel 1956/7, p. 591)

> Much of his life was directed toward creating among Indonesians a sense of enlightened self-interest which would enable them to understand what Western culture would do for them. In this realm of cultural synthesis, Snouck Hurgronje was to conduct his greatest and most thankless work. (ibid., p. 593)

However, the times when Snouck was paid deference and respect have passed. Not just have his analyses been corrected or even disproved, but there has been much criticism from Indonesians and Dutch who have criticized his methods of fact-finding and his performance. Isa Anshary, for instance, one of the most popular Islamic scholars in Indonesia, called Snouck Hurgronje "a mufti of Dutch imperialism" (quoted in Boland 1982, p. 13). Snouck misrepresented the trustfulness of his Acehnese informants to deliver the information which was demanded by the colonial government.

> Since many I daily associate with Natives regardless of their position, in a more intimate way than could be the case with a Civil Servant, considering his official position. In order to achieve such an intimacy one has, so to say, to absorb oneself within the native society, and to have at one's disposal the instruments which may eliminate, as far as possible, the barriers that separate the native world from our due to the difference in language, custom, way of thinking and race. (quoted in Wertheim 1972, pp. 323–24)

Snouck pretended friendship with the Acehnese to conceal his cloak-and-dagger activities. Although he often spoke of sympathy for the Acehnese, that sympathy is not always to be found in his writings.

> ...that Acheh, with its hopeless internal discord, its lack of any central authority, its deeply rooted contempt for kafirs (unbelievers), the treacherous und utterly unreliable character of its population, cannot be won over for a civilized intercourse, nay, cannot be made harmless unless through a complete submission. (quoted in Wertheim 1972, p. 325)

So, was this all an unscrupulous breach of trust in favour of his own scholarly reputation, at a time when only utilizable scholarship was sought after and when independent research was not financially supported? Or, was Snouck just more or less a child of his time — a time when imperialistic thinking was omnipresent — who was smart enough to assess the state of global affairs and to bind himself and his services indispensably to the colonial government? At the point when his analysis came to an end, his political and strategic advice started. The importance of his recommendations could only be estimated since they have long been kept secret.[34] Parts of his findings were modified and published in a two-volume publication *De Atjehers* (1893–94), but of course, not his strategic conclusions for ending the war. The publishing of his *Verspreide geschriften* (collected writings) in 1923/24 disclosed some previously kept secrets about Snouck Hurgronje's work, but only with the voluminous publication of the *Ambtelijke adviezen* (official advices) in 1957 did all information became accessible and traceable (Wertheim 1973, p. 92).

THE IMPACT OF THE ACEH WAR ON THE PRESENT

Until its second phase, the war in Aceh was mainly a matter for the Dutch military (KNIL and *Korps Marechaussee*). Since solely military action (expeditions and "concentration systems") had proved insufficient, civil-military measures were added and double strategies were tried (co-option and counter-insurgency). The war was won not only because of Dutch logistical and technological superiority, but also due to the lack of cohesiveness, which would have resulted in a more nationalistic resistance, on the Acehnese side.

Although the Aceh War could be categorized as a small war, when considering the violence of its operations, this should not belittle its short- and long-term consequences. The label of "small war" inherently downplays the suffering caused by the war, but looking at the approximate number of victims produces a different perspective: about 7,700 soldiers of the Netherlands Indies army lost their lives, and about the same number suffered severe bodily injuries. On the Acehnese side, the losses were more drastic: between 30,000 and 100,000 people died as a consequence of the war but also because of an outbreak of epidemics (cholera and malaria) during the adverse wartime conditions (Bakker 1993, p. 58). In some parts of Aceh, the diminution of the population was particularly acute. For instance, in the heartland of Aceh Besar, only a quarter of the pre-war population was to eventually survive.

As well as the enormous financial burden which was caused by the war on both sides, the war gave rise to grave psychological after-effects not only on the side of the losers, but also on the winner's side. Aceh became a prime example of harsh resistance. It was no wonder that the Dutch avoided reoccupying Aceh on their return after the Second World War.

The long-term consequences of the Aceh War are astonishing and they have lasted until today. Hasan di Tiro, a descendant of Teungku Cik di Tiro (1836–91), exploits the Aceh War to drum up support for the armed independence struggle of his Gerakan Aceh Merdeka (GAM; Free Aceh Movement) that has been fighting for almost thirty years for the separation of Aceh from the unitary state of the Republic of Indonesia.

In his publications and official statements, Hasan di Tiro always refers to the anti-Dutch resistance and equates that struggle with the present separatist activities of GAM by calling the Indonesian states the neo-colonial successor to the Dutch.

> Even Acheh Sumatra was given to the Javanese instead of being returned to the Achehnese, the indigenous people of that country, who have more claim to the territory because the Dutch had taken it from them and not from the Javanese.... Yet instead of returning the country to the people of Acheh Sumatra, the Dutch gave it to the Javanese. In doing so, the Dutch violated all the known rules of international law and decolonization procedures of the United Nations.... (Hasan di Tiro 1986, p. 66)

According to other writings of Hasan di Tiro, Aceh was never completely defeated by the Dutch. Henceforth, Aceh should not have been integrated against its will, but should have remained the legal successor state of the sultanate and therefore, has the right to full sovereignty. Hasan di Tiro especially stresses the kinship connections of the Tiro family and the conferment of the royal seal on his ancestors to enforce his demands (Aspinall 2003, pp. 139–41; Aspinall 2002, p. 13).

It seems that almost none of the other powerful clans were as influential as the Tiro clan, from whom many significant *ulama* descended. Teungku Cik di Tiro had not only several thousands guerrillas under his command, he was also known for dispensing powerful written appeals for the continuation of resistance. His family members were also involved in fighting the Dutch and some of them even lost their lives on the battlefield. Two of his sons, Teungku Mat Amin and Teungku di Boekit, died in 1896 during the fighting in Anakgalong, and one of his grandchildren, Teungku Ci Amat di Tiro, was killed in 1911 (Bakker 1993, p. 67).

In order to legitimize the independence struggle of GAM, a big arc has been drawn — spanning from the Aceh War against the Dutch to today's uprisings. Antithetic events that took place in between are neglected or seem meaningless to GAM propaganda (Missbach 2005, p. 116). In Hasan di Tiro's published diary, there are many references to the anti-Dutch war, for example, about how his relatives died and about their burial places, which are described as places of worship. At the beginning of GAM's independence struggle, at the end of the 1970s, Hasan di Tiro also introduced a new type of calendar in Aceh which contains ten official holy days — eight of which are dedicated to Acehnese heroes of the Aceh War (Hasan di Tiro 1984, p. 50). Without going into the details of Hasan di Tiro's ideological premises, the eclectic characteristics of GAM's ideology and the permanent reference to Aceh's former magnitude and its alliances have to be noted.[35]

Without ignoring all the political or economic factors which have played a key role in initiating the armed resistance of GAM, the repercussions and long-term consequences of small wars on following developments — such as in Aceh — must also be taken into consideration when analysing current conflicts.

Notes

1. Snouck did not enjoy such a good reputation among influential Indonesian Muslims (Boland 1982, p. 13).
2. The Ethical Policy was initiated primarily by C. T. van Deventer, a lawyer and

parliamentarian, who pointed out all the advantages enjoyed by the Netherlands by exploiting its colony in his publication *Een Eereschuld* (A debt of honour). Consequently, he pleaded — bearing in mind the white men's burden — for some kind of compensation for the colonized. With paternal "generosity", development projects for the Indonesian population were set up following Western guidelines (*mission civilisatrice*) and under Dutch authority. Highlights of this policy, which was officially announced in 1901 by Queen Wilhelmina, were education, irrigation and transmigration. This change of policy was possible mainly due to the military consolidation of its hegemony that had been achieved by the colonial government of the Netherlands Indies (Ricklefs 1993, pp. 145–47). Generally, a distinction has to be made between the Ethical Policy as ideology and its genuine implementation in detail (Otterspeer 1998, p. 204).

3. This was also the case at the royal court in Aceh, where certain symbols and rituals, which were Hindu in origin, lived on (Brakel 1975, pp. 60–62).
4. There were four queens who ruled Aceh in the seventeenth century, but admittedly the autonomy of the "pepper kings", who controlled the harbours in the peripheries, was enlarged during their reign (Reid 1975, pp. 52–54).
5. With this treaty, signed on 6 July 1663, the coastal areas of Minangkabau, including Padang (south of Aceh), became a protectorate of the VOC, which in return was responsible for preventing raids across the border from Aceh.
6. This group consisted of traditional leaders of trade, who were theoretically subordinate to the sultan, but in reality were independent of him and his power, which consequently caused tension from time to time. Large parts of the pepper trade and its logistics lay in their hands. They did not have fixed relations with the territories which were granted to them, and only in exceptional cases did they intervene politically (Siegel 1969, pp. 9, 16, 23, 32). Since the beginning of the nineteenth century, they had become more and more independent of the sultan's taxes (Christie 1996, p. 140).
7. For more information on British-Acehnese relations, Lee Kam Hing (1995).
8. In 1819, Sir Thomas Stamford Raffles, who had formerly served as the governor general in Java, concluded an agreement with the Acehnese sultan, Jauhar Alam, that reappointed him as the legal head of Aceh but also demanded, at the same time, a guarantee of free trading rights for the British, the acceptance of a British legal adviser to be appointed to his court and the prevention of permanent settlement of other Europeans in Aceh (Tarling 1963, pp. 17–19). The British feared that Aceh might become weakened through succession conflicts and, in that case, the Dutch would enjoy a walkover.
9. For example, the Padri Wars (1821–35), the assimilation of the Sultanate Siak (1858) and, later on, the Batak Wars (1872–95).
10. Since oil had been found in Aceh's hard-fought territories and because of increasing global demand, the Royal Dutch Oil Company (*Koninklijke Nederlandsche Petroleum Maatschappij*) also exerted more pressure on the governments in Batavia and The Hague (Ricklefs 1993, p. 145).

11. For the exact wording of the contract, see Reid (1969, Appendix 2).
12. Piracy was defined broadly to ease intervention from the British side. For more information on concrete cases of what was suspected to be piracy in Aceh at that particular time between the London Treaty and the Sumatra Treaty, see Tarling (1963), pp. 186–206.
13. In the introduction to his book *The Acehnese*, Snouck refers in a very detailed way to this phenomenon and cites it repeatedly as a cause to justifying armed intervention in that "old pirate state" (Snouck Hurgronje 1906, pp. vii–ix).
14. See Chapter 2 in this volume for details.
15. In 1893 again, the Acehnese sultan tried to contact the Ottomans by post, but his letter was confiscated/intercepted and dropped into the hands of the Dutch (see Chapter 2 in this volume).
16. Letter from James Loudon to the governor general, van de Putte, on 25 February 1873, as quoted in Reid (1969, p. 95).
17. Altogether, the Dutch army numbered about 28,000 men, and was, hence, relatively small. Considerably more than a quarter was sent to Aceh (Schulten 1988, p. 62).
18. His successor, Muhammad Daud Syah, was only ten years old at that time (Reid 1969, p. 158).
19. The Dutch even constructed a railway in Aceh in order to transport and supply their troops more easily.
20. *Zakat* is the obligatory alms tax which is one of the five pillars of Islam, but in this case it was a tax-like source of revenue for war purposes.
21. Whether this transfer of power was temporary or also applied to his descendants, who continued to resist the Dutch after Cik di Tiro himself had passed away, remains strongly disputed (Aspinall 2002, p. 13).
22. Founded in 1890, it was a special unit of local patrolmen (mainly from the Moluccas) who served under Dutch general command.
23. The duration of his stay is contended. See Freitag (2003), p. 41.
24. It seems the case, at least, that Snouck Hurgronje not only recognized certain advantages of Islam but also made use of them. He was allied to two Muslim women but kept his marriages secret, fearing a negative impact on his reputation (Freitag 2003, p. 54).
25. Although these scholars were highly regarded among the Acehnese population, the conception of reform — "to leave behind the ties of kinship in order to unite as Muslims" (Siegel 1969, p. 74) — was never to be realized.
26. A translation from Acehnese into Indonesian of some of the most famous lyrics was edited by Ibrahim Alfian (1992).
27. Besides being an active resistance fighter, she was also the wife of the renegade Teuku Umar.
28. The Dutch colonial government also used taxes from the Netherlands Indies to finance its war (Ricklefs 1993, p. 145).
29. Snouck Hurgronje was not very convinced of Umar's trustworthiness, and his

opinion of him was not very complimentary: "[…] he was a typical Achehnese in his complete untrustworthiness and in his slavery to opium and gambling, but he differed from most Acehnese headmen in his energy and consummate tact in his relations with all sorts and conditions of men" (Snouck Hurgronje 1906, p. xii).

30. Snouck Hurgronje and van Heutsz had known each other since their boyhood in Breda and later on they also met in The Hague where Heutsz attended the *Hogere Krijgsschool* (High Military Academy) (Van't Veer 1980, p. 195).
31. In 1905, he was exiled by the Dutch because he had written a petition to the Japanese consul in Singapore (Reid 1969, p. 259).
32. Due to his decision to surrender, Polem was later granted a high post under the direct suzerainty of the Netherlands (Ricklefs 1993, p. 146).
33. Siegel generally regards the *uleebalang* more as "business people" than as administrative authorities (Siegel 1969, pp. 9–11).
34. Admittedly, it is not unusual for state archives to remain closed for twenty-five years or more.
35. Not for nothing does the flag of GAM bear such an enormous resemblance to the Turkish flag (see Chapter 2 in this volume).

4

FROM COLONIAL TIMES TO REVOLUTION AND INTEGRATION

Fritz Schulze

Without any doubt, the Aceh War, which started in 1873, was the bloodiest and most fiercely fought in Dutch colonial history. It is difficult to establish when exactly the war was really over. The Dutch side declared the end of the war in 1903. By that year the Sultan had surrendered, and in the same year the Dutch succeeded in establishing an *uleebalang*-led administration. Nevertheless, the Sultan had not officially handed over power, and the resistance of *ulama*-led guerrilla groups continued. In 1904, the Gayo and Alas districts were subdued by extensive brutality. And only between 1910 and 1912 were the Dutch able to break the open resistance of the *ulama* in the area of Tangsé. The Acehnese claim that the war only ended with the arrival of the Japanese in 1942. Moreover, they claim that the Netherlands had never really controlled Aceh and that Aceh had never been a subject of Dutch colonial sovereignty because the Acehnese had never surrendered and the Sultan had never handed over state power to the Dutch. Indeed, the open war was over, but the violence continued. Several smaller uprisings took place in the twenties. The most remarkable was the Bakongan Revolt, which resulted in several skirmishes between 1924 and 1926. Being unable to continue the open *jihad* successfully, many Acehnese turned to individual attacks, which would nowadays be called knifings and in those days, *Atjeh moord* (Aceh murder). However, on the surface Aceh had been subdued now. However, the military success of the Dutch was only one point of interest. The other was the profound change which the Acehnese society has experienced and which was still underway in the twenties and thirties.

In the course of the war, leadership and hierarchy in Acehnese society had already experienced substantial changes.[1] The authority of the *uleebalang* was not accepted any more by the peasants of Aceh. The old *adat* system had eroded. Not only the military leadership in the course of the war, but also the spiritual leadership was now in the hands of the *ulama*. Although the Dutch had installed the *uleebalang* as heads of the administration, they had lost their traditional social function as *adat* chiefs. They completely depended on the Dutch for their authority — the Dutch colonial government being their only source of legitimization. This was, of course, dangerous in a society which had suffered so many losses and had experienced so many grievances in forty years of war against this very authority. Moreover, the former economic basis of the *uleebalang* had also dwindled. Now they were no longer able to control the trade in pepper as well as the trade in local agricultural products. The Dutch had stopped the cultivation of pepper. Instead, rice cultivation had been expanded significantly. The local trade was now dominated by Chinese merchants. Since the old sources of income had diminished, many *uleebalang* turned to arbitrary measures to enrich themselves.

The destruction of the traditional political system had removed the *uleebalang* from their position of social leadership. Now the ordinary people had only the *ulama* left to turn to, although many of them had lost their lives during the war. However, this was not the case for all of them. The *ulama* of Aceh now played a central role in society. However, this new position could not be filled in the traditional way, which was hundreds of years old. Now they had to cope with a modernizing colonial society. To uphold their traditional function, which had developed within the framework of a feudal society, could only mean to lose control. The challenges of modern times were clearly visible. Certainly, the Acehnese people did not like the foreign intruders. However, the development of the modern market economy and especially, the imposition of a modern educational system eventually would have eroded Acehnese self-confidence and national identity.

The preconditions for the change in social leadership were favourable for the *ulama*, not only because of the unstable situation of the *uleebalang*, but also because of the change in religious attitude within the ranks of the *ulama* as well as among ordinary people. In the course of the war, religion had developed into a potent political force. Formerly, the influence of the *ulama* had been restricted to religious issues. The Friday prayers were held in Arabic, and no political influence was exerted. However, in the course of the war, the *ulama* established a network which allowed them to communicate and to make the *dayah* and mosques places of political propaganda and a focus of their political power. By entering into a holy war against the infidel intruders, the *ulama* transformed religion into a highly political issue. Of course, when the Dutch imposed their colonial administration, the conditions changed once more. However, the newly developed attitude in the fields of social leadership and resistance against the Dutch remained. A greater part of the Acehnese *ulama* quickly adapted to the new conditions. They knew that there was no way to return to the time prior to the Dutch invasion. Historical romanticism would not be able to liberate the Acehnese people. The answer, for a significant number of the *ulama*, was to turn towards reformism.

Reformism was not only a matter of urgency in Aceh, but also in other parts of the Dutch East Indies, especially in Sumatra and Java. Indeed, the Acehnese *ulama* used whatever opportunities they had. There were mainly two ways in which they came into contact with modernist ideas. First, several *ulama* got in touch with Islamic modernism via the Middle East, when they made the *hajj* to Mecca or studied at Middle Eastern universities. The second way was through the fast-growing Islamic education system, especially in West Sumatra, where modernist Muslim leaders established several *madrasah* which attracted Muslim pupils from all over the archipelago, including Aceh. A further factor was the establishment of reformist Muslim organizations in the Dutch East Indies, above all the Muhammadiyah. Although the Muhammadiyah was founded in 1912 as a unitary organization for the whole of the Dutch East Indies, the Acehnese *ulama* did not integrate themselves into that organization but, instead, chose their own way. This circumstance alone shows that the Acehnese regarded themselves as separate and not as an integral part of the colony. The influence of the Muhammadiyah was restricted to the bigger towns in Aceh, especially Kutaraja. The same was true for the Sarekat Islam, which also could not take root in Aceh.

It would not be proper to assume that the coming of modernism was only due to political aims. Modernism was the genuine result of the social and political conditions in Aceh; education was the main issue. The traditional system was not able to meet the needs of a modernizing society. According to the old system, which was still prevalent at the beginning of the war, education was only based around the *dayah*. It concentrated on religious subjects, especially Islamic jurisprudence and learning the Qur'an by heart. Secular subjects were considered not only useless, but even dangerous, because they distracted students' minds from the important issues which were aimed at the hereafter. The only relevant language to study, besides Acehnese and Malay, was Arabic. European languages were considered to be products of "unbelief", and should, therefore, not be studied. Furthermore, the introduction of a Western education system was also considered dangerous, as it might turn the younger generation away from Islamic religious values and bring them closer to the ideas of the foreign intruders. The only answer could be the establishment of a modernized Islamic education, which would not only bring a new attitude to Islamic doctrines, but also teach secular subjects, such as mathematics, Malay and so on, which were so important to cope with modern times. In this way, the modern *madrasah* combined traditional religious teachings — though with new modernist aspects — with secular subjects. One *madrasah* in particular became something of a model: the Jamiatul Diniyah, which had been founded by Muhammad Daud Beureu'eh in 1930 at Garot in the vicinity of Sigli. Such *madrasah* became very popular in Aceh. In order to provide teachers who were able to fulfil the needs of a modern Islamic education, a teacher training school, the Sekolah Normal Islam, was established in Bireuen. When founding this school, the Acehnese reformist *ulama* took a similar school, which had already been established in West Sumatra, as the working model. In this way, the anti-Dutch resistance changed from being backward-looking and focused on the re-establishment of the old *adat* system to being of a modern religion-based anti-colonial orientation. Of course, not all Acehnese *ulama* followed this new orientation. A split developed within the ranks of the *ulama*, separating the modernists, on the one hand, and the so-called *ulama kolot* (old-fashioned *ulama*) on the other.

Education was one focus and political propaganda among the people in general another. For the latter purpose, the so-called *tabligh* became popular. *Tabligh* were a kind of public speech which were held from time to time in the mosques or related places. There were several renowned *ulama* who travelled from place to place to disseminate their political views through the *tabligh*. One of the most prominent of them was Teungku Muhammad Daud Beureu'eh, who later became the leader of the Acehnese revolution and after independence also the leader of the Acehnese rebellion against the central government in Jakarta. Since there was no substantial national secular political movement as in other parts of the Dutch East Indies, especially in Java, the reformist *ulama* of Aceh became the sole leading anti-colonial political force in the country. So, it was only natural that its next consequent step was to establish an organization of its own. This happened in 1939, when the Persatuan Ulama Seluruh Aceh (PUSA; All-Aceh Ulama Association) was founded.

However, only three years later, conditions changed profoundly, when Japanese troops invaded the Dutch East Indies, including Aceh. In general, the Acehnese welcomed the Japanese, because they ousted the Dutch and promised to liberate the Indonesian peoples. For this reason, several Acehnese *ulama* conspired with the Japanese even before the invasion took place.

The most important among them was Said Abu Bakar, who lived in exile in Malaya. After the Japanese occupation of Malaya, he collaborated with the Japanese and went back to Aceh to provoke a rebellion. This rebellion broke out in mid-February 1942 in Seulimeum under the leadership of Tengku Abdul Wahab and cost the lives of the Dutch *controleur* and the director of the Aceh railway. On 7 March, a full-scale rebellion began in Aceh, with the result that the Dutch began to evacuate the northern part of Aceh. A few days later, on 12 March, the Japanese troops landed near Kutaraja and Peureulak. It is notable that the rebellion not only was lead by PUSA *ulama*, but also was particularly strong where the few anti-Dutch *uleebalang* supported the rebellion. Aceh was the only place in the Dutch East Indies where the Japanese invasion was preceded by a local upheaval. As a result, the Japanese invaders met with the growing self-confidence of the Acehnese.

As elsewhere in the Dutch East Indies, the Japanese were warmly welcomed by the local people. However, the PUSA *ulama*, in particular, quickly realized that their support of the Japanese did not earn them any immediate advantage. Not only did the Japanese not favour the *ulama* party, in general, they paid no special attention to the Islamic religion. Moreover, they were suspicious of the anti-colonial zeal of the *ulama*. For this reason, they relied more on the traditional *uleebalang*. So, it is not surprising that the lower levels of the administration and the central advisory board mainly consisted of *uleebalang* besides several *ulama* of different origins. Moreover, religion was not allowed to play any political role. So, PUSA was kept away from having any political influence or responsibility. Since the Japanese paid no attention to local traditions and exercised a brutal rule, they were quickly regarded as barbarians by many Acehnese. This attitude and their neglect of local conditions led to the first revolt, which took the Japanese by surprise in November 1942. The uprising was led by a young conservative *ulama* at Bayu near Lhokseumawe. He not only preached against the Japanese, but also against their PUSA supporters. He did not want "the dogs exchanged for pigs". The showdown took place on 10 November and left him and about a hundred of his followers dead, as well as eighteen Japanese soldiers. After this, the Japanese were even more suspicious of political Islam. PUSA was reduced to a mere religious organization of the same level as the Muhammadiyah. When the Majlis Agama Islam untuk Bantuan Kemakmuran Asia Timur Raya (MAIBKATRA; Islamic Council for the Development of the Greater Asia Co-Prosperity Sphere) was installed as a religious propaganda instrument, the parity of PUSA and Muhammadiyah was kept. Of course, this council had no political significance. However, it gave its members the opportunity to travel across the country and to address the people openly. Daud Beureu'eh, for instance, made wide use of this opportunity.

As pointed out earlier, religious leaders and organizations were kept as far away as possible from the administration. However, the revolutionary zeal of the PUSA youth especially was exploited for another purpose in 1943. The position of the Japanese army became more and more critical, especially in Sumatra and Malaya, which both were administered by the 25th Army. Aceh became a focal point, because the Japanese expected an Allied assault there. By the end of 1942, young Acehnese had already been recruited for police operations in Malaya to quell the communist resistance there. However, in 1943, Acehnese were recruited on a large scale for the *Heiho* — the indigenous auxiliary defence forces, which were part of the Japanese army — and later the *Giyugun* — volunteer forces which were not part of the Japanese army, but were instead auxiliary forces which were intended to resist an Allied invasion as guerrillas (in Java, they were known as *Peta*). As a result, the *Giyugun* forces of Aceh were the strongest in Sumatra and included more than twenty companies or 5,000 to 6,000 men. Later, these military units were to become the nucleus of the national army.

At the end of 1943, the Japanese announced the introduction of "political participation". However, this turned out to be merely a smokescreen. The newly established councils in each district had no political competence or power. On the contrary, they were used by the Japanese to enact their demands on the Acehnese people, that is, to functionalize the Acehnese people to meet the needs of the Japanese occupiers. These demands quickly became excessive. The Acehnese had to deliver rice, to provide labour, and so on. Soon, the members of the councils became the focus of the people's anger. This was, in the long term, very dangerous. Generally, the great majority of the council members were chosen from the ranks of the traditional nobility, the *uleebalang*.[2] This meant that the *uleebalang*, who had already been disliked since Dutch colonial times, were about to be labelled as collaborators of the hated Japanese occupiers too. In the course of the war, conditions worsened continuously. Eventually, all males between the ages of 16 and 45 were obliged to do forced labour. The population went hungry because much of the rice produced had to be delivered to the Japanese. Nothing could be bought, including clothes, because there was no sea trade any more between Sumatra and its neighbours. All ships were needed for the war in the Pacific. This brought the *uleebalang* into a precarious situation. If they refused to enforce the Japanese's demands, they could be killed. If not, they became the enemies of the people. The role of the *ulama* was much more comfortable, although they also were involved in spreading propaganda for the Japanese. As they only operated on the level of ideology, they were not forced to enforce the intolerable demands of the occupiers. On the contrary, in the countryside, they were able to direct their propaganda against the *uleebalang* — a portent of doom.

As already pointed out, the situation continually worsened. For this reason, the Japanese tried to obtain broader support among the local people. The Japanese military's secret service advised relying more on the progressive *ulama*. One means of doing this was through the introduction of a new legal system which gave more influence to them. The traditional courts, which were under the control of the *uleebalang*, were abolished and two new types of court established: a secular and a religious one. Both courts were separated from direct *uleebalang* influence. The appointment of *kadhi* (judges dealing with Muslim affairs) was in the hands of a central religious court in Kutaraja. When positions in the secular courts needed to be filled, the *Aoki* (the judicial official of the Japanese) turned directly to PUSA to ask for suitable candidates. This behaviour was very much like a putsch and deprived the *uleebalang* of any influence on the courts. However, these legal reforms were made at the 25th Army's headquarters in Bukittinggi, but the Japanese governor of Aceh, Iino Shazaburo, was suspicious of the PUSA activists. Through his interference, the *uleebalang* again gained influence, not just on the appointment of judges in the secular courts but also on the appointment of the *kadhi*. Iino also tried to reduce the influence of PUSA at the central religious court in Kutaraja, which led to some dispute between the governor and the PUSA *ulama*. Nevertheless, the establishment of the religious court was a propagandistic victory for the *ulama*. Although their direct influence was still limited, they now had gained further ground.

Iino's pro-*uleebalang* policy and his suspicious attitude toward the *ulama* was probably also the reason why there was no training of native guerrilla forces in Aceh, in contrast to other regions in Sumatra, where the Japanese tried to prepare for an Allied invasion.

Another means by which they tried to obtain the support of the suffering people was the promise of independence by the Japanese Prime Minister Koiso on 7 September 1944. This was a political move in the face of impending defeat in the Pacific. The military headquarters in Bukittinggi did not support this step, but had to give in. Although there were almost no actual consequent actions, the propagandistic effect was strong. Moreover, the nationalists in Sumatra gained several important advantages. The first benefit was that they were now able to meet, because every province sent delegates to the meetings, which were now being held in Bukittinggi. Aceh sent Teuku Njak Arif, an ardent nationalist *uleebalang* and the right hand of governor Iino Shazaburo, as well as Daud Beureu'eh. In the eyes of the people, cooperation with the Japanese suddenly seemed to be meaningful and positive. In Aceh, this development had an interesting side effect. For the first time, a sense of nationalism, which reached beyond the boundaries of Aceh, arose and became the basis for the willingness of the Acehnese to join an Indonesian unitary state.

By the end of the Japanese occupation, the situation in Aceh had become desperate. Famine and forced labour meant that the situation was spiralling out of control. Japanese often came under attack from people who could not endure their suffering any more. Besides this, the social system had eroded because there was no functioning relationship between the social groups any more. The Japanese had forced the *uleebalang* to exploit their own people to the utmost degree, and the religious leadership was unable to provide substantial help. To further strengthen their grip on the people, the Japanese created a new Aceh-wide unitary organization for all local citizens — the *hôkôhai* — and dissolved all other civil organizations. Again, Teuku Njak Arif became the first leader, but he quickly resigned, maybe because he realized that it would be better for him to seek his political future elsewhere. Daud Beureu'eh became the leader of the religious section of *hôkôhai*; it was the first time the Japanese governor had conferred on him such a high-ranking position. But time was running out, and the *hôkôhai* had no future.

While preparing for independence, the headquarters in Bukittinggi, in the meantime, decided to set up an all-Sumatran advisory council, which first assembled on 26 June 1945. Again, Teuku Njak Arif was Aceh's representative. However, yet again, the military administration was very reluctant to promote any measures geared towards independence, notwithstanding the supposed independence of Indonesia as a unitary state. The Japanese army preferred maintaining Malaya and Sumatra under its own political control. The only further step they took was the formation of a Sumatran committee to investigate the possibility of granting independence to Indonesia. Despite this reluctance, the Japanese government decided to declare 7 September the day of Indonesia's independence. Most likely, it was due to the delaying tactics of the 25th Army that none of the Sumatran leaders were sent to Jakarta, but only two persons of secondary rank. Nonetheless, in Aceh the preparations for independence had far-reaching repercussions. Teuku Njak Arif was chosen to replace the Japanese resident in the event that independence was granted. Similar measures were undertaken in the other regions, where future assistant residents were determined. However, on 14 August, when the atomic bomb fell on Hiroshima and ended the Second World War, Sumatra and Aceh were not properly prepared for independence.

After the surrender of the Japanese, the situation in Aceh became precarious. Nobody knew what the future would bring. Many people expected the Dutch to return to the Indies and to Aceh in particular. For this reason, many of the *uleebalang* quickly contacted their old Dutch acquaintances, who had been interned in prisoner-of-war camps in North Sumatra. The position of the Japanese army was unclear as well. Many Japanese only wanted to get out of the country safely. However, in contrast to the other regions in Sumatra, the administration in Aceh was not in disarray. The *uleebalang* who have been appointed as district heads kept on working, and Teuku Njak Arif was appointed successor to Governor Iino.

Things became more complicated when the Allied Forces sent a small party — including the Dutch major Knottenbelt — to Kutaraja to supervise the post-war development of the state. The state of things, indeed, could not satisfy the Allies. Teuku Njak Arif, for instance, tried to maintain the military structures that had been put in place during the occupation, which by 12 October were restyled the Angkatan Pemuda Indonesia (API; Indonesian Youth Forces). This quasi-army was closely connected with nationalist youth organizations that had emerged in the Kutaraja area and mainly consisted of young intellectuals with strong pro-Indonesian leanings. They called themselves the Badan Pemuda Indonesia (BPI; Indonesian Youth Agency), and were later renamed the Pemuda Republik Indonesia (PRI; Indonesian Republic's Youth). On 12 October, an Aceh-wide congress established the BPI throughout Aceh. The leading figures in the rural areas were almost all adherents of PUSA.

On 15 October, the Acehnese took over power from the Japanese administration, notwithstanding the protests of Knottenbelt. This was the beginning of an independent national administration in Aceh. At the same time, Daud Beureu'eh issued a declaration of *jihad*. This time, modernist and conservative *ulama* were united. On the basis of this declaration, Islamic armies were founded — the Mujahidin in Pidie and the Hizbullah in Aceh Besar. As a result, two power centres emerged: the *uleebalang*-dominated territorial administration and the Islamic militia, which were led either by PUSA or by conservative clerics. Some *uleebalang*, especially in the Pidie region, used their power to seize back their hold on the judicial system, which had been taken away from them in 1944. This dangerous development became even more complicated when Teuku Njak Arif used about 200 former KNIL soldiers (KNIL had been the colonial army of the Dutch) to form a special police force. When tensions increased, Knottenbelt was forced to retreat and was sent back to Medan by Teuku Njak Arif. From this point onwards, Teuku Njak Arif — who himself was an *uleebalang* — was deeply mistrusted by the PUSA Youth and PRI.

In the following period, each side remained eager to arm their forces. The Japanese army was the only source of arms at that time. Sometimes, the Japanese handed over their weapons voluntarily, and sometimes under massive pressure. At the same time, the PRI, which had renamed itself the Pemuda Sosialis Indonesia (PESINDO; Indonesian Socialist Youth), founded a further army of its own, the Divisi Rencong. Several Japanese soldiers deserted and helped the Acehnese to build more professional armies. Obviously, the Japanese were unable and unwilling to fulfil their obligation to keep order in Aceh until the arrival of the Allied Forces. Except for some regions along the North Sumatran border, the Japanese army left Aceh in the course of December 1945. However, the quest for weapons triggered what would later be called the Acehnese social revolution.

The so-called Cumbok War began in December 1945, when several parties tried to get hold of the weapons at the Japanese garrison at Sigli in the Pidie region. In Pidie, the *uleebalang* and the PUSA clerics stood fiercely opposed to each other. There was no moderate party that might have been able to work out a reconciliation between the two. When the time came to disarm the only remaining company of Japanese soldiers, a bitter conflict arose. On 4 December 1945, *uleebalang* followers fired on the PRI's men. A fierce battle broke out. Although the official Acehnese army, the Tentara Keamanan Rakyat (TKR; People's Safety Army), was present, they could not stop the fighting. The PRI and PUSA got more and more support from the population, who were eager to get rid of the *uleebalang* once and for all. The *uleebalang* of Pidie were in fear now and gathered around the hardline *uleebalang* Teuku Mohammad Daud. His plan was to frighten the other side by a show of force. They raided the homes of PUSA followers. However, despite an initial military success, the result of this campaign was not as intended. Outrage broke out. Finally, the group around Teuku Mohammad Daud was declared traitors and enemies of the republic. Units of the TKR, as well as other units, for example the Mujahidin from Seulimeum, were sent to Pidie. The latter were led by Teungku Hosain Almujahid, who in pre-war times was the leader of the PUSA Youth. The final attack was launched on 12 January 1946. Finally, Teuku Mohammad Daud and his followers were captured and executed. Following that, the remaining ruling *uleebalang* of Pidie, except for two, were also killed. Ordinary members of their families were also slaughtered by the mob.

In the meantime, another front opened in the area around Langsa in the east. Revolutionary forces tried to oust the remaining Japanese garrison. Heavy fighting brought no result. However, after the victory in Pidie, revolutionary forces, including the powerful Mujahidin unit from Seulimeum, rushed eastwards to help their comrades. Their targets were not only the Japanese, but also the *uleebalang*-dominated civilian administration and police. The onslaught took place on 12 February, and the *uleebalang* leader, Teuku Ibrahim, was finally captured on 16 February 1946. After this success, the victorious Mujahidin, now renamed the Tentara Perjuangan Rakyat (TPR; People's Struggle Army), purged the north coast of Aceh between Langsa and Kutaraja of the remaining *uleebalang*, who were captured or killed, especially in the Lhokseumawe region. Hosain Almujahid, the leader of the Mujahidin/TPR was now at the peak of his power. The arbitrary power of the *uleebalang* had been wiped out all over Aceh, including in the west coast. The survivors were interned at Takengon, the capital of the Gayo lands. Several other political adversaries, including the leading Muhammadiyah cleric and veterans of the 1942 uprising, were detained. Teuku Njak Arif was also detained and replaced by Teuku Mohammad Daudsjah. However, Almujahid's rise to power was short-lived. The concentration of power in just one hand and the risk of another arbitrary rulership was not tolerable for many others. Above all, it was pressure from Deud Beureu'eh which made Almujahid and his forces retreat from Kutaraja. Deud Beureu'eh himself was then appointed deputy resident. Later, in August 1947, he became the military governor of Aceh.

The war in Pidie and the following events had changed the political landscape. It marked the end of traditional rule in Aceh. The door to a more democratic and egalitarian society had been opened. The *uleebalang* were replaced by an interim commission. After a period of five months, the head of every region would be elected by the people. The property of the *uleebalang*, especially the land, was redistributed. A part was retained by the government, another given to the peasants, and a third part had to be returned to the surviving members of the *uleebalang* families. In fact, much was taken over by followers and activists of PUSA and the now numerous related organizations. The same went for important positions in other sectors of the economy. For instance, Hosain Almujahid became director of the North Sumatran Oil Company, and Said Abubakar — the organizer of the anti-Dutch rebellion prior to the coming of the Japanese — became manager of several state-owned estates. In this way, the Acehnese *ulama* split into two factions: the *ulama* who entered secular professions and the *ulama* who continued to uphold their religious functions.

The situation in Aceh was quite different from other developments in Sumatra and Indonesia as a whole. In East Sumatra, for instance, a social revolution had taken place as well. However, the outcome there was a very unstable political situation, which was partly due to the ethnic diversity there, as well as the competition between several political groups. Except for some minor disturbances, the political situation in Aceh was rather stable and the country well administered. Considering their historical experience and the fact that the social basis for a return of colonialism had been wiped out, it is hardly surprising that the Allied Forces and later, the returning Dutch did not try to enter Aceh any more. From 1945 until 1950, the Indonesian republic was busy maintaining independence in the face of successive Dutch aggression. Therefore, the government did not pay Sumatra and Aceh much attention. When the Republican leadership shifted from Java to Sumatra during the second Dutch military campaign at the end of 1948, Aceh was even promised autonomy within the state of Indonesia. So, on the surface, things were going well for Aceh. However, the roots of the coming conflict had already been laid. The leadership in Java was dominated by nationalists and left-wing politicians. In Aceh, nationalism was comparatively weak and had been mainly employed as a means of unifying the people against colonial rule and to help them become a free people with a firm desire for self-determination. Nobody in Aceh was prepared to drown in a unitary state dominated by Java or secular values. In fact, on 17 December, the central government granted Aceh the status of an autonomous province, although it did so reluctantly, feeling under pressure from Acehnese nationalists. Daud Beureu'eh became the first governor of this province.

When Indonesia became an independent federal republic on 27 December 1949, all efforts were concentrated on turning the country into a unitary state. Aceh had to play its role in this ruling enforced by Jakarta. This concept left no room for autonomy or regional identity. Furthermore, the nationalist-dominated central government was suspicious of the religion-dominated Aceh province. They were not prepared to accept any demands from Aceh. On the contrary, they wanted to destroy Aceh as a political unit and to try to enforce old plans to incorporate Aceh into a larger province of North Sumatra, that was to include Aceh, parts of former East Sumatra and the densely populated and Christian-dominated Tapanuli areas. The capital was to be Medan. A committee, whose task was to prepare for the establishment of this province, was founded as early as 1 August 1950. To the Acehnese, this step by the central government came as a shock. The short-lived euphoria at being part of an independent Indonesian state was replaced by a quickly deepening sense of alienation and the feeling that they were the losers in this newly established state. The attitude of the nationalists becomes clear from what the first governor of North Sumatra had to tell the people: "Our state is based on amongst other things the nationalist feelings of a united Indonesian people; there is no room in it for an Acehnese people, a Batak people or a Malay people. As far as the State is concerned there is only one people, the Indonesian people ...".[3]

On 25 January 1951, a governor for the new province of North Sumatra was installed. At the beginning, no substantial replacements took place within the ranks of the local Acehnese administration. However, tensions began to arise when local opposition forces — the Badan Keinsyafan Rakyat (BKR; People's Awareness Agency) — joined the attacks on PUSA and its allies. Things deteriorated even further when Indonesia-wide mass arrests took place in August 1951. These arrests were directed against communists and radical Islamists who allegedly endangered the stability of the state. However, in Aceh, these apparent dangers were only a pretext for the anti-PUSA actions of the military, which was in charge as a "State of War and Siege" had been declared in North Sumatra. The central government had already been able to secure the loyalty of the army leadership in North Sumatra by a policy of demobilization, active replacement and the exchange of military units. In the latter case, Acehnese units were transferred to other parts of Indonesia, and non-Acehnese troops, including Batak and former KNIL soldiers, were brought to Aceh. Now, the central government and the internal opposition party, the BKR, stepped up the pressure to overthrow the local civilian administration, which was still PUSA-dominated. The situation continuously deteriorated.

In early 1953, former guerrilla leaders, like Almujahid, gathered demobilized guerrillas and united them to become the Persatuan Bekas Pejuang Islam Aceh (BPA; Association of Former Acehnese Islamic Fighters), which was to become the core of a new guerrilla army. At the same time, Daud Beureu'eh and his companions established contact with Kartosuwirjo, who had led an Islamist uprising in West Java to establish an Islamic state, the Negara Islam Indonesia (NII). Now, the time had come to prepare for a new Acehnese uprising. Beginning with two Islamic congresses in Medan and Langka in April, Islamic leaders started a campaign to propagate the idea of an Islamic state. All the old organizations, which had formerly been associated with PUSA, including PUSA itself, were revived. The most important of these, besides the above-mentioned BPA, were the PUSA Youth and the Acehnese Boy Scout Movement. Of course, such activities could not have remained unnoticed. However, the central government was reluctant to take action, because it feared adding to the troubles it was already facing with the NII uprising in Java. In the meantime, many people started to leave Aceh, especially adherents to Jakarta's policies, members of the PNI (nationalists) and the PKI (communists). However, even PUSA's followers began to feel insecure, because they feared the possible reactions of the central government and the military.

Now, the government in Jakarta came under mounting pressure because of its reluctance to act. What followed seems to have been a calculated political move in order to provoke a showdown. Left-wing politicians spread the rumour of an imminent uprising in Aceh. After this, the government allegedly drew up a list of 190 Acehnese to be detained immediately. News of this was leaked in Aceh, where the leaders of Acehnese nationalism still remembered the detainments of 1951. Consequently, the Acehnese leaders felt compelled to take action. On the night of 19 September 1953, the attack started. Several towns were taken by the rebels. However, the troops of the NII were not able to defend the occupied towns for long. A quick counter-attack by government forces drove them out of the towns and forced them to retreat to the countryside and the mountains. This was the beginning of a long-lasting guerrilla war. Although the Acehnese rebels were not able to seize power in Aceh, the central government, on the other hand, was not able to pacify Aceh.

It is outside of the scope of this chapter to describe the following course of events. However, the impact of all these events on the Acehnese awareness of self should be pointed out. The revolution in Aceh, starting with the upheaval against the Dutch in 1942 and continuing with the social revolution in 1945/46, was mainly aimed at restoring Acehnese self-determination and abolishing *uleebalang* feudalism. In the course of this fight, the PUSA *ulama* adopted the option of integration into the Indonesian national state and even declared the fight for it a *jihad*. By the beginning of the 1953 rebellion, the attitude of the Acehnese had changed profoundly. Now, the Indonesian nation-state had became a new threat. It was regarded as a new type of imperialism — this time of the Javanese, who, it was believed, wanted to restore the old Javanese Majapahit Empire. Furthermore, the Indonesian state was identified with secularization and a growing communist influence. For this reason, the new rebellion acquired a distinctly religious colouring. Daud Beureu'eh also declared Aceh an autonomous state within the NII. That meant that the attitude towards the Indonesian nation-state had changed completely and to this day, that alienation between Aceh and the central government (or Java) has never been bridged again. Indeed, both sides have to realized that they are not able to win this war.

Aceh was promised that it would become an autonomous province in 1956. Ali Hasjmy, a former leader of the PUSA Youth, was appointed its first governor. However, only after quarrels within the rebel forces and after Daud Beureu'eh had been toppled in March 1959, Daud Beureu'eh and his few remaining followers finally surrendered in May 1962.

The war was over, but no lasting peace had been achieved. In the following years, especially after Soeharto seized power in 1966, Aceh became an object of ruthless exploitation and political suppression, as well as a target of massive transmigration from Java. The result was mounting hatred and alienation, until the Gerakan Aceh Merdeka (GAM; Acehnese Freedom Movement) was founded and another bloody rebellion started in 1976 under the leadership of Hasan di Tiro, a veteran of the 1953 rebellion.

Notes

1. For more details, see Chapter 3.
2. Cf. Reid (1979, p. 121).
3. Cited by Van Dijk (1981, p. 287).

PART II

Contemporary Economy and Politics

5

ECONOMIC MODERNIZATION AND ITS INFLUENCE ON THE SOCIAL SYSTEM IN ACEH

Nazamuddin, Agussabti, and Syamsuddin Mahmud[1]

INTRODUCTION

The process of economic modernization in the Western world vastly differs from that which has taken place in Aceh. In the West, the process of modernization emerged as a normal consequence of internal and natural developments in capitalist industry. This process is called "natural" because the path that economic modernization has taken was not deliberately planned or directed. The government has played a passive role, and if there was direct intervention, it has been limited to managing market forces. Conversely, intervention by the central government in Jakarta, characterized as centralistic and paternalistic, has actively directed the process of modernization in Aceh with the aim of "catching up" with the rest of the world in terms of development. This race to modernize Aceh has not accounted for pre-existing traditional values within Acehnese society. In many respects, while older values no longer retain their function, recently introduced values are also ineffective. Hence, the process of modernization has resulted in ambiguous values and apathy among the community itself.

This article discusses the various phenomena involved in such a transformation in the social system in Aceh as a consequence of the economic changes and modernization that have taken place since the 1970s. This includes observations regarding changes in values, attitudes, institutions and traditions within society, and relating these to government policies of intervention and exogenous changes, with the former aiming at economic improvement and the latter a consequence of globalization.

STRUCTURAL TRANSFORMATION AND ECONOMIC MODERNIZATION

Structural transformation has been taking place in Aceh since the 1970s, during which time Soeharto's government gave priority to economic growth. All resources were extracted or exploited for the sake of development. This included the centrally-organized exploitation of natural resources, such as timber, oil and natural gas. Profits from these went to fill the wallets of the central government and flowed back to Aceh in the form of project proposals, handed down from Jakarta. The regional government's autonomy in managing its revenue and its budget was extremely limited.[2] Similarly, society was oriented towards a social system instructed from above. Local tradition and government gradually became powerless, as part of a uniform pattern that was enforced throughout Indonesia.

The discovery of natural gas in Arun (Northern Aceh) in 1974 and the production of liquefied gas beginning in 1978 were pivotal moments in this process, altering the economic structure in Aceh drastically. In 1975, the contribution from the agricultural sector was still fairly high at 47.35 per cent, while the mining and oil and gas extraction sectors were relatively low at just 16.66 per cent. This situation had reversed by 1979, as contributions from agriculture had fallen to 25.27 per cent, while the mining and oil and gas extraction sectors had risen to 54.16 per cent. Five years later (in 1984), agricultural contributions had fallen to 16.84 per cent, while mining and oil and gas extraction continued to grow, reaching 66.58 per cent.

Changes to the economic structure in Aceh, with the relative decline in the role of the agricultural sector in terms of regional output, did not necessarily result in a rapid transformation in the economic activities of society at large. However, it has had an impact on the government's revenue and also on subsequent economic activities that are influenced directly or indirectly by the budgets of the (central and regional) government. In this regard, construction has become an important activity, together with other businesses that are largely dependent on the government's budget. Small-scale economic activities of the broader society, especially in agriculture and trade, have also intensified due to this role of the government, although generally not as much. The result is an economic dualism in which modern economic activity grows in line with market needs (such as transportation, banking, insurance, shipping and other services), alongside a traditional economy that is only slowly utilizing more developed technology and a higher degree of monetization.

In accordance with Law No. 18, 2001, Special Autonomy (*Otonomi Khusus*) for Aceh took effect at the beginning of 2002. Since then, the budget for the provincial government of Nanggroe Aceh Darussalam (APBD NAD) has increased to more than five times that in 2001.[3] The regional government has become a dominant driving force behind the economy. As the economy of the common people (*rakyat*) remains mainly agrarian, the government's main emphasis is on activities such as food cropping, fishing, the handcraft industry, and the production of construction materials and household goods (e.g. bricks, wood and furniture), as well as small-scale and seasonal plantings. At the same time, activity in professional services remains low. Besides oil and gas, farming remains dominant in the primary sector, contributing more than 56 per cent.[4] The two agricultural activities that stand out the most, economically speaking, are food cropping and animal husbandry.[5] Meanwhile, industrial activity outside of oil and gas has not yet developed substantially,[6] which is an indicator of how much Nanggroe Aceh Darussalam is lagging behind in the process of industrialization. Outside of oil and gas extraction, as well as related industries (such as fertilizer production), modernization is taking place, and only to a limited extent, within the sectors of agriculture and farming.

Regarding labour, almost half of the work force in Aceh in 2003 still worked in the farming sector, while those in industrial production amounted to less than 4 per cent. It is only the services that stand out, comprising nearly one-fifth of the 48 per cent of the work force. A large portion of these are most likely informal activities categorized as services. If compared to the conditions in 1971, in which almost three-quarters of the work force was involved in farming, arguably a significant transformation has taken place in the relative employment structure. The percentage of labour force employed in trade and in hotels and restaurants rose from 6.31 per cent in 1971 to 20.76 per cent in 2003. During the same period, the number of those in other services doubled from 7.49 per cent to 18.63 per cent. Relatively speaking, however, the rough percentage of the labour force in industrial production has not changed significantly, from only 3 to 4 per cent.

Although the above statistics suggest that industrialization in Aceh has been slow, the intensity of overall economic activity continues to increase. Similarly, modernization carries on in the application of new production and distribution methods. New methods in farming, commerce and services bring with them structural and institutional change, contributing to changes in the social life of the community. Structural transformation takes place through four processes: firstly, through the process of accumulation, which is indicated by an increase in the use of capital and an increase in private and public savings. Accordingly, along with this growth in per capita income, the tax base also expands, leading to an increase in expenditure for education and health care. At the same time, because of the decrease in the dependency ratio, the general function of the common people is shifting, from being a "burden" to becoming a "productive asset". Nevertheless, albeit as assets, the majority of the labour force is still working in the informal sector with low productivity.

Second, the process of allocation is signalled by changes in the structure of domestic demand. With regards to consumption, the largest part of household expenditure is shifting from foodstuff to the consumption of non-food goods. Even in terms of the former, consumption is changing from self-prepared meals to meals cooked by somebody else. This has resulted in a fairly rapid increase in the food market, leading to a rising demand for industrial food products (e.g. flour, flavouring and food colouring), and packaging (e.g. paper, plastic, etc.). On the other hand, there has also been a shift in government expenditure, increasing the share of public goods.

Structural shifts in production, partly as a result of changes in consumption within society and partly because of the expanding role of the government in the economy, have continuously taken place in Aceh. Better infrastructure and education have also resulted in economic growth, which no longer focuses solely on farming and the manufacture of foodstuff but also on the small-scale manufacture of goods and services for the local market. Although the agro-industry and agro-business sectors are not yet well developed, the economic activities of the broader society in the production and distribution of agricultural products continue to increase and expand in centres of economic activity, such as the traditional markets. Local markets (*uroe peukan*) that are open only on certain days of the week,[7] with sellers coming from around that area, have gradually lost their importance due to the ongoing process of agglomeration, which has been facilitated by better infrastructure (e.g. roads and shops). Such agglomeration demonstrates efficiency, which is also driven by market development on par with population growth. The scale of the economy, along with competition, increases if the trade in manufactured goods and modern services remains dominant. Generally, these goods and services are imported, for instance, from Java or from outside Indonesia.

Third, the ongoing demographic change is indicated by the ever-increasing proportion of the population of working or productive age, the decline in the dependency ratio, the creation of new jobs outside of the agriculture sector, and the increase in urbanization and agglomeration. This condition persists in Aceh to such an extent that its impact can be seen throughout the entire social system.

The fourth structural transformation is in the process of distribution, in which government policies often favour producers over consumers, capitalists over workers, urban society over the village community, and modern over traditional sectors. Such a situation is common in the initial stages of economic development. However, in Aceh this took place during the 1980s and 1990s, during which time modern forestry and plantation businesses (PTP and privately owned) and large-scale fishing rapidly increased. This growth has been enhanced by the extension of credit by the banking sector, which has experienced similar rapid growth. One effect of this has been a widening gap between those with capital and the workers, and between the modern and traditional sectors. Rather than effecting strategic long-term solutions, the centralistic welfare programmes[8] of the government have made society dependent on the government.

THE TRANSFORMATION OF THE SOCIAL SYSTEM

The philosophy of *Adat Bak Po Teumeuruhom, Hukum Bak Syiah Kuala*[9] is a major foundation of the life view, shaping values, attitudes and traditions, in Acehnese society. According to this philosophy, religion and *adat* are equally valid *zat ngon sifeuet* or essences with specific attributes. Fundamentally inseparable, elements from both Islamic law (*syariat*) and *adat* are unified in one Islamic order. As such, *adat* does not challenge Islamic religious law, because conceptions of value (i.e. what actions are allowed or not allowed) in Acehnese society are always in accordance with both *adat* and Islamic law. The value system associated with *adat* shapes and determines patterns of social relations within Acehnese society in synergy with the values upheld by Islam. Due to the strong influence of Islamic values in Acehnese society, the region has been nicknamed *Serambi Mekah* (The veranda of Mecca).

Economic modernization in Acehnese society is a consequence of the force of government intervention in economic development. The influence of globalization has also contributed to changes in values, attitudes and institutions. The process of economic modernization in Aceh began in line with the second Five Year Plan (Rencana Pembangunan Lima Tahun Tahap II, REPELITA) in the 1970s. In this plan, modernization encompassed the field of agriculture in general, and food cropping in particular. The latter reached its apex during the "Green Revolution", which was nationally known as the Bimbingan Massa (BIMAS). In addition, the process of modernization encompassed the industrial, commerce and service sectors. Indications of this can be seen in the construction of large-scale (multinational) industries in Aceh — such as PT. Arun, Exxon Mobil, the fertilizer factories PIM and AAF in the district of North Aceh, and ASAMERA (which is in the oil drilling business) — as well as wood (e.g. plywood) and copra oil processing plants in East Aceh. In the field of trade, economic modernization was signalled by the opening of Sabang free port in 1978, which has greatly contributed to economic progress in Aceh (although it was later closed, to only be reopened during Megawati's presidency in the Reformasi period). In the service industry, modernization is represented by the rapid construction of the transportation system, and electricity and telecommunications services, as well as the development of education services throughout the entire region of Aceh. Such aspects of modernization have greatly influenced changes to Acehnese society in several ways.

AGRICULTURE AND THE ECONOMY

The modernization of the agriculture sector in general, and of food cropping in particular, was initially introduced through accelerated intervention by the central government during the period of the New Order, which emphasized economic growth by meeting production targets. During this time, a number of innovations and new technologies were introduced into Acehnese society. The implementation of modern planting methods alongside traditional ones also effected social change in Acehnese society. Various elements of the pre-existing social system were transformed as a result of economic modernization in agriculture.

Firstly, there was a change in orientation, from mere subsistence farming, where food production for private consumption was the main goal, to a commercial (market) outlook.[10] Local growers and manufacturers shifted to meet the needs of a global economic system, selecting commodities that are in demand internationally, such as coconut oil, cocoa and coffee, as well as non-agricultural goods.

As production shifted from subsistence to market-oriented farming, this affected decisions on what should be planted and when. Prices became the deciding factor. As a result, agricultural production moved from being labour-intensive, employing little or no technology, to being a heavily mechanized agro-business. In the past, farmers tilled the soil with human or animal labour, planting traditional seeds. Now, people in Aceh are accustomed to using tractors, fertilizers and high-yield seeds. Instead of husking the rice with *cheumuelo*, machines are now used; similarly, the use of *jeungki* to grind rice into flour has been replaced by rice mills. This has been accompanied by a shift in focus from food cropping to horticulture (e.g. of the Bangkok durian) and the plantation cultivation of commercial crops such as coconuts and cocoa. Effects of this shift, from subsistence to market-oriented farming, include a striking decline in the number of family-owned rice fields in villages throughout Aceh. The produce from a single rice harvest that before would have been the family's food reserve until the next harvest season is now merely stored according to quality, and more frequently, is sold directly to local distributors.

Second, the demands of modernization have also meant that the importance of traditional *adat* institutions has given way to that of national institutions. Some traditional Acehnese institutions that once functioned in association with the village administration include *kejruen-blang*, dealing with wet rice farming, *petua seuneubok* for field planting (swidden or *berkebun*), *panglima laot* for the fishing trade (*kelautan*), *pawang uteun* for forestry, and *mugee* or *toké* for monetary and marketing matters. After the economic modernization of agriculture, such traditional institutions were pushed aside, became dysfunctional and were finally replaced by institutions initiated by the state, such as the Association of Water-Using Farmers (Kelompok Tani Pemakai Air, P3A), the Association of Fish Breeders (Kelompok Tani Nelayan Andalan, KTNA), the Association of Coral Fishers, the Agricultural Cooperatives (Koperasi Tani, KOPERTA), and community-based NGOs (Lembaga Swadaya Masyarakat, LSM).

Third, structural changes in patterns of social relations have occurred in the sphere of cultural traditions. For example, traditionally, the *blang* and *peusijeuk* ritual meals would have been performed prior to the start of wet rice planting (*sawah*) and before initiating communal projects, respectively. Performing such rituals had a positive influence in that they functioned to strengthen social interaction between members of the community by promoting relations of mutual help and support, cooperation and reciprocity. Such aspects of traditional culture are disappearing under the force of agricultural modernization. Social interaction and ties are being replaced by the principles of monetization and commercialization, which place such a premium on efficiency that individualism is becoming more apparent. Thus, the disappearance of traditional culture in Aceh has had an alienating effect on social interaction and relations.

Fourth, the priority given to communal and collective needs has shifted, and emphasis is now placed on the individual's needs. The concept of *pangulee' hareukat meugoe* (farming is the primary source of livelihood) no longer holds, as sources of livelihood continue to diversify and polarize. The religious-traditional beliefs that everything is imbued with a hidden (cosmic) force, whether it is a mountain, the sea or a rice field, have changed to one of a more rational religious belief. Subsistence behaviour and a pre-capitalist economy of mutual dependency have given way to commercialism and dependence upon the modern economic system. This has caused a sharp decline in the value of the old traditions as well as in the value of harmony and collective responsibility.

Fifth, there has been a transformation in the decision-making process by landowners and in the structure of society, from a system based on familial and governmental control to control by the market. Government domination over agricultural development has gradually been replaced by market forces. The traditional bases of power, such as the ownership of land, are shifting to new forms of wealth, besides agriculture, and therefore social status is no longer dependent upon the possession of large tracts of land.

OUTSIDE THE SPHERE OF AGRICULTURE

Outside the field of agriculture, the introduction of large-scale industries to the region initiated economic modernization in Aceh during the first few years of the New Order (ORBA) under Soeharto's government. Industrial modernization has had two main effects. First, there have been transformations in production methods and community needs. Production is now based on the market and competition. Farming is no longer the dominant means of making a living. The choice of livelihood for the Acehnese is increasingly expanding to sectors outside of agriculture, such as small business, industry and services. Some people have become civil servants, factory workers, merchants, and so on. Urbanization has accompanied this diversification; not only have people moved from their villages to the city, villages have also developed into cities (e.g. the region of Banda Aceh, or the city of Banda Aceh). This has, in turn, meant changing social needs that require modern institutions like banks and insurance houses.

Education

The influence of economic modernization on education can be seen in the development of infrastructure and materials for general education, such as the creation of elementary, junior and high schools, vocational schools, and schools for higher education. This has meant a move from a socio-religious system of education to one that is focused on the economic future, thus, affecting the role of religious schools such as the *pesantren* (traditional Islamic schools). Traditional modes of education within the *pesantren*, which traditionally have been naturally interwoven into Acehnese society, are being displaced by modern systems of education.

The decline in the dominant role played by the traditional religious education system and the corresponding shift in favour of modern institutions of education have influenced the values, behaviour and traditions in Acehnese society. The socially-oriented behaviour taught in the *pesantren* schools is changing, and actions are increasingly informed by the modern economy and basic education. Today, a general modern education is considered more valuable than a religious education. Wealthy parents are reluctant to send their children to the *pesantren* because education is seen as a means to enhance one's future chances in the job market and as an economic investment in the future. At the same time, the majority of those who do enrol their children in *pesantren* are typically poor and backward.[11] Hence, the resulting inequality between the rich and poor concerning who has access to, and to what type of, education is so extensive that the social values grounding behaviour in Acehnese society are increasingly diverging.

Today, teacher-student relations are not as close or as limited as they once were. Traditionally, the instructor (*guru*) was considered the sole point of reference and source of knowledge for their students. References and resources are now more diverse. Changes in educational institutions have been accompanied by a transformation in the concepts and views held by society, resulting in a conceptual polarization within the spheres of both religious and secular knowledge.

The Service Sector

In the service sector, economic modernization has been accompanied by the widespread development of infrastructure (i.e., transportation, electricity and telecommunications networks). Such development has intensified society's mobility and contact with the outside world, and has provided easier access to diverse sources of information. This condition consequently has contributed to changes in social relations, values and behaviour. Similarly, improvements to the transportation system have also changed people's lives. The field of health care in Aceh has changed from one dominated by traditional medicine (*pengobatan dukun*) to one of (Western) medicine via national health programmes such as PUSKESMAS, Family Planning (KB) and Posyandu. In the area of finance, the local *toké* and *mugee* have been replaced by corporate bodies and banks, as well as new organizations such as the BPR. Besides these organizations and bodies, several other national institutions were introduced into Aceh as part of the national mission to development and its idea of what modernization means.

The effect of expanding the power supply and telecommunications networks has been quite substantial in terms of how it has changed the pattern of social relations within Acehnese society. For instance, the introduction of television and satellite dishes has had both positive and negative effects on social behaviour. Positive effects include, for instance, easier access to different sources of information, which is necessary in order to gain new knowledge and views about global changes. One negative effect is that children's ability to wake up early in the morning to pray and study has declined because they watch television until late at night. In addition, children no longer have time to listen to stories and legends told by their parents and grandparents about holy and pious people — stories that pass on noble Acehnese values and traditions. Instead, a lot of time is spent in front of the television watching soap operas (*sinetron*). The increasing adoption of foreign culture as portrayed in the media is an impediment to the passing on of Acehnese cultural values.

Government

The *desa* (village)[12] is the smallest governmental unit in Aceh. The village head is called the *Keuchik* and is democratically elected through direct elections. The person elected as *Keuchik* is usually someone with special qualities, and who is educated, experienced, of good character and of good social status, and who has a grasp of local issues. Therefore, the *Keuchik* are usually long-time inhabitants of the village they administer. However, in some areas, the Acehnese term *Keuchik* has recently been replaced by the Indonesian term *Lurah*, and the area which they govern is now called the *Kelurahan*. While it is no longer necessary that the *Lurah* be from the area (*asoe lhok*), they still must possess significant social status in the village.

In matters of religion, the *Keuchik* is assisted by a *Teunku Imum* or *Imum Meunasah* who functions as the *imam* (leader of the prayer) during the common prayer in the prayer hall (*meunasah*) and who presides over religious ceremonies, including the *peusijuk* and other ceremonies. Like the *Keuchik*, the *Imum Meunasah* are democratically elected by those (among the community) who possess a good knowledge of religion, a presence of authority, and good character. In the Indonesian (national) system of government, *Imum Meunasah* did not used to be involved in village-level government. However, since the implementation of special autonomy in Aceh in 2002, the *Imum Meunasah* have been informally recognized as civic leaders and given a monetary honorarium called the *Minyeuk Panyot* for the upkeep of the *meunasah.*

The *Keuchik* and *Imum Meunasah* can be considered to be the executive body at the village level, while the legislative body of each village has traditionally consisted of the *Tuha Peut* (four members) who make decisions (*keputusan*) and approve all important decisions that affect village society. In addition, the *Tuha Lapan* (eight members) — basically an extension of the *Tuha Peut* — also carry out the function of consensual decision-making at the village level (*musyawarah desa*) and are always included in the preparation of common decisions and in resolving important neighbourhood (*kampung*) problems. Besides these (i.e. the *Tuha Peut* and the *Tuha Lapan*), in traditional forms of government there are informal posts such as the *Keujruen Blang, Peutua Seuneubok, Panglima Uteun* (*Panglima Glee*), *Syahbanda* and *Panglima Laot,* each with their own respective tasks.[13]

The next larger administrative unit after the village used to be the *mukim,* comprising of several villages (*gampong*), which was governed by an *Imum Mukim.* Their function was to coordinate and resolve inter-village issues. Typically, every *mukim* had a large mosque, which was administered by the *Imam Mesjid.* This level of local government has faded out over the decades, but the role of *Imam Mesjid* is still needed in some respects.

Although once playing an important role in society, traditional village organizations, such as the *Tuha Peut,* have been replaced with national institutions such as the Organization of the Village Community (Lembaga Masyarakat Desa, LMD) and village security organizations (Lembaga Ketahanan Masyarakat Desa, LKMD). Now, the formerly powerful Organization of Mukim Administration (Lembaga Pemerintahan Mukim) has disappeared from the Acehnese system of government.

Economic Organizations

Gala is a system of borrowing in which a person puts up their land, gold or other goods as collateral during hard times (typically so that he has enough cash to meet basic daily needs). The formerly unwritten binding agreement is giving way to formal written contracts, but without specific deadlines. *Gala* gives the lender the right to make use of the land given as collateral until the borrower has paid back the loan. The produce obtained from working the land is considered a service in return for the act of lending rather than for the sum of money borrowed, and is therefore not considered interest. Land rights are transferable only through the consent of its owner (i.e. the borrower). In the event that the borrower is unable to pay back the loan, the collateral may be sold to a third party with the proceeds used in payment of the loan. The lender may also choose to buy the land, paying its original owner the remaining cost subtracted from the outstanding loan. Here, customary law differs from national agrarian laws in that *gadai* can last for up to seven years. After which time, the land must be returned to its original owner.

Customary *gala* law is still practised among village society in Aceh, but its frequency is declining. Landowners who need money for daily needs, as well as for investments and financial capital, tend to borrow from banks that already have local branches in their village. In certain cases, landowners wishing to avoid the complex procedures governing bank loans, borrow from private money lenders (*rentenir*) at a rate of interest that has been mutually agreed upon (and which is usually higher than those offered by banks). As the process is easy and based solely on mutual trust between two parties, this type of money-lending has become commonplace in Acehnese society. This is especially the case in urban areas where merchants, who do not have access to formal credit, need to take out short-term loans (sometimes daily or weekly). Economic modernization in this regard has already deeply affected traditional methods of money-lending in Aceh and has effectively replaced the *gala* system.

Mawah is a slightly different system where a person gives the right over certain assets (usually land or cattle) to another person, who then works on the owner's behalf for a negotiated percentage of the profits. In a sense, *Mawah* is a type of profit-sharing. Negotiated profit-sharing depends on the cost of production, including hard costs such as animal feed and the more burdensome labour costs, in terms of time and effort. For example, if a wet rice field is close to the village, the landowner may receive one-third of the profits, while the one who works on their behalf receives two-thirds. If the field is far from the village, the profits may be divided in a ratio that is less favourable to the landowner (e.g. one-quarter to three-quarters respectively). Today, profits are relatively less due to the utilization of increasingly intensive and expensive farming methods. The amount of "net operating income" is less today than in the past due to new costs, in addition to the usual use of pesticides (to combat blight), fertilizer, and so on. There are also many cases where the one who takes over use of the land needs to rent a tractor or other equipment and hires other farm labourers, paying them hourly or daily wages. Hence, profit is less because of the increase in operational costs. In terms of *mawah ternak* or *mawah* animal husbandry, profit shares are estimated against net operating costs, namely the animal's selling price measured against the time spent raising the animal, beginning from the moment the transfer agreement began. In cases where female animals are included in the transfer, profit-sharing involves the net selling price of the animal. If the animals are still young and have not yet produced offspring, then the owner receives one-quarter of the profits and the herder three-quarters. Therefore, profit shares are always in accordance with the net profit after accounting for the potential gains against the financial expenses and labour costs.

Modern modes of profit-sharing began to grow after the emergence of modern payment systems such as venture and bank capital based on Islamic *syariah* law (e.g. as offered by Bank Syariah Mandiri, Bank Danamon Syariah, Divisi Syariah BPD, etc.). For instance, the calculation of profit shares as done by PT. Sarana Aceh Ventura (SAV) calculates the net profit from an investment project (not limited to farming and animal husbandry) and divides this based on percentages, for example, fifty-fifty or sixty-forty. For owners of small and medium-sized businesses, who are relatively well educated, calculating in percentages is not a problem. However, for village farmers and ranchers, it is easier to understand simple fractions. Urban dwellers are already accustomed to the *syariah* banking system of profit-sharing, such as *Mudharabah*, *Murabaha*, *Musyarakah*, and so on. This system of calculating shares is possible because these businesses have used hard currency from the beginning. This differs from the *mawah* system that uses money only when the profits are to be divided, in other words, after the sale of the animal, for example.

In the fishing sector, the system of profit-sharing is somewhat more complicated and unique. Unlike other sectors, particularly in industrial manufacturing where workers are paid hourly or daily wages, plus overtime that is usually higher, the fishing industry uses a system similar to a piece rate scheme. This form of profit-sharing can differ from one *Lhok* to another,[14] from one region to another, and from one type of boat to another. The description below gives examples of how a haul of fish is shared in the area of Aceh Besar and Banda Aceh. The first is specific to a type of fishing known as Pusat Rational (Pusat Aceh) and the second involves the use of a *Thep-thep* (a boat of two to three gross tonnes).

Traditional *pukat* fishing uses a small boat (usually made from wood) to stretch the *pukat* net out until it is approximately 200 metres from the beach. This is then manually pulled in from the shore. Not all of the catch is to be sold. Instead, a portion of it is divided among the net crew. The method for dividing up the fish is as follows. Suppose that the entire catch fills ten buckets. Two of these are divided among the net draggers (*penarik pukat*) who consist of: (a) the *Pawang Pukat* (10 per cent), (b) the crew of four to five people (40 per cent), and (c) the assistant *Tarek Pukat* or

Teumupoh/Awak Teumarek, consisting of members of the local community (50 per cent).

The profits from the remaining 80 per cent of the catch are also divided after the fish is sold. The *Pawang* gives the profits to the owner of the boat. From this, the *Pawang* receives 25 per cent (1 *Kaja*), which is usually collected once a week (usually on a Friday as no boat goes out to sea on that day). The remainder belongs to the boat's owner. Sometimes the *Pawang* shares his portion with the boat crew. Those who work harder receive a larger percentage. This presents an interesting incentive for hard work within the system of profit-sharing.

When fishing using a *Thep-thep* (*Pancing*), measuring between two and three gross tonnes, a small part of the catch is taken home to be eaten as a side dish (*Eungkot Bu*). The rest is sold by the *Toke Bangku* who waits at the dock/pier and functions like a broker. The proceeds from the sale are divided as follows: the *Toke Bangku* receives 10 per cent, 2.5 per cent is given to a place of prayer (this is viewed as a tithe *Zakat*), and approximately 30 per cent goes to covering operating costs. The remaining 57.5 per cent is given to the *Pawang* (also called the *Tekong*, or the one responsible for the boat) who then divides it into the following portions: one-third for the owner of the boat, and one-third for the *Pawang*, *anak buah kapal* (ABK), watchman and boat cleaner (usually 1 or 2 of the ABK double as watchman and cleaner). While the final third is for the watchman, he typically receives half of the share of the ABK person.

In addition to what they receive directly from the sale of the fish, every Friday the *Pawang* gets an additional share from the *Toke Bangku* and the owner of the boat, each contributing 30 per cent. The role of the *Toke Bangku* is very important in this process because, besides being the manager who ensures that the profit-sharing continues in accordance with the tradition of consensus, they also function as marketing agents, trying to get the best price for the catch. In many respects, the *Toke Bangku* also plays a stabilizing role by lending money to the *Pawang* and ABK during times when the catch is not large enough to meet daily expenses. The *Toke Bangku* is also always prepared to provided an advance to cover operational costs during the time the boat is out to sea. In the event the catch is not large enough to repay these upfront costs, the debt is rolled over and redeemed later against a more successful catch.

As traditional line fishing in Aceh is generally of the *Pukat Tradisional* type and the *Perahu Thep-thep* has limited capacity and uses simple fishing gear, the traditional system of profit-sharing discussed above is still in use. The same system is also used for larger boats, such as the *Pukat Labi Labi* (of twenty to twenty-five gross tonnes) and the *Pukat Langga/Purseine* (of thirty-five to fifty gross tonnes). Such traditional forms of profit-sharing still prevail because, in the field of fishing, market intervention and capitalism around the docks is not the same as that in the farming economy. Moreover, investors in larger boats are often the owners of capital or have other businesses on land. They use their assets in order to get even more capital for their fishing business, such as buying a new boat.

Religion

Islam, as the religion of the majority of the population in Aceh,[15] colours everyday customs (*reusam*), both of the individual and his or her relationship with society. *Reusam* is seen in the customs surrounding circumcision (*sunatan*), the life of bachelors, marriage ceremonies and the everyday life of married couples, pregnancy and childbirth, the education of children, the building of houses, the planting of rice, behaviour when going out to sea, and so on. Its forms are various, beginning with the *peusijuk ingá* ritual meals and ritual ceremonies. Besides declining in frequency, how these activities are carried out has also changed. While all such activities usually are accompanied by prayers, they have been simplified in certain aspects. For example, their duration has been shortened. Some ritual meals and ceremonies have even disappeared altogether.

These shifts have led towards fundamental changes to the very nature of Acehnese society. These changes have come in many forms. First, there are those that deal with social structure and relationships. The domination of men over women has begun to decrease. The central importance of the elderly, to whom the younger generation must listen, has begun to shift. Social layers that used to be important because of landownership are yielding to other forms of wealth outside of agriculture, so much so that landed gentry (*tuan tanah*) are now less and less common in Aceh. Additionally, the cultural values upheld by most people are becoming more diverse due to the influence of foreign cultures (through globalization).

Second, there has been a change in people's values, beliefs and behaviour. Belief in mysticism has been replaced by scientific reasoning. Whereas Acehnese once went to a traditional mystic healer (*dukun*) if they were sick, they have now begun to go to doctors or to the nearby PUSKESMAS health station. The introduction of family planning (KB) in Aceh has meant a change in the conviction that "the more children, the greater the reward". The influence of foreign culture can be observed, among others, at parties where food is no longer served to the guests in the old way, but instead *ala prasmanan* (à la France, i.e. in the French way). The reading of the Qur'an (*selawat badar*) and the traditional poetry (*pantun*) exchange during some parts of the wedding reception have given way to pop songs and popular *dangdut* music. Parties that once took place at home have moved to reception halls. Once collectively (*gotong royong*) organized, parties are now catered. All of this has been embraced for practical reasons and is related to principles of economic expediency in terms of time, cost and the labour involved.

Third, there have been changes in the structure of political and economic power. This is the result of the move from a horizontal system of conflict resolution, based on a tradition of communal deliberation and decision-making (as suggested by the proverbs *uleu beu matee', ranteng bek patah, and meunyoe taleung panjang, meunyoe ta lingka paneuk*, which describe a type of win-win solution), to a vertical stratum of political and economic control.

VIOLENT CONFLICT, REFORMASI AND THE TSUNAMI

The nearly thirty years of physical conflict in Aceh that even went on during the euphoria of the Reformasi era, as well as the terrible catastrophe of the tsunami, are landmark events that have fundamentally altered the economic and social equilibrium in Acehnese society. The destructive effects of these historical events have led to Aceh's plummeting economic position and the sundering of its social structure. On the economic side, it will require several years for the Acehnese people to recover their source of livelihood. It may be that the mental state, character of, and social interaction among and between the people have also altered.

The conflict in Aceh, which claimed an estimated 3,000 victims, has left an indelible mark on the social and economic life of the Acehnese people in general. For instance, the *ulama* have been incapable of preventing the killing in Aceh, and the local government and institutions that once had an important role, are now ineffectual. Dignity and human rights have been buried under the power of weapons. The process of economic modernization in Aceh, therefore, has been slow, causing many large factories to close. Only the many local NGOs that have emerged have given the Acehnese wider access to the outside world.

The arrival of a number of foreign NGO workers following the devastating earthquake and tsunami on 26 December 2004 also affected the pre-existing values of the people. Possible changes to the social system have included the emergence of a new communalism (resulting from the close social interaction from living in barracks, tents and temporary shelters), structural changes in employment (e.g. fishermen switching to farming or factory work), and the appearance of new economic institutions. If this is not addressed carefully, this may lead to some Acehnese people becoming psychologically dependent on foreign aid, adding an increasingly precarious note to the ideology of modernization in the future.

CONCLUSION

The ongoing economic modernization during the last thirty years has altered the values, attitudes and institutions in general in Aceh. Such non-economic and non-quantifiable factors have proven important to the social order and have become the measure of contentment for the Acehnese people. For example, the role of traditional property rights in the allocation of resources and the distribution of the profits has had a significant influence on economic change and the prosperity of the community. Although special autonomy for Aceh has been in effect since 2002, it would seem that only the regional government has gained an important role, while local social institutions, to a certain extent, have become less significant, weakening the degree of the community's self-reliance.

For more than thirty years, Aceh has experienced a series of setbacks to its economic and social development, not only because the social order has systematically dissolved to be replaced by the New Order system of government, but also because of the natural process of change owing to external influence. Continuing economic modernization has had an impact on transformations in the social system; it has affected values, traditions and democratic institutions. Every change in a social system resulting from external influences always has its positive and negative aspects. However, it is important to remember that some of the existing local knowledge/wisdom in Acehnese society needs to be preserved and even cultivated as something beneficial to economic modernization in Aceh in the future.

Notes

1. Translated by Amanda Rath.
2. Law No. 5, implemented in 1974, regarding Regional [Self] Governance did not afford much of an opportunity for autonomy.
3. The provincial government's budget (i.e. the APBD NAD) increased from Rp250,270,148,697 in 2001 to Rp1,572,094,258,442 in 2002.
4. The 2003 regional output in Aceh (Regional Gross Domestic Product, or *Produk Domestik Regional Bruto*) was as much as Rp21.973,19 billion.
5. 17.05 per cent and 17.82 per cent respectively. Forestry and fishing contribute 6.28 per cent and 6.43 per cent respectively.

6. This sector contributes less than 10 per cent. Industries outside of oil and gas, consisting primarily of food and beverage as well as tobacco production, contribute 4.22 per cent. Other industries, such as the production of textiles, leather, lumber and other forestry products, paper and printing materials, cement and non-metal mining, transportation tools, machinery, and equipment, combined contribute 9.88 per cent. The fertilizer, chemical and rubber industries contribute only 2.16 per cent of the PDRB in 2003.
7. Usually taking place once a week, on a Wednesday or Saturday for example, these markets — locally called *uroe peukan*, or *uroe ganto* — differ from location to location. Travelling merchants from one village will typically go from one market to another in order to offer their goods and services (e.g. travelling salesmen for medicaments).
8. Including, among others, programmes to feed the poor (literally known as "rice programmes", *Raskin*), the Farming Credit Plan (Kredit Usaha Tani; KUT), the Health Card, etc.
9. A well-known *hadih maja* among people in Aceh.
10 The Acehnese have a saying about such changes in orientation: *Jaroe bak langai, mata u pasai* (hands hold the *bajak*, eyes point towards the market).
11. The original expression is *miskin dan terbelakang*. "*Miskin*" refers to their poverty in material terms, while "*terbelakang*" literally means "backward" in terms of outlook and orientation, which can also imply disenfranchisement because of external forces.
12. In most of Indonesia, the official term for the governmental unit of the village is *desa*. In Aceh, the local terms *gampong* or *meunasah* are also often used.
13. The *Keujreun Blang* administrates water management for *sawah* (wet rice farming); the *Peutua Seuneubok* oversees the customary law governing garden-like plantations (*perkebunan)*; the *Panglima Uteun*, the forest; the *Syahbanda*, the ports; and the *Panglima Laot* takes care of customary law regarding the sea.
14. A *Lhok* is literally a shore. Its geographical area is not necessarily defined according to the boundaries of government administration. It is headed by a *Panglima Laot* who is unanimously elected by the fishermen of a particular *Lhok*. *Panglima Laot* have the authority to manage and issue sanctions against infractions to traditional fishing ordinances (e.g. fishermen caught breaking the rule forbidding fishing on Fridays will not be allowed to go out to sea for between three and seven days.
15. 97.3 per cent of the inhabitants of Aceh are Muslim.

6

THE ECONOMIC DEVELOPMENT OF ACEH SINCE 1945

Manfred Rist

How is it that a resource-rich country like Indonesia is so poor? What is the reason why a province like Aceh, with its wealth of oil and gas reserves, which produces and exports a large part of the resources of the whole country, is so bitterly poor? What is the explanation for the fact that a province, which once had a flourishing trade with the outside world, nowadays has disappeared from the scene economically? Finally, why is it that a strictly religious province like Aceh, which initially actively supported the war of independence in Indonesia and which — unlike Timor — had been part of Indonesia since the beginning, later should become embroiled in one of the bloodiest and most persistent underground wars?

These subjects are all interrelated. They indicate a paradoxical development in a nation which nowadays poses yet another complex question: Why should a country so rich in oil and who is a member of OPEC be suffering so badly from the rise in oil prices?

The answers to all these questions can be found in the tragic effects that have resulted from the intertwining of economics and politics, the vicious circle of poverty, violence and counter-violence. Economic policy and mismanagement have played an important part. The Jakarta-designed New Order policy reaped disorder, which first affected the outlying areas of the country and then later, Java. Even today, the country is still suffering from its after-effects. Given the circumstances, it appears that, throughout the implementation of the New Order policy from 1965 to 1998, the mental distance between Banda Aceh and Jakarta seemed to be even greater than the enormous geographical distance of 1,700 kilometres.

The civil war in Aceh, which now — after the signing of the peace agreement — will hopefully come to an end, may be one of the reasons for the severe underdevelopment of this province. Violence, terror and insecurity do not just deter foreign investors; these factors also paralyse the domestic market. They tie up and block resources, including human resources, which could otherwise have been applied to the development of a great variety of economic networks; these could be either formal sectors, or — as is widespread in underdeveloped countries — informal ones, which are just as essential.

However, to declare the civil war to be the one and only explanation for the lack of development in Aceh is far too simplistic. The absence of war in itself — implying relative order or peace, in fact — is by no means a guarantee of economic progress. Compared with other countries in this region, like Vietnam or Cambodia, Indonesia can look back on decades of peace, at least until 1965. Undeniably, again between 1970 and 1996, the country underwent rapid economic development, which opened up opportunities in domestic fields. Nevertheless, this giant nation is still — and again — considered to be a developing nation. And, it is considered to be poor. Just before the outbreak of the Asian economic crisis, in the mid-1990s, approximately 15 per cent of the population was living below the poverty level. The situation can be compared with that in the Philippines. However, in the Philippines the process has been even more dramatic. This once rich and promising Asian nation with a relatively highly educated populace has degenerated into a chaotic state, whose average income per head has fallen under the ASEAN mean value.

This suggests another perspective from which to view the situation in Aceh. Are the reasons for the conflict in Aceh possibly mere economic ones? Could it be that lurking behind the call for independence and freedom is simply the desire for economic development and wealth, which has been beckoning seductively since the exploration of Aceh's oil resources at the beginning of the 1970s? Although religious and political motives can readily be put forward to explain the conflict, economic considerations — as will be shown later — should certainly not be ignored. Various authors such as Shari (2002) and McCulloch (2000) have come up with the same hypothesis. Even quotations from Hasan di Tiro (1984) point in that direction. At any rate, it is conspicuous that, as early as the rebellion of 1953, economic reasons have played an important part in stirring up discontent. In this context, it is remarkable that the formation of Gerakan Aceh Merdeka (GAM) in 1976 occurred after the exploitation of fossil fuels, and so the armed resistance gained new impetus from the discovery, keeping pace with the oil and gas bubbling up from the Acehnese soil.

Superficially, this may seem highly relevant, but it is also necessary to pose the question of whether natural raw materials are indeed a source of wealth. Economic theory often states that rich resources are a good starting point for economic development. If this is the case, then Indonesia is a poor example of it. Some authors even talk about the "curse of the raw materials" (Ross 1999, p. 297) or the "petro-paradox" (Seda 2005, p. 179). The presence of these materials do not always bring the "blessed" country the expected rich yield. Unhappily, the reverse is very often true and pollution and overexploitation are often the only lasting effects. Evidence of the truth of this is easy to supply; the complete deforestation of tropical forests, the overfishing of lakes and rivers, and the polluted air in Jakarta are but three examples of how things can go horribly wrong. In hardly any other East or Southeast Asian country is the lack of understanding about matters of environmental or human health as deeply ingrained as in Indonesia. The root of this problem might be traced back to the fact that Indonesia has — or perhaps, had — plenty of water, land, timber, people, and rich animal and plant life.

HUMAN TRAGEDIES AND THE ECONOMIC DAMAGE

After the tsunami of 26 December 2004, the human victims were understandably given priority. According to the latest estimates, there were 165,000 dead, innumerable injured or traumatized, and 550,000 left homeless ("Ocha Report", May 2005; "HIC Situation Report", May 2005). The extent of the suffering was so huge and the corresponding images so dramatic that, immediately after the catastrophe, it seemed almost indecent to mention the economic damage in the same breath. On 28 December 2006, the *Neue Zürcher Zeitung* published an article in its financial pages which pointed out that the economy in the affected countries would probably be no more than grazed in spite of the catastrophe. This article provoked indignation among various readers (*Neue Zürcher Zeitung*, 28 December 2006). Economic considerations in the face of such a cataclysmic occurrence did not strike a resonant chord with the public mood.

Nevertheless, economic damage is an inescapable part of any disaster. When all is said and done, it is undeniable that the unparalleled international solidarity shown and the determination to rebuild what was lost were inextricably connected with the extensive destruction of the infrastructure and micro-economy in the coastal areas, though such a rational economic analysis seems positively heartless. The ravages caused enormous harm to the people, but the economic damage was — when viewed from a distance — relatively insignificant. The stock market in Jakarta barely blinked; the world market not at all.

It stands to reason that the more highly developed a country is, the higher will be the economic damage it will suffer after a natural disaster, like the 2004 tsunami. Conversely, wherever only a small amount of capital is available, the damage will be correspondingly minor. Capital in this context, as De Soto (2000, p. 41) has pointed out, should not be understood merely to be financial capital but factual capital. Wherever then little — or more appropriately, underrated — factual capital is available, the losses are concomitantly few. For example, the loss of a simple fishing village on the north coast of Aceh represents, for its inhabitants, their economic livelihood as well as, more intangibly, social stability and security. It literally means the world to them.

The consequences were indeed disastrous; the material loss in Aceh and Nias was estimated at US$4.3 billion (SIIA, May 2005). That is, with the exception of the oil and gas plants spared from the torrent, 97 per cent of the gross domestic product (GDP) of Aceh. The data available for 2003 shows that the GDP of Aceh amounted to around US$4.5 billion, which equals aproximately 2.3 per cent of the Indonesian GDP.

But in a report on the economic damage, Morgan Stanley wrote:

> Given that the energy (mainly oil and gas) production facilities in Aceh or Northern Sumatra have survived the tsunami, the overall damage to Indonesia's economy appears to be minimal. (United Press International, 7 January 2005)

In the same article, United Press International (UPI) quotes David E. Samuel of the Danareksa Research Institute (Jakarta) as saying:

> The (tsunami) disaster is expected to have little impact on the country's economic growth in 2005, and be far less significant than the Bali bombing in 2002. (UPI, 7 January 2005)

The Asian Development Bank assumed a GDP growth of 5.5 per cent in its economic forecast for 2005 — which would have been above that of the previous year — and noted the following in April 2005:

> The December earthquake and tsunami caused heavy loss of life and great destruction in Aceh ... These disasters were devastating for communities, but not for the country's main economic production centres. (ADB News Release, 6 April 2005)

The ambiguity in comparing the economic impact of the disaster between rich and poorer countries is obvious. The economic damage in Phuket, Thailand, for example, could be assessed quickly because of the better developed tourist infrastructure and because it fitted in better with Western ways of thinking and values. What is more, to calculate the damage in Phuket, it was possible to quote insurable values, that is, the insured indemnities. This amount, which is always brought up in cases of catastrophes but which in fact gives no information about the real damage wrought, had nonetheless virtually no significance for Aceh. According to the General Insurance Association of Indonesia (Asosiasi Asuransi Umum Indonesia, AAUI), there were just twenty-two landed properties in Aceh which were insured against earthquakes, to the total value of Rp800 billion (around US$90 million). More than a third of it covered the property of the state-run enterprise Telkom. According to the National Insurance Association, PT Jasindo, only 877 insurance policies with a total of 15,030 property policies offered protection against natural catastrophes. The result was that even if the destruction in Aceh had been total, capital-wise it would have been relatively modest, and insurance-wise it would not have been worth speaking of.

ACEH'S BACKBONE — THE RURAL ECONOMY

As with all other Indonesian peripheral areas, Aceh is classed as a traditional agrarian province. In 1920, the population of Aceh was registered at 735,355 people, of whom a major part worked in agriculture, stock-farming and weaving (*Meyers Lexikon* 1928). This did not change much during the ensuing decades, regardless of the oil boom which started in the 1970s. A comparative analysis between Aceh and the Malay member states of Perlis, Kedah and Penang shows that, in 1971 in Aceh, 80 per cent of the population worked actively in the primary sector, and that the agrarian sector still produced 58 per cent of the added value of the whole province. The corresponding numbers for the three Malaysian provinces were at that time between 60 and 38 per cent. A more recently published manual about Aceh refers to the fact that in 1997 more than 80 per cent of the population was still working in the primary sector (Mahmud Bangkaru 1997, p. 29).

Following the road from Medan to Aceh along the east coast, it is still fascinating to see the luxuriant green rice fields. According to the Aceh manual of 1997, approximately 1.1 billion tons of rice were harvested from these fields (Mahmud Bangkaru 1997, pp. 29–30). Other agricultural products included peanuts (19,000 tons), soybeans (118,000 tons), maize (22,000 tons), coffee (34,000 tons), betel nuts (7,000 tons), and rubber (15,000 tons). Since then, newer statistical data shows some alterations: in 2001, the yield of soybeans fell to 68,000 tons, the cultivation of maize had more than doubled to 45,000 tons, and only 5,000 tons of peanuts were harvested. These harvest yields fluctuate year by year and can be correlated to the intensity of the conflict in the civil war. According to statements by an International Committee of the Red Cross (ICRC) assistant, regional tensions bring larger tea and coffee plantations to a complete standstill, because the army classifies everybody who stays outside the villages as GAM members.

It is important to note that within Indonesia the economic backwardness of Aceh is not exceptional. The underdevelopment of the whole nation in this same period has manifested itself in many ways, such as the high degree of illiteracy and the low life expectancy. In 1960, the life expectancy in Indonesia was still no higher than forty-seven years, which pales in comparison with Malaysia's sixty-seven years, the Philippines' sixty years, or Hong Kong's seventy-two years (Tan Ngak Yong 2002, p. 71).

All over Indonesia, approximately 50 per cent of the population is still employed in the agrarian sector. In 1970, this was roughly 65 per cent (World Bank 1999). The decrease can be traced back to the industrialization efforts of the New Order government, which, in the 1980s and 1990s (to 1997), led to a massive rural exodus and an equivalent rise in the population in cities like Jakarta, Surabaya and Medan. However, the decrease in the size of the agrarian sector should be seen in the right context. Many households have simply initiated a kind of "diversity" in the process of industrialization, which is comparable to the processes which occurred at the beginning of the industrial era in Europe. Within this extension of the basic income, farming still usually plays an important part in acquiring an adequate income or indeed providing the basic livelihood for a family (Booth 2004, p. 16). This pattern is still particularly valid in the periphery of the country. For instance, whereas 46 per cent, on average, of the households in the country still declared that farming was their main source of income in 1995, the corresponding percentage in provinces like Maluku or Papua (as well as East Timor) was a much higher 72 per cent (Booth 2004, p. 18).

The natural fertility and the traditionally agrarian character of Aceh also explains another early plan by the Indonesian government, which is not widely known. In the context of the first Five Year Plan, which set out the course of the economic ventures of the New Order, there was a discussion about transforming Aceh into an agrarian province and establishing it, to a certain degree at least, as the rice provider for all of Indonesia. This idea can best be understood against the background of the rice shortages during the 1950s and 1960s and the agricultural Green Revolution which followed. During this period, Indonesia was in fact the largest importer of rice in the world.

With the use of improved methods of cultivation and a supply of chemical fertilizers and artificial manure, and boosted by the cultivation of new species, the so-called high-yielding varieties, the Green Revolution solved the anticipated scarcity in food — a fear that was bolstered by the strong increase in the population. During the Green Revolution, the yield in Java, for instance, which still hovered around 2.6 tons per hectare in 1970, had doubled by 1990 to 5 tons. Thus, since 1985, Indonesia has been self-sufficient in rice production. Moreover, the discovery of petroleum and gas at the beginning of the 1970s brought great changes in its wake: Aceh did not need to become the planned rice barn of Indonesia, but — owing to the black gold beneath its soil — it soon became a most important provider of foreign exchange for Jakarta.

DISAPPOINTED EXPECTATIONS — REBELLION AND THE CIVIL WAR

The key events below are essential in understanding the economic development of Aceh:

1. Indonesia's Declaration of Independence on 17 August 1945, which was also supported in Aceh.
2. The rebellion, which started on 21 September 1953, under the banner of the Darul Islam.
3. The conceding of Aceh's "special region" (*daerah istimewa*) status in 1959.
4. Soeharto's usurpation and the onset of the New Order in 1965.
5. The discovery of petroleum and gas under the aegis of the New Order.
6. The formation of GAM and the increase in Acehnese regional consciousness and pride.
7. The abrogation of the recognition of Aceh's autonomy in 1989 by Jakarta and the military repression in Aceh through the DOM (Daerah Operasi Militer).
8. The economic crisis of 1997 which entailed the breakdown of the central state and which led to new autonomy laws.

Although the economic development of Aceh displays its own idiosyncrasies, it cannot be viewed as a process working separate to that of the state of Indonesia. The hunger for basic commodities which grew immensely during the process of industrialization, which began in 1970, should be seen as one of the principal causes of the current conflict. And, since the beginning of the 1970s, as the strategy of exploitation quickened its pace and grew more blatant, the conflict has become increasingly brutal. Therefore, Robinson too points out that, from a historical point of view, the resistance of the Acehnese has always been rooted in the control and sharing of resources (Robinson 1998, p. 134).

From the point of view of Jakarta, the political importance of Aceh to the state has been first and foremost that of a province, i.e. only that of a region within the nation as a whole. However, it was remarkable that between 1945 and 1949, Aceh remained completely beyond Dutch attempts to re-colonize it. Given its exceptional position, Aceh was initially granted a remarkable degree of economic freedom and space to negotiate with Jakarta. Even more importantly, on account of its position during the birth of the new republic in 1945, expectations were high in Aceh that the province would be granted a generous measure of economic autonomy (Nazaruddin Sjamsuddin 1985, p. 6). Thus, the rebellion of 1953 should by no means be associated only with the Darul Islam movement. It tended to be more concerned with winning the guarantee of a fairly independent commercial position, which was perceived to be threatened by grasping centralism (McGibbon 2004, p. 6).

To analyse the persistence of underdevelopment in Aceh and to try to comprehend the economic backwardness of this province, the legacies of the Dutch and the badly managed development of their colony must inevitably be reviewed.

The Dutch failed to contribute much to either the advancement of the infrastructure or to the education of the population in Aceh (Tan Ngak Yong 2002, p. 13). On the eve of independence, 47 per cent of the population was still illiterate. Pragmatically, the colonial rulers had indeed focused themselves on the governance of the sea routes and coastal towns. Occasionally their trade involved Chinese merchants, who had always lived on somewhat strained terms with the Dutch in Batavia, but the indigenous people remained largely beyond the purlieus of the colonial system. The vast majority of the population in the colonial empire lived modestly and earned a living as cultivators, livestock farmers or fishermen. Aceh was no exception.

The agrarian structure offers clues to the fact that Aceh was not always so economically deprived. From a historical point of view, the underdevelopment and poverty of Aceh today contrasts with its often cited "golden age" during the reign of Sultan Iskandar Muda at the beginning of the seventeenth century. Even two centuries afterwards, during the eighteenth and at the beginning of the nineteenth century, a dynamic export trade, operating beyond the Dutch sphere of influence, and with close links to Penang and Singapore, was recorded (Booth 1998, p. 25). At the beginning of the nineteenth century, for example, the pepper trade brought new wealth and a temporary increase in influence to Aceh. At that time, the province produced half of the world's pepper crop. Besides this, there was a flourishing, traditional gold- and silver-working industry. The riches did not stop here. The northwest corner of Sumatra was abundant in timber, rubber, tobacco and coffee.

This economic renaissance was of relatively short duration owing to the later war against the Dutch. By the beginning of the twentieth century, Aceh's connections with the outside world had stopped, largely because of the chaos wrought by the war, which was followed by the virtual subjugation of Aceh after 1913.

The agreement between the two great powers of Great Britain and the Netherlands in the Sumatra Treaty (1871) gave the Dutch the go-ahead to launch an intervention in Aceh. This Sumatra Treaty rescinded the first Anglo-Dutch agreement of 1824, which declared Aceh formally to be an independent region under a Dutch zone of influence. The attempt to assimilate Aceh into the Dutch colonial empire unleashed a war which officially lasted thirty years but which actually dragged on much longer and definitely brought an end to the sultanate's dreams of reviving its prosperous past.

PETROLEUM AND GAS — ACEH'S *FATA MORGANA*

As it was primarily oriented towards an agrarian economy, Aceh was badly prepared for the oil boom. Amidst the incipient industrialization, which was basically concentrated in the Lhokseumawe Industrial Zone (ZILS), the population was virtually overrun. The infrastructure was bad and, at the beginning of the 1970s, not a single technical academy existed in Aceh (Kell 1995, p. 16). This had sad consequences for the employment situation. Only a few local labourers could be absorbed into the industry. As the land of the indigenous population was systematically expropriated, numerous industrial labourers from other provinces were recruited. In 1976, this trend had contributed to the formation of the Free Aceh Movement (GAM) (Heiduk 2004, p. 7).

The industrialization of Aceh could be said to have begun almost literally overnight and was caused by the discovery of petroleum in what had seemed to be a purely agrarian province. During the start-up phase, local unskilled labourers could be absorbed, but there were no educated domestic specialists to operate the oil plants in the province. In this context, Emmerson notes that the industrial zone (ZILS) could be referred to as an enclave. In absolute contrast to the provincial structure, this enclave was "high-income, capital-intensive, urban, non-Muslim, non-Acehnese". The province, on the other hand, could be described as "low-income, labour-intensive, rural, Muslim, Acehnese" (Emmerson 1983, p. 123).

This influx of foreign employees, who in places tripled the population, not only caused social tensions, it placed enormous pressure on the existing infrastructure (Kell 1995, p. 17). These economic and social changes fertilized a slumbering resistance in the early 1970s, and since outward and visible signs of resistance caused repression, violence begot counter-violence. Caught in the crossfire, the economy was unable to evolve. The result of this suspense-filled and unequal process is still visible today in the enclave of Lhokseumawe. Immediately after the tsunami, Bruce Harker wrote: "The contrast between the corporate enclave and the shabby town is sharp" (Harker 2005).

To reiterate, the political course which was to vitalize and reinvigorate the resistance in Aceh was set early on in distant Jakarta, with the year 1965 considered to be the turning point. Between 1945 and 1949 and — after the rebellion of 1953 — between 1957 and 1965, Aceh enjoyed a remarkable degree of autonomy. However, the political situation suddenly changed drastically after 1965. Under the New Order government, the administration of the country was systematically centralized to a high degree, de-ideologized and de-politicized. All economic decisions were, henceforth, to be made in Jakarta. The administration of resources was also Jakarta-centred. In Jakarta, favouritism flourished within Soeharto's powerful circle and was strongly tied to the granting of concessions for the utilization of resources. The power of the military which, by order of Jakarta, was responsible for cohesion within the archipelago and which was to play a fatal role in East Timor in 1975 and then later in Aceh, began to rise under the new political regime, and it became involved in both legal and illegal economic activities.

The fact that, in the course of the New Order regime, Soeharto had increasingly employed technocrats in the administration of Aceh rapidly led to a situation in which Aceh fell more and more under outside rule. From 1965, anyone who entertained such an idea would not have far to search for confirmation. They would merely have to observe the exploitation of the region's resources. Those local technocrats who complied with Soeharto's methods were mostly descendants of local *ulama*. Their reward was that they could benefit from an education and privileges in Jakarta and all they had to do was to acquiesce in aligning themselves to Soeharto's GOLKAR party. This growing sense of living under "foreign" rule was exacerbated by the increasing brutality of the Indonesian army. The Indonesian military reacted to the formation of GAM by stepping up their repression of the province.

This oppression assumed an alarmingly and utterly unbridled extent after the denial of autonomy to Aceh by the central government and this resulted in violence carried out in the course of the DOM (Daerah Operasi Militer).

Soeharto quickly realized that the enormous supply of Indonesian natural resources held the key to industrial success, and that the extensive exploitation of these resources would only be possible with foreign help (Budy P. Resosudarmo 2005, p. 2). The foreign policy course pursued by Soekarno, which has sometimes been labelled "adventurous", also encompassed a rapprochement towards China. Under Soeharto, this gave way to a decidedly Western orientation, with the United States and Japan as the main goals. Correspondingly, liberal economic laws were already being passed in 1967 (i.e. Law 1/1967, Law 5/1967, and Law 11/1967), which granted individuals and companies the right to exploit resources and gave foreign companies free reign to extract whatever they wanted. At the beginning of the 1970s, foreign oil companies, including Mobil Oil, struck a bonanza in Aceh. For this reason, the economically insignificant province of Aceh became the motor of Indonesian economic development within a decade.

With the discovery of petroleum, Aceh suddenly became rich, at least from the point of view of Jakarta and certainly on paper. Thanks to the discovery of petroleum and gas, the gross domestic product per capita of this region was almost triple the Indonesian average (Tan Ngak Yong 2002, p. 20). The impact of the discovery of petroleum and gas in Aceh on the industrialization of Indonesia can hardly be overestimated; by the end of the 1980s, the province had contributed 30 per cent of Indonesian petroleum and gas exports. Between 1975 and 1990, these amounted to approximately half the public revenue, and in the peak year of 1980 was actually almost 80 per cent (Alisjahbana 2005, p. 110).

The influence of this new motor on the economic acceleration of Indonesia can be read from the growth data. Between 1950 and 1970, the country registered an average economic growth of 3.5 per cent per annum (Tan Ngak Yong 2002, p. 58). Between 1970 and 1980, a new phase of rapid growth started, which brought in an average increase in GDP of 7.2 per cent, attributable to the high prices of oil between 1973 and 1979. The government backed a policy of import substitution and the setting up of secured public enterprises, which were designed to lessen dependence on foreign countries. Although, in retrospect, this created inefficient public enterprises, which were unable to vie with foreign competition, it nonetheless developed a domestic economic motor, which enabled Indonesia to make an immense push towards modernization. Only when oil prices collapsed in 1980 — resulting in a depression which lasted almost a decade — did growth promptly weaken as well. Between 1980 and 1990, the Indonesian economy increased by only approximately 6.1 per cent per annum. In the same period, the proportion of petroleum and gas revenues contributing to the total public revenue sank, owing to the fall in prices from 75 to 25 per cent (Alisjahbana 2005, p. 110).

At the beginning of the 1990s, Indonesia supplied 40 per cent of the world's liquefied natural gas (LNG) requirements, with the production in Aceh from the gas fields of PT Arun as the key source. This production reached on average 12 million tons of LNG per year. In 1992 and 1993, the revenue from LNG exports amounted to US$4 billion per year. This occupied 14 per cent of the total exports at that time. While LNG was directly conveyed by ship from the refineries in Aceh to the whole world — with Japan, South Korea and Taiwan as its bulk purchasers — scarcely any of the revenue it generated remained in Aceh. The proceeds were passed on to the state, the petroleum company Pertamina, and the consolidated foreign operator Mobil Oil (which merged with Exxon to form ExxonMobil in 1999). Not only for Indonesia, but also for Mobil Oil, Aceh remained a focal point; its local oil and gas operations provided the company with a quarter of its business income at the beginning of the 1990s (Martinkus 2004, p. 16).

Thus, contrary to original expectations in Aceh, practically all profits from the LNG boom flowed to Jakarta, into the hands of Pertamina and the foreign oil companies. Fifty-five per cent of the plants belonged to Pertamina, 30 per cent to Mobil Oil and the remaining 15 per cent to a Japanese syndicate (Jilco). Only approximately 5 per cent of the profits flowed back to Aceh (Heiduk 2004, p. 7). This swiftly became another source of disillusionment. As the profits for the Indonesian state dramatically increased, the flow back to the province in the form of investments failed to materialize (Tan Ngak Yong 2002, p. 19). The consequences were noticeable in the long run. Even at the beginning of the 1990s, Aceh — with 40 per cent — had the highest number of villages which remained below the poverty line.

On paper then, the impact of the petroleum and gas industry on Aceh has been high. According to the Asian Development Bank (ADB), this industry has contributed 43 per cent of Indonesia's GDP (though according to official Indonesian state statistics, it is 39 per cent), which was estimated at US$4.5 billion for 2003 (ADB 2005). While the population of Aceh amounts to 1.9 per cent of the total Indonesian population, the proportion of the GDP contributed by the province adds up to 2.3 per cent. At first glance, this would therefore seem to indicate a higher per capita income in Aceh, at least until the fact that just a tiny fraction of this US$4.5 billion was ploughed back into the province is taken into account. The underdevelopment and stark inequality of the situation in Aceh then becomes more palpable.

Anne Booth is convinced that the standard of living in Aceh should have had no trouble reaching the level in Malaysia, if the distribution of income from the oil and gas business had been equitable (Booth 2001).

A REBELLION FOR ECONOMIC REASONS ONLY?

In connection with these economic considerations, it is interesting to refer to the causes of the earlier rebellion of September 1953. Various authors have decided that the proximate reasons for this riot were political and religious. This involved the protection of Islamic culture in the broadest sense (Robinson 1998, p. 132). Hence, the Darul Islam movement was based on the desire for a more Islamic Indonesia. However, it was not oriented towards the foundation of its own state separate from the republic (Robinson 1998, p. 133). Religion was indubitably important but economic considerations certainly played an important part as well. The Darul Islam movement also drew its energy from the determination to maintain Aceh's economic autonomy, which it had enjoyed until 1949.

Coupled with the consistent build-up of Indonesia as a centralistic state after 1949, economic considerations increasingly made themselves felt. Between 1945 and 1949, a brisk trade between Aceh and Penang, as well as between Aceh and Singapore, had developed. Rubber, copra, palm oil, nuts, imported textiles, firearms and munitions were exported (Morris 1986). Aceh enjoyed a largely unlimited freedom of trade, which came under threat from the strengthening centralist tendencies of Jakarta. To a mounting degree, after 1950, the sense in Aceh was that its people had assisted the Indonesian nation financially during the hour of its birth, but that this loyalty was not being requited because of the centralization which was growing apace.

This judgement was not far wrong. The growing economic self-reliance of Aceh and its definite separation from North Sumatra had aroused apprehension in Medan. Fears were voiced that the port city of Aceh, Kuala Langsa, could outpace Medan as the central point for the transhipment of exports. More pressingly, since the beginning of the 1950s, it was known that Aceh was abundant in raw materials. The export of agrarian products from the plantations, which was traditionally transacted via Medan, seemed to be in jeopardy as well. When these factors are taken into consideration, it is clear that the plan to dissolve the province and subsequently to absorb it into the province of North Sumatra obviously had an economic motive.

The straw which broke the camel's back and which ultimately contributed to the rebellion was the abolition of direct trade between Aceh and Penang and Singapore, which was imposed by Jakarta in 1952. To make matters worse, trading licences had to be obtained in Medan and the competition faced by merchants rose dramatically. The ban on external trade, which from the Acehnese point of view seemed to be nothing more than an arrangement by Jakarta to benefit Medan, hit the farmers badly as many of them were not only rice farmers, but also did other jobs, such as working on coconut and palm oil plantations. Sjamsuddin indicates that this was not all. The government in Jakarta did not honour its promise to mend the irrigation systems, which had been badly maintained during the war years. As a consequence of the meagre harvest in 1952 — one year before the rebellion — only 10,000 tons of rice could be exported from the province (Nazaruddin Sjamsuddin 1985). Also, the infrastructure, primarily the road network, had been neglected. Hence, the resentment against the central government smouldered more strongly.

Since the beginning of the petroleum and gas bonanza in the 1970s, which proved to be a mere *Fata Morgana* for the Acehnese, the feeling of marginalization had increased. After 1976, it had loomed ever larger that the real purpose of the resistance to the central power of Jakarta was no longer to uphold the province's cultural identity or to regain economic autonomy, but to become independent of Indonesia.

In this context, it is revealing that, in 1974, a local businessman's application to construct an oil pipeline for Mobil Oil was rejected and the contract awarded instead to an American company (*Forum Asia*, 2004, p. 69). This local businessman was Hasan di Tiro, who established the rebel organization GAM two years later and absconded soon afterwards to live in American and Swedish exile.

IT'S THE ECONOMY, STUPID

Nowadays, the question of whether economic neglect was the real cause of the conflict seems more relevant than ever. Since the oil crisis of 1973, the rebels have been able to proceed on the assumption that petroleum is not only the basis for wealth, but possibly the economic basis for the creation of a separate nation as well, and their claim is all the more justified by how the state has hoarded almost all the wealth exclusively for itself. Now, after being sparked off by economic considerations, the rebel's political demands have gone on to lead a vibrant life of their own.

The proposition that the conflict had economic roots in the first place opens a window to a fascinating perspective. If the cause of war lies in the economy, then the economy holds the key to peace in its hand. The realization that not all inveterate political and cultural animosities have goaded the province into its current stance, but that the fault lies in economic considerations as well, is changing the view on how peace can be achieved in Aceh. The importance of this has increased since the formal waiver of independence. If the state in the memorandum of understanding should be successful in allotting the profits from Aceh's resources fairly and developing the province economically, then the risk of conflict should also decline. And the billions which were donated to Aceh after the 2004 tsunami could also be seen as a contribution to peace-keeping in this context. The legendary slogan of the Democratic Party's election campaign during the 1992 American presidential, "It's the Economy, Stupid", would be applicable to Aceh.

The sense of economic exclusion, which had already stoked the rebellion, was forcefully expressed in Hasan di Tiro's declaration of independence in 1976:

> During the last thirty years, the people of Acheh, Sumatra, have witnessed how our fatherland has been exploited and driven into ruinous conditions by the Javanese neo-colonialists... Acheh, Sumatra, has been producing revenue of over 15 billion US dollar yearly for the Javanese neo-colonialists, which they used totally for the benefit of Java and the Javanese. (Tan Ngak Yong 2002)

This assessment, that neglect should be seen as an important root of the conflict in Aceh, is shared by Dr Bachtiar Effendy of Paramadina University in Jakarta. In his opinion, the civil war raging since 1976 has had nothing to do with religion or interpretation of the Qur'an; he sees the principal cause as the inequitable treatment of Aceh by Jakarta (Bachtiar Effendy 2005).

THE ECONOMY AND THE MILITARY

The role of the army, which through its brutal use of force essentially contributed to the alienation of the previously loyal province and to the revival of anti-colonial emotions, can be observed from an economic point of view as well. Because this giant nation and its government lacked the capacity and the necessary funds to do so, the army was given the go-ahead to "develop" the periphery as early as the 1950s. The *Dwifungsi* doctrine, under which the military acted as a security force and socio-political power under Soeharto, is well known and was unchallenged for a long time. Less known is the fact that the military was given a third duty, namely the economic "development" of the country. In this context, McCulloch coined the term *Trifungsi* (McCulloch 2000). In a nutshell, this meant that the military, which could satisfy only 30 per cent of its expenses from the government's coffers, had to acquire the rest itself from alternative sources.

In a situation like this, it would be fair to say that the colonial legacy was maintained to a certain extent by the military. In 1957, the Indonesian army absorbed the nationalized Dutch companies and continued their business (Kingsbury 2003, p. 199). With the help of adequate carte blanche for the utilization of resources (like forests, for example), the collection of road taxes, the leasing of military materials, and the offering of security services, the military not only stabilized its internal finances, but unburdened the military budget as well. A profitable system of incentive emerged for officers, who could "carry their wages" as it were for their duties in remote territories. The malign consequences of this war economy, which should be classified as a legal grey area, were that the military had no economic incentive to leave the tension-ridden periphery, and, when all was said and done, was not interested in peace. After all, insecurity and violence jacked up the price of safety and the military's income correspondingly, whereas peace undermined the money to be made from security jobs.

Kingsbury differentiates between the official, grey and black market activities of the army (Kingsbury 2003). He refers to the first as the roots of the economic activities of the army. Among these official activities were the management of its own businesses, such as Mandala Airlines, established in 1969, the logging business, and providing security services for several foreign companies. According to an inquiry set in motion by the Indonesian human rights organization Kontras, in the year 2000, no fewer than seventeen military and police station — encompassing approximately 1,000 members of local security forces — were employed by ExxonMobil. The magazine *Tempo* postulated that figures could be as high as 5,000 soldiers. Sofyan Dawood, spokesman for GAM, declared in January 2001 that an adequate wage per soldier amounts to Rp3 million per month. This is about US$300. In comparison, the average income of an agrarian household in Aceh came to Rp1,987 million in 1993 (Booth 2004, p. 19).

Deforestation unhampered by any official restrictions, the leasing of military stock — like construction equipment — or less transparent security tasks form part of those grey, semi-official activities that the army also takes on. The systematic or arbitrary collection of tolls, that falls within the scope of control of movement, can also be added to this list. Well-known black market activities pursued by the army include prostitution, drug trafficking and the arms trade. One of the great ironies of the conflict in Aceh has been that GAM was a bulk purchaser of those arms.

The deforestation, which has amounted to some 75 per cent of the land area in Aceh, has always occupied an exceptional position in the economic activities of the Indonesian army. This process commenced in 1949 under

Soekarno's presidency when concessions could be traded as incentives and rewards for political cooperation. This system proved most popular in the outlying and troubled provinces of the archipelago — initially in Kalimantan and West Papua, and then later in Aceh — in places where the military had to be kept in line. Controlled by Soeharto, the legal and illegal exploitation of timber reserves met the needs of the rapidly growing national economies of Japan, South Korea and Taiwan. Between 1968 and 1979, the export of timber rose from 0.3 million to 10 million cubic metres. The seemingly unlimited treasure trove of trees also fuelled an increase in plywood production. The export of this product rose from 1.25 to approximately 9 million cubic metres between 1982 and 1991.

Until very recently indeed, all ceasefires and peace negotiations were fraught with the uncertainty of whether the army would join in. According to President Susilo Bambang Yudhoyono, the more optimistic appraisal of the newly initiated peace process of 2005 is that it could be lasting and will not be disturbed by the military, based on the fact that the military was included in the peace negotiations with GAM from the beginning (Susilo Bambang Yudhoyono 2005).

PERTAMINA — ONE MORE SYMBOL OF EXPLOITATION

The state-owned oil company Pertamina has been playing another key role in the economic exploitation of Aceh. This company literally holds the key to the economic development of Indonesia (and Aceh), and its connection to the military impressively illustrates the functionality of the New Order government.

About this Robison writes:

> Pertamina constituted the channel through which the bulk of state's revenue flowed, as well as the largest and most concentrated source of contracts for construction and supply. Pertamina therefore was the strategic focus of economic power and the crucial source of revenue. The autonomy and hegemony of the military was closely dependent upon its ability to maintain its control over this terminal and to prevent its absorption by any regularised state apparatus. (Robison 1986, p. 234)

The history of Pertamina, whose monopoly on the supply of fuel was only relaxed as recently as 2006, provides a striking example of the mismanagement which has continued to expand untrammelled under the New Order regime from the beginning of the 1970s. Although the oil boom, which commenced in 1973, could have transformed Pertamina into a gold mine, the company went bankrupt two years later. This bankruptcy had less to do with oil, and more to do with poor diversification, corruption and careless external financing. Under the New Order system, Pertamina had already been turned into a confusing conglomerate in 1973. It was anchored in numerous industries, which had nothing at all to do with petroleum. As a consequence, Pertamina had to be reorganized after its bankruptcy and refinanced by the government, but, from the 1980s onwards, the company enjoyed new sources of income from the LNG-boom (Budy P. Resosudarmo 2005, p. 181).

The reasons for the corruption within its ranks can be directly linked to Soeharto's style of leadership and the government's New Order system. Thanks to the oil boom, the centralist policies and his authority, Soeharto was able to create a widely ramified system of rewards and patronage, which proved unbreakable until 1997. Pertamina's earnings from the oil business had only a minimal effect on the welfare and hardly any on the standard of living of the population of Aceh. This can be traced back to the fact that revenues were lost in a quagmire of corruption, or were invested in government-owned establishments, which never made a profit (Seda 2005, p. 189). Although the Indonesian economy grew between 1970 and 1996, the economic growth was sub-optimal and concentrated on government-owned establishments. Hence, the impact on Aceh remained marginal.

The Soeharto-sponsored industrialization may have been accompanied by corruption and enterprising mismanagement, but by 1996, it had created a middle class. However, this was barely noticeable in Aceh on account of the virtual lack of connection with the local economy.

The petroleum and gas industry on the east coast of Aceh was much better incorporated into the growing East Asian national economies than its own interior (Dawood 1989, p. 116). The ZILS has always been an economic special area — an industrial enclave and expatriate enclave. Public greens behind high safety fences and a modern security system still illustrate this today. Outside those security fences, Aceh continues to be deprived of a sound infrastructure, poor and agrarian.

Panggabean writes:

> Aceh is an example of an economic mishandling that has produced one of the slowest growing provinces in Indonesia that contributes to poverty and further fuels local suspicions of foreign influence. (Panggabean 2003*b*)

This may have been true but then neither the shipbuilding nor the traditional rattan or clothing industries received modernizing impulses from the oil boom. Whether this lack of integration can be traced back to some conscious policy by Jakarta or to the latent, smouldering civil war must remain open in this case. Both may have played a part.

CRISES, DISASTER AND A CHANCE AT PEACE

To stop the mechanisms of exploitation and to stop the civil war in Aceh it was obviously going to take more than a radical change of political and economic thinking in Jakarta. It seems, as has been mentioned in the discussion over and over again, that a human and economic catastrophe like the tsunami was necessary to initiate a new dialogue.

The Asian crisis of 1997–98 did advance the requirements for an easing of the situation in Aceh, as much as the framework for the democratization of Indonesia and the development of civil society in Indonesia made the civil service and the economy more transparent. Increasing international pressure forced the government in Jakarta to take note of the violation of human rights in Aceh. However, the transitional government of President Jusuf Habibie reneged on the concessions made. Towards the end of 1998, when secession tendencies began to loom in East Timor at the other end of the archipelago, the situation in Aceh was exacerbated yet again, particularly as the attacks by GAM, rearmed by the Acehnese diaspora in Thailand and Malaysia, increased (Heiduk 2004, p. 8).

After the downfall of Soeharto in May 1998, the economic situation in Aceh was impeded by hostilities in spite of the change of government, and it was burdened and aggravated even more by the fallout from the Asian crisis. One of the upshots of this was that thousands of Acehnese, who had been able to earn money as foreign workers in Malaysia, now had to return home without either a job or an income.

Despite these setbacks, the rise in poverty attributable to the Asian crisis seems to have been less notable in the province than it was in the rest of the country or in Jakarta. According to an inquiry by Said and Wisyanti, between 1996 and 1999, the number of poor people in Aceh increased by only 27.1 per cent, to 569,085 (Said and Widyanti 2001, p. 52). Compared with this, the total percentage rise reached 189.4 per cent in Jakarta and 121.5 per cent in West Java. On average, the overall rise in poverty in the country amounted to 52.9 per cent. The less dramatic aggravation of poverty in Aceh can be traced to the fact that the province was less affected by the Indonesian economic breakdown because of its weak, selective industrialization.

From the point of view of Jakarta, the integration of Aceh, with its wealth of raw materials, into the national economy gained high priority as it sought to repair damage caused by the crisis; from the point of view of Aceh, the political and economic breakdown at the centre of power seemed an affirmation of the soundness of its intention to secede. This was expressed most vehemently in the increasing call for a referendum in the manner of that in East Timor. Inevitably, this led to an escalation of tensions and, as a consequence, both parties confronted each other, apparently more unappeasable than ever.

Only when Abdurrahman Wahid became the new Indonesian president was there a temporary easing of tension. During Wahid's term of office, the future relationship between Aceh and Jakarta was made clear as well. As the independence of Aceh represented neither a viable option for Jakarta nor for the international community, any compromise could include only a solution involving autonomy. And one of Wahid's first official acts was to initiate proceedings smoothing the path for just this solution.

The earliest steps to achieve this were taken in April 2000. At that time, the parliament in Aceh suggested to the government in Jakarta a plan for the sharing of responsibility and income from its natural resources. From the Acehnese point of view, the autonomy concessions of 1999, which also included a new plan for fiscal sharing, were just passable. After elaborate discussions, this suggestion resulted in Law No. 18/2001 (Special Autonomy for Nanggroe Aceh Darussalam). The law was signed on 19 July 2002. Article No. IV of this law, among other matters, delineates a redistribution of the profits from Aceh's natural resources. Whereas the regulations in the old Law No. 25/99 still designated Aceh's share as being just 6 to 12 per cent of the petroleum and gas profits, these shares were raised to 55 to 40 per cent in the new law.

However, this gesture of autonomy did not stretch far enough to preserve peace in Aceh. The legacy of the New Order government and the influence of the military had been entrenched for too long. With the declaration of martial law by President Megawati in May 2003, which temporarily established her position a year before the presidential election, another regression in relations took place. Only with the fourth president after Soeharto, Susilo Bambang Yudhoyono, and only after the tsunami, which vividly showed the absurdity of this conflict, did Jakarta and Aceh seem willing and prepared to make peace.

The Memorandum of Understanding (MOU) between the two includes, within the scope of autonomy, a new allotment formula for the profits from local resources. Details still have to be worked out, but basically, Aceh can claim broadly 70 per cent of all its land and sea resources. A fundamental difference of this new treaty with previous agreements is that this treaty stipulates that, in addition, the provincial government of Aceh will be allowed to collect taxes and charges. Another remarkable contrast with former arrangements is that autonomy has been granted to Aceh to manage its own air and sea ports — a point of friction which had previously caused tension with Jakarta. Besides countless concessions in the political and cultural spheres, on paper at least, the economic concessions that have been granted this time as well provide hope for a more optimistic appraisal of a chance of peace.

7

THE ACEH CONFLICT DURING THE NEW ORDER AND THE FOLLOWING DEMOCRATIZATION PROCESS

Patrick Ziegenhain

INTRODUCTION

This chapter seeks to provide an overview of political developments in Aceh between 1965 and 2004. It will analyse, from a historical perspective, why and how the conflict between the separatist movement and the Indonesian central government escalated, and what attempts were undertaken to end the fighting in Aceh. The main focus lies on the years after 1998, when Indonesia started its way on a bumpy road towards a more democratic political system. Within this transition process, the intensity of the conflict in Aceh was not diminished but rather fuelled. In order to assess the background of the Aceh conflict, the roles and the behaviour of the main actors involved, such as the Indonesian military (Tentara Nasional Indonesia, TNI) and the Free Aceh Movement (Gerakan Aceh Merdeka, GAM) must be analysed, and for the assessment to be complete, a careful literature review and expert talks have been conducted by the author.

ACEH DURING THE NEW ORDER

When the military under General Soeharto took over power from long-time President Soekarno in 1965–66, the consequences for Aceh were initially relatively minor. The installation of the New Order (Orde Baru) regime was mostly supported by the Acehnese since they expected more economic and political stability after the chaotic last years under President Soekarno. Aceh "was one of the areas where the new government received a particularly warm welcome, primarily because of its strong anti-Communist stance" (Kell 1995, p. 13).

Moreover, the anti-Communist purges, which in some areas of Indonesia had killed hundreds of thousands of people, were not so heavy in Aceh, since the Communist Party of Indonesia (PKI) had no stronghold in this province. The province's status as a special region (*daerah istimewa*), which Soekarno had granted to Aceh, also remained untouched.

However, while the region's status left them some autonomy in the fields of education and Islamic affairs, the centralist state structure of the Unitary State of Indonesia (Negara Kesatuan Republik Indonesia) became now more noticeable to the people in Aceh. Soeharto's administrative reforms brought the province more tightly under the control of the national government in Jakarta. The New Order regime had no intention of giving a wider scope to regional, especially Islamic, organizations but rather tried to curb the influence of all countervailing sources of regional power.

Government and political power became increasingly centralized during the New Order era. Such a "concentration of power was accompanied by major changes in the structure of society, as government policy and rapid economic change favoured particular classes and elites and resulted in the decline of others" (Kell 1995, p. 13).

Important political positions, such as that of the province governor and even district leaders (*bupati*), were appointed directly by President Soeharto, on whose behalf they were responsible for the affairs of government in Aceh. By making the choice himself, Soeharto made it clear that the governor was absolutely loyal to the central government and did not favour any support for more regional autonomy. All governors in Aceh during the New Order government were from Soeharto's GOLKAR party. The limited pluralism of the authoritarian regime, however, allowed two other parties (the Islamic Partai Persatuan Pembangunan (PPP) or United Development Party and the nationalistic Partai Demokrat Indonesia (PDI) or Indonesian Democratic Party to compete with GOLKAR in manipulated parliamentary elections. In these elections, the Islamic PPP usually received a higher percentage of the votes in Aceh than at the national average. In the 1977 and 1982 elections, the PPP even garnered more votes than GOLKAR, which was markedly unique compared with the election results in all the other Indonesian provinces during the New Order. However, the power to rule was nearly completely yielded in a "coalition consisting of the all-powerful and ubiquitous army, and the civilian provincial government led by the [Jakarta-controlled] technocrats" (Kell 1995, p. 29).

The emergence of these political forces in Aceh were accompanied by a forced decline in terms of the traditional Acehnese elites. However, in the initial years of the New Order, they continued to be highly influential, especially in the rural areas. Later though, traditional Islamic leaders, such as the *ulama*, who in the beginning had mainly supported the introduction of the New Order regime, were increasingly sidelined. The regime regarded political Islam as a potential danger for the two main targets of the New Order: development and stability. Consequently, traditional Muslim elites in Aceh were, as far as possible, removed from political and societal influence. State institutions, such as the MUI (Majelis Ulama Indonesia; or Ulama Council of Indonesia), were established to maintain control over the local Islamic elites. More and more, the central government was successful at co-opting the local elites, so that by the mid-1980s "the Acehnese ulama had both lost their position as a cohesive, independent, and powerful social and political group, and been drawn into the New Order 'network'" (Kell 1995, p. 52). This led to their alienation with ordinary Acehnese, who felt that their interests were no longer being represented by these traditional elites (Kell 1995, p. 60).

They also did not trust the Jakarta-controlled civil politicians, not least due to economic reasons. The natural resources of Aceh, especially gas and oil, had been managed by the state-owned company Pertamina, which had given far-reaching concessions to Western oil companies such as Mobil Oil. The high income generated by the sale of oil and gas from Aceh, however, did not remain in the province but rather had gone directly to Jakarta or to international companies. Thus, the central government had controlled the revenues that had been accrued from the province's export industries. In sum, Aceh's natural resources had been exploited for the benefit of the central government.

Jobs in lucrative industries were often not given to local people but rather to people from other parts of Indonesia, mainly Java (Sulistiyanto 2001, p. 440). While the local economy continued to be based on small-scale agriculture and fish farming and the local population lived in rural villages, the hired migrants lived often in better-equipped, segregated housing complexes.

Thus, the economic growth, which Indonesia had witnessed in the 1970s and 1980s, was not enjoyed by the Acehnese to the same extent as other regional groups. Until today, the large majority of native Acehnese are still subsistence farmers, so their contribution to the economic development of Aceh has been limited. While other parts of Indonesia have made significant economic progress, the economic development of Aceh has stagnated.

Resistance against the central government has a long tradition in Aceh. The Acehnese local elites soon became aware that under the Soeharto regime their chances of exerting any influence on political and economic matters in the province were very limited. The Indonesian central government's policy of blatantly disregarding Acehnese cultural and historical peculiarities was also not welcomed by many Acehnese. Thus, Aceh's aversion towards the central government and the army is the result of the social, political and economic changes described above, which many ordinary Acehnese feel has left them at a disadvantage.

A member of the traditional Acehnese elite, Tengku Hasan di Tiro, whose family has a long-standing tradition of resistance, became leader of the Free Aceh Movement (Gerakan Aceh Merdeka, GAM). Founded in October 1976, the GAM demanded independence from Indonesia and the creation of its own Acehnese state, called Nanggroe Acheh Darussalam. Their leaders regarded Indonesia as an unnatural geopolitical entity and believed that it needed to be broken up into a number of independent states (Kell 1995, p. 62). According to them, Aceh needed to be liberated from Javanese colonialism and so they called for an independent Aceh.

The GAM punctuated their demands with some acts of violence against Indonesian military troops in the province. President Soeharto, whose authoritarian government tolerated neither opposition nor separatist demands, increased the number of military units in the province and tried to crush the initially-very-small independence movement.

Since then, Aceh has always been in a state of civil war, though the intensity of the conflict has varied over the years. In the early 1980s, the violence by both sides was rather low and GAM leader Hasan di Tiro went into exile in Sweden. By 1989, however, "rapid urbanization, the incursion of the non-Acehnese, land seizures, pollution, and competition for jobs in the industrial sector all contributed to tensions that facilitated GAM's 1989 re-emergence" (Ross 2003, p. 15). The conflict escalated again when GAM attacked Indonesian police and army units, killing some two dozen officers. The group also targeted civilian authorities, commercial property, suspected government informers and non-Acehnese settlers in the Lhokseumawe area (Ross 2003, p. 17). This led the Indonesian government to declare Aceh a military operation area (Daerah Operasi Militer, DOM). The armed forces of Indonesia (Angkatan Bersenjata Republik Indonesia, ABRI) were given far-reaching powers to fight GAM fighters and supporters. Over the following years, the military in Aceh faced virtually no accountability for their actions;

police and military units could conduct their operations with impunity. Their main victims were the local civilians, whose lives were threatened when they were suspected of being GAM supporters and whose property was destroyed or stolen by army personnel.

During the authoritarian rule of President Soeharto, Indonesia was rife with human rights violations. They happened all over the huge archipelago but were particularly prevalent in Aceh. The military's operations and their brutal violence did not decrease the number of separatists but rather had opposite effect. Acehnese "secessionist nationalism became a mass phenomenon only after military operations began against an initially tiny secessionist challenge" (Aspinall 2003, p. 145). It is questionable whether disaffection with the Soeharto regime can be translated into broad support for outright independence, "but in the absence of political alternatives the separatist movement would have held an obvious appeal for the Acehnese, as a way of expressing regional sentiment" (Kell 1995, p. 85).

REFORMASI AND ITS IMPACT ON ACEH

After the declaration of the DOM, the Indonesian military soon gained dominance in Aceh. Thus, in the years between 1991 and 1998, separatist activities in Aceh were low, and many observers even believed that the GAM did not exist any more (Missbach 2005, p. 96). All this changed, however, when political, social and economic developments in early 1998 discredited the long time authoritarian rule of President Soeharto's New Order government. Accompanied by huge anti-government demonstrations and riots in May 1998, political and military elites forced Soeharto to step down on 21 May 1998. This date marked the end of the authoritarian New Order and the beginning of a transitional process towards a more democratic political system.

The escalation of the Aceh conflict in the post-Soeharto era is closely connected with the way the regime changed. The transition from authoritarian rule to a more democratic system happened incrementally and with the inclusion of powerful actors from the *ancien régime.* In Huntington's terms, it is justified to speak of it as a "transplacement", which he defines as being the result of negotiated pacts among reform-oriented opposition and moderate ruling groups (Huntington 1991, pp. 151–53), or that of a "pacted transition". In such modes of regime change, no radical break with the authoritarian past occurs since some parts of the former authoritarian elite hold on to their vested interests.

However, immediately after the regime change — in the Indonesian case, the resignation of Soeharto in May 1998 — the former elites have to rearrange themselves, while the former more-or-less united opposition splits up into various groups and parties. Temporary uncertainty about what are the appropriate decision-making procedures, which is a typical result of the transition process, leads to new constellations within the political elite. In Indonesia, the military, as one of the main pillars of the New Order government, was discredited in the eyes of many Indonesians. The ABRI had to change their attitude to bring together various opinions about the future role of the military to form a common strategy. These internal struggles weakened the ABRI's ability to act effectively for some years.

On the other hand, former opposition groups and other societal movements saw, after the regime change, their chance to break into the power vacuum that Soeharto's resignation had left.

Thus, the Indonesian state, which had formed the New Order system and which was founded on a powerful military, a loyal bureaucracy and the ubiquitous state party GOLKAR, eroded. The loss of authority and control by the central government over the provinces of the archipelago resulted in many areas turning into lawless regions. Regional and separatist groups could gain local power and influence, which had not been possible under the strong and authoritarian rule of Soeharto. Regional demands were voiced bluntly after the regime change, especially in resource-rich provinces such as Aceh. More regional autonomy was explained "as both democratic, in that it would restore control over their own affairs to local communities, and equitable, as it would give the regions a greater share of the wealth produced within their own borders" (Aspinall and Fealy 2003, p. 2). However, some regional organizations, such as the GAM, stated flatly that they would not be convinced by any offer of regional autonomy but rather demanded independence from Indonesia.

Additionally, the lifting of many of the New Order's political controls and the resulting new freedom of expression, assembly and association, gave the GAM a broader scope of action, enabling them to mobilize popular support and establish links with other local societal organizations. Rabasa and Haseman wrote that the GAM "exploited the disarray in Jakarta and the growth of popular support for independence in Aceh to expand its presence in the province, step up its attacks, and begin to set up an alternative administration" (Rabasa and Haseman 2002, p. 100).

The national economic crisis in Indonesia also made the separation of Aceh from the rest of the country a more attractive choice for many Acehnese. In such a way, they could gain full control over their natural resources, which seemed to be a viable solution for overcoming the economic hardships they were facing. Although unrest and violence had become a feature in many provinces of Indonesia, most observers agree that Aceh and the easternmost province of Irian Jaya (Papua) are different from the rest. In both provinces, there exists a strong local nationalism linked to an antipathy towards the central government, which has resulted in the demand for independence (Cribb 2001, p. 298).

Furthermore, the nationalism of the GAM is based on a simple concept: the glory of Aceh's own national past contrasted with the situation under Dutch colonial rule and — in the words of the GAM — the current Javanese colonial rule. Such a simplified construction, which ignores the existence of minorities within Aceh, appeals to many local people. However, the conclusion that independence would solve all problems and lead Aceh to a glorious future is an illusion. As Donald L. Horowitz has argued, secession can not create a homogeneous successor state and, thus, cannot generally be viewed as a desirable solution to the problems of ethnic conflict (Horowitz 2003, p. 6).

While in Java and most other provinces the motivating catchword of the democratization process was *reformasi* (reform), most people in Aceh used the word *keadilan* (justice) as their main motivation for political change (Bertrand 2004, p. 174). Members of Acehnese civil society demanded the withdrawal of military troops, investigations into human rights violations, and the prosecution of the perpetrators. In their eyes, democracy meant not only an institutional and personal reorganization of the state, but also a serious discussion about its authoritarian past and misdeeds.

The revelations of past human rights abuses and the following public discussion on these matters made independence for Aceh seem more attractive and discredited the policies of the central government in Jakarta. However, despite the many changes made to the political and economic system during the reform period, the situation on the ground in Aceh did not change completely.

All these factors led to a further loss of public confidence in and ruined the credibility of the Indonesian government. This shift in public opinion made it easier for the GAM to recruit new members and perhaps to raise funds among many Acehnese (Ross 2003, p. 24).

ACEH DURING THE PRESIDENCY OF B.J. HABIBIE

After the resignation of Soeharto, Vice-President Habibie became, in accordance with the constitution, the new president of Indonesia. With his new policies, including the relaxation of restrictions on the press and political organizations, the reform process gained momentum. Political prisoners — among them, some from Aceh — were granted amnesty and released by the post-Soeharto government (Schuck 2003, p. 77). Of special importance for Aceh was the lifting of its status as a military operation area (DOM) in August 1998. This was a significant break with the past, which ended, temporarily, nearly ten years of heavy military pressure on Acehnese civilians.

All Indonesian governments after Soeharto have voiced their rhetorical support for demands to investigate past crimes of the military in Aceh. Also the MPR (Majelis Permusyawaratan Rakyat), the highest Indonesian state assembly, passed a decree during their annual session in 1999, which promulgated an investigation and prosecution of human rights violations in Aceh (Arifadillah 2001, p. 325).

However, Indonesian state institutions have showed no political will and only a half-hearted commitment to a thorough investigation. Military leaders have voiced clearly their resentment and state institutions have bowed to their pressure. A parliamentary fact-finding mission established in late 1998, for example, was headed by Lieutenant General Hari Sabarno from the military. The mission held public meetings in Aceh and West Papua, where local people provided evidence of abuses (Crouch 1999, p. 136).

ABRI Commander Wiranto even apologized for possible military wrongdoings — an unprecedented step in Indonesian history. However, no concrete legal action against military human rights violators followed. To make things worse, a legislator of the Indonesian parliament from Aceh and vice chairman of the above-mentioned commission, Nashiruddin Daud (of the PPP), who was well known for campaigning for the prosecution of accused military members, was abducted, tortured and killed by still unidentified men in January 2000. Amnesty International suggests that his murder may be connected to his activities and efforts to find those responsible for past human rights violations in Aceh.[1]

The results of all fact-finding commissions have showed clear evidence of widespread human right violations in Aceh. However, no serious effort has been undertaken to prosecute the accused members of the military. This lack of action has fuelled support for the separatist movement. Many people in Aceh "might have supported reformasi and participated in an Indonesia-wide movement for deepening democratic reforms, if the government had responded to claims for justice and shown a desire to break with the past" (Bertrand 2004, p. 175).

Habibie visited Aceh on 21 April 1999, a day after a bomb blast rocked the basement of the Istiqlal Grand Mosque, the largest mosque in Banda Aceh. On this occasion, he delivered a speech full of promises to the Acehnese and apologized for past abuses by military forces. Among others, he pledged to aid the region's economy, to help children orphaned by the conflict, and to establish a commission to examine human rights abuses by security forces.

Additionally, President Habibie announced a decentralization programme to appease many troubled provinces which had insisted on more autonomy. In Law No. 22/1999 and 25/1999, the districts (*kabupaten*), but not the provinces, were given far-reaching competencies. With such a policy, the Habibie administration hoped to ease the pressure on local communities and simultaneously encourage certain provinces not to persist in their desire to separate from the state. The decentralization policy was implemented under the term "regional autonomy" (*otonomi daerah*), while the term "federal system" was consciously avoided. The negative association of federalism with attempts by the Dutch to weaken Indonesian nationalism during the struggle for independence has led to a psychological legacy, which until today makes the word "federalism" a taboo among a large majority of Indonesians. The two laws on regional autonomy and fiscal balance between the central and local governments became effective in January 2001. Officially, Law No. 22/1999 has restored Aceh's special autonomous region status.

The main problem, however, was with the implementation of the proposed laws. The majority of the Acehnese did not see them realized, resulting in an even further distrust of the central government. Michael L. Ross wrote that: if the government's pledges in 1998 and 1999 were credible, the notion of independence — a risky option that appeared to have little popular support before the late 1980s — should have been unappealing to most Acehnese. But if these commitments were not credible, then the only way that the Acehnese people could be certain they would no longer suffer from the Indonesian military's brutality, and would retain control of the province's resource wealth, was to secede from the rest of the country (Ross 2003, p. 21).

ACEH DURING THE PRESIDENCY OF A. WAHID

The Indonesian democratization process entered a new stage when the relatively free and fair elections of June 1999 produced a new parliament (Dewan Perwakilan Rakyat, DPR), of which more than 60 per cent were newcomers who could be expected to stand for a different approach towards the difficulties in Aceh. Additionally, the news of the election of moderate Muslim leader Abdurrahman Wahid as new Indonesian president in October 1999 was greeted in most parts of Aceh. In the days after his election, huge demonstrations in the Acehnese provincial capital of Banda Aceh were held to demand a referendum on self-determination or even independence. Wahid seemed personally not to repudiate these demands. He was quoted as saying,

"I don't know when, but I support a referendum [for the Acehnese], of course. That's their right. If we can do that in East Timor, why can't we do that in Aceh?" (quoted in O'Rourke 2002, p. 333).

Indeed, the successful referendum for independence in the East Indonesian province of East Timor in September 1999 had a demonstrative effect on the Acehnese psyche. Immediately and in the months after the election of Abdurrahman Wahid as the Indonesian president, massive parades in support of a similar referendum took place across Aceh. In November 1999, hundreds of thousands of people came to the Acehnese capital, Banda Aceh, to hold a rally in support of the announced referendum. After their experience in East Timor, where nearly 80 per cent of the population voted for independence from Indonesia, the officials in Jakarta then clearly expected a similar result in Aceh.

President Wahid stuck to his opinion on a referendum for Aceh on several semi-private occasions, but then the military intervened and forced Wahid to retract his statements on Aceh. In November 1999, Major General Edi Sudrajat declared that Wahid may have talked about his personal opinions, but that his statements on a possible referendum in Aceh were not made in his capacity as president of the Republic of Indonesia (Gorjão 2003, p. 17; O'Rourke 2002, p. 334). The Coordinating Minister for Political Affairs and Security, the powerful General Wiranto, pointed out that solutions to the Aceh problem should not violate the 1945 Constitution of Indonesia, which promulgated the territorial unity of the country (Gorjão 2003, p. 17). Legislators in the DPR from nationalistic parties also demanded that Wahid should refrain from making such controversial statements.

By the end of 1999, Wahid had to declare publicly that a referendum in Aceh was not possible. However, his administration pushed forward a plan for special autonomy for the province. In January 2000, new talks with the GAM leadership started under the auspices of the Swiss-based Henry Dunant Center, which, after three meetings, ended in the Joint Agreement on Humanitarian Pause signed by both parties on 15 May 2000.

This temporary ceasefire, however, did not have a lasting effect in reducing the level of violence in Aceh. The Indonesian army (TNI) "believed that the GAM was taking advantage of the pause for renewed military operations" (Rabasa and Haseman 2002, p. 103). The fighting between the GAM and the military kept going and the victims continued to be mostly civilians suspected of working for the "other" side. There was evidence that the TNI considered anyone its forces killed in conflict areas, to have been an armed rebel (U.S. Department of State 2005), while the GAM also employed violence against civilians to coerce support for their own side and to deter support for the other side (Rabasa and Haseman 2002, p. 101).

More and more, Wahid departed from his initial stance for a political solution to the conflict. In April 2001, finally, Wahid issued a presidential decree authorizing TNI to restore law and order in Aceh. This decision "symbolized his final capitulation concerning his diplomatic approach towards the pro-independence movement" (Gorjão 2003, p. 18). As a result, the structure of the security forces in Aceh was reorganized in such a way that the number of regular troops was augmented considerably. Additional paramilitary units were engaged and the use of special military personnel, such as KOSTRAD and KOPASSUS, was strengthened (Rabasa and Haseman 2002, p. 104).

The intensification of military operations to crush the GAM led to an immediate escalation of violence. In a report by the Indonesian human rights organization Kontras, which was delivered at the fifty-seventh session of the UN human rights organization UNHCR in 2001, the situation in Aceh was described as being "the same as it was when Indonesia was under the authoritarian regime of Suharto. Civilians are still being killed and the government is not doing anything to stop it" (quoted in Buendía 2002, p. 47).

President Wahid's efforts to curb the military's influence on national politics met with heavy resistance. From the beginning of the reform period until after 1998, the Indonesian army was opposed to recognizing limits to its powers, to accepting its effective subordination to a civilian government, and to decreasing its intervention in political affairs.

ACEH DURING THE MEGAWATI PRESIDENCY

In July 2001, the MPR dismissed Abdurrahman Wahid as Indonesia's president because of his erratic policies and because he had alienated all the other political forces in the country. The nationalistic Megawati Soekarnoputri automatically became his successor. Together with the army's leadership, she shared the view that Indonesia had to be a unitary and centralized state. In the eyes of the military, she was much better fitted for a hard-line military approach to cracking down on any Acehnese rebellion. Abdurrahman Wahid was blamed by senior military members for "his off-the-cuff remarks and accomodationist inclinations [that] effectively had encouraged separatist movements both in Aceh and Irian Jaya" (Honna 2003, p. 185).

Unlike her predecessors, Habibie and Wahid, President Megawati Soekarnoputri did not place human rights as a priority during her government.

Her administration favoured territorial integrity and national security over human rights (Juwana 2004, p. 57). However, Megawati and her Coordinating Minister for Political Affairs and Security, the retired general Susilo Bambang Yudhoyono, initially adopted a conciliatory stance towards the Aceh problem. Megawati apologized for the military excesses of the past and signed a law (Law No. 18/ 2001) which granted the province a much higher proportion of the revenue earned from its resources. This gave Aceh control of 70 per cent of its oil and gas revenues for eight years, after which the arrangement would be subject to review. It would also partially implement Islamic law in Aceh, establish Islamic courts, introduce direct elections for the province's governor, and give the governor greater control over the Acehnese police force.

However, the failure in this lay in the implementation of this autonomy law. The Acehnese provincial assembly made little to no progress in adopting the regulations needed to implement the new law. Additionally, the central government's control of Aceh was too tenuous to implement the autonomy law's provisions. Moreover, the government decreased the credibility of the autonomy plan by placing even more military pressure on the province, and by failing to prosecute the military for its human rights abuses (Aspinall and Crouch 2003).

Eventually, the military started a new major military offensive against the separatists. Despite some military successes, such as the killing of GAM's longtime military commander Abdullah Syafi'ie, "breaking up the GAM units into isolated bands" (Rabasa and Haseman 2002, p. 105), the military option soon showed its limitations.

Thus, a new round of dialogue with the GAM was initiated by the Megawati administration, which finally, in December 2002, led to another agreement between the two sides in Geneva. Both sides adopted a Cessation of Hostilities Framework Agreement, which was hailed as the first step towards a settlement of the conflict. Although it led to a sharp fall in the casualty rate, it was abandoned in May 2003 after being undermined by both the GAM and the Indonesian military (Aspinall and Crouch 2003). Soon after the signing of the Cessation of Hostilities Framework Agreement, the Indonesian military and the GAM both accused each other of ceasefire violations. Both sides then could not agree on a date for a negotiation meeting to discuss these matters. Wiryoso, a negotiator for the Indonesian government, wrote that his side "had taken all pains to be flexible even when its patience was stretched to the limit. On the other hand, the GAM was not only inflexible without any clear reason; it also displayed a streak of obstructionism and disdain for the Government's demonstration of goodwill" (Suryoso 2003, p. 279).

The Megawati administration then again saw no other way to solve the crisis but through military means. It imposed martial law in Aceh in May 2003 and launched a new wave of military operations to crush the separatist movement. Local and foreign journalists were prohibited from reporting independently from Aceh. Following the introduction of martial law, more than 603 school buildings in Aceh — the majority of them elementary schoolhouses — were burned. The government attributed the arson attacks to the GAM, which they vehemently denied responsibility for (U.S. Department of State 2005). The state of martial law, which was previously limited to a maximum of six months, was extended for another six months in November 2003.

On 19 May 2004, the first anniversary of the enactment of martial law in Aceh, Jakarta officially downgraded the territory's status to that of a "civil emergency", shifting authority from the military (TNI) to the civilian government. Despite the change, a strong military presence remained, leaving local authorities to assume control over domestic restrictions, like press censorship, curfews and house searches.

The first direct presidential election in Indonesia's history took place in two rounds in July and September 2004 and ended the presidency of Megawati Soekarnoputri. Just like her predecessors, Abdurrahman Wahid and B.J. Habibie, she was not able to significantly contribute to peace in Aceh. All three presidents had different conceptions of how to "manage" the province, but the outcome was nearly the same. All governments largely failed to hold soldiers and police accountable for extrajudicial killings and other serious human rights abuses in Aceh and could only temporarily halt the violence in the province. In October 2004, the directly-elected president, Susilo Bambang Yudhoyono, and his vice-president, Yusuf Kalla, took over their offices and initiated a new dialogue with the GAM under the auspices of the former Finnish president, Martti Ahtisaari.

THE HELSINKI PEACE AGREEMENT

At the end of 2004, the northern Sumatra region, including Aceh, was struck by an earthquake and the resultant tsunami, which left an estimated 240,000 persons dead or missing. Additionally, the tsunami caused extensive destruction of the infrastructure in the mentioned regions. Admittedly, it is mere speculation whether this huge natural disaster had any impact on the dialogue between the GAM and the Indonesian government, but in August 2005, there was a breakthrough in their talks. On 15 August 2005, both sides signed a peace treaty in Helsinki. As Chapter 8 of this book will focus on the process and outcome of this peace treaty, only some short comments on it shall be included here.

The Helsinki agreement is an important milestone on the way to peace in Aceh but is not the solution to all the problems of the conflict. Of great importance is how the agreement will actually be implemented in the field. The GAM, for instance, regards the regulations of the peace agreement as an important step, which gives Aceh more independence from Jakarta's interference. However, according to the GAM's advisors during the Helsinki peace talks, the overall goal of independence for Aceh has not been given up.[2] The question remains, therefore, whether the GAM can really transform into a political organization, which peacefully represents the interests of the Acehnese.

On the Indonesian government's side, much depends on the overall political development of the country. A deepening of democratic consolidation in Indonesia would have a positive impact on resolving the conflict in Aceh. If the central government had effective control over the military, it could help stop excessive military action against the alleged rebels. Additionally, an effective prosecution of offenders who have tried to destabilize the peace process must go along with a responsible dealing with the past.

CONCLUSION

In the years after the independence of Indonesia in 1945, especially after the introduction of the authoritarian New Order in 1965–66, more and more Acehnese felt that they were getting a raw deal by the central government in Jakarta. There were several reasons for this political alienation of the Acehnese population. Firstly, the central government's control over Aceh's natural resources had created grievances over the distribution of the revenue and jobs they generated. Secondly, the use of military means to guard the state's territorial integrity and the brutal suppression of separatism had united the Acehnese even further against the central government. The feeling of justified self-defence against military occupation has increased enormously over the last few decades. The Indonesian state, more and more, has not been regarded as a guardian or advocate of Acehnese interests but as a repressive military power, which has perpetually violated basic human rights. Thirdly, the political paternalism, which the government in Jakarta had exercised for decades over the Acehnese, while ignoring their regional uniqueness, resulted in a strong desire for political self-determination.

After the end of the authoritarian New Order regime, many Acehnese saw a window of opportunity to change their situation. Spearheaded by a militarily organized separatist movement, the GAM, their demand for the independence of Aceh confronted the weakened central government in Jakarta. At the same time, the military actions of the GAM and the Indonesian army escalated again at the expense of local civilians. The following years, until 2005, were characterized by constant violence in the province, only temporarily interrupted by provisional ceasefire agreements. The subsequent Indonesian governments made the same mistake as the Soeharto regime by trying to crush the separatist group with more military violence. With such an approach, the resistance of many Acehnese to the central government, unsurprisingly, did not decrease.

What has changed, since the regime change in 1998, is how the successive administrations have willingly entered a dialogue with the GAM, where once the Soeharto government refused to have anything to do with them. After several preliminary agreements failed to create conditions for a sustainable peace, the Helsinki peace agreement in 2005 offers better chances. However, it is obvious that this is only a first but important step, which has to be followed by tangible actions on the ground. The people of Aceh are tired of decades of armed conflict, during which more than 10,000 people, mostly civilians, have died. The time is now ripe for peace.

Notes

1. Amnesty International Appeal, "Indonesia: Acehnese human rights defenders under attack. Nashiruddin Daud, Acehnese parliamentarian" <http://web.amnesty.org/library/print/ENGASA210092000> (accessed 12 March 2003). However, the murder could have also been committed by GAM members, as Acehnese politicians who have cooperated with Indonesian institutions have often been their target as well.
2. Personal interviews with members of the GAM advisory team in October and November 2005.

8

THE ACEH PEACE PROCESS

Damien Kingsbury

INTRODUCTION

On 27 January 2005, representatives of the government of Indonesia (GoI) and the Free Aceh Movement (GAM) met for the first time since May 2003 to discuss the possibility of resolving the almost three-decade-long conflict in Aceh. The conflict resulted from a claim to Acehnese independence, which was proclaimed in 1976 (ASNLF 1976), being met with a military response from Jakarta. The talks, held at Koenigstedt Manor in Riipila, Vantaa, about twenty-four kilometres northwest of Helsinki under the auspices of the Crisis Management Initiative (CMI), followed the massive 2004 Boxing Day tsunami that killed around 180,000 people in Aceh, made homeless hundreds of thousands more, and destroyed much of low-lying Aceh.

This document outlines the Aceh peace process from its inception to the signing of the eventual peace agreement on 15 August 2005. The intention of this paper is to show how the agreement was reached, and why it reflected its particular details. Whether or not the Aceh conflict has in fact permanently ended as a consequence of the peace agreement is too early to say at the time of writing. However, the fact that a peace agreement, and not just a ceasefire, has been reached, for the first time ever, itself appears to be of some moment.

HOW THE PEACE TALKS CAME ABOUT

While the tsunami was clearly the catalyst for the peace talks, there had been earlier communication about returning to the negotiating table. During that time, however, the GAM leadership in Stockholm had treated all discussion on returning to talks with polite disdain, remaining committed only to the possibility of reinvigorating an earlier process under the auspices of the Henri Dunant Center for Humanitarian Dialogue. The election of Susilo Bambang Yudhoyono as president of Indonesia in September of that year, and his commitment to finding a resolution to the Aceh conflict, however, was a primary contributor to this return to talks. Another contributing factor was that the military budget allocated to the Aceh conflict had been vastly overspent without achieving its goals. Finally, Indonesia lacked foreign investment, especially in the critical oil and liquefied natural gas industries, which meant it had become an oil importer at a time of world record high prices. This had damaged the economy, and forced the government to look towards creating a more conducive investment climate, especially in energy-rich areas such as Aceh. Yudhoyono thus appointed Vice-President Jusuf Kalla with the responsibility of overseeing a negotiated settlement to the Aceh conflict.

The Crisis Management Initiative had been approached by Finnish businessman Juha Christensen to act as a mediator between GAM and the GoI, if talks could be arranged. Christensen had been trying, since 2003, to broker talks between the two parties after approaching Deputy Social Welfare Minister (for Health) Farid Husein. Similarly, other government attempts to restart talks through intermediaries in Malaysia had fallen on deaf ears. Following the election of Yudhoyono as president in 2004, further approaches were again made to GAM, in October and November of that year, which were also treated with caution. However, a formal invitation from the CMI for GAM and the GoI to meet was issued on 24 December 2004, two days before the tsunami struck Aceh. Following the tsunami, this invitation was accepted.

ROUND ONE

Indicating how seriously it viewed the talks, the Indonesian delegation was the highest ranking it had sent to such talks. It included the Coordinating Politics and Security Minister Admiral (retired) Widodo Adi Sucipto, with the Minister for Justice and Human Rights, Hamid Awaluddin, as chief negotiator. Other members included the Minister for Communication and Information, Sofyan Djalil (an ethnic Acehnese), the Deputy Minister for Social Welfare (Health), Farid Husein, the Director for Human Rights and Security for the Ministry of Foreign Affairs, I Gusti Agung Wesaka Pudja, and the Director for Law and Human Rights, Usman Basyah. The TNI (Tentara

Nasional Indonesia) sent, as its formal representative, the commander of Korem 012 for Aceh since the late 1990s, Major General Syarifuddin Tippe. There were also three unnamed GoI advisors. The GAM delegation was headed by the Prime Minister of the Government of the State of Aceh and the Acheh-Sumatra National Liberation Front, Malik Mahmud (ASNLF is the formal name — GAM is the common but informal name of the same organization), the Foreign Minister, Dr Zaini Abdullah, spokesman Bakhtiar Abdullah, and political officers Mohammad Nur Djuli and Nurdin Abdul Rahman. U.S. citizen William Nessen and the author joined the GAM team as unofficial advisers for the first round. The Finnish government funded the first "unofficial" round of talks, with subsequent rounds becoming more official and being funded by the European Union.

The talks began on 27 January 2005 with former Finnish President Martti Ahtisaari stating to GAM that the condition for the talks was GAM's acceptance of the GoI's 2001 imposition of "special autonomy" in Aceh. Ahtisaari also told both parties that there would be no settlement that was not complete and final (Ahtisaari 2005). This precluded any chance of a ceasefire while the talks were underway, or as a precondition of the talks progressing. The first formal discussion ended with a statement of both sides' positions on the conditions for the talks, with GAM refusing to accept any preconditions. Thus, the first day of the talks ended in crisis, with an apparent impasse having developed, which appeared would preclude any further progress.

On 28 January 2005, GAM opened by focusing on what it regarded as common ground between the two sides, including supporting the international aid effort in Aceh and the necessity of achieving a ceasefire. Farid Husein ended the day's talks by confirming that the GoI wanted a ceasefire.

The following morning, on 29 January, the GoI delegation returned to the talks insisting that a ceasefire should be predicated upon acceptance of "special autonomy". By midday, it again appeared that the talks would collapse, and there was a brief break. GAM reiterated their "common ground" approach, and held out the possibility of a politically negotiated settlement after achieving a ceasefire. The GoI team responded by again demanding their acceptance of "special autonomy", for the province — the terms of which could be negotiated after their acceptance. It also offered GAM members full amnesty, jobs or land for GAM fighters, and oil palm plantations and money for the leadership.

This first round of the talks ended with Ahtisaari saying to the media that progress had been made and future talks would be held within the context of acceptance of "special autonomy". GAM had decided that it also needed to consult and work with significant elements of Acehnese civil society, to ensure support for its position in the peace process. The GAM leadership felt it could work with those elements of civil society that shared a basic common position around the ultimate desirability of some form of self-determination, although there was reticence about working with elements of Acehnese civil society that had openly attacked GAM in the past. The third and probably most significant initiative was that GAM had moved to consider, as a possibility, an alternative political approach to its existing position of complete independence.

One view within GAM was that it could accept the broad outline of "special autonomy" and then construct functional independence within that while still preserving Indonesia's territorial integrity. This corresponded to earlier observations by the author put to GAM as a possible solution to the conflict, with discussion within GAM moving towards the idea that there could be some form of self-determination that was neither full independence nor "special autonomy". The GAM leadership was prepared to consider what should be its first principles: was the goal independence as such, or was independence a means of achieving something else, and if so, was this achievable by other means? After having been earlier criticized for its inflexibility, GAM had thus started to become more creative in its approach to finding a resolution to Aceh's conflict. The biggest impediment to a politically negotiated outcome remained with the TNI, which continued to kill and harass Acehnese apace during the talks.

Following the criticism of Ahtisaari's statement for the context for talks, he rephrased the CMI's invitation to the second round of talks, which was accepted for 21 to 23 February 2005. Following an intercession from the Finnish Foreign Minister, Ahtisaari modified his position on "special autonomy", stating that he wanted to find out if the

> special autonomy concept could offer an opportunity to reach an end to the conflict … That does not mean that your advance acceptance of the "special autonomy", but it does mean that you are prepared to enter into serious discussions on its possible contents and other issues related to a comprehensive settlement to the conflict in the framework of special autonomy. (Ahtisaari 2005)

This showed a more nuanced approach to the process by Ahtisaari.

ROUND TWO

The key moment in round two of the talks was when, on 21 February 2005, GAM responded to the Indonesian position by proposing "self-government", which Ahtisaari promptly overruled. The meeting broke up with the GAM team saying that the talks were deadlocked over their refusal to accept Indonesia's offer of "special autonomy". That the TNI had also launched two significant attacks against GAM positions in Aceh at that point in time, even though they had limited success, further added to the bleakness of the occasion.

The previous evening, Ahtisaari had, in Finnish, changed his choice of word for the translation of "special autonomy" (*erityisautonomia*) to *erityisitsehallinto* (self-government) and this had been printed in the morning's newspapers. In Finnish, these terms are actually interchangeable as both indicate self-determination (*itsemisoikeus*). However, translated into English, or Indonesian, these terms take on a somewhat different meaning, with "special autonomy" referring to the maintenance of the status quo, and "self-government" to something along the lines of self-determination or genuine autonomy.

When first approached about this, Ahtisaari said he was not prepared to consider changes to language. However, when confronted with the difference between the Finnish words for "special autonomy", "self-government" and "self-determination", and asked to confirm that he had in fact used the term for "self-government", Ahtisaari acknowledged that this was the word he had used and, on further questioning, said that he thought it was acceptable. He then agreed with the GAM delegation's request to accept the use of this term, and said he would propose its use to the Indonesian delegation. However, he stressed that this would not alter his intended meaning of "special autonomy" and not "self-government". The GAM delegation then pointed out that if the term was to retain his original meaning of "special autonomy" then there would in fact be no negotiation, but simply the imposition of the pre-existing government position. Ahtisaari also accepted this, and said he was prepared to consider variations on this theme, to be addressed within the context of the existing agenda.

When the two parties met again at Koenigstedt the following morning, Ahtisaari outlined what he saw as a practical outcome for both parties, including provincial elections with local political parties (in contrast to the existing law on political parties having a national presence with representative offices in half of the districts in half of the provinces at least), the introduction of unarmed external monitors from the militaries of sympathetic countries (most probably the EU and ASEAN), and a consideration towards limiting the TNI's powers in Aceh. The Indonesian delegation accepted, in principle, Ahtisaari's outline, which marked a distinct shift in the talks, and agreed to take the term "self-government" back to Jakarta for consideration. This was the first turning point in the process. Ahtisaari also called on both parties to exercise the utmost restraint in the field — a comment which was primarily directed at the TNI. This appeal was comprehensively ignored by the TNI, and eventually by the AGAM (Angkatan GAM) as well.

The issue of "self-government" was to become a major point of discussion in Jakarta over the coming months. The main question was what was meant by a concept that was still being negotiated. While most of the commentary was critical and negative, it helped place the talks firmly on the agenda in Jakarta, as well as put on the agenda the possibility of an outcome other than the simple acceptance of "special autonomy". During this time, the GAM also began to work towards meeting with a number of Acehnese civil society representatives to both ensure the acceptance and socialization of its "self-government" proposal and to seek further input into what it could ultimately mean for the province.

Following round two, GAM had to come back to the negotiations with a plan for what it wanted to achieve. Keeping in mind that there could be a realistic but still optimal claim, and a much less optimal but probably more realistic claim, it constructed a Plan A and a Plan B as a fall-back position. These plans were based in part on Ahtisaari's agenda (CMI*a* 2005), the existing legislation on Aceh, and the sorts of claims that could reasonably be made under the self-government model. The plans covered issues such as politics, the economy, human rights, the law, and so on. Plan B was much the same as Plan A, except that it retained, as a major concession, the continuing presence of some TNI in Aceh at the end of any agreed process. Plan A subsequently became the basis, with little change, of the proposal that GAM tabled during round four of the negotiations, and thus formed the basis over which the negotiations were conducted. In the give and take of negotiation, taking into account some unmovable realities and the nature of compromise, the large number of points that were agreed to in round four and which subsequently ended up in the resultant MOU between the two parties much more closely reflected Plan B than Plan A.

On 22 March 2005, the author met with Christensen, Awaluddin and Husein in Jakarta and discussed the issue of political parties for Aceh. Awaluddin rejected the option of creating local political parties. The other key point was that of the presence of the TNI and Polri in Aceh. It was agreed that this would probably create the biggest obstacle to an agreement, given that the TNI would certainly object to its removal, and that there might not be sufficient political will in Jakarta to tackle this problem head on. The following day, the author met with Vice-President Jusuf Kalla, the two ministers, Awaluddin and Husein, and Christensen (see *Kyodo*,

28 March 2005, for a sensationalist account of this meeting). The primary outcome of this meeting was a plan to reach an agreement on the less controversial issues in the negotiations first, and then to move on to more difficult subjects towards the end of the process. The intention was to build goodwill, and to have the process fall over, if at all, at the end, and not at the very beginning.

ROUND THREE

For round three of the talks, General Tippe did not return. Christensen said it was because Kalla had him removed from the team as he had been an unhelpful influence, but another version was that TNI headquarters had ordered him not to attend as a means of expressing its lack of desire to recognize this process. More importantly, however, Widodo was also notable by his absence, which he said reflected his unwillingness to support this "unofficial" process (AFP, 14 July 2005), while Commission I on Foreign Affairs and Defence in the Indonesian legislature, the Dewan Perwakilan Rakyat (DPR), became a site of outspoken criticism of this process. The vice-chairman of Commission I, Effendy Choirie, said that the sole purpose of the talks was to allow the TNI more time to organize further attacks against GAM. He also called on the talks to be halted, and for any further discussion to be held only within Indonesia (*Kompas*, 18 April 2005).

Shadia Marhaban was invited by GAM to attend round three as an expert in field monitoring, having worked in the Cessation of Hostilities Framework Agreement process. That Shadia was a woman in a male-dominated process also made GAM appear more progressive in its thinking, since her appearance led to objections by the GoI delegation, on the grounds of her sex.

On the GAM side, the Dean of Political Science at UKM, Professor Palanisamy Ramasamy, joined the GAM team for two rounds, replacing Dr Vacy Valzna, who had in turn replaced William Nessen after the first round. More notably, however, the GAM team was joined by Irwandi Yusuf who had been jailed for seven years for treason. Irwandi had been in prison in Banda Aceh when the tsunami struck on 26 December 2004. He managed to break a hole in the prison roof as his cell was filling with water and then clambered onto the roof. In the following chaos, he simply walked away to find his family, then left Aceh via a circuitous route that led him to Stockholm and then to Helsinki. As an escaped political prisoner, his presence was a major affront to the GoI delegation, and they said that if he was present at the talks, they would lodge a formal protest with the Finnish government and might even walk out. To save embarrassment to their hosts and to ensure the continuation of the talks, it was decided that Irwandi would stay at the GAM hotel with telephone and computer access.

The GoI delegation came to this round of the talks saying they wanted GAM to accept that foreign affairs, currency, formal recognition and defence would remain with the republic. This was viewed by GAM as acceptable, if it allowed negotiation over all other matters, and appeared to open up again the possibility that the talks could move forward. Nurdin then put forward GAM's comprehensive rejection of the NAD law, which was debated but ultimately accepted. This was a further major step towards constructing an alternative political outcome. In the following session, Malik put forward the idea of genuine democracy and political participation with local parties. The GoI delegation responded by saying that local political parties were not possible, but Malik said this was GoI's problem, not GAM's, and that it would have to change the law. Out of this discussion came an agreement in principle to accept a democratic framework for an outcome, which indicated to GAM that self-government, or whatever it was to be called, had moved one small but important step closer to becoming a reality.

On 13 April 2005, the GoI delegation confirmed its agreement to audit revenues from natural resources, the allocation of future resources, and the letting of contracts for the exploitation of resources. GAM proposed that Aceh retain control over the letting of contracts, which drew a more muted response. Ahtisaari then suggested that Aceh undergo a transitional economic process and, following from the GAM proposal, put forward the suggestion that there be a GAM-managed police force. He also raised the issue of compensation for GAM fighters, and suggested that the decommissioning of GAM weapons, which would have to be part of the process if it were to succeed, could be handled by GoI officials.

Nur Djuli responded on behalf of GAM, saying that any issue of compensation for GAM fighters could be undertaken by a future Aceh government and that this responsibility should not remain with Jakarta. He also noted that talk of the decommissioning of weapons was premature and would be the last part of process to be discussed. On human rights issues, Nur Djuli further noted that there could be no acceptance of any possible GoI amnesty for GAM members without also implementing a proper system of justice for criminal acts committed by the military in Aceh. At the second morning session of 13 April 2005, the GoI and GAM teams received separate military briefings on a possible external monitoring mission by Brigadier General Jaako Oksanen.

During the afternoon session that day, the use of the Indonesian currency, the rupiah, was discussed and accepted, and the issue of the capacity to raise loans, for local taxation and for the allocation of resources, was accepted only in principle by Hamid Awaluddin, while Sofyan Djalil was clearly not happy with the direction of the discussion and walked out. Based on a request from Ahtisaari to have documents concerning the key issues in the talks ready to be tabled, GAM segmented its Plan A proposal and, with some minor changes, handed them over for tabling for the session starting on 14 April. In them, the term *wilayah* was used as a more neutral reference to Aceh, being a territory rather than a province.

Given the GoI delegation's reluctance to engage with GAM's political claims, this session ended in a stalemate, and discussion of political issues was deferred until after other matters had been resolved. The issue of economic policy also arose, with Christensen attempting to persuade the GAM delegation to accept the GoI's position. The GAM delegation then tabled that section of the lightly redrafted Plan A as its economic paper.

Although the peace talks were supposed to be held in confidence, on 18 May 2005, Djalil was quoted as saying that GAM would not be allowed to contest elections as a local party. "If we allow local political parties, all of those negative potentials could emerge like a party based on language, a party based on tribe, a party based on segmented religious beliefs. And then, you can imagine, an extreme religious party could emerge," said Djalil, himself an Acehnese. However, Djalil did also say that GAM could set up a political party with a different name under existing party laws, which was "a tough prospect given the negative view many Indonesians have toward separatists and likely opposition to the establishment of branches outside Aceh" (Reuters, 18 May 2005).

Just ahead of round four of the peace talks, on 23 and 24 May 2005, GAM met with representatives of Acehnese civil society groups just outside Stockholm, under the auspices of the Olof Palme International Center. GAM outlined the key developments in the peace talks process to show them, what it hoped to achieve and what problems it had faced and was expecting to face. In particular, GAM outlined its position on the questions of independence, self-government (everything but independence) and democratization in Aceh. It then took questions and offered clarifications on questions about how the peace process had developed and GAM's pre-tsunami and post-tsunami positions. Questions from these civil society representatives addressed the key issues of GAM's position on "special autonomy" and the NAD law, the meaning of "self-government" within the Republic of Indonesia, local law and the judiciary, political parties, human rights issues, the allocation of resources, the future of the TNI and police in Aceh, the separation of forces, peacekeeping, administration and the rule of law, who would oversee local elections, the creation of a transitional authority, and what are the final outcomes.

GAM identified the following as major problems it had encountered: the lack of basic knowledge and general intransigence of the CMI, the attitudes of Widodo and Tippe, dealing with the assertion of "special autonomy", the refusal to agree to a ceasefire, the continued incarceration of GAM negotiators, and continuing attacks by the TNI. Problems that GAM expected included the rise of nationalism in Jakarta, the formation of political parties and legislative issues, the reallocation of resources and possible consequent constitutional changes, human rights trials, and security issues regarding the TNI, militias and peacekeepers.

Civil society representatives questioned GAM and offered their own views as to what should be achieved. There was overwhelming support for the idea of a referendum within Aceh that would allow the people of Aceh to determine their own future. To this end, the civil society group drafted a statement in support of the peace process (CS 2005).

That night, the GAM delegation left Saltsjöbaden for Stockholm, where it received the Indonesian response to their two initial working papers. The response reflected the rhetoric that had been coming out of Jakarta prior to this round, primarily revolving around the talks producing a result under the NAD law on special autonomy, and that political parties should comply with existing laws.

ROUND FOUR

Round four of the talks began on 26 May 2005, with the first day being inconclusive. On 27 May, the author ran through GAM's papers on politics, economy and law, in a smaller session with only Awaluddin, Ahtisaari, Malik and Zaini. A second session also included Nur Djuli, Usman and Sofyan Djalil. These two sessions produced a high level of agreement around key points, with only minor matters remaining outstanding. It was agreed that local parties for Aceh should exist in principle, and Awaluddin proposed that a constitutional court mechanism might be one means of achieving this outcome.

The GoI delegation formally responded to GAM's politics position paper with one of its own on 15 April, to which GAM responded on 23 May. The GoI delegation's response also included the claim that as "the spirit of autonomous regions" had been granted and secured under the constitution, there was "no reason to be sceptical that the provision of autonomy will be arbitrarily changed in the future" (GoI 2005, point 6).

Similarly, the GoI claimed that "The people of Aceh have wisely chosen the name of Nanggroe Aceh Darussalam as the official name of the Aceh Province to pay tribute to the richness of its historical backgrounds and bears a noble meaning, namely the home of peace. The name of the province of Nanggroe Aceh Darussalam has been fully accepted and carried out by the Acehnese people" (GoI 2005, point 8). Finally, the GoI rejected the call for local political parties, saying such a development "will trigger other provinces to also establish their own parties based on ethnicity and at worst on religious extremisms".

Awaluddin had accepted that there could be local political parties in principle, saying they could possibly be achieved through an appeal to the constitutional court. However, as Awaluddin's proposal was unlikely to succeed, there was no agreement on the mechanism by which local political parties could be achieved. On 28 May 2005, the negotiating teams again met, while GAM fine-tuned its political, economic, human rights and security papers for re-presentation or, in the case of the security paper, for first presentation. Importantly, it was at this point that GAM accepted that the nomenclature to be used in Aceh, for its chief executive and various elected offices and districts be left open for the new government itself to decide. It was also at this point, that the term "self-government" was formally dropped, and for this issue to be decided by that form of government. This was acceptable as the term had only ever been a vessel for other ideas: the main one being some form of genuine autonomy or self-determination within the over arching state. It had also been a vessel for carrying the process away from the language and hence, legislation of "special autonomy", and in this, it had fully served its purpose.

The last day of round four of the talks was conducted at the Palace Hotel near the waterfront. A meeting was arranged between Awaluddin, Malik, Zaini and the author, with Christensen present. At this meeting, Awaluddin retreated from the idea of political parties for Aceh. With this clear indication that the GoI was returning to a more hard-line position on this most critical point, it again looked as if the talks had run their course.

The next day, the author wrote the following assessment, which was circulated among the GAM team, Ahtisaari and a small number of supporters outside:

> In particular, the issue of the establishment of local political parties, the timing of the elections of a local legislature and the repealing of the Special Autonomy legislation are each critical points over which the process would fail without inclusion.

On 30 May 2005, Sofyan Djalil made the observation that if there were fresh elections in Aceh, current legislators would be unhappy if they lost their seats. However, if these legislators genuinely represented the wishes and interests of their constituents, they should not fear being unseated from office. In reality, with such a high level of external intervention in the selection of candidates and such notoriously overwhelming corruption in Aceh's political process, with 374 cases of corruption reported but not prosecuted in 2001 and 766 in 2002 (Miller 2004, p. 346), there is a good chance that many and perhaps most would be unseated. This reflection of their lack of popularity, and arguably legitimacy, is a strong argument for fresh and openly contested elections. Should existing legislators be returned in such elections, their political legitimacy would have been confirmed. However, assuming there are no restrictions on local political parties, a refusal to allow fresh elections would disenfranchise both those political aspirants who were excluded from the 2004 election process, and voters who would have voted for alternative candidates had they been able to stand.

Unless the GoI is prepared to genuinely move on this matter, and offer a compromise equating to that of GAM not bringing independence to the negotiations, it would appear that this peace process has failed to reach its objective of finding a position between the two parties upon which there can be an agreement (Kingsbury 2005).

The idea of more meetings between GAM and various Aceh civil society groups had taken hold within GAM, among civil society groups and with the facilitator, the Olof Palme International Center. The Palme Center had regarded the first civil society meeting as a considerable success and saw it as an important means of widening and deepening support for the peace process. GAM was keen to continue to promote the idea. The second civil society meeting at Lidingo, just outside Stockholm, on 8 and 9 July 2005 was an expanded version of the first GAM-Aceh civil society meeting, in that it included a number of participants who had been quite critical of GAM. This meeting followed the format of the first, with a major concern being expressed by civil society participants being the lack of a referendum among the proposals being considered in the talks. There was also concern about the inclusion of wider social issues, including education, health and women's rights.

On 1 July 2005, the CMI issued the first draft of the proposed memorandum of understanding. Ahtisaari also asked Malik to provide details of GAM troop numbers and weapons, and his thoughts on a dispute settlement mechanism and the establishment of a truth and reconciliation commission.

SECURITY ISSUES

It was clear from the outset that while it would be difficult to reach a political solution to the conflict, the real test would involve security arrangements. There were two components to this: the first being the decommissioning of GAM and its weapons, and the second the non-combatant status of the TNI and Polri (Indonesian National Police, or Polisi Republik Indonesia).

At a meeting on 29 May 2005, the whole GAM team worked through a complex discussion about what level of the TNI's presence it would regard as acceptable in Aceh. This was a fundamental recognition that it would be virtually impossible to get all of the TNI out of Aceh. The question was how many it would be acceptable to let remain, and what their function would be. The decision about whether or not to accept any TNI forces was taken by consensus. None of them wanted any TNI presence at all, but all but one recognized that there was probably little choice in accepting some level of presence, and the question would be how much to accept and how to achieve that number. In the end, the GAM team agreed on accepting TNI forces in Aceh solely for the purpose of external defence. The key elements of this were that the TNI in Aceh would be funded by the official military budget, there was to be no Kodam (Komando Daerah Militer, or Regional Military Command) presence below the battalion level, internal security would be the sole preserve of the police, and the Aceh Kodam would have a maximum of 6,000 personnel.

Furthermore, GAM would accept just four strategic locations for the TNI forces to be stationed at and military personnel would not be allowed to carry weapons beyond their barracks, except on deployments sanctioned under Point 11 of the agreement. This is in keeping with the conventional practice of militaries in non-conflict zones. GAM also accepted a limited naval and air force presence. Most importantly, however, GAM stipulated that any incident that occurred between soldiers and civilians was to be investigated by civilian police and any matter requiring legal proceedings would occur under the jurisdiction of the civilian courts.

While some of these conditions found their way into the final agreement, the issue of the number of TNI to remain was not pursued by the leading GAM negotiators. As a result, there was no commitment from either GoI or Ahtisaari on the number of TNI to remain. However, at the beginning of round five of the talks, the European Union's Pieter Feith outlined his assessment of how many TNI would remain after the withdrawal, which was in broad accordance with the GAM proposal. From the time the EU delegation met both the GoI and GAM during round four, it was clear that it was committed to the monitoring process.

The main tasks of the Aceh Monitoring Mission (AMM), as it became known, were to:

- Monitor and report the pullout of national military and police troops
- Monitor the decommissioning of GAM armaments and confiscation of illegal weapons
- Monitor the human rights situation
- Monitor the process of legislation change
- Monitor and report the general security, economical (*sic*) and political situation
- Conduct inspections and investigations, car and foot patrols
- Inquire into complaints and alleged violations of the MOU
- Establish and maintain liaison and good cooperation with the parties
- Promote peaceful settlement of disputes
- Provide good services to the parties

(CMI*b*, Terms of Reference, unpublished document).

The "minimum strength of the AMM is approximately 270 persons, including 200 foreign monitors and 70 locally employed persons" (CMI*b*, 13 May 2005, Deployment). However, due to poor budgetary planning, as the AMM was being implemented after 15 August, it became clear that the proposed number of EU staff would be substantially cut, and that the total number of 200 would be comprised of both EU staff and ASEAN personnel. EU staff, who had already been offered jobs were told, after 15 August, that they had to formally apply for the positions that they had been requested to fill, and informed that there would be fewer positions than personnel invited to apply.

As earlier agreed between the parties, the government of Indonesia would be responsible for the security of all AMM personnel in Aceh. "The mission personnel do not carry arms." (CMI*b*, 13 May 2005, Security). This was the primary condition placed on the AMM by the GoI, and in this respect replicated the security arrangements that had applied to the UN in East Timor prior to and just after the ballot in 1999. It was clearly a problematic model, but it was again the only one available.

One important point that Feith made was that it would be up to the GoI to provide weapons collection points. He noted that members of the mission had spoken with the TNI officers about the number of GAM weapons, which they had estimated at about 1,300, with around 4,000 active GAM members. The decommissioning of these weapons was intended to be completed by the end of the year, and it was agreed that decommissioned weapons would be immediately destroyed (EU, 12 July 2005) The process of decommissioning of the GAM's weapons would be in parallel with the withdrawal of GoI forces, on the basis of 25 per cent per month for four months, to occur on a district by district basis (EU 12 July 2005).

ROUND FIVE

The fifth and final round of the Aceh peace talks commenced on 12 July 2005. The key element of the talks on this day was the further outlining of the security arrangements by Pieter Feith, who said that the TNI and Polri should reduce the size of their forces by 31,000 members by the conclusion of the monitoring of the withdrawal period. It was noted this would still leave about 20,000 or more TNI and Polri. Feith replied that the TNI and Polri would be reduced to a figure of about 4,800.

On the following day, 13 July, the move back to the issue of local political parties came as debate on this issue was stepped up in Jakarta. Awaluddin again rejected the idea of local political parties because, he claimed, their establishment would not comply with the constitution. However, it was quickly shown that Law 31/2002 was in fact a piece of legislation and not a part of the constitution, and could thus be changed if there was sufficient political will. Awaluddin then progressed from proposing that GAM join existing political parties to that of establishing GAM as a political party in itself. To achieve this, he said that the major political parties in Jakarta had agreed to support GAM by donating members to help it establish branches in half of the provinces and in half of the districts of those provinces, as stipulated under Law 31/2002. It was at this point that Christensen interjected, saying that GAM must dissolve as an organization. This interjection from a person whose role was solely as a facilitator shocked and angered the GAM team. There had never been any discussion about GAM dissolving, not even from the GoI team.

Speaking on behalf of the GAM delegation, Nur Djuli rejected the GoI proposal on GAM being set up as a political party with assistance from Jakarta-based parties, as a "sweetheart deal" between the Jakarta-based parties and GAM, which would disadvantage other political parties that might oppose GAM. The right for anyone to contest elections was, he said, a basic democratic principle. Nur Djuli also noted that even if this basic principle was ignored and a back door deal arranged, it had no prospect of lasting and could not secure the political future of Aceh. GAM had committed itself to basic democratic principles and demonstrated a genuine desire to improve the lives of the people of Aceh.

The following session in the afternoon addressed some practical security issues that would come out of any proposed agreement. GAM was told that the number of organic forces to remain in Aceh would be given after GAM provided its own numbers. Both sides agreed that organic police forces would remain responsible for law and order in Aceh, while organic military forces would be responsible for upholding external defence in Aceh. The timeline for the withdrawal of those Indonesian forces that had agreed to leave was laid out on the basis that the TNI would not be able to effect changes immediately following the decommission/withdrawal process, and that troops and police would be removed from Aceh according to logistical readiness.

The GAM was now pressing hard on the local political parties issue. Having committed itself to the formation of local parties, GAM had the opportunity to take the high political ground by emphasizing how its own stand was based on fundamental democratic principles. The GoI was left in the position that it either rejected the GAM's stand and hence compromised on its own claims to democracy, or it asserted its own claims of accepting full democratic principles and hence acceded to GAM's demands. Attempts at back door deals and obscurantism by the GoI could be, and were, portrayed as such. The debate on this issue went back and forth, with the GoI delegation offering variations on its original offer to help establish GAM as a national political party. The GoI also accepted that the next head of the Aceh administration and more junior positions could reflect GAM's interests.

The following day, 15 July, GAM formally replied to the GoI's proposal on local political parties with its own interpretation of the acceptable wording for the MOU. Discussion on local political parties was clearly bogged down, and it appeared that there was an unbridgeable divide between the two teams (Siboro 2005). GAM began to move towards the position of accepting the failure of these talks, while taking a draft of the MOU as a blueprint for future negotiations, rather than backing down on the issue of local political parties. Meanwhile, Awaluddin continued to press for his offer on the creation of an Acehnese national party to be accepted.

The negotiations had developed into a contest of ideas, with each side taking turns in asserting its own agenda. It was, in this sense, a conventional debate, largely conducted in public. However, the problem would always be that winning the contest of ideas would not necessarily translate into "winning" the negotiations. Indeed, "winning" in the negotiations could have inspired a more negative reaction in Jakarta. The rhetoric was therefore about establishing the parameters of the debate and finding a middle ground within that. However, the further the parameters moved in GAM's direction, the further the centre would be towards GAM's basic position.

The debate on the wording of the draft MOU went back and forth. The changes were relatively minor at one level, but at another, were important markers of the limitations of the GoI and the authority of the new self-government. The formal debate, now in writing, continued with GAM proposing:

> 1.1.2. The new Law on the Governing of Acheh will be based on the following principles:
>
> Acheh will exercise authority within all sectors of public affairs except in the field of foreign affairs, external defence, basic monetary and fiscal matters and the national application of justice, the policy on which belong to the Government of the Republic of Indonesia. These sectors will be administered within Acheh in conjunction with the civil and judicial administration of Acheh.
>
> 1.1.5. Acheh has the right to use regional symbols including a flag, a hymn and a crest, the latter of which shall also be displayed within Republic of Indonesia passports carried by residents of Acheh issued by immigration offices located in Acheh.
>
> 1.1.7. Administrative structures in Acheh will reflect traditional administrative structures, including the appointment of a Wali Nanggroe, including all ceremonial attributes and entitlements.
>
> 1.4.4. The appointment of the Chief of the organic police forces and prosecutors shall be approved by the Chief Executive of Acheh. The recruitment and training of organic police forces and prosecutors shall be under the direction of the Chief executive of Acheh in compliance with applicable national standards. (Draft MOU, 6 p.m., 15 July 2005)

With this accepted by the GoI delegation, the last hurdles were being overcome with most of the outstanding issues now being agreed upon, it appeared that the two parties were moving closer to a final agreement.

On the final day of the fifth and final round of the talks, all parts of the MOU had been agreed upon, except the thorny issue of the creation of political parties. The GAM had submitted its proposal in response to the Indonesian one that had been incorporated into the draft MOU the previous evening. The morning session produced no results and the afternoon session was cancelled while the GoI delegation discussed the draft MOU with Jakarta, and, just before 6 p.m., they came back with yet another version of their existing proposal. The view within the GAM delegation was, given that day was formally over, having ended at 6 p.m. that Indonesia had not come back with a meaningful offer, and that the process had ended. The GAM delegation began to pack in preparation for returning to the hotel, thus ending the talks. The author then drafted a media statement entitled "Acheh Peace Talks End Without Agreement For Peace".

In reading and re-reading the Indonesian proposal, however, while it was 99.9 per cent clear it was not agreeable to GAM, the prospect of walking away from the talks without even the faintest possibility that it could have been salvaged was overwhelming. Nur Djuli went to the Indonesian meeting room and asked if Sofyan Djalil would be prepared to come back and talk about the GoI's proposal. The GAM delegation and Djalil sat in a circle in the GAM meeting room and discussed the GoI's proposal. It was noted that, for GAM, there were two main problems with the proposal: one was clarity and hence, its intentions and commitments, and the other was the timelines for action, which did not exist. Djalil said that he accepted this.

Djalil agreed to change the Indonesian proposal from "be willing to" create local political parties to "will" but said that he needed to consult with Hamid Awaluddin regarding the timeline for action. Awaluddin came in and went back through the proposal. Awaluddin agreed to the inclusion of the word "will". The timeline was discussed in relation to the legislative process, producing an outcome that was regarded as both practical and agreeable to both parties. The redrafting began, and it became clear that both parties were now working towards a mutually acceptable text that would make clear the creation of local political parties.

Three drafts later, each of which was only very slightly different from the previous, at about 9.30 p.m., or more than three hours after the talks had formally ended, there was an agreement in principle on the issue of local political parties. The key element in place was that the GoI would facilitate the creation of local political parties for Aceh within twelve months and no later than eighteen months. Some of the language was awkward and the rest was less than perfect, but it was enough. Awaluddin faxed the proposal to Jakarta for approval. The CMI then produced a draft MOU which incorporated the agreed text on local political parties. The agreement was confirmed the following morning when President Yudhoyono approved the negotiated text.

At midday on 17 July 2005, the agreement was to be initialed. Before the initialing, Malik was to hand over the GAM troop figures, and their number and types of weapons. These details would then be included in the MOU along with the number of TNI and Polri to remain in Aceh. At ten minutes to noon, the GAM team was shown that the number of TNI personnel to remain in Aceh, penned into the MOU, was 13,000. Discussion over this saw the initialing delayed by over an hour and very nearly cancelled. Moreover, the GAM team had made an error in being slow in handing over its own numbers, and hence had not had access to the TNI's numbers. GAM noted that while the 13,000 was supposed to consist of organic troops, the TNI had been artificially inflating that number and that it was a much larger number of "organic" troops than would ordinarily be stationed in a province (TNI 2005*a*; TNI 2005*b*). Ahtisaari responded by saying that what was important was that the TNI be focused solely on external defence and be under civilian authority. He added that the police would be under local command. Finally, Nur Djuli, Malik and Zaini agreed that they had not followed through adequately on this aspect of the process and that they had been trapped. That being the case, that they were trapped was their own fault and the agreement as it existed, even with artificial numbers that did not add up, had to be accepted. GAM's public statement that day on the initialing was that it was a "leap of faith". In the final version of the MOU, the TNI's troop figures went up to 14,700, while the size of the police force was reduced slightly, producing a slightly higher overall figure. Similarly, a sentence that referred to the disarming of militias was removed without consultation ("MOU", point 4.9).

With the continuing support of the Palme Center, GAM organized its third meeting with members of Acehnese civil society. The intention was to have this meeting much closer to Aceh than the previous two, which had been held in Sweden. Nur Djuli took over the organization of this meeting, which was held on 8 and 9 August 2005 at the NIOSH complex in Selangor, Malaysia. More than 230 people registered to attend the meeting, with most coming from Aceh itself, though there were Acehnese from other parts of Indonesia, as well as many who had been living in Malaysia, and a small contingent from Australia and Sweden. The meeting followed the format of the previous two, although GAM also received reports from representatives of a range of specific civil society groups. While there were many in this diverse group that did not support GAM, support for the peace process was unanimous and the meeting was characterized by a great sense of cohesion and happiness.

On 15 August 2005, GAM and the GoI returned to Helsinki to sign the memorandum of understanding. That day, AMM personnel were deployed in Aceh for the first time, to start demilitarization on 15 September 2005. In Jakarta, despite earlier reluctance, there was increasing support for the agreement, with some commentary even suggesting that it be used as a model for resolving other similar disputes.

It is unclear if the peace agreement is going to be successful in the long term, either in ensuring permanent peace or the establishment of a sustainable local democratic process. It does have that potential, but there are very many factors working against it, not least of which is a reluctant TNI. In the final analysis, this agreement is very much a compromise. It contains many basic flaws, too many of which were a consequence of errors on the part of the GAM team. However, it also contains a number of important positive points. Whatever the perspective, this MOU is the best that could possibly have been achieved by the GAM team given the circumstances.

PART III
Foundations of Religion and Culture

9

ACEHNESE CULTURE(S) Plurality and Homogeneity[1]

Susanne Schröter

INTRODUCTION

Nanggroe Aceh Darussalam is a multicultural province within a multicultural state. Hence, its political leaders not only face the need to integrate ethnic and cultural diversity into a regional framework, but also have to define Aceh's role within the Indonesian nation. During its violent past, which was characterized by exploitation and military oppression, there were good reasons to emphasize sameness over diversity and to build up the consciousness of a unified Acehnese identity. From both an emic and an etic perspective, it is today widely accepted that there is such a thing as a homogeneous Acehnese culture which is rooted in a glorious, though troublesome, history of repression and rebellion and shaped by a strong Islamic piety.[2]

Even if it is true that Acehnese history has created a strong regional identity, it must not be forgotten that people living in this area belong to various ethnic and cultural groups, and that they represent a rich variety of different cultures rather than simply a single, homogeneous culture. As a matter of fact, the practices and discourses of Islam have also vary depending on the cultural background of the people. As elsewhere in Indonesia and beyond, world religions have to adapt to local customs, have to be appropriated by the local people, and have to be indigenized. This is the reason why *adat* still continues to play a role in every local context, even if it has been treated with suspicion in many parts of Indonesia since the Dutch colonial administration began using it as a counterforce against Islam in order to implement their divide-and-rule strategy.

With this chapter, I wish to shed some light on the complexities of Acehnese culture, as it encompasses numerous very distinct local cultures and this reflects on the general significance of culture for the construction and reconstruction of post-tsunami Aceh.

Writing on Acehnese cultures is not easy due to a lack of reliable written sources for the post-colonial era. Colonial Aceh, however, is quite well documented. Until the middle of the twentieth century, Aceh's cultural landscape was described in detail by travellers who put their experiences to paper and by members of the colonial administration who wrote on indigenous cultures and languages;[3] most notable among these are the brilliant ethnographies written by Snouck Hurgronje.[4] Thus, there is quite an excellent stock of colonial anthropology. More recent or contemporary empirical data, however, is rare. This is partly due to the war between the separatists and the Indonesian military that has been ongoing for the last thirty years and the very limited number of research permits that have been granted to foreigners. The difficult political situation and the high risk has discouraged all but a few anthropologists to conduct fieldwork. Therefore, it is not surprising that the culture of the people of Aceh receives no mention, even in volumes on North Sumatra.[5] On the other hand, ethnographic reports are available for the Gayo of Central Aceh, the Alas of the Alas Valley, and the so-called Acehnese, who consider themselves the original inhabitants of the area.

MULTICULTURAL ACEH

Aceh was first mentioned in Chinese annals dating from the Liang Dynasty in the sixth century AD. These refer to a Buddhist polity named Po-Ii, which existed in North Sumatra. Hinduism arrived in the seventh and eighth centuries, followed by Islam one hundred years later. Marco Polo, who reached Sumatra in 1292, chronicled a state named Peureulak (now Perlak), which he described as inhabited by Muslims. The Portuguese called the region, which they entered in the sixteenth century, Achem and the Dutch changed it to Achin. Both peaceful and bellicose cultural contacts have left their marks on the population, whose physical features bear lasting testimony to the intercourse that has taken place between Europeans, Indians and Arabians. Acehnese are proud of their mixed cultural heritage, and people still pass on their awareness of their foreign descent to their offspring.

Because of its position in international trade and because of its being the source of valuable agricultural products, such as pepper, the region has for centuries been a destination for temporary or permanent migration, and it continues to attract migrants to this day. Apart from the previously mentioned settlers from South and East Asia, and from India and Europe, there has also been migration from within the archipelago, particularly from Nias,[6] Minangkabau and Batak.[7] Most of these migrants have mixed with the local population and have been indigenized. Descendants from Nias who married autochthonous partners are now called the Kluet and live in South Aceh, while the descendants of Minangkabau settlers from West Sumatra, who moved to the southwest,[8] are referred to as the Aneuk Jamu or Aneuk Jameu — a designation that means "child of a guest" and, thus, recalls their foreign origin. Migrants from East Sumatra came to form yet another new ethnic group, the Tamiang.[9] Javanese settlers dwell in Central and East Aceh and Chinese merchants live in urban communities and both have retained their pre-migration identities. Two of the biggest ethnic minorities[10] — the Gayo[11] and the Alas[12] — are of Batak, mainly Karo Batak, origin and came to settle in the Barisan Mountains.[13] Generally, ethnic minorities inhabit the rather sparsely populated mountain areas, while the Acehnese, who constitute the largest ethnic group, dwell in the fertile lowlands of North and East Aceh.

The Acehnese

The Acehnese number about four million and they emphasize how their physical appearance shows some Arab and Portuguese heritage.[14] Their language belongs to the Malayo-Polynesian strata and is closely related to the Cham language of Cambodia. Their economy relies on rice cultivation,[15] the growing of cash crops (like coffee), fishing and trade — the latter formerly (together with pepper) being the source of wealth and social stratification in Aceh.

Historically, they formed a unique sociopolitical system composed of four distinct groups, between whom a precarious power balance existed. Most interesting was the group called the *uleebalang* — merchants who controlled the trade between the Acehnese cash-crop[16] producing areas and the outside world.[17] Their income was derived largely from taxes[18] or from entrepreneurial activities. The *uleebalang* tried to use their wealth to gain political power, but their attempts were hampered by the dominance of the court and their lack of ties to the peasantry. Because they derived their livelihood from entrepreneurial profit and taxes and had no alternative way to assert their status other than by violent means, the *uleebalang* came to be viewed by others as infamous parasites and tyrants who exploited the people. Later, they were also accused of collaborating with the Dutch colonialists.[19]

A second power group was the court. The sultan restricted the *uleebalang*'s autonomy (LeBar 1972, p. 15) tried to benefit from their income, and competed with them to control trade. While the court only gradually succeeded in exacting tribute from them, it did manage to break their control of foreign commerce.

A third influential group was the *ulama* — religious teachers who had separated themselves from their village of origin at an early age to pursue an education at an Islamic boarding school, called a *dayah*.[20] As is well known, it was the *ulama* who had led the anti-colonial struggle.

The majority of Acehnese, however, did not belong to any of these groups. They were peasants — small landowners who lived off the land. Furthermore, Acehnese society was and is still primarily based on kinship and locality, but in the modern urban context, increasingly also on the nuclear family. Villages (*gampong*) are composed of several related kin groups and lead by a religious authority (*Teunku Imum*) and a village head (*Keuchik*); both are technically elected but are, in fact, genealogically determined. The authority of the *Teunku* and *Keuchik* is limited by a council of adult village men. Several villages comprise a *mukim*, which is spiritually and administratively headed by an *imam* (or *imum*). In the past, the *mukim* were parts of larger territorial units which were largely autonomous and which vied with the *uleebalang* for power.

This quite elaborate economic and political structure is today cross-cut by a more simple dichotomy that distinguishes between the people of the hinterland (*ureueng tunong*) and the people of the coast (*ureueng baroh*), that today roughly follows the increasingly important distinction between rural and urban groups. In Aceh, like the world over, a modern social stratum has emerged mainly in urban centres, which have sprung up since the 1970s partly as a consequence of industrialization and development[21] and partly as a result of expanding higher education in the provinces.

Kinship was and still is central to Acehnese social structure. It was the importance of kinship that according to Snouck Hurgronje, underlay the practice of marrying girls off at a very young age, particularly if they were daughters of the nobility, who were forbidden to marry hypogamously.[22] In societies where kinship constitutes the dominant mode of organization, marriages are the most important means of building alliances and of allaying feuds, although the latter practice is no longer common.[23] Consequently, marriage was not only a matter between two clans but affected a whole village. In addition, the principles of kinship and locality frequently overlapped, since there was a strong tendency to intra-village marriages and also to marriages between paternal cousins, even if the latter is forbidden by Islamic law.[24]

According to LeBar, Acehnese descent is bilateral among societies living on the coast and patrilateral among societies settled in the mountain areas, while residence is generally uxorilocal. He further mentions a "perfectly symmetrical bilateral reckoning … [and a] sharp distinction between older and younger relatives on the same generation levels" (LeBar 1972, p. 17). Most authors, however, stress that Acehnese society is matrilocal and uxorilocal.

Thus, after marriage, a man may continue to live in his mother's house and visit his wife, or he may reside with the latter.[25] Upon marriage, a woman receives from her parents a house and a piece of land, to which she has rights of usage, but does not yet formally own. After a few years, a ceremony is held that officially transfers the house to her. From this point on, she is considered independent of her parents (*geumeuklèh*). With each child that she bears, her parents confer upon her additional lands. The birth of the first child constitutes the central right of passage for a woman and is celebrated in a sequence of rituals that are spread over several months and which serve to prepare her for the ardours of her role as an adult woman. Children, according to Siegel, are the most important part of a woman's adult life; they are treated with affection and leniency. Mothers fulfil all their children's wishes, particularly the wishes of their sons. Disciplinary measures are something experienced only outside the mother's home, at the *dayah*, where children receive not only an Islamic education, but are also socialized accordingly. While children remain such for their mothers and are spoiled unconditionally, Islamic institutions, such as the *dayah*, inculcate boys and men with the understanding that becoming a man means following the rules.

With regard to inheritance practices, sources are contradictory. While Kennedy[26] claims that women inherit the house while men inherit the land, Siegel (2003, p. 139) reports that sons inherit land only if their sisters have not yet been accorded all of it upon the death of their parents. In such a case, one of the daughters will then receive the house while the remaining property will be distributed among the children according to Islamic law. The extent to which women are associated with houses is strikingly manifest in the idiomatic term for a wife as "the one who owns the house" (*njang po rumoh*).[27] Ideally, the houses of women and their daughters are located next to each other so that the village centre is typically made up of matrilineal clusters. Women live their entire lives together and comprise a socio-economic cooperative unit.

Gender segregation structures Acehnese society in several respects. Boys are separated from the maternal household at an early age and reside in the *meunasah* — a community centre which serves both as a meeting point and a place where the youth are educated in reciting the Qur'an. Boys often remain in the *meunasah* and spend their lives exclusively among males. Upon marriage, a man is only loosely connected to his maternal kin group, but at the same time, he will not be integrated into his wife's family.[28] However, he does have economic obligations to fulfil towards them. As long as his wife has not been "separated" from her mother, he should contribute gifts to both her and her parents. Once she has formally been accorded her own land, it is expected that she provides for herself. As the father, a man is merely obliged to make a contribution to providing for his children. The lightness of his responsibilities is a consequence of men's poor economic capacities. Therefore, men are expected to leave their families and go to another village, province or island, in order to earn money — in the past, as workers on pepper plantations or as traders. This practice is called *merantau* — an enterprise that can last for years or, even, for a lifetime. Siegel mentions that in Pidie, where he did his fieldwork, men who had been engaged in the coffee trade visited their families only for the month of Ramadan.[29]

The absence of males from the local community affects not only the Acehnese economy, but also their conception of masculinity and feminity. Siegel and Snouck Hurgronje both emphasize how little women were affected by the extended absence of their husbands; for the most part, women regarded men to be utterly superfluous.[30] Both authors quote from interviews with men who felt they were little more than guests in their wife's house. Relegated to such a marginal position, men emphasize their obligation to financially support their families, for example, to finance construction on the house or to buy their daughters rice fields. The women, on their part, expect such support, even if their husbands own rice fields of their own and are able to contribute to the household's subsistence. Conflicts between couples generally amount to squabbles over money. Women expect their husbands to give them the money they have earned while working abroad and treat them with respect until the money is spent. At that point, they pressure their husbands to get out and earn some more.[31] The money is not vital to the family's subsistence, since women also have rights of usage over their husband's land. Given that, Siegel concludes that men are relatively powerless in the family.[32] He writes that "although men tried to create roles as husbands and, especially, as fathers, women thought of them as essentially superfluous" (Siegel 2003, p. 55). More than ninety years before, Snouck Hurgronje has been under the same impression and characterized men as "guests in their wives' houses" (Snouck Hurgronje 1906, vol. 1, p. 339).

Generally, men have had a difficult time finding their place once they return from their *merantau* to their villages and their wives' homes. Siegel quotes one woman as saying, "He is like a child. He walks around the house looking for something to do. Then he goes back to the road and sits on the bench with the other men. The longer they sit the stupider they get." (Siegel 1969, p. 180). Contrary to male anthropologists, female ones stress the positive aspects of this matrifocality, even though the empirical data is the same. Nancy Tanner emphasizes female centrality (Tanner 1974, p. 141), while Jaqueline Siapno focuses on "gender egalitarianism" (Siapno 2002, p. 65) instead.[33]

However, generally, conflicts do not result primarily from a man's insecure position in local society. Rather, conflicts arise because not only do a man's wife and her family demand financial support, but his family of origin does so as well.[34] Consequently, the divorce rate is high.[35] In the nineteenth century, Tanner and Siapno agree that men carried the burden of numerous obligations and few rights. According to Siegel, Islam offers a way out this state of affairs: boys and men can stay at the *dayah* and experience a totally different cultural world. At these Islamic boarding schools, social life, values and notions on religion and gender differ from the village; in an environment shaped by Islamic values, men can derive a feeling of superiority from pursuing a proper Islamic way of life. Thus, men can opt out of their unsatisfying village role by emphasizing religion over geographic and social identity.

The Gayo

Gayo territory is located in the Barisan Mountains — a densely populated area in South-Central Aceh.[36] According to linguistic data, the Gayo first settled on the coast of North Aceh, from where they moved to their current home in the mountains.[37] They speak an Austronesian language which is close to Batak and even contains words from the Mon Khmer family.[38] Aceh chronicles, dating from the seventeenth century, mention them as inhabitants of the outskirts of the kingdom of Aceh Darussalam and they probably converted to Islam at that time.[39] During the Dutch colonial expansion and the Aceh War, Gayo rulers tried in vain to remain neutral but finally joined the anti-colonial resistance, adopting Acehnese anti-colonial rhetoric in poems, narratives and metaphors. Particularly popular were accounts that cast the struggle as a holy war against infidels (*hikayat prang sabi*).[40]

Unlike other ethnic groups, the Gayo are well documented ethnographically in the publications of Snouck Hurgronje[41] and the American anthropologist John Bowen.[42] While Snouck Hurgronje's monograph is based on data obtained through questionnaires he sent to Dutch officials, via the reports written by military personnel and two key informants, Bowen conducted extensive fieldwork in the region.[43] Interestingly, these authors came to very different conclusions regarding Gayo social structure. Struck by the fact that kin groups occupied separate longhouses (*umah*), Snouck Hurgronje believed kinship to be the dominant factor in structuring society.[44] In his view, the ostensibly kin-based Gayo thus contrasted with the territorially organized Acehnese. However, Bowen criticized the findings of his predecessor. According to his historical research, three elements determined pre-colonial social structure: kinship, village, and the wider community. Furthermore, he described how "each level contained a dynamic tension between two ideas of authority: descent from an indigenous founder and power from an external source" (Bowen 1991, p. 49). Depending on intra- and inter-kin relationships, the communities could be characterized as either tendentially egalitarian or hierarchical. In pre-colonial times, after the Acehnese expansion in the seventeenth century, domain lords were imparted their authority by the sultan of Aceh, which was represented by and embodied in the *bawar* (a ceremonial dagger). In exchange, regular tribute was paid, but the Sultan did not interfere in day-to-day village affairs. With the coming of colonialism, Bowen saw a shift in the relationship between the two groups, from one of equality and exchange to one characterized by hierarchy and competition.[45] During this time, political authority was strengthened and social divisions intensified.[46]

Today, the Gayo number some 200,000 people. Ethnically, they have strong ties to the Karo Batak, who were their slaves in pre-colonial times and were considered to be non-Muslim Gayos of sorts. Many subsequently converted to Islam after slavery was abolished by the Dutch, married Gayos and became integrated into the local population. Apart from the Gayo, the region is also inhabited by Javanese and Chinese migrants. The Javanese came to the Gayo hills during colonial times in order to work on the dammar pine estates. Today, their descendants dwell in "Javanese" villages near the capital city, Takèngon, which is situated at the edge of Lake Tawar, and is inhabited by about 21,000 people. As is characteristic of peoples living in a diaspora, they have retained their distinct cultural identity, kept the Javanese language and retained their agrarian way of life. Takèngon is a multi-ethnic city in which the Chinese dominate commercially. The Chinese own shops, but often do not speak Gayo. The city's multi-ethnic make-up, which Bowen characterized as an "intermingling" rather than a "blending", has made urbanized Gayo more ethnically self-conscious, but has also made them more at ease than other ethnic groups with respect to the Indonesian language and culture.[47] Bowen describes the town as modern and, since the 1920s, as increasingly "Indonesian".[48]

In 2000, inter-ethnic conflicts occurred between Acehnese coastal people and members of the so-called Jago.[49] A further source of tension was the income inequality between the local population and Javanese transmigrants who had arrived on the east coast between 1960 and 1980 and then settled in central Aceh. The latter had received land and money to aid in their settlement and often found work on the palm plantations and in firms that serve as suppliers to the gas industry. The ease with which these Javanese migrants were able to enjoy relative economic success thus left the indigenous Gayo with the impression that they had been short-changed.

Kinship is the locus of social organization and considerable importance is accorded to "choosing the correct form of interaction" (Bowen 1991, p. 23) in the kinship network, which predicates on adequate knowledge of modes of kinship. Kinship is conceived of in two ways: through uxorilocal ties and virilocal ones. The latter are assumed to be the stronger, and the transmission of land through a line of genealogically-related men is a symbol of strength.[50] Since formal rules allow men and women equal access to property, this becomes a source of intra-village conflict when, in practice, men gain certain advantages.[51] Generally, descent is traced through the male line, while spiritual and magical powers (i.e. healing abilities) are passed on through the female line. The divorce rate is high and even increased during the economic crisis in the late 1990s. Villages are managed by headmen, the secretaries to the headmen, and the *imam*. The primary social unit in pre-colonial times was the *sarak opt* — a settlement of related individuals who were represented by a local ruler (*reje*) of limited authority.

The Gayo speak of four "debts" they have to their children: naming and introducing the baby to the natural and social world on the seventh day after birth, the provision of education (meaning an Islamic one) and regular schooling, circumcision of the boys at the age of five and subincision of the girls at one or two, and finally marriage, which constitutes the threshold to the world of adulthood.

The impact of world religions on local cultures always leads to tensions and challenges local actors to redefine their own customs. This is particularly true in cases where purist or revivalist movements occur. In the early twentieth century, the Gayo area witnessed the rise of such a movement, called the "young group" (*kaum muda*), which was inspired by scholars from the Middle East and spread to the Gayo hills, carried by migrants from Aceh and Minangkabau. The movement sparked controversy over proper religious practice, which became particularly heated over the custom of using Qur'anic verses for rituals related to ancestor worship. As Bowen argues, unlike the Acehnese, pressure was high on the Gayo to make their *adat* consistent with Islam, since they continued to rely heavily on local kin networks. Even the most modern Gayo could not conceive of a life wholly detached from the village.[52] In order to reconcile the demands of Islam with local practices and beliefs, they distinguished between religion and the demands of daily life, and accordingly played down the meanings implicit in these ceremonies.[53] Also common was to embed the significance of practices in Islam by means of exegesis or contextualization. Thus, people explain their local ritual practices by referring to Islamic texts or link them to Islamic traditions more generally. This has allowed Gayo Muslims to continue believing in local spirits and in saints and to practise rituals to appease them or beg them for help.[54]

The Alas

The Alas, also known as the *Urang Alas* or *Kalak Alas*, live in the Alas River Valley in the district of Southeast Aceh (Kabupaten Aceh Tenggara). They number approximately 70,000 and are descendants of immigrants from other parts of Sumatra, particularly the Batak region. This is supported not only by oral tradition, but also by linguistic data. Like the Gayo in pre-colonial times, they were subjects of the sultan of Aceh and had, by the seventeenth century, converted to Islam. In the capital, Kutacane, the commercial elite was comprised of Batak, Malays and Minangkabau. In 1903, the Dutch conquered the area in a bloody campaign which claimed the lives of between one quarter and a third of the male population.[55]

Up until the middle of the twentieth century, the Alas lived in longhouses of varying size. In the village of Batu Mbulan, for example, it was reported, in the mid-nineteenth century, that twenty-four families lived in one single house, while other longhouses harboured far fewer people (Iwabuchi 1994, p. 88). Each patrilineal nuclear family had its own hearth. Such longhouses, however, are a thing of the past. Today, the Alas build smaller houses, often with corrugated sheet iron roofs, in which separate rooms provide a degree of intimacy. Until the birth of their first child, couples generally reside in the house of the husband's father; after that, they build a separate house in the husband's village. Oftentimes, though, these houses stand wall-to-wall next to each other and are internally connected by a door. Most of the homes studied by the Japanese anthropologist Akifumi Iwabuchi housed only two generations or, at most twelve persons. Residence, however, is conceived of rather loosely and leaves ample room for personal preference and economic necessity. Adults may live temporarily on their rice fields, youths often sleep at the homes of their friends or girlfriends, and older boys commonly spend the night in unused rice storehouses or in community halls.

Relations between the sexes are structured hierarchically and subject to the principle of male dominance. This hierarchy is not only manifest in the terms of address between married couples, but also in the fact that women must walk behind their husbands or brothers and in how men and boys enjoy a number of daily privileges, such as being able to eat first, while women and girls eat in the kitchen whatever the men have left. Formally, households are headed by the oldest male member, who is designated the *kepale rumah tangge*. For the most part, women are not visible in the public sphere and do not participate in rituals.

Gender-specific socialization begins at around the age of five, when boys begin to orient themselves towards their fathers or other male relatives, while girls begin to assist their mothers, older sisters and aunts with their daily tasks. At this age, the children are also circumcised, although female subincision receives far less ceremonial attention. Through marriage, individuals attain adult status and customarily, at some point in time after the marriage, the father will perform a special ritual for his son that is known as the "separation from the parents". The young man receives a number of useful objects, including a rice pot and a pan, which symbolize his independence. Iwabuchi describes the relationship between fathers and sons as potentially problematic, especially when men divorce their wives and the sons side with their mother.[56] Relations between siblings are usually very close and highly emotive, but are also subject to the hierarchies dictated by seniority and gender.

The Alas trace descent along the male line, although, according to Iwabuchi, the rules of inheritance also give rights to female descendants, who are entitled to only half of that accorded to males, in line with the rules of inheritance as stipulated under Islamic law. Social organization is based on a patrilineal kinship system — the smallest unit of which is the patrilineal household. Several households comprise a lineage and several lineages a sub-clan. The distinction between sub-clan and lineage, however, is not always clear, and the local terminology indicates that it is not always possible to distinguish between the two. Depending on the dialect spoken in the area, both organizations may be called a "*belah*" or "*urung*". In other areas, however, only sub-clans are referred to by these terms, while the term for lineage is "*jabu*". Lineage genealogy, according to the information collected by Iwabuchi, extends back between four and six generations. The members refer to themselves as *sade asal* (of the same origins) and male members of the same generation refer to themselves as *senine jabu* (lineage brothers) or as *anak jabu* (lineage children). When male and female members form close ties of friendship, these may find expression in lifelong relations of mutual support, which are called "*turang perasat*" — a classificatory term that refers to a closely linked brother or sister. Lineage members are integrated into a network of obligations that come to bear not only in ritual contexts or during key phases of life, but in daily life. Formerly, lineages also constituted strong economic units.

The most inclusive kinship category is the clan (*merge*). In 1988, Iwabuchi counted twenty-seven clans — each of which was known by its own name, could trace its origins back to a common ancestor, and was subject to certain dietary prohibitions. These origin myths mention a migration from central Sumatra, primarily from the Batak area, but also a migration from India. Because of their size, clans only serve as a vague point of reference in establishing the identity of clan members. The same holds true for sub-clans.

Kinship is the central framework that organizes community life, and members endeavour to strengthen their networks through strategic marriages or adoptions. Among the Alas, both children and adults may be adopted, with the adoption of adults serving as a mechanism by which to ritually integrate individuals into the group. Marriages are arranged according to the principles of prescriptive connubium, i.e. the idea that certain marriage alliances are preferred, while others are prohibited. Preferred is a man's marriage to his cross-cousin, i.e. the mother's brother's daughter or the father's sister's daughter. The former alliance is called "*ngulihken taruk jambi*" (to return to the squash's vine). The bond between in-laws (*dekawe*) is strengthened by the exchange of gifts upon marriage and subsequently reactivated and confirmed periodically by numerous ceremonial obligations. In this, the mother's brother plays an important role, for it is he who has important ritual duties when it comes to circumcision, marriage and burial.

Very poor families who find themselves unable to provide the required gifts for exchange and who are unable to pay an acceptable bride price, resort to an exchange of sisters, which means that a man gives his brother in-law his own sister in marriage. This type of marriage is called "*sambar gawang*" (the food-box exchange).[57] In this form of union, the wife moves into her husband's family's house, which generally means that she must move to another village. In exceptional cases, residence may be uxorilocal, and the man moves in with his wife's family. This happens when a family has no sons of their own and needs a man to help in the fields, or when the man cannot afford to pay the bride price.

However, the cost of marriage has sunk drastically in the last one hundred years, which has resulted an increase in the divorce rate. Men take advantage of the relatively simple Islamic divorce procedure when their wives do not bear them any sons, when their children die or when they just get tired of them. Childlessness is also one of the reasons for the widespread practice of polygyny. However, beyond kinship, territorial ties also play an important role in daily life among the Alas, and the village (*kute*) is an important point of reference.

The economy is based primarily on wet rice cultivation. Other important cash crops are coffee and candlenuts, while fruits and vegetables are grown primarily for individual consumption. Land is privately owned and is also leased. Until the mid-twentieth century, there was a surplus of arable land, and the Alas Valley was therefore a popular destination for migrants. Under the Dutch colonial administration, there was an effort to attract settlers from the Batak region; later, landless Gayo, Acehnese, Singkil, Malays and Javanese followed. Today, land is scarce. Rapid population growth and over-cultivation have caused a radical change in living conditions. Moreover, deforestation in the mountains has led to more frequent landslides, fishing using poison and dynamite has destroyed the river fauna, and the hunting of reptiles has led to a concomitant increase in the rodent population. Iwabuchi fears not only environmental[58] and economic deterioration, but also sees indigenous culture in peril as modernity encroaches on village life and as the Indonesian language and culture permeate local society.[59]

ETHNIC DIVERSITY AND THE BUILDING OF AN ACEHNESE NATION

Politics and Ethnicity

Aceh's multi-ethnic structure has always been an issue of political importance. Representatives of the Indonesian government tried to use the province's ethnic diversity to their advantage by strategically recruiting mainly migrants and Javanese settlers, but also members of other minorities, for their anti-guerrilla campaign.[60] These recruits were armed with weapons and organized into village militias, and also recruited into the intelligence apparatus. While the central government emphasized and promoted diversity, the Free Aceh Movement (Gerakan Aceh Merdeka, or GAM) insisted on the homogeneity of their culture. Moreover, their leader, Hasan di Tiro, did take the province's ethnic diversity into consideration: in order to legitimize his claim to being the sole legitimate representative of all inhabitants of the province, he propagated the idea of Aceh being a nation comprised of nine ethnic groups. Thus, members of different ethnic groups were acknowledged as having been part of the movement and were also taken into account in staffing the leadership.[61]

The notion of Acehnese cultural homogeneity is based on a sense of unity that derives from its former status as a well-known centre of trade and from its long history of suffering and resistance that began with the war against Dutch colonial rule and continued into post-colonial times under the banner of the Free Aceh Movement. Without a doubt, this history of suffering, oppression and resistance does more or less unify all inhabitants of Aceh. These experiences have given rise to a sense of community which has, in the decades since Indonesian independence, served as the basis for a collective identity that has been asserted against the central government in Jakarta. The push for secession and autonomy, as well as the formation of an all-Acehnese liberation movement, has been based on this sense of unity and historical homogeneity. History was, thus, strategically deployed over culture to rally all inhabitants in a common cause against Jakarta.

Following the well-known patterns of ethnic construction, GAM speakers outlined Acehnese culture as fundamentally different from Indonesian culture and fundamentally incompatible: being Acehnese and being Indonesian thus became mutually exclusive commitments.[62] Generally, "Acehnese-ness" was held to be incompatible with "Indonesian-ness", and for this reason, the Indonesian concept of "unity in diversity" was rejected. The Acehnese construction of collective self-identity and its difference from the "Indonesian identity" has been both the basis for political demands and a strategy for popular mobilization. Political analysts and anthropologists have interpreted the construction of an Acehnese culture, independence movement and nation mainly as an effort to form an "Acehnese" ethnicity by transforming cultural values and practices into politicized symbols. Ethnicity and ethnic identity as proto-nationalism[63] have been used instrumentally both as mobilizing forces and political weapons. Since they feed off the notion of the "Other", who serves as a foil, leading figures of the GAM have turned their propaganda against Javanese migrants (Brass 1991, p. 19). Particularly in the 1990s, they used "anti-Javanism" as a political strategy to build up popular support.[64] Migrants were accused of being spies for or collaborators with the Indonesian military and thus, were attacked viciously. In the mid- and late 1990s, attempts at anti-Javanese ethnic cleansing caused dozens of casualties and thousands of refugees to flee from northern Aceh. Similar attempts were made in 2000 and 2002 in North, East and Central Aceh.

The psychological basis for these aggressions against non-combatants was diffuse anti-migrant sentiments which existed for various reasons. Economic envy has been suggested as one such reason, since a remarkable income gap had evolved between the highly paid non-Acehnese who worked in the gas industry[65] and the local population. Transmigrants in the countryside also received financial support from the government, which stirred feelings among locals that they were being put at a disadvantage. Another common complaint against migrants was that the behaviour of these newcomers was un-Islamic.[66]

Although, the strategy of drawing on widespread xenophobia, in many cases, had the desired effect, there were other cases in which such a strategy was not successful. This was so in Central Aceh, where the Gayo people had respected Javanese settlers as neighbours for generations. Many of them had arrived during the colonial period as workers on coffee plantations; others came in the 1980s and 1990s motivated by the national transmigration programme. GAM members targeted these Javanese coffee farmers in order to extract so-called "taxes". Those who refused were intimidated, maltreated, even tortured and killed. The local population, however, did not support this behaviour. On the contrary, they declared their solidarity with the Javanese and formed ethnically mixed defence groups.[67]

Although "Javanism" has been equated with neocolonialism, this would only hold true if ethnic identities in Aceh were deeply rooted. The reality is quite the reverse and they can be abandoned easily, if no longer needed. The signing of the memorandum of understanding in August 2005 was the turning point. Since then, the emphasis on the incommensurateness of Indonesian and Acehnese culture has been rapidly waning and is being replaced by nationalist sentiments.[68]

Local Culture in Danger?

However politically isolated it has been for nearly thirty years, Aceh is part of a rapidly changing world, where local culture responds to foreign influences, and where scraps of different cultures are adapted, appropriated and reassembled in new contexts. This process has been called "glocalization" by the sociologist Roland Robertson, in order to emphasize local agency over global hegemonies (Robertson 1992).

Today, Aceh faces contradictory developments. On the one hand, we see a rediscovery and even a revitalization of culture, but at the same time, observers have lamented the disappearance of local traditions.[69]

Triggered by the presence of foreign aid workers, journalists, scientists and diplomats, cultural consciousness is growing among Acehnese intellectuals and activists. Contemporary Acehnese reflect on who they are and how they want to present themselves to the world. At the same time, the presence of foreigners stirs a sense of unease and raises questions as to whether they can be trusted. Particularly in the early phases of foreign engagement after the tsunami, rumours spread that members of Christian organizations had tried to proselytize locals.[70] Radical Muslims even accused foreign aid workers of having "a hidden agenda of robbing Acehnese from their culture and religion" (Abdurrahman Wahid 2005).

Interestingly, such fears regarding the possibility that foreigners might be a threat to Islamic values and practices were not stirred vis-à-vis the laws and practices based on *adat*. Indonesian societies are well known for their ability to bridge the gap between religion (*agama*) and local culture (*adat*). Indigenization, syncretism and the creation of parallel ceremonial cycles have been some successful modes of integration.[71] Local people have felt and continue to feel that they must reconcile the demands of world religions to which they belong with their local culture. How this is accomplished varies from individual to individual and depends largely on the social stratum to which the person belongs. Usually, members of the urban middle class distance themselves more radically from *adat* than farmers and villagers. This is also true in Aceh. The task of reconciling the two encounters difficulties particularly with respect to social structure and kinship.

As anthropological findings from East Indonesia,[72] West Sumatra[73] and Negri Sembilan[74] show, a matrifocal social structure is much more vulnerable and unstable than a patri- or virifocal one. Urbanization and increasing individualism weaken local clan-based structures and existing legal pluralism. Increasingly, Islamic law is now recognized as being more important than *adat* law and more commensurable with modern life. Unlike in Minangkabau, where the integration of matrilineal *adat* and Islam is widely debated among intellectuals[75] and where both systems are recognized as central pillars of society, the Acehnese middle class stress the superiority of Islam. This seems to have led to a weakening of traditional social organization, specifically the matrifocal structure which is already waning among members of the urban middle class.

This development is rooted in the general difference between *adat* and Islam: the former being associated with a backward, insular mindset and the latter being viewed as a form of globalization, particularly in the sense of belonging to a global *umma*. In this, Snouck Hurgronje and Siegel underscore the role of the *ulama*, in particular, who distinguish themselves from ordinary villagers and even look down on them.[76] Trained in a *dayah* outside of their home region, they are alienated from their culture of origin and have turned to Islamic principles instead. Asserting their religious authority, they accuse villagers of neglecting Islamic commitments and of practising un-Islamic rites. Furthermore, they deploy a rhetoric that pits the modern and educated against the illiterate and backward in order to establish a dichotomy that casts *adat* "as the rule of the unreflecting villager versus universal Islam as a scriptural guide for the learned individual".[77] Yet, turning to modernist Islam has also been a strategy for resolving social conflicts resulting from the matrifocal kinship order.

The disparagement of Acehnese *adat* is all the more effective given that it has often been identified with the colonial order. Although during the early phases of colonial rule Dutch authorities did not intervene in local Islam-based legal systems, they changed their policy in the 1920s and essentially created *adat* as a means of keeping Islam in check.[78]

Interestingly, one of the arguments in favour of strengthening Islam as a counter-force to *adat* is the role of women in society. While anthropologists like Jaqueline Siapno,[79] Nancy Tanner and James Siegel view autochthonous gender relationships as rather egalitarian, even matricentric, Acehnese Muslim women activists see it as a source of discrimination against women and feel a need for action. Many of them are organized in Islamic political parties, like the Partai Amanat Nasional (PAN), and argue using feminist re-interpretations of the Qur'an for women's empowerment.[80]

Liberal interpretations of the Qur'an and emphasis on gender-egalitarian *adat* might, however, succumb to recent developments related to a resurgence of fundamentalist Islam. In 1999, the Aceh Council of Ulama issued a *fatwa* stating that Islamic dress for women should cover the whole body except for the face, hands and feet. In their legal findings, the *ulama* were supported by leaders of the Free Aceh Movement, who also required women and girls to be veiled. Violence against unveiled women began in 1999 when young men threatened those who were not dressed "properly" and, in some cases, even shaved their heads. In 2000, Islamic law was implemented and since then, the pressure on social deviants has continued to increase. The whipping of women and the arbitrary arrests of youth by the *shari'a* police indicate that local culture and its modernization, within the framework of liberal, middle-class discourse, are being endangered by this particular form of religious revitalization.[81]

Apart from the rather unique problems of having to define tradition and culture in order to restructure society, Aceh faces some difficulties with modernity that are common to many other parts of the world, namely the disappearance of local languages. Throughout Indonesia, Bahasa Indonesia has been introduced as the language of instruction, administration and, more generally, of modernity. It is taught at every school in the nation, and classes are consequently conducted in Indonesian. This exerts considerable pressure on local people, and today, even in villages, ambitious parents will speak Indonesian with their children in order to equip them better for their future career. Consequently, people's knowledge of their autochthonous language is vanishing. For the Gayo, this development has been analysed by Guilio Soravia.[82] According to him, the Gayo language is acutely endangered, even if one takes into account the government programmes that have been launched in order to preserve it. Measures to protect local languages, he criticizes, exist *de jure* but not de facto. There are no publications nor broadcasts in Gayo and no effort is made to distribute music cassettes in Gayo. Urban areas, particularly Takèngon, are dominated by Bahasa Indonesia and Acehnese — languages to which locals accord a high degree of prestige. The long-term effect of these processes is not to be underestimated, even if the Gayo do continue to use their language in daily conversation and during rituals.[83]

Post-tsunami Culture Politics

Acehnese culture has recently become a political issue. According to Hazballah M. Saad, Indonesia's former Minister of Justice and Human Rights and one of Aceh's most influential intellectuals, post-tsunami reconstruction should focus not only on the economy but also incorporate culture. The Acehnese, he explained to me, should maintain their culture, learn about it and present it to the outside world. This would prevent them from losing their identity in the wake of globalization and would make them proud of who they are. In order to strengthen Acehnese culture and make people aware of it, he and a group of local intellectuals had founded the Institut Kebudayaan Aceh (Aceh Cultural Institute). When I asked him what exactly he intended to accomplish with the establishment of this institute, he outlined his ideas on how local heritage could be preserved. In particular, the tsunami had destroyed a collection of ancient manuscripts which had been kept in the local museum. Hazballah felt that by demanding to have copies of these from the archives in the Netherlands he could restore what had been lost and make an important contribution to conserving local heritage.

Cultural heritage is becoming a central theme in the Acehnese engagement with culture today. Apart from the Aceh Cultural Institute, there are at least four more organizations which are devoted to documenting and preserving Acehnese culture: Pusat Dokumentasi Aceh (Aceh Documentation Centre), Lembaga Kebudayaan Aceh (Aceh Cultural Foundation), the international Lestari Heritage Network, and Yayasan Komunitas Lestari Pusaka Aceh (Aceh Heritage Community Foundation)[84] which runs the Internet portal Aceh Heritage. In explaining the importance of their mission, which is to promote culture, the organization declaims cultural heritage as a keystone essential to a stable identity: "The heritage of Aceh contributes to the psychological well-being, social pride and identity of the Acehnese. Heritage plays a role in cross-cultural exchange within Indonesia and abroad. Identification, rescue, safeguarding and conservation efforts must begin now, during the rebuilding process" (Lestari Heritage Network). Among the objects listed as belonging to Aceh's cultural heritage are monuments like the *kraton* complex, mosques, colonial buildings and the home of the national heroine Tjut Nyak Dhien in the subdistrict of Lhok Nga.

The process of rebuilding Acehnese culture has been supported and funded by foreign institutions, such as the German Goethe Institute, which is engaged in financing the reconstruction of the Province Library and which organized an exhibition on *Rumoh Aceh* in the capital, Banda Aceh, in 2005.

One might say that these efforts amount more to the preservation of folklore than the preservation of local culture, and in this does lie a certain degree of truth. Today's Acehnese prefer to live in modern buildings made of concrete and bricks and an exhibition reminding them of their cultural heritage will probably not change their preference for the comforts of modern life. The reality is that if they wish to work as something other than a farmer in the countryside, they would need to speak Indonesian and ideally should also know some English. As more Acehnese opt for lives outside the traditional village milieu, the clan-based social structure also seems to be becoming a thing of the past and, along with this, the matrifocal line of decent and residence system as well. However, Acehnese culture does not exhaust itself in what is shown at exhibitions in cultural heritage museums.

Selectively, this culture has even been used in contemporary politics. One of the most impressive performances of "traditional" culture was to be seen in early August 2005 — a few days before the peace agreement between the government and the Free Aceh Movement was signed. Political activists organized a two-day Rapa'i Pase — a peace festival that involves the beating of traditional drums (*rapa'i*[85]), which originated from Pase in North Aceh. Two hundred and eighty-eight drummers engaged in a rally and toured through the capital city of Banda Aceh. This event marked the first time in decades that such a parade had been organized. In fact, most of the drummers were older men, since the skill of drumming had not been passed down to the younger generation. As this case shows, traditional culture can be revitalized and appropriated in a modern context. Even if people no longer believe that such a ritual can actually bring about peace, the ritual helped to publicize the peace effort and rallied support for the treaty to be signed. The *rapa'i* itself is, in reality, the product of cultural hybridization. According to Bukhari Daud, its origins have been attributed to the mystic Ahmad Rifa'i[86] and are associated with a ritual called the *rapa'i daboh*, in which men drum themselves into a trance and supposedly make themselves invulnerable to sharp blades, like daggers or *parang*.

Using a tradition, like the *rapa'i*, in a contemporary political context shows that culture is not only something that exists to be conserved by collecting folklore or by establishing museums, but can be a useful part of a modern life.

Notes

1. The author thanks Werner Kraus, Roman Patock, Katja Rieck and Susanne Rodemeier for their helpful comments.
2. To a certain degree, contemporary Acehnese identity had been constructed as an anti-Javanese identity. However, even if we take some anti-Javanese riots into consideration, Aceh has never experienced the sort of ethnic clashes that took place in Kalimantan or the Moluccas, where ethnic and religious conflicts at the turn of the century claimed the lives of thousands.
3. Among them Beets (1933), Bernhard (1904), Broersma (1925), Jacobs (1894), Jongejans (1939), Kennedy (1935), Kreemer (1922–23), Lekkerkerker (1916), Loeb (1935), Palmer van den Broek (1936), Voorhoeve (1955), and Zentgraaff (1938).
4. These extensive monographs on the Acehnese (1893–94) and the Gayo (1903) are still discussed by contemporary anthropologists.
5. Cf. Carle (1987).
6. Most people from Nias came as slaves.
7. Cf. LeBar (1972, p. 15), Loeb (1935), and Siegel (1969).
8. In Aceh Selatan, Aceh Barat and Daya.
9. The district in which they live is called Aceh Tamiang.
10. The second biggest group, the Tamiang Malay, who make up 9 per cent of the population, live in the lowlands.
11. These make up 10 per cent of the population.
12. They comprise 2 per cent of the population
13. The Gayo dwell in Aceh Tenggah, Aceh Timur, Beher Meriah and Gayo Lues; the Alas live in Aceh Tenggara.
14. Portuguese origin is ascribed to the so-called "blue-eyed Acehnese" in particular.
15. However, the amount of rice grown in Aceh is not sufficient to feed the population and Aceh still relies on imports.
16. These cash crops were mainly pepper and rice.
17. Trade outside of Aceh was dominated by Chinese merchants.
18. Siegel mentions the *wasè djalan* (Siegel 2003, p. 22) levied on roads used by peasants to transport the pepper harvest to the harbour and the *wasè lueng* imposed on irrigation channels (Siegel 2003, p. 23).
19. Cf. Reid (2005), pp. 94–96.
20. In Bahasa Indonesia, they are called *pesantren*.
21. Cf. Fachry Ali (1989), and Kell (1995), p. 46.
22. Cf. Snouck Hurgronje (1906), vol. 1, p. 296. His interpretation of this rule as particularly Islamic overlooks the widespread occurrence of hypergamy.

23. Cf. Snouck Hurgronje (1906), vol. 1, p. 297.
24. Cf. LeBar (1972).
25. Cf. Sugihen (1982), p. 17.
26. Cf. Kennedy (1935).
27. Cf. Siegel (2003), p. 51.
28. Cf. Siegel (2003), p. 54.
29. Cf. Siegel (2003), p. 141.
30. Cf. Siegel (2003), p. 55, and Snouck Hurgronje (1906), vol. 2, p. 356.
31. The whole system has recently encountered further difficulties, since men have begun to emigrate permanently and have married local women.
32. Cf. Siegel (1969), p. 145.
33. For further discussions on matrifocal social structures in Indonesian societies, see also Kato (1982), Sanday (2002), and Schröter (2006).
34. A similar conflict setting is reported among the matrifocal Negri Sembilan of Malaysia. Cf. Peletz (1995).
35. After divorce, a man is expected to continue to provide for his children, which he often does not. Cf. Siegel (2003), p. 141.
36. The Gayo live in the following parts of the province: Central Aceh, the northern part of Southeast Aceh, the western part of East Aceh, and small strips of northern South Aceh and southern North Aceh.
37. Cf. Bowen (1991*a*), pp. 14–15.
38. Cf. Kennedy (1935), p. 44. Their language belongs to the Mon Khmer group.
39. Historical texts written in the fourteenth century characterize them as a people who were reluctant to convert to Islam, but obviously, they ultimately did.
40. Cf. Bowen (1991*a*), p. 67.
41. Cf. Bowen (1991*a*), p. 36.
42. Cf. Bowen (1988, 1989, 1991*a* & *b*, 1992, 1993, 1996, 1997, and 2003).
43. To be specific, his empirical research was conducted in the village of Isak — a community of 1,000 people who, into the 1970s, engaged primarily in wet rice cultivation, but who, since the late 1980s, have also begun to grow coffee and other crops in the mountains thanks to improvements in the local infrastructure.
44. Cf. Snouck Hurgronje (1903), p. 131.
45. He examines this together with an analysis of poetic discourses. Cf. Bowen (1989).
46. For a detailed analysis of Gayo historical development and cultural changes, see Bowen (1991*a*).
47. Cf. Bowen (1991*a*), p. 17.
48. Cf. Bowen (2003), pp. 32–33.
49. Jago is the short form of Java-Gayo.
50. In Bahasa Indonesia, this is called *turun-temurun* (coming down one after the other).

51. Examples are given in Bowen (2003), pp. 35–37.
52. Cf. Bowen (2003), p. 37.
53. For further discussion on this problem, see Bowen (1997).
54. Cf. Bowen (1991*a*).
55. Cf. Reid (1969), pp. 187–88.
56. Cf. Iwabuchi (1994), p. 111.
57. Cf. Iwabuchi (1994), p. 217.
58. The focus of his criticism is the construction of a road through the Leuser National Park, which was financed by USAID.
59. Cf. Iwabuchi (1994), p. 259.
60. Cf. Reid (2003), p. 14, Schulze (2004), p. 43, and Sukma (2007).
61. Thus, the commander of Aceh Tengah is a Gayo, as are two of the four GAM chiefs in Tiamiang.
62. Cf. Burke (2005).
63. Bertrand characterized the Free Aceh Movement as an example of an ethno-nationalist movement (Bertrand 2004, p. 174), while Eriksen (1994), p. 14 speaks of it as a proto-nationalist movement. Both approaches can be useful in distinguishing the particular use of ethnicity, as applied to indigenous people or urban ethnic minorities.
64. Cf. Ross (2003), pp. 27–28.
65. This is particularly problematic in the region around the city of Lhokseumawe on the northeast coast of Aceh, where the state enterprise Pertamina has exploited the gas resources.
66. Cf. Ross (2003), p. 17.
67. Cf. Schulze (2005), p. 44.
68. This finding is based on observations and interviews conducted during the celebration of Independence Day in 2005.
69. Bowen (1991*a*, p. 93) characterizes Gayo history as the struggle to redefine society and culture around the challenges of modernist Islam and nationalism. Reflecting the response to a speech he delivered at a meeting of the Jakarta Gayo community, he realizes that underlying the lively discourse on modernity is a fear that a loss of cultural values may lead to a breakdown of society and a radical alienation from their own past. Others, however, have not been so concerned about this and have emphasized the integration of the region into the nation instead.
70. It is not easy to prove the veracity of these stories. My Acehnese interlocutors told me of having heard about these occurrences but had never met one of these missionaries. Roman Patock, however, who travelled through Aceh in March 2005, apparently witnessed them in Meulaboh. Cf. personal communication.
71. I have analysed these processes for the Ngada of Central Flores. Cf. Schröter (1999 and 2000).
72. I examined this with respect to the Ngada in eastern Indonesia — a nominally Catholic population which became matrifocal in the early twentieth century

and which is now going through a process of patrifocalization triggered by inter-ethnic marriage and urbanization. Cf. Schröter (2006).

73. Acehnese gender structures have often been contrasted to those of the Minangkabau of West Sumatra, and there are even stories that it was frustrated female Acehnese leaders who established matriarchal Minangkabau culture in response to a wave of patriarchalism that shook Aceh in the seventeenth century. Cf. H.S. Smith (1997), p. 9.
74. Cf. Stivens (1996).
75. Cf. Kato (1982), p. 246, and Reenen (1996), p. 5.
76. Cf. Siegel (2003), p. 57, and Snouck Hurgronje (1906), vol. 2, pp. 31–33.
77. Cf. Bowen (2003), p. 38. He described this modernist strategy being used by the Gayo.
78. Up until then, intervention in local legal systems affected mainly Java and Madura, while other parts of the colony were largely unaffected. For a brief examination of *adat* in colonial and post-colonial state politics, see Bowen (2003), pp. 44–66.
79. In her monograph, Siapno stresses women's agency in traditional Acehnese society and criticizes Western feminists' misunderstanding of autochthonous gender relationships. Cf. Siapno (2002), pp. 181–83.
80. They, thus, position themselves as part of a pan-Islamic feminist movement, which focuses on rereading the Qur'an and the *hadith*. According to these women and men, patriarchy violates the principles of Islam and should, therefore, be reformed. Prominent representatives of this movement in Indonesia are Lily Zakiyah Munir (1999) and Siti Musdah Mulia (2005).
81. This has been problematized by some women's organizations, like the Flower Aceh Foundation. Cf. Suraiya Kamaruzzaman (2004 and 2005).
82. Cf. Soravia (1987).
83. Cf. Bowen (1991*a*).
84. The Aceh Heritage Network is part of the international Lestari Heritage Network — a section of the Asia and West Pacific Network for Urban Conservation (AWPNUC). The AWPNUC was established in 1991 in Penang and links cultural organizations from East, South and Southeast Asia with Australia and the Pacific. <http://www.awpnuc.org/background.html>.
85. A *rapa'i* is a tambourine made of wood and covered with goat skin. In the Samudra Pasa'i kingdom, the *rapa'i* was beaten to signal the people to gather. Today, it is used to accompany traditional dances, such as the *geleng rapa'i*.
86. Cf. Bukhari Daud (1997), p. 256. Ahmad Rifa'i founded the Sufi order Rifaiyyah, which was introduced in Aceh by Nurudin ar-Rainiri in the seventeenth century.

10

ISLAM IN ACEH Institutions, Scholarly Traditions, and Relations between *Ulama* and *Umara*

Hasan Basri[1]

Experts have yet to make a comprehensive study of Islam in Aceh, despite the fact that Aceh is the part of Indonesia that first came into contact with Islam. Later, Islam spread from Aceh to Java, the Lesser Sunda Islands, Borneo (Kalimantan), Sulawesi, Maluku, and even Melaka and other territories of contemporary Malaysia. Islam spread primarily by word of mouth as *ulama* (Muslim religious teachers), traders and professional Islamic missionaries entered regions that had already been touched by Hinduism and Buddhism, mysticism and faith. Efforts to spread the teachings of Islam were gentle and peaceful; the religion passed though trade, persuasion and the conversion of powerful kings, and eventually through marriage as well.

This paper attempts to consider Islam in Aceh from historical, sociological and political perspectives. The observations from these three perspectives are based, respectively, on three fundamental facts: first, scholarship about Islam in Aceh is inseparable from the history of Islam's entrance in that region; second, because of its location along the shipping channels that connect many parts of the world, Aceh is both a home port and a place of transit for many different peoples; and third, politically speaking, Aceh has existed as a sovereign nation, with its own monarchy, since the thirteenth century. From that time onwards, the kingdom of Aceh has forged diplomatic and trade networks with many other nations. Before dissecting these connections for analysis however, a general understanding of Aceh is required.

THE HISTORY OF ISLAM IN ACEH

Before Islam made its way to Aceh, Aceh had already established trade relations with India, Persia, Arabia, China and several other countries. These economic interactions had significantly influenced the lives of the Acehnese people. From India, for example, came Hinduism which influenced Acehnese culture both directly and indirectly. How great was this influence cannot be known with any great certainty. Though according to Mukti Ali, "the Islamic religion that entered Indonesia was mixed with elements of Hinduism" (Mukti Ali 1964, p. 4). However, this statement would be correct only if we were looking at Islam as practised by the Javanese community. This would not be entirely true for Islam in Aceh. This is because Islam in Aceh was brought in directly by Arab merchants, and in Aceh, the teachings of Hinduism were not as well rooted as they were in Java.

Almost all historians say that Aceh is the part of Indonesia where Islam first entered the country. Among experts, however, there is a difference of opinion concerning the year in which this happened. In connection with this, three ideas have developed and gained prominence. First, some claim that Islam gradually came to Indonesia, beginning in the first century AH — that is, the first century of the Islamic calendar or about AD 700–800. These people claim that it came directly from the Arabs. Second is the idea that Islam spread within Indonesia by means of peace, and not by the sword or by force. And third, it is believed that because of Islam's arrival in Indonesia, learning and high culture have become a part of the Indonesian identity (Ali Hasjmy 1993, pp. 38–39).

Regarding Islam's arrival in Indonesia, Azyumardi Azra acknowledges that, as far as the introduction of Islam in the Indonesian archipelago is concerned, there have been discussion and debate concerning three problems on the subject: first, the question of where Islam was originally introduced; second, the question of who brought it in; and third, the question of when it was brought in. According to Azra, the various theories and discussions that have tried to answer these three questions have not yet been fully successful. This is not only because of the limited data available that could support any particular theory, but also because of the one-sidedness of the various theories (Azyumardi Azra 2004, p. 2).

Most Dutch scholars put forward the idea that the origin of Islam in the Indonesian archipelago was the Indian subcontinent, not Persia or Arabia.

The first scholar to propose this theory was Pijnappel. Later, the theory was popularized by Snouck Hurgronje, who stressed the fact that Islam had a strong foothold in several port cities of the Indian subcontinent. They were intermediary points which connected the Middle Eastern merchants with traders from the Indonesian archipelago. Later on, these traders came to the Malay-Indonesian region directly, as the first disseminators of Islam. There is also a related theory that states that Islam in the Indonesian archipelago originated in Bengal (ibid., p. 3).

We see, then, that theories on how Islam arrived in Indonesia can be divided into two groups: first, those who say that the arrival of Islam in Indonesia came directly from the Arabian Peninsula; and second, those who suggest that Islam came to Indonesia via Persia and Gujarat.

After discussing the various theories on Islam's arrival in the Indonesian archipelago in a detailed manner, Azra concluded that Islam had been brought to Indonesia directly from Arabia, and that it had been introduced by "professional" teachers and poets — that is, those who specifically sought to spread the words of the Qur'an. Most of these missionaries and "professional" disseminators of Islam came to Indonesia between the twelfth and thirteenth centuries AD and those who first embraced Islam were the rulers of the region. Based on this analysis, it is possible that Islam was introduced into the Indonesian archipelago as early as the first few centuries AH (ibid., p. 12).

An Islamic history seminar on the topic of Islam's entry into Aceh was held in Banda Aceh in 1987, as a continuation of the seminar that had been held beforehand in Medan in 1963. This seminar stressed that Islam had been introduced in the Indonesian archipelago in the first century AH, coming directly from Arabia. Later, participants in the seminar agreed that the part of Indonesia that had first encountered and accepted Islam was Aceh (Ali Hasjmy 1993, p. 52).

Nevertheless, after a careful study of the history of Islam and the theories on Islam's arrival in the Indonesian archipelago, it cannot be ignored that Islam may have come to Aceh through two different routes. First, Islam arrived directly from Saudi Arabia, and then, Islam later returned via the *ulama* (Muslim scholars) from Persia and Gujarat in India. These scholars came to Aceh by boat and on ships. Among them, there were those who came specifically to proselytize, but there were also those who came simply to trade and who spread Islam as well as their wares. Thus, Islam could not be separated from economic activity, and some traders helped to spread Islam to the inhabitants of whatever port they stopped at. There is a strong indication that the Acehnese were affected by Islam's disseminators in a myriad of ways. For example, in the Acehnese community even now, there are traditions that resemble those in India, Persia and Arabia; this is especially evident when one looks at conduct, clothing or food in the region.

ISLAMIC INFLUENCES ON THE ACEHNESE COMMUNITY

Islamic influences on the lives of the Acehnese can be seen in at least two aspects: in their Islamic traditions and Islamic law, and in the community's attitude towards Islam.

Tradition and Islamic Law

Adat refers to the set of traditions that the Acehnese community has practised for generations; these were eventually codified by legal practitioners. In addition to thinking of *adat* as codified law, however, it should also be understood as a code of behaviour and guidance from past generations, which have been continuously passed down to later generations through traditional institutions. The *adat* constitutes written and unwritten norms that have become a moral compass within a people. Moreover, in the Acehnese community, *adat* and law may not be incompatible with religion. Everything that is decided by a leader or ruler must be in accordance with the provisions of the religion and with *shari'a*. If tradition is not compatible with religion, then these traditions are not valid.

Islam's arrival in Aceh in the seventh century AD (or the first century AH) influenced Acehnese customs and traditions. In carrying out traditional law, the Acehnese community is very careful to do so in accordance with Islamic *shari'a*. From the perspective of the Acehnese people, *adat* must be based on *shari'a*. Moreover, the Acehnese practise Islamic law precisely as they have learned it from religious teachers and Islamic scholars. They are guided by the Qur'an, Sunnah, *ijma'* and *qiyas*.[2] To remind the people about the application of Islamic law, the Acehnese created a life philosophy called the Hadih Maja, which includes information about which authority is in charge of enforcing which laws. An example follows:

Adat bak Poteu Meureuhom
Hukom bak Syiah Kuala
Qanun bak Putroe Phang
Reusam bak Laksamana
Hukom ngon Adat lagee Zat ngon Sipheuet

(Authority over tradition is in the hands of the Sultan
Authority over the law is in the hands of the *ulama*, the Muslim scholars[3]

Social functions are arranged by the *Putri Pahang*
Traditional ceremonies are arranged by the *Panglima*
Law and tradition are like soul and body.)

This life philosophy contains three important insights:

a. The life of the country and its people must be animated by and based on Islam.
b. State politics and Islam in the Acehnese community are one.
c. Cooperation between the *ulama* and the Sultan is harmonious and enforcement of the law is carried out by involving all the relevant people, both religious and secular.

The people of Aceh are also rich in culture and tradition, art, and dance, though each regency featured differences and variations. These can be seen in marriage ceremonies, childbirth, how they work in the rice fields, how they fish at sea, variations in *peusijuek*,[4] the way communities celebrate the Prophet Muhammad's birthday, the way they tell the story of being given the Qur'an, and in numerous other ways as well. Moreover, the shape of a unifying culture can be seen in its ornamentation and calligraphy, traditional architecture, and advanced religious education, which in Aceh features Islamic art and music, including chanting and the playing of the tambourine. Other traditional motifs can be seen in gold jewellery, silverware, ceramics and various ornamented surfaces, including Acehnese gravestones, bridal daises and traditional clothing (Badruzzaman Ismail 2002, p. 69).

So great has been Islam's influence on Aceh that standard greetings and goodbyes now make use of the statement "*Assalmu'alaikum Warahmatullahi Wabarakatuh*" (it is hoped that Allah's safety, tranquillity, affection and blessings are showered upon you), or the shortened form "*Assalamu'ailaikum*". When someone accepts a gift from another person, he does not use the usual expression, which is "*terima kasih*" (thank you), but rather "*Alhamdulillahi Rabbil 'Alamin*" (all glory be to Allah, Lord of the Worlds) or, more briefly, "*Alhamdulillah*" (praise the Lord). This phrase is also said when finishing an activity or at the end of work. Good or pleasant work is often begun with the phrase "*Bismillahir Rahmanir Rahim*" (in the name of Allah, the Most Beneficent, the Most Merciful). When making a promise to someone, the people of Aceh usually add the phrase "*Insya Allah*" (God willing). And, if they hear of or experience a disaster, such as sickness or death, they say, "*Inna Lillahi Wa Inna Ilaihi Raji'un*" (we belong to Allah and to Him we shall return). It is said that these sentences are a reflection of one's faith in God, and so they are uttered spontaneously. According to Islamic practices, saying these holy sentences is a religious duty to Allah, and the person who says them will receive a reward from God.

In the social life of the Acehnese, the right hand and the left hand do not have the same value. The right hand is usually used for things that are good and clean, whereas the left hand is used for those things which are ugly and dirty. Therefore, greeting someone by waving or lifting the left hand is considered impolite. Likewise, to give or accept something with the left hand is not considered polite. Indeed, it is an insult. Eating and drinking, taking things, and giving or receiving is always done with the right hand.

The public gathering place in each village is known as the *meunasah*.[5] The word *meunasah* comes from the Arabic *madrasah*, which refers to a religious school or a place of study. The *meunasah* serves several functions in the lives of the Acehnese people. It is used as a place to study the Qur'an, to learn about religion, or to gain other knowledge and useful skills. Its other function is as a place of prayer, for which it is used five times a day. Because of this, the position of the *meunasah* must be different from that of a normal house, so that a person can immediately identify which house is a place of residence and which one is the place of religious duties. When a *meunasah* is established, the most important consideration is the orientation of the building and the *kiblat* (the direction in which people must face when praying, i.e. towards Mecca). In Aceh, as in the rest of Indonesia, the *kiblat* faces westward. Even the common man knows to pray towards the west. Therefore, when someone urinates or defecates, it is unjustifiable to face the west or the direction of the *kiblat*. However, for all good actions, including sleeping, it is better to face towards the *kiblat*.

The other function of the *meunasah* is as a gathering place — a place to meet and conduct business, or as a general meeting place for members of the community. Moreover, a *meunasah* also functions as a playground for children and adolescents, as a place for single people to sleep, and as a place where people can recite the Qur'an, talk about religion, and make their obligatory prayers. It is a place of peace and the place where marriage ceremonies are held, as well as the place where communal banquets are held while observing public holidays like the Prophet Muhammad's birthday and the *qurban* rituals (when animals are sacrificed for Idul Adha and during the *tashriq* days).[6]

Every *meunasah* is led by an *imam* (or *imum*, in Acehnese). The *imam* plays a role in leading communal prayers and is responsible for the *meunasah* as well as its congregation. He is helped by a *bilal* (or *bileue*, in Acehnese), who is assigned to be the muezzin, that is, the person who issues the call to prayer. Other than that, the social system includes the *Keuchik*, or village headman, and the *Tuha Peut* (four elders who have been chosen by the members of their community to lead them and who are considered to have influence and respect as well as sufficient knowledge to guide the community). A village also has an organization called the *Tuha Lapan*, or Eight Elders, which makes the *Tuha Peut* more complete by including four other kinds of people in the decision-making process: intellectuals, young men, women, and the wealthy people of the village. In addition, there is the *Tuha Adat* — a leading figure who is known to be the most knowledgeable and experienced when it comes to village traditions. If there is a conflict or dispute between the citizens of the community, then the *Keuchik*, the *Imum Meunasah*, the *Tuha Peut*, the *Tuha Lapan* and the *Tuha Adat* will come together to reconcile the two quarrelling sides. Today, however, social governance has been modified by the addition of the Lembaga Ketahanan Desa (LKMD; the Agency of Rural Endurance) and the Lembaga Masyarakat Desa (LMD; the Agency of Rural Community).

The Acehnese Community's Attitude towards Islam

As a result of the transformation and socialization of the Islamic teachings that have been carried out by religious teachers and Muslim scholars from the time of Islam's entry into Aceh, the Acehnese people have become intensely devoted to Islam. This attitude motivated the Acehnese to fight against Dutch colonization for dozens of years; indeed, this fanaticism brought the Acehnese courage to oppose all forms of evil, as well as any movements against Islam. Ali Hasjmy says that the bravery of the Acehnese people has been motivated by the enthusiasm of their religious practice. With their fervour in opposing the Dutch infidel, who they saw primarily as the enemy of Islam, the Acehnese people who died in the fight valued their sacrifice as a form of *jihad* (in Acehnese, *syahid*) and believed that they would be given entrance into a heaven that would be both a place of rest and full of pleasures. Their fervour was further fired up by the *Hikyat Prang Sabil*, an epic story of holy war.[7]

The Dutch writer Paul van't Veer explains in his book, *De Atjeh-oorloog*, that the Acehnese war on the Netherlands continued to flare up over a long period from 1873 to 1942. It is significant that Aceh never surrendered to the Dutch even though the Sultan and some other dignitaries had been caught. Van't Veer divided the Acehnese war against the Netherlands into four periods: (1) The first Aceh War in 1873; (2) the second Aceh War from 1874 to 1880; (3) the third Aceh War from 1881 to 1886; and (4) the fourth Aceh War from 1897 to 1942 (Van't Veer 1969). These wars lasted sixty-nine years in total and claimed many fatalities and inflicted great costs on the Dutch side. Nonetheless, despite all hardship, with the spirit of *jihad* driving them forward and the sense that they were following in the path of Allah, the Acehnese people did not submit to the Dutch.

The Acehnese people's devotion to their religion not only helps them to do very great things, however, but also helps them to make everyday progress which cannot be separated from their Islamic values. The Acehnese are known today for the great care they take over religion, for the fact that they can read the Qur'an fluently, for the way they obediently perform their religious duties, for having nobility of character, and for the way they shun immoral behaviour and crime. There are, however, some Acehnese people who merely choose to be identified as Muslims on their Residency Card (the Kartu Tanda Penduduk, KTP), without practising their faith consistently on a day-to-day basis. However, these people will still defend Islam to the death and will oppose those who do identify with the infidels. For these people, being Acehnese is identical to being Muslim. Anybody who is Acehnese must be a Muslim.

When it comes to marriage, both according to *adat* and according to *shari'a*, the prospective husband or wife must be a Muslim; marrying someone of a different religion is not allowed. And, in any case, it is very rare for an Acehnese to convert to or follow a different religion. A young woman or man must understand the teachings of Islam before rushing into marriage. Moreover, in certain communities, the prospective husband is required to be able to read the Qur'an fluently and to obediently perform his religious duties, especially praying the obligatory five times a day.

However, it must be noted that the Acehnese community's dedication to Islam does not make individuals "stiff-necked" or inflexible. Rather, the people's Islamic values continue to grow with each new challenge that they meet. Though occasionally, of course, there are some Acehnese who are caught committing crimes or other wicked acts.

During the marriage ceremony, the people's devotion to Islam can be seen particularly clearly. If there are several different versions of the ceremony, including some with particular local characteristics, then the one which most agrees with Islamic law is favoured. Right before the ceremony, the prospective husband is guided in reading of "*bismillahir rahmanir rahim*", says "*astaghrifullahal 'azhim*" (I ask pardon for all my sins from Allah), reads a *shalawat* (a prayer to the Prophet Muhammad), and says the *syahadat* (a confession of faith) twice. In order to be all the stronger, the last of these is read out both in its original language and also in translation in the Acehnese or Indonesian language. Immediately after finishing all this, the wife says *ijab* (i.e. offers a contract — in this case, a marriage contract) and the husband returns by saying *gabul* (i.e. that he accepts the offer). Then, once the witnesses agree that the marriage is legal, there is a sermon containing advice about how to serve Allah, how to be faithful and charitable to one another, how to get along with each other, and how to love and appreciate one another. For this, one often invites a respected Muslim scholar, in the hope that his sermon will provide stability and strength. As the closing prayer is read out by the *ulama*, he again asks Allah to bless the couple and requests that both of them be brought together in goodness, happiness and peace, and that they be given virtuous children (Taufik Abdullah 1983, pp. 120–21).

The *Ulama* and the Organization of Islamic Education

Someone may be elevated to the status of an *ulama* on two conditions: first, he must have substantial Islamic religious knowledge; and second, the community must acknowledge that fact. The first condition can be fulfilled only after a long period of study. The second condition, however, can be fulfilled immediately once the community sees the quality of a person's morals, the depth of his knowledge, and his obedience towards the teachings of Islam. Knowing what is the right thing to do without acting on this knowledge is not enough to acquire acknowledgment from the community. In Aceh, an *ulama* generally graduates from a *dayah* (an Islamic school).[8] University graduates are not acknowledged to be members of the *ulama*.

Traditionally, in the Acehnese community, an *ulama* receives the honorary title of "Teungku" in front of his name. Descendants of the Sultan are called by the honorary "Tuwanku", while descendants of the *uleebalang* (the nobility), who generally held power during the period of Dutch colonization, are addressed as "Teuku". Members of the Acehnese community who have connected themselves with the descendants of the family of the Prophet Muhammad generally add "Habib" or the more popular "Said" in front of their names. However, social position of this sort does not bring with it special rights; rather, one's privileges depend upon one's capacities and the strength of one's efforts.

The organization of the social system through religion and religious agencies is deeply rooted in Aceh. Religious organizations, like the *dayah*, have formed the moral character of Acehnese society. In Aceh, the Islamic school has become the model around which the Muslim consciousness has been built and formed. These schools are generally led by charismatic *ulama* who have become examples for their students. However, unlike the Islamic schools in Java, the students in Aceh do not glorify or revere the *ulama*. If an *ulama* violates the teachings of Islam, he will immediately fall in stature and will no longer be honoured by either his students or the surrounding community.

Religious agencies, like Islamic schools, are also the educational homes of those with high morals, and they are regarded as very potent forces in building and protecting the community; this has been true for a long time, is still true today, and will continue to be so in the future. At the same time, religious agencies are important in bringing reform, especially in Islamic thinking. Religious organizations in Aceh have, for a long time, played a part in educating the community, so that it can be full of thinkers, leaders and intellectuals. In the beginning, these religious agencies were the only institutions capable of instilling religion in the younger generation and able to take on the role of providing public education in Aceh. The Islamic school or *dayah*, therefore, played a critical role in bringing civilization and reform to Aceh during Islam's golden years. However, the educational role of the Islamic school diminished after the Dutch colonizers came. The Dutch separated theology from public knowledge, so people who went to the Islamic schools were only permitted to study *ubudayah* (religious affairs).[9] Nevertheless, the Islamic schools, as well as the *ulama*, continued to build up the spiritual life of the younger generation. In other words, the Islamic school was an institution that maintained stability and harmony in the Acehnese community.

The Acehnese community very much appreciates the *ulama* (the devout person) because an *ulama* is both a *waratsatul anbiya'* (an heir to the prophet) and a public guide along the path of Allah. Moreover, the *ulama* makes himself fully subservient to the community, never involving himself in overt political activity. An *ulama* who does engage in politics gives the community reason to doubt him. This is because, from the perspective of the Acehnese community, the *ulama* who is active in politics or the government is disgraced by his association with deviant behaviour, like corruption, abuse of power, and distance from the common people. As a result of this attitude, the *pesantren* and other Muslim schools have historically been reluctant to accept funding from the government, because they consider these contributions to be closely tied to with political activity; this was particularly true during the New Order period. Usually, the development of a *dayah* or *pesantren* is done by an *ulama* in cooperation with the surrounding community, not with the government. An *ulama* who is already known for his piety and authority becomes the school's leader and also the person to whom members of the community turn to ask about religion and other matters as well. In return, the citizens of the village sometimes give *zakat* (alms) and *infaq* (charity) to the *ulama*; this shows that the community trusts the honesty of the *ulama* more than that of the state apparatus. By extension, we can see that the

Muslim scholar has often been regarded as more honest than the government officials in the area.

The values and behaviours associated with life in Aceh show the features of Islam in almost all of their aspects. More than anything, this has been caused by the existence of socializing institutions that shape public behaviour, especially the *dayah* education system, that was the result of efforts by *ulama* who never tired of leading the people towards a deeper understanding of religion and greater Islamization. Indeed, since the rulers, including the Sultan, got most of their education from the *ulama*, they were more inclined to accept their *fatwas*.

In past eras, Acehnese education was completely under the control of the *ulama*. Among the most well-known members of the *ulama*, both in the Acehnese sultanate and during the period of the sultanate of Malikul Sale in the kingdom of Aceh Utara, were Hamzah Fansuri, Syeikh Abdurrauf, Nuruddin ar-Raniry and Syamsuddin as-Sumatrani. There were, in addition, several important *ulama* who played an important role in the struggle against the Netherlands: Teungku Chik Di Tiro, Teungku Chik Pante Kulu, Teungku Chik Kuta Karang and Teungku Fakina (a woman). The influence of these Muslim scholars was enormous, since the *ulama* were not only educators and spiritual leaders, but also motivators in the fight for freedom.

Islamic theology spread throughout the Indonesian archipelago from Aceh. In the same way that many Islamic theologians came to Aceh from the outside, so too did many Acehnese leave home to gain religious knowledge elsewhere, journeying to Saudi Arabia, India, Egypt, Turkey and Iran. From local oral traditions, we can deduce that both traditional and more modern educational systems developed very quickly in Aceh. Over the course of history, there have been four kinds of educational institutions in Aceh, which we will consider in greater detail.

THE TRADITIONAL EDUCATIONAL INSTITUTIONS

The most traditional form of educational institution is the *dayah* or *pesantren* (an Islamic school), which is led by an *ulama*. Such traditional schools open today include, among others: (1) Dayah Darussalam in Labuhan Haji, Aceh Selatan; (2) Dayah Teungku Tanoh Mirah in Samalanga; (3) Pasantren Budi in Lamno, Aceh Barat; (4) Dayah Inshafuddin in Aceh Besar; and hundreds more.

The *Madrasah*

These institutions follow the "pure school system", as set out by the Indonesian Department of Religion. Under this system, education is divided into several levels: kindergarten (Taman Kanak-Kanak, TK); six years of primary school (Madrasah Ibtidaiyah Negeri, MIN); three years of middle school (Madrasah Tsanawiyah Negeri, MTsN); three years of high school (Madrasah Aliyah Negeri, MAN); and finally a minimum of four years at the university level at either the Islamic State University (Universitas Islam Negeri, UIN) or the National Islamic Institute (Institut Agama Islam Negeri, IAIN).

Public Education

These educational institutions fall under the control of the National Department of Education, which is also known as Depdiknas (a contraction of its full name: Departmen Pendidikan Nasional). Like the *madrasah*, these schools are divided by age and educational level, but they focus less on religious knowledge.[10] Public education parallels that of the *madrasah*, and a student in this system would also begin with kindergarten and then move into six years of primary school (Sekolah Dasar Negeri, SDN). This would be followed by three years at a junior secondary school (Sekolah Menengah Pertama Negeri, SMPN), three years at a senior secondary school (Sekolah Menengah Umum Negeri, SMUN), and at least four years at the Universitas Negeri (UN), the state university.

Combined Education

Since 1985, a combined educational system has also been developed in which traditional *dayah* education is united with modern public education. These schools are commonly called integrated *dayah* or *dayah terpadu*. The *dayah terpadu* try to integrate Islamic knowledge with scientific knowledge. These institutions often operate as boarding schools, like Dayah Bustanul 'Ulum in Langsa, Dayah Jeumala Amal in Lueng Putu, Pidie, and Dayah Umar Dian in Indra Puri, Aceh Besar. This kind of integrated system is hardly new and in other parts of Indonesia, we see older examples of this, such as Madrasah Thawalib in Padang Panjang, Sumatera Barat, and Pondok Modern Gontor in Ponorogo, Jawa Timur. The difference between most integrated education and traditional education systems is found in the curriculum. Traditional education is limited to the study of Islamic knowledge and the study of the "Yellow Book",[11] whereas pupils in the integrated educational system study not only the "Yellow Book" but also science and life skills, such as livestock breeding, agriculture, machinery and shop skills, sports, art, and music. Moreover, they are taught leadership through involvement in the scouting movement. In these schools, classroom activities are conducted primarily in Arabic and English.

These four modes of education each have a place in the heart of the Acehnese people. During Dutch colonization, most Acehnese chose to send their children to religious schools, like the *dayah* or *madrasah*, rather than public schools. Few people wanted to go to those schools because, at that time, the public schools were run by the Dutch. Moreover, only a small part of the Acehnese community, primarily the nobility, were given the opportunity to attend Dutch-run schools. At the same time, most Acehnese people believed that the schools run by the Dutch did not have curricula that were in line with Islamic teachings, and they considered those who studied there to be infidels. During that period, then, most Acehnese communities had a strongly negative attitude towards public schools. Later on, however, this attitude changed and people began to take a real interest in public education. Nevertheless, religious educational institutions continue to be favoured, especially when integrated with other kinds of education, such as in the *dayah terpadu*.

CONNECTIONS BETWEEN THE ULAMA AND THE UMARA[12]

Cooperation between the *ulama* and the *umara* (government), has been an important part of Acehnese society since the time of the sultanate of Malikul Sale, in the thirteenth century. This tradition was continued by later sultans and achieved its greatest momentum in the sixteenth and seventeenth centuries, when the Acehnese kingdom was at the height of its brilliance in several fields, and when it had everything from strong religious, social and political systems to a well-developed economy and impressive scientific and cultural achievements.

The harmony between *ulama* and *umara* can be seen in the way that the palace reserved a special place for the Muslim scholar. The *ulama* played an important role in the development of science, as well as in spreading Islam not only within the royal territories (and above all, within the royal family) but also more widely throughout the Indonesian archipelago: to the east and west coasts of Sumatra, to Java, to Ternate, to the Bugis who lived in Sulawesi, to Malacca, and even to Malaysia. At this point, the Acehnese kingdom could be said to be the centre of government, the centre of science, and the centre of Islam for the entire Indonesian archipelago. The *ulama* was the Sultan's guide on life, his advisor, the bearer of truth, and the person who reined in and controlled his power. For that reason, judicial authority was given to the *ulama*; only a Muslim scholar could hold the position of *kadhi* (judge). The *kadhi*'s decision was final, and always had the force of authority behind it (Ali Hasjmy 1978, p. 56). For this reason, the *ulama* became the determining factor in the administration of justice, and they held authority and power in equal measure.

It is important to point out that this mutual cooperation brought about a very harmonious relations between the Acehnese *ulama* and *umara*. When Sultan Iskandar Muda governed the Islamic Kingdom of Aceh Darussalam (1607–36), he chose Syeikh Syamsuddin as-Sumatrani to be his advisor, as well as choosing him to be the *mufti* responsible for religious affairs. Nuruddin ar-Raniry was chosen to be the *Kadhi Malikul Adil* and *mufti* during the reign of Sultan Iskandar Thani from 1636 to 1641; this *ulama* was assigned not only religious duties, but also economic and political responsibilities. Syeikh Abdurrauf al-Singkili was retained as *mufti* and *Kadhi Malikul Adil* during the reign of four different Acehnese queens, from 1641 to 1699 (Ali Hasjmy 1977*a*, pp. 175–76). Apart from these Muslim scholars, in the following period, there were also several *ulama* who found a respected place in the palace, for example Syeikh Saiful Rijal, Syeikh Jalaluddin at-Tarusani, Syeikh Jamaluddin al-Asyi, Syeikh Muhammad Zein, Syeikh Abdul al-Asyi, Syeikh Muhammad ibn Ahmad Khatib Langien, Syeikh Abbas (Teungku Chik Kuta Karang), and Syeikh Daud Rumy.

After the Dutch captured Sultan Alaiddin Muhammad Daud Shah in 1903, he could not support the Muslim scholars any longer and so many Acehnese *ulama* returned to their respective villages to build educational institutions, although in doing so, they had to obey several conditions set by the Dutch government. Other *ulama* continued to fight against the Netherlands. After the sultanate was eliminated by the Dutch, the potential for the *ulama* to join with the community against the colonizers became increasingly strong and together they gained the strength to declare a *jihad* on the Netherlands.

The *ulama* and *umara* never stopped working together to expel the Dutch colonizers. When Aceh struggled against the Dutch and, later, against the Japanese invaders, the nation's energy was concentrated on the physical struggle and everybody took up arms. The *umara* were never suspicious of the motives of the *ulama*. Rather, the *ulama* were treated as informal leaders with great influence in the community, who could rally the population to fight to release themselves from the shackles of colonization. During these times, it was indeed the case that the role of the *ulama* tended towards politics and political action. However, we should note that this was inevitable since the *ulama* have not only played a role in popular education, but have also had a duty to respond to the problems that might have emerged or developed in their community. For that reason, the *ulama* have tried to position themselves so that they have not been completely separated from social authority and politics.

This kind of conflict can also happen when an *ulama* holds the position of *kadhi* and is a tool of the *uleebalang* (a noble with political power), who profits from the arrangement. When Habib Abdurrahman az-Zahir gave an *ulama* religious jurisdiction where before authority had been reserved for a particular *uleebalang*, who was a Dutch collaborator, then conflict was unavoidable because of their different attitudes towards the Netherlands. The *ulama*'s position, which was shared by Abdurrahman, the Panglima Polem, and a very religious *uleebalang*, was that they must continue their opposition to the Netherlands without surrendering. By contrast, the *uleebalang* who fought for the Panglima Tibang — a military commander — believed in coming to terms with the Dutch (Tim Penulis 2003, pp. 96–97).

In the following period, the *ulama* were organized into the Ulama Association of All Aceh (PUSA), and their position and prestige increased accordingly. At the same time, the *uleebalang* were pushed to the edges of the sociocultural landscape because they had been close to the Dutch. As a result, the *uleebalang* accused the *ulama* of forming PUSA in order to compete with them politically. Even more radically, it was suggested that the intent of PUSA was to destroy all Acehnese *uleebalang*. Unsurprisingly, the conflict escalated and *ulama-umara* relations increasingly worsened. Furthermore, through PUSA, the *ulama* hoped to expel the Netherlands completely from Acehnese lands. One of their strategies was to clear the road for Japan to enter Aceh in order to help expel the Dutch (ibid., pp. 96–97).

After entering Aceh with ease, owing to the help of the *ulama*, the Japanese began to recruit Acehnese *ulama* to control the territory. These *ulama* took up positions that before had been held by the *uleebalang*. Moreover, Japan gave the *ulama* greater power in several other organizations as well. These concessions, so beneficial for the *ulama*, were balanced by a reduction in power for the *uleebalang*. Gradually, the conflict between *ulama* and *uleebalang* reached a peak, and the whole thing culminated in the outbreak of civil war in Cumbok. The Cumbok War led towards increasing social revolution and finally to the bloody incident of 21 September 1953, in which PUSA chairman Daud Beureu'eh played a major role.[13]

After this, the fate of the *ulama* took a turn for the worse. After Indonesia gained its independence, the *ulama* had less opportunity to inform and control the policies of the government. The *ulama* became little more than a political commodity used for the legitimization of power and authority. Even more tragic, during the time of Indonesia's New Order government, Acehnese *ulama* were used to mobilize the masses in order to win the general election for GOLKAR, a political party. In return, the *ulama* were given money, cars and even their own *dayahs*, where they could teach students loyal to them.

In the end, the prestige of the *ulama* began to fade. Some communities began to call the *ulama* "money-lovers" and even "bossmen-*ulama*" because they had so much money that they began to run their own businesses, and bought empty land and padi fields as investments.[14] Indeed, there were some *ulama* who went so far as to enter the political arena by nominating themselves to be members of the DPR, the new country's main legislative body. Regretfully, it might be said that today there are no true *ulama* left in Aceh, but rather that there only exist pseudo-*ulama* who are controlled by those with political power. This even includes those Acehnese *ulama* who sit on the *ulama* discussion council (i.e. Majelis Permusyawaratan Ulama, or MPU) as a substitute for the Indonesian *ulama* council (i.e. Majelis Ulama Indonesia, or MUI), as well as those who sit on the Dinas Syari'at Islam Aceh (the Acehnese *shari'a* board).

In short, we could say that in the Acehnese community, which is known to be very religious, the socially elite *ulama* occupy a significant role. Despite egalitarian ideals, the community is characterized by a pyramid-shaped social stratification. The majority fill the lower and middle strata, while the *ulama* sit at the top. This stratification is based on the degree of intensity with which the different groups approach Islam. The *ulama* is acknowledged to be the most concerned with his religious studies and is expected to put his energies into the teaching of Islam, and the community recognizes the superiority of his religious knowledge. Therefore, the Muslim scholar is considered the source of moral strength for the group, the source of Islamic socialization through his teachings, and the source of the group's strength and social solidarity, which is a result of shared faith and firm piety.

THE MOSQUE AS THE CENTRE OF ACTIVITY FOR THE ACEHNESE COMMUNITY

It cannot be doubted that the Acehnese people truly love their mosques. A Muslim's piety and obedience is marked by his perseverance in visiting the mosque at least five times a day in order to pray. These prayers are an essential part of Islam — second in importance only to saying the *syahadatain* (the Islamic statement of faith). Anybody who consciously says the *syahadat* twice, uncoerced, is considered to be a Muslim; for him, it becomes obligatory to pray daily. Praying maintains the second pillar of Islam; ignoring prayer destroys this pillar. For this reason, the Acehnese people urge their children to pray regularly from a very young age. When a child reaches six or seven years of age, his parents will begin to teach him how to pray properly and how to read religious materials. By ten years of age, a child is usually asked to accompany his parents to the mosque to pray with the rest of the congregation. It is important that obligatory prayers be done in a mosque even at a young age, but it is better for optional prayers to be done at home. From the Islamic point of view, prayers are the key to heaven; as a result, the Acehnese believe that anyone who prays sincerely and devoutly will go to heaven.

The Indonesian word "*masjid*" (mosque) came from the word "*sajada*", which is the name for the bow that one makes while praying, when moving from a kneeling position into a position where one's head touches the floor. Literally then, the mosque is the place of *sujud* and, by extension, of prayer. In Aceh, as elsewhere, when Muslims moved into several adjacent villages, in large enough numbers to allow them to gather to make the obligatory prayers and to join together for Friday services, they then would build a mosque. Generally, each district, consisting of several villages, has its own mosque. In some districts, however, the more populated areas might have as many as three mosques per village. This is an indication of the fundamental importance of the mosque for the Acehnese people, and of its great importance in their lives.

The main function of the mosque is as a place to carry out prayers and other religious duties; the mosque is the vehicle by which a person can bring himself closer to Allah. A Muslim who goes to the mosque specifically in order to bring himself closer to Allah might even practise *i'tikaf* (a special kind of devotion and dedication in which he does not leave the mosque for a period of several days). By doing *i'tikaf*, a person receives spiritual strength and guidance from Allah. Each person who loves the mosque will get Allah's protection on Judgement Day, when there will be no place to hide.

The mosque is not just a place of religious duty, however; it is also the centre of many social activities. Religious classes held in the mosque are good for children, teenagers and adults. Public Islamic holidays are celebrated in the mosque too, and one of the ways that the community comes to more fully understand Islamic teachings is by experiencing them through the celebration of these holidays. Many people visit the mosques during celebrations to commemorate the birth of the Prophet Muhammad, to remember his journey to the Al-Aqsa Mosque in Palestine and his later ascension to heaven (the *isra'* and *mi'raj*), to celebrate the Islamic New Year, to commemorate the receipt of the Qur'an, to pray during the month of Ramadan, to engage in religious discussions, and to celebrate the public holidays of Idul Fitri and Idul Adha. Moreover, the pilgrim making his obligatory trip to Mecca starts his journey in his local mosque. In this atmosphere, a sense of brotherhood and friendship forms among the members of the community, and they truly feel the beauty of their religion. The mosque functions as a unifying place.

Moreover, for the Acehnese community, the mosque generates the inspiration and the motivation for *jihad*. The congregation absorbs a fighting spirit from the mosque and so loves their mosques that they will not allow them to be bothered or damaged. When, in 1873, the Dutch tried to burn the Masjid Raya Baiturrahman, which was located in the heart of the city of Banda Aceh, the Acehnese people worked hard trying to save it.

CONCLUSION

Due to limitations of space and time, this article has not been able to fully consider all aspects of Islam in Aceh. The knots that we have untangled only partly reflect the characteristics of Islam in Aceh over the course of its history. Of course, Islam in Aceh today reflects both a shift in and a distortion of earlier Islamic teachings; some old Islamic values remain vibrant in the life of the people, while others have disappeared with the passing of time. Nonetheless, the spirit of Islam still flares in the hearts of the Acehnese, especially among those who have grown up in religious families. On some issues, there are Acehnese who embrace change and modern progress, but others, especially those who are older, still continue to cling firmly to the traditional ways. Islamic ethics continue to influence their lives, and lead them to act with obedience, tenderness, friendliness, hospitality and cooperativeness.

However, some of the younger generation are now beginning to distance themselves from traditional Islamic ethics. They choose the life of the outside world, adopting the conduct, dress, food, drink and lifestyle of other cultures. These people tend to copy what they see in films and on television. Young people fill roadside stalls that provide food and drinks, and the social distinctions between men and women have been blurred to such an extent as to be almost indistinguishable. Things that were once regarded as improper are now commonplace. It is not rare for there to be conflict between parents and their children when these values collide; the parents' values are shaped by customs and traditions, while their children see things according to the here and now. For that reason, very few members of the younger generation care about conserving Acehnese traditions or the culture of the past.

The life of the Acehnese is closely connected to their social organization and religion, as can be seen from the important roles that are played by the *meunasah*, the mosque, the *dayah*, the *madrasah*, and the government's office of religious matters. The intimate relationship between the people and these organizations was traditionally due to their shared religious roles. Although occasionally, due to weak faith, some people did not perform their religious duties in their entirety or in a disciplined way, a feeling of sympathy for their religion has nonetheless always been very prominent. Religious and social organizations have been at the centre of any community, and even though their immediate functions have been different, their ultimate purpose has been the same. These organizations are constructive institutions that have provided guidance for the community, helping solve both religious and social problems, and creating a sense of shared nationhood.

Thus, in order to understand the dynamics of Islam in Aceh, we have investigated, among other things, the history of Islam's introduction in the Indonesian archipelago, the role of the *ulama* and *umara*, the function of educational institutions, and the ways in which the Acehnese understand and practise Islam. This last can be seen in the social life of the Acehnese community, which is marked by the harmonious application of the pillars of Islam: fasting, giving of alms, going on a pilgrimage, and above all, praying. The Acehnese community sees prayer as the defining feature of a Muslim, while fasting is carried out every year only during the month of Ramadan. Those who are economically well-off are obliged to give alms, and similarly, the obligation to go on a pilgrimage to Mecca only applies to those who are physically and financially able to do so. On a day-to-day basis, Islam's influence on people's lives is greatest during the celebration of public holidays, like Idul Fitri, Idul Adha and the Prophet's birthday, and during the fasting and prayers of Ramadan, as is the case among Muslims worldwide.

Fundamentally, there is not much difference between Islam in Aceh and Islam in other areas. The uniqueness of Acehnese Islam is located in the spirit of strict adherence to religion — a thing that is so part of the Acehnese identity that they continue to be known for their religious fervour, even when they do not fully carry out the religious duties that they profess to follow. Moreover, the Acehnese community has made devotion to Islam the standard of goodness in their social system and in their customs and traditions. Tradition cannot be separated from *shari'a*, and *shari'a* must be based on the Qur'an and the Hadith. Separating these things is considered to be a deviation from Allah's law, and each deviation is considered a thing of the infidel and, therefore, heresy. For this reason, the *ulama* has become the first recourse for the people when they want to know the right way to deal with their problems.

Notes

1. Translated by Shawna Kim Lowey-Ball.
2. The Qur'an is the word of God that was given to the Prophet Muhammad — the reading of which is a religious duty. The Qur'an is the first source of law

in Islam. The Sunnah is the tradition of the Prophet's good deeds — a standard feature of Islamic teaching that can be found in the Hadith. The Sunnah is considered to be the second most important source of Islamic doctrine after the Qur'an. "*Ijma*" refers to consensus among Muslim scholars about whether a law is legal or not and whether a particular object or action is acceptable or forbidden. These decisions are based on the Qur'an and the Sunnah. Finally, "*qiyas*" is a legal analogy that can be made by reference to another law when the application or determination of a legal question is not clearly answered in either the Qur'an or the Sunnah.

3. Also known as the Syiah Kuala. This is the title that was given to Sheikh Abdurrauf as-Singkili, the important *ulama* who was appointed *mufti* and Kadhi Malikul Adil during the reigns of the four queens of Aceh (Queen Safiatuddin, Queen Naqiatuddin, Queen Zakiatuddin, and Queen Kamalat Syah), from 1641 to 1699. For further information on the four queens, read Ali Hasjmy (1977*a*).
4. "*Peusijuek*" comes from the word "*sijuek*" meaning "cool, cold, peaceful, fresh and calm". In Aceh, the *peusijuek* is a traditional ceremony that is carried out to give respect to certain people, for instance, when welcoming a guest, newlyweds or public figures, or for the sake of the souls of people who have been stricken by disaster. *Peusijuek* involves sprinkling flour into water, mixing it with foliage and unhusked rice, and then placing the sticky mixture on the right ear of the honoured person. All of this is carried out with humility, and the ceremony ends with a prayer to request for the safety of the honoured guest and a blessing from Allah.
5. In Western Sumatra, this is known as a *surau*, and in Java it is called a *langgar* or *mushalla*.
6. The *meunasah* also has various socio-religious functions, such as providing an educational space for the community — the *meunasah* is said to be a person's first school. The social system and social solidarity are formed in the *meunasah*. It is also unusual for more mature men who remain single to sleep in a house, and so, most sleep in the *meunasah*; if they were to sleep in a house, this would be considered embarrassing. As for the *qurban*, it is one of the religious duties of Islam. Through the *qurban*, one becomes closer to God by sacrificing animals like cattle, water buffalo or goats on the tenth, eleventh, twelfth and thirteenth of the month of Zulhijjah each year. The aim is to provide meat for the poor, but some animal meat may also be enjoyed by rich people.
7. This epic was written by a famous Muslim scholar, Haji Muhammad Pante Kulu, better known as Teungku Chik Pante Kulu. It contained stories about: (1) Ainul Mardhiyah; (2) Pasukan Gajah, or the elephant cavalry; (3) Sa'id Salmy; and (4) Kisah Muhammad Amin, a slave who died and later came back to life. The *Hikayat Prang Sabi* stoked a fire in the souls of the Acehnese who opposed the Dutch colonists. For further information, read Ali Hasjmy (1977*b*). Also, see Ali Hasjmy (1976).
8. The word *dayah* appears to be a modified version of the Arabic *zawiyah*, a

special place that is used for the teaching of Islamic mysticism. This term was later adopted by the Acehnese *ulama* to mean the place where people recite the Qur'an or study Islamic theology. In Java, the preferred term is *pesantren*.

9. *Ubudayah* was a narrow term focused only on human relations with Allah. One could formally study only religious duties in the *dayah*, without thinking about worldly affairs in the process. One of the strategies of the colonizers was to give the colonized communities the opportunity to undertake their religious duties while restricting their movement in more political spheres of activity.
10. All students in Indonesia are required to take classes in one of the five recognized religions (Islam, Hinduism, Catholicism, Protestant Christianity, and Buddhism), whether at a public, private, or religious school. (Translator's note).
11. The term "Yellow Book" or "*Kitab Kuning*" was used by students at traditional *pesantren* because they studied the thirteen books of Islamic Law in Arabic, and these books came with pages that have turned yellow with age. Studying the "Yellow Book" took many years, indeed, sometimes dozens of years. Later on, the term "Yellow Book" became associated with traditional education despite the fact that the books were no longer yellow, but rather used white paper like that generally used in printed books today. For further information about the "Yellow Book", see Van Bruinessen (1999).
12. To the Acehnese, the word *ulama* refers to a person who focuses serious attention on the study of Islam and who intends to act upon that knowledge and to develop himself both through the processes of studying and teaching and through talk or preaching. Usually an *ulama* leads a *dayah* (an Islamic school) and has several pupils (who in Acehnese are called "*aneuk meudagang*"). He is also the person to go to with various social problems or religious questions. "*Umara*", by contrast, refers to the government, the ruler, or the leader who formally holds authority in a particular place. The word is plural, and derives from the singular "*amir*" or "*emir*", with which many are familiar. For the Acehnese, the paired terms "*ulama*" and "*umara*" have a strong cultural significance. The *ulama* and *umara* are seen as two inseparable elements of righteousness and stability; both terms refer to a leader who undertakes the mandate of Allah — God's will on earth.
13. For detailed information about PUSA and the Cumbok War, see M. Nur El Ibrahimi (2001).
14. The actual terms used were "*gila uang*" and "*ulama toke*". "*Gila uang*" suggests not merely love of money, but rather an infatuation to the point of obsession and perhaps, even insanity. It might be equally translated as "money-crazy". "*Ulama toke*" has several connotations which are bound up in the multiple meanings of "*toke*". The first of these meanings is "lizard" — a well-known insult. However, this term can also refer to Chinese bosses, employers or shop owners. In Indonesia, the Chinese have suffered much abuse and are stereotyped as money grubbing, very rich, fairly immoral, and absolutely un-Indonesian. All of these connotations are present in the slur "*ulama toke*". (Translator's note).

11

THE SHATTARIYYA SUFI BROTHERHOOD IN ACEH

Werner Kraus

Aceh was, during the sixteenth and seventeenth centuries, the intellectual centre of Malay Islam and the hotspot of Islamic mystical thinking as well. One of the giants of this discourse was Abdurrauf al-Singkili. He introduced the Shattariyya Sufi (in Indonesian, *tarekat*) order to Aceh and the Malay world. This chapter traces the history of the Shattariyya in India, Arabia and Aceh to the present day. It documents that this *tarekat*, like others as well, went through a constant process of reinvention and recreation. The Shattariyya that was introduced into Gujarat in the fifteenth century had very little in common with the Shattariyya brought to Aceh in the seventeenth century. And, the present Shattariyya communities in Aceh are a different story again. What is known to us by the name of "Shattaríyya" has been over the centuries, a highly unstable institution that has been influenced by local and regional Islamic developments and interpretations. In this respect, it mirrors other Acehnese Islamic institutions as well.

Mysticism in Islam is not, as in the case of Christianity, a marginal phenomenon. Rather, it is the complementary opposite of Islamic law, the *shari'a*, and as such, one of the two poles of the authentic and creative manifestation of Islamic religious life. The two poles — law and mysticism — are the expression of the apparently contradictory Qur'anic God-man relationship. One pole presents God as the almighty creator of all things and beings, in whose hand the fate of the universe is decided anew from one second to another. Man, on the other hand, is a weak, fragile, mortal being, who can only submit to the will of God. His breath pervades Adam's body and He is "nearer than the artery of man's throat" (Qur'an 50:16).[1] Thus, God's presence is omnipresent and all-permeating. "To God belong the East and the West. Wherever you turn, you have God's countenance before you" (Qur'an 2:115). From this tension between transcendence and immanence, nearness and distance, and incomprehensible otherness and absolute proximity have developed the two poles of law and mysticism — the exoteric and esoteric understanding of the Qur'an. Only the two together offer the chance to understand the entire mystery of the Islamic revelation that reached the world through the Prophet Muhammad.

In the Malay archipelago, Islamic mysticism was, for centuries, more than just a complementary opposite to the law. It was the centre both of popular and of elite religiosity. Not mysticism but the law — the Islamic legal system to be precise — played a marginal role in Islamic Southeast Asia right up to the twentieth century. The *shari'a* remained, for a long time, a concept about which a small group of scholars could debate impressively, but was of little importance in the everyday legal practice of the local Muslims organized in tribal communities or in highly unstable states. Ernest Gellner's interesting thesis (with reference to North African society) postulated that "urban Sufi mysticism was an *alternative* to the legalistic, restrained, arid [as it seems to its critics] Islam of the *ulama*. Rural and tribal 'Sufism' is a *substitute* for it" (Gellner 1981, p. 115). This could apply to the Southeast Asian situation as well. Since, however, in Southeast Asia (unlike in North Africa) up to this century, no stable urban tradition of Sufi mysticism could develop, the gap between the two traditions has not been quite as pronounced as in Algeria or Morocco. In the Malay archipelago, it was the rural religious centres — the *pesantren*, *dayah*, *surau*, *pondok*, or however they were designated in the local idiom — which acted as centres of urban and rural Sufism at the same time. While the ordinary people were happy to learn some rudimentary forms of the daily ritual and receive more or less powerful amulets, the more sophisticated members of the religious community climbed the philosophical and mystical heights of Islam, at the same religious institution, as well.

Islam reached Southeast Asia as Sufi Islam. Sufis made the decisive contribution to the Islamization of the Malay archipelago. All major reform movements in Malay Islam up to the modernists of the twentieth century, the Salafiyah, were reform movements in the Sufi context. The great opponent of the Acehnese mystic poet Hamzah Fansuri, Nuruddin ar-Raniry, was not just a dry *fuquah* (supporter of the law), but was himself a representative of Islamic mysticism. Ar-Raniry followed a different tradition of theological interpretation, but was not opposed to mysticism (in Indonesian, *tasawuf*) itself. The conflict between the two was a conflict within the paradigm of Islamic mysticism (and most probably a conflict about influence and worldly power as well).

Malay Islamic mysticism was, of course, not a rigid system that remained unchanged over the centuries. Sufism in Southeast Asia has to be regarded as a dynamic system: a system which grew and declined, expanded and contracted. New interpretations of mystical concepts found their way from the centres of the Islamic world to the archipelago, replacing old ideas when social and cultural conditions were ready to receive them.

And, the concepts of mystical systems were transferred to other areas of culture, social organization or architecture as well.[2] The organization of the Malay Sufis in associations, called orders or brotherhoods, also changed over the centuries. During the seventeenth and eighteenth centuries, Islamic mystical brotherhoods were not well organized nor were they clearly structured social units, but rather, loosely structured schools of thought that had developed around a certain mystical system. Sufi brotherhoods as "corporate groups" (i.e. as active religious and social units), in my opinion, first appeared in the Malay context in the nineteenth century. Neither local nor Dutch sources permit us to assume the existence of highly organized brotherhoods in earlier times.

Certainly, I do know that the Acehnese mystic Hamzah Fansuri claimed affiliation with the Qadiriyya brotherhood and that his rival, Nuruddin ar-Raniry was supposed to have been a member of the Rifaiyya.[3] It is also true that Abdurra'uf al-Singkili brought the Shattariyya to Aceh as early as the seventeenth century and Sheikh Yusuf Makassari brought the Khalwatiyya and Naqshbandiyya to Banten. However, and this is the crucial difference, these and other local mystics founded no brotherhoods in the sense of "corporate groups". Instead, they propagated, for the most part, a system of mystical, esoteric knowledge (*ilmu* and *ngelmu*). In Southeast Asia, brotherhoods, as a religious and social category in the modern sense, first arose under changing social conditions during colonial rule and under the influence of the reforming Sufi tradition of the eighteenth and nineteenth centuries. They then became bearers of the strong wave of Islamization that transformed many regions of the Malay archipelago from *Dar ul-Harb* to *Dar ul-Islam*.

Nevertheless, we do not have to deal much with the history of Islamic mysticism. Orientalists have already done that in great detail. Two representative names can be mentioned here: Annemarie Schimmel and Spencer Trimingham. Monographs about individual brotherhoods or descriptions of the history of brotherhoods in certain regions of the Islamic world have been, on the other hand, rare. However, over the last twenty-five years, more and more serious works about the nature and activities of Sufi brotherhoods, in the local context, have appeared. These include the works of Hamid Algar, Michael Gilsenan, Abu Nasr, John O. Voll, Richard Eaton, Sayid Athar Abbas Rizvi, Warren Fusfeld, D.B. Cruise O'Brien, Louis Brenner, Frederick de Jong, Mark Sedgwick, and many more.

However, in the past the Sufi brotherhoods of Southeast Asia attracted little attention. Only recently have they aroused the interest of academics. Here, Denys Lombard and Martin van Bruinessen should be mentioned. Van Bruinessen's book about the Naqshbandiyya in Indonesia is a milestone: an important contribution to the history of *sufi tarekat* in Indonesia (Van Bruinessen 1992). The author of this contribution has also published work on the *tarekat* in Indonesia (Kraus 1990).

The obvious mystical dimension of Indonesian Islam was recognized quite early by colonial scholars, but as a rule, it was considered to be merely a historical phenomenon. In accordance with the evolutionary understanding of the nineteenth century, the Dutch regarded Indonesian Islamic mysticism as a "survival" — a relic of the animistic and Hinduistic cultural traditions of the islands. Dutch administrative officials and scholars were, for the most part, convinced that this *bijgeloof* (superstition) would yield in the long run to the enlightening force of the European spirit. Even the Indonesian Islamic modernists of the 1920s and 1930s shared this conviction. They, too, regarded the rituals, images and customs of the mystical brotherhoods as deviations (*bidah* — forbidden innovation) and strictly rejected them. They understood the modernist reinterpretation of Islam essentially as a force for enlightenment that would cleanse and renew the confused ritual landscape of Indonesian Islam. The Salafiyah did not want to get rid of Islamic mysticism per se. They accepted *tasawuf* as important part of the Islamic tradition. However, they imagined a *tasawuf moderen* as cleansed of all ecstatic elements and oriented towards orthodoxy.

For quite some time, Western social sciences succumbed to the ideas of their (mostly modernist-minded) Indonesian informants and regarded the brotherhoods as a dying institution in Indonesian society.[4] However, the Islamic mystical orders have survived the death prophesied for them in the best of health and have grown and flourished over the last few years.

At the same time, Islamic scripturalism and fundamentalism carry the day and capture our imagination about Islam in general and Acehnese Islam in particular. The introduction of *shari'a* criminal law in Nanggroe Aceh Darussalam, the public floggings in front of the mosques across the province, which started in 2005, and the strictly enforced dress codes and prayer attendance are all signs that Acehnese Islam is orienting itself more and more along Middle Eastern practices. It will be seen if this kind of social engineering is successful in a society that needs — after the catastrophe of the tsunami and the end of regional fighting — social solidarity more than anything else.

TAREKAT IN PRESENT DAY ACEH

While it is true that Islamic mystical schools and brotherhoods reached the rest of Indonesia via Aceh, it is at the same time true that Sufi *tarekat* never gained the same importance in Aceh as it did in West Sumatra, Java or South Sulawesi. Sufi brotherhoods, as corporate organizations, developed in Indonesia during the nineteenth century, especially in regions under colonial control. Wherever local government was weak or non-existent, *tarekat*, as a kind of political and cultural counter force, developed. Aceh, at that time, was still under local rule and there was no need for the development of a clandestine Islamic structure. The long Aceh War as well did not encourage the development of quietist and contemplative movements. Therefore, Kreemer's statement that there were almost no *tarekat* to be found in Aceh (in the 1920s) was certainly true. Only some small pockets of Shattari communities survived the long anti-colonial struggle.

However, new orders were introduced in the meantime and today, it would be wrong to state that Sufism has no place in Acehnese Islam. Besides the Naqshbandiyya, which is the most prominent brotherhood in Aceh as well as in North Sumatra, there are traces of the Haddadiyya and, of course, the Shattariyya. No major research has so far been done on the situation of the different *tarekat* in Aceh. Besides the chapter on Aceh in van Bruinessen's book about the Naqshbandiyya in Indonesia, we only have a number of *skripsi* (BA or MA theses) submitted to Fakultas Ushuluddin of the IAIN Ar-Raniry in Banda Aceh.[5] All of them concern themselves with the Naqshbandiyya and give us valuable insights on the local workings of this brotherhood. Political ramifications of *tarekat* affiliation, like the Naqshbandiyya affiliation of Syeikh Muda Wali of Labuhan Haji during the troubled times of the Acehnese rebellion against the Republic of Indonesia in the 1950s, is never touched by these *skripsi*. His strong commitment to PERTI (Persatuan Tarbiya Islam, or Islamic Education Party) and the fact that the Naqshbandiyya in West and South Aceh was a cultural marker for the Minangkabau-speaking Aneuk Jameu is again not been researched.[6] While the Naqshbandiyya-Khalidiyya in South Aceh (Labuhan Haji) was directly introduced from West Sumatra, another line of introduction of the same brotherhood runs through the Naqshbandi centre of Babussalam in Langkat, North Sumatra, which ultimately also derived from West Sumatra. This again points to the immense importance that West Sumatran schools had for the Acehnese during the last century. Almost all leading modernist Acehnese *ulama* spent some time at a Minangkabau religious school.[7]

Today, Sufi brotherhoods are not very visible in Aceh. And, certainly, they are not part of public discourse in the press. However, as an important element of Islamic culture, they still are part of the Islamic tradition of Nanggroe Aceh Darussalam. Sufi brotherhoods still play an important role as a spiritual and emotional resource for Acehnese Muslims.

THE SHATTARIYYA BEFORE ITS ARRIVAL IN INDONESIA

Around 1661, Abdurrauf al-Singkili brought the Shattariyya from Medina to Sumatra. Abdurrauf had been a pupil of the Medinese scholars al-Kushashi and al-Kurani. From them, he received permission (*ijazah*) to spread the *tarekat* in his homeland.

The word "Shattariyya" is derived from the Arabic "*shatr*", which means "to move in a certain direction". A Shattari, in the language of the brotherhood, is a believer who "with great speed and great zeal seeks the vision of God" (Nizami 1950, p. 57).

The spiritual genealogy — the *silsilah* (chain) — of the Shattariyya follows the line of the so-called "Khorasan Brotherhoods", that is, the genealogy running through the ecstatic Iranian mystic Bayezid Bistami, and through Ali back to Muhammad. Bistami, in mystical ecstasy, called out, "*ana wahdi la sharik li*" (I am one and have no companion) and was condemned by many as a heretic. He introduced the concept of *fana* (extinction) into Islamic mysticism, which means the complete and final union of the saint with God, being absorbed into Him. This shows that the Shattariyya is rooted in a tradition that could be regarded as rather heterodox.

The first saint who used the attribute "Shattari" was Shah Abdullah Shattari, who brought the brotherhood to India. He was sent from Iran by his master 'Arif and appeared in public not as a poor fakir or admonishing ascetic, but took on a princely aura (Schimmel 1980, p. 40). With his disciples, he donned military uniform, travelled overland with drums and flags, and in every town he visited, he had someone call out, "Is here anyone who wishes to be shown the way of God?" (Nizami 1950). Shah Abdullah died in 1485 in Mandu, the capital of the petty kingdom of Malwa, having wandered through most of northern India.

The more important representatives of the Shattariyya in India and the direct predecessors of the Sumatran Abdurrauf in the *silsilah* of this brotherhood are Muhammad Ghawth Gwaliyari who taught a very eclectic form of mysticism, Wadjih al-Din al-Alawi who guided the brotherhood towards the orthodox path, and Shah Sibghat Allah who introduced strong anti-Shi'ite elements and who made the order acceptable to the scholars of Medina.

Muhammad Ghawth Gwaliyari (1502–63)

Muhammad Ghawth Gwaliyari was regarded by a lot of his contemporaries as an extremely heterodox thinker. During his time, the Shattariyya brotherhood was "the most syncretic of all medieval Sufi orders" (Lawrence 1982, p. 39) in India. He spent thirteen years as a hermit in the mountains north of Benares and then, for the rest of his life, taught a highly eclectic form of Islamic mysticism. In his book, *Awrad-i ghawthiyya*, he described his ascension (*mi'raj*) to heaven, in a similar way to how Abu Yazid al-Bastami had done before him. His *Jawahir-al khamsa* is a rapturous description of ecstatic mystical states, which attracted harsh criticism from many *ulama*. In another work, *Bahr-ul-Hayat*, he attempted to combine Islamic mystical thought with Hindu astrological theories and yoga meditation methods. According to his own account, he was a descendant of the important Persian Sufi poet Fariduddin 'Attar, who in turn had been inspired by the spiritual self (*ruhaniyya*) of the great mystic Mansur al-Hallaj. When Muhammad Ghawth returned from the solitude of the mountains, he became, like many Shattariyya sheikhs before him, closely associated with the Mogul court, and reportedly, at least for a time, was highly revered by the Emperors Babur and Hamayun. However, because of his affiliation with Hamayun, he had to seek exile in Gujarat, after Hamayun faced defeat by Sher Shah Suri in 1540. After eighteen years — when Hamayun had come back to power — Muhammad Ghawth Gwaliyari finally was allowed to return to Gwalior (Ernst 1999, p. 418).

As mentioned above, most *ulama* regarded Muhammad Ghawth Gwaliyari with critical distance because of the syncretic nature of his works. Only one felt attracted to him and defended him against all censure, the famous Hadith scholar, Wadjih al-Din al-Alawi Gujarati, who finally became the *khalifa* of Muhammad Ghawth in Gujarat.

Shah Wadjih al-Din al-Alawi Gujarati (d. 1589)

Shah Wadjih al-Din was one of the most important Islamic scholars of his time. Over three hundred books and treatises have been attributed to his pen. The Mogul historian Bada'uni wrote of him, "There was hardly a standard work from the treatises on the accidental properties of light to books of law and medicine ... which he had not annotated and adorned with a commentary" (Lawrence 1982).

He was a typical urban Sufi who resided in Ahmedabad, Gujerat, and whose pupils came from all classes of the population. The *madrasah* he founded continued to exist into the nineteenth century. In contrast to his master, Muhammad Ghawth Gwaliyari, he abstained from ecstatic practices and did not even participate in *soma* (musical performances which lead to a trance-like state), which are so popular in India. Perhaps that is the reason why, in spite of his scholarship and his reputation, he never became one of the highly regarded Sufi masters of Gujarat. His grave in Khanpur, Ahmedabad, still exists, but its *baraka* (power of blessing) is considered to be limited and it is only a local pilgrimage site.

Wadjih al-Din accepted the transcendence of God's existence and brought the Shattariyya back to a strictly orthodox line, which would later be its distinctive feature in Arabia and Sumatra. According to the orthodox view, the mystical path of the Sufis (*tariqa*) should follow Islamic law (*shari'a*). The law and the transcendence of Allah are the necessary points of departure for the mystical journey of a Shattari. That is why Wadjih al-Din refused to follow the common practice of his day to accept Hindus among his pupils too. Under his leadership, the Shattariyya became an urban order — one that had made its peace with the local political authorities and was integrated into orthodox Islam. Starting with Wadjih al-Din, Shattari Sufism acquired the reputation of a scholarly order.

Wadjih al-Din is said to have had fourteen hundred *khalifa*. One of them was Muhammad ibn Fazlullah Burhanpuri, who had written the important book *at-Tuhfa al-mursala ila'n-nabi*. This work, described by A.H. Johns[8] as the watershed of Malay mysticism, is the source of the Martabat Tujuh (the seven emanations or degrees of being): a mystical theory which played a major role in the speculations of the Sufis in Sumatra and Java from the seventeenth to the nineteenth centuries.

The important Medinan scholar of the seventeenth century, Ibrahim al-Kurani, who knew about the importance of this work in the archipelago, wrote a commentary on the *at-Tuhfa al-mursala ila'n-nabi* for his Malay disciples. In his biographic dictionary, Mustafa al-Hamawi writes:

> Our Shaykh Ibrahim al-Kurani told me that one of our Jawi companions — and he was reading the Tuhfa with him at the time and we were present — informed him that this treatise and the matter it treats was popular and famous in the lands of the Jawi, and that it is read in their religious schools, and that the youth study it as a minor treatise on the rudiments of their studies. (Johns 1978, p. 477)

This clearly shows that even before Abdurrauf, Shattari thoughts were widespread in the "lands of the Jawi" and that his devotion to this tradition was not exactly a coincidence. Probably, he had become acquainted with the Shattariyya even before his departure from Aceh.

Shah Sibghat Allah (d. 1606)

Shah Sibghat Allah follows Shah Wadjih al-Din al-Alawi Gujarati in the *silsilah* of the Shattariyya brotherhood. Sibghat Allah was born in the Gujarati harbour town of Broach as a member of a Persian immigrant family (Azyumardi Azra 2004, p. 13). Soon, he moved to the provincial capital, Ahmedabad, where he became a pupil of Wadjih al-Din. Around 1590, he left his master and went on a pilgrimage to Mecca. On his return, he settled in Bijapur in the Deccan. Under the rule of the Adil Shah dynasty, Bijapur had advanced to become an important Sufi centre on the subcontinent. Sibghat Allah reached Bijapur in AH 1000 (AD 1592). Throughout the entire Islamic world, the beginning of the second millennium was linked to a hope for the appearance of a religious renewal. While, in north India, these expectations were concentrated on the Naqshbandi Ahamad Sirhindi, Sibghat Allah seems to have been the focus of similar hopes in the Deccan. The nineteenth-century historian Ibrahim Zubairi assumes that Sibghat Allah came to Bijapur mainly to bring Sultan Ibrahim II, who was friendly to Shi'ism, back along the path of orthodox Sunni Islam (Eaton 1976, p. 113).

Sibghat Allah became known in Bijapur, above all, for his strong anti-Shi'ite attitude. It seems that his family had to leave Iran because of Sunni persecution after the victory of the Safawites. The Safawites, who started out as a Sufi movement, themselves turned very strongly against Sunni Islamic brotherhoods after they came to power. This and the serious clashes between Sunni and Shi'ite Bohras during the second half of the sixteenth century, which he had experienced in Gujarat, made Sibghat Allah a determined enemy of Shi'ism. His aversion increased during the reign of Shah Abbas I (1588–1629), who had ordered the execution of thousands of Sufis. During this time, many Shattaris fled to Gujarat.

His repudiation of Shi'ism was not limited to words. When, during the feast of 'Ashura in 1596, a procession of Shi'ites passed before his *madrasah*, he sent out a pupil to destroy one of the symbols being carried by the Shi'ites. This incident set off bloody riots in Bijapur. Sibghat Allah, as the author of these religious tensions, was promptly banished from Bijapur. He returned to Mecca, where he built a *ribat* (a Sufi centre) which was regarded as the headquarters of the Shattariyya brotherhood in the Haramayn. He introduced

Muhammad Ghaut's controversial work, *Jawahir-I Khamsah*, to the local scholars and died as a highly regarded *alim* (Islamic scholar) in 1606.

Abu'l Mawahib al-Shinnawi (d. 1619)

Sibghat Allah's *khalifa* in the Holy Cities was the Egyptian scholar Abu'l Mawahib al-Shinnawi, whose life and intellectual development was admirably researched by Azyumardi Azra (2004, p. 15ff). Abu'l Mawahib al-Shinnawi was born into a scholarly Egyptian family in 1567. He was especially interested in Hadith studies and developed a highly regarded expertise in this field. In Mecca, he befriended Sibghat Allah and studied the Indian tradition of Sufism with him. Through his knowledge of the Hadith and *tasawuf,* his study circle was visited by a wide variety of students. One of the more remarkable among them was Ahmad al-Kushashi, to whom he gave his *tarekat* (Shattariyya), as well as his daughter in marriage. Al-Kushashi has to be regarded as the primary teacher of Abdurrauf, who finally brought the Shattariyya to Sumatra.

Ahmad al-Kushashi (d. 1661)

Sheikh Safi al-Din Ahmad b. Muhammad b. Yunus al-Madani al-Dagani al-Kushashi, born in Medina in 1583, came from a family which originated from the city of Jerusalem (*Encyclopaedia of Islam*). He studied with various teachers in Yemen and then, with Sibghat Allah and al-Shinnawi in Medina. Al-Kushashi was a member of various brotherhoods, including the Shattariyya, Qadiriyya, Naqshbandiyya and Dubrawiyya, and is said to have authored over fifty books, especially Hadith commentaries (*Mystical Illustrations*, p. 5). As a Hadith scholar, he was widely known. In the history of Islamic scholarship up to that point, it had been exceptional for a Sufi to concern himself with the Hadith. The Hadith — the collection of handed-down sayings and actions of the Prophet Muhammad — served mostly as a source of answers to new social and political questions. The primary interest of the Sufis, however, had been the individual experience of salvation. Not the conditions of this world, but the overcoming of the world was the focus of Sufi thought. For reasons that cannot be explained here, in the seventeenth and eighteenth centuries this changed, and the study of the Hadith assumed an important place in Sufi circles. Al-Kushashi was an important person in this process of reorientation. For this reason, the American Islamic scholar John Voll describes him as a precursor of so-called neo-Sufism.[9] Al-Kushashi died in 1661 in Medina.

In the same year and perhaps as a consequence of al-Kushashi's death, Abdurrauf went, after spending almost twenty years in Arabia, back to

Sumatra in order to spread the Shattariyya and its version of reformed Sufi Islam.

Ibrahim al-Kurani (d. 1690)

The most influential teacher and friend of Abdurrauf was, however, not al-Kushashi, but al-Kushashi's pupil and successor Ibrahim al-Kurani. Abdurrauf maintained correspondence with him even after his return to Aceh. Al-Kurani, whose person and work have attracted little attention in orientalist circles, is a key figure for the later development of the doctrine of the school of Ibn al-Arabi. He had a large group of students from all over the Islamic world, including many from India, Sumatra and Java. Apparently, his descendants remained a gathering point for Jawi students, because later Shattari *silsilah*, which reached Indonesia only in the nineteenth century, were firmly linked to the family of al-Kurani. His son, Abu'l Tahir, was a teacher of Shah Wali Allah, the great renewer of Indian Islam. On the other hand, the intellectual *isnat* (genealogy) of Muhammad ibn 'Abd al-Wahab (founder of the Wahabis) and Muhammad ibn 'Abd al-Samman (founder of the Sammaniyyah) can be traced back to Ibrahim al-Kurani as well. With that, he clearly stands in the middle of a great period of reform in Islam. The work of al-Kurani, as well as his relationship with Abdurrauf, have been researched by A.H. Johns and were published in his article "Friends in Grace" (Johns 1978). Voll (1975), Van Bruinessen (1987) and, in particular, Azyumardi Azra (1994) round out the picture.

From this summary of the last developments in the Shattariyya *silsilah* before its arrival in Sumatra, it is clear that the theology of the brotherhood at this time was moving in the direction of being law-abiding, orthodox, and even reformist. There is no evidence at this time that it was syncretistic in character or inclination. It also lacked the impatience of earlier reformers like Sibghat Allah or ar-Raniry. Al-Kurani and his friend Abdurrauf had been profoundly shaped by a humanist simplicity; both were exemplary models of the great, central tradition of Islam — the tradition of tolerance and reconciliation. Abdurrauf wrote in seventeenth century Aceh, "It is dangerous to accuse someone of heresy. If you make the charge and it is true, why lose so many words? If it is not true, however, the accusation will fall back on you" (Johns 1955).

In Arabia, the Shattariyya soon was removed to secondary importance by other brotherhoods, like the Naqshbandiyya and Khalwatiyya, but it never completely faded away. In India, too, the stage was soon dominated by the Naqshbandis and Qadiris. The Shattari *silsilah* was a "spent bullet in the seventeenth century" (Nizami 1950, p. 70). This, however, does not mean that the brotherhood completely disappeared from India. Important *ulama* continued to hold it in esteem. Sheikh Abu Tahir Muhammad (d. 1733), the son of Ibrahim al-Kurani, for example, initiated the great reformer Shah Wali Allah into the Shattariyya in Medina.

The development of the brotherhood in Southeast Asia was a different one. Here, the Shattariyya would remain, for a long time the only *tarekat* of importance and even today, it is found in many parts of Malaysia and Indonesia. Its presence is strongest in West Sumatra and Java. In order to gain an understanding of the historical and contemporary importance of the brotherhood, the following will map out the history of the Shattariyya brotherhood in Aceh.

THE SHATTARIYYA IN ACEH

Although the Shattariyya certainly reached the Malay world through Aceh, it is only weakly represented there today. The present *silsilah* tradition suggests that it only reached Aceh in the nineteenth century.

However, we know that the *at-Tuhfa al-mursala ila'n-nabi*, the compendium of the seven degrees of being (Martabat Tujuh), which was read mainly by scholars belonging to the Shattariyya tradition, was known in Aceh in the early seventeenth century. All Acehnese mystics (with the exception of Hamzah Fansuri) referred to this system (Johns 1961, p. 153). This could mean that the Shattariyya was already known in Aceh at the beginning of the seventeenth century. Abdurrauf is the first Shattari sheikh known to us by name, but it is possible and even probable that he had predecessors. Unfortunately, there is no documentation to support this hypothesis and we have no Shattari *silsilah* from Indonesia, neither in manuscripts nor in oral tradition, that refers to a lineage prior to that of Abdurrauf.

Abdurrauf returned to Aceh in 1661 and promoted the spread of the Shattari version of Islamic mysticism that he had acquired from al-Kushashi and al-Kurani in Arabia. Soon after he had gained the confidence of Sultanah Safyat al-Din, he became the *Shayk al-Islam* of the sultanate and the most important teacher of his time. As his fame developed, he attracted students from many parts of the archipelago: from Aceh, West Sumatra, Trengganu and Java. The most well known of his students were Burhanuddin Ulakan from West Sumatra, who played an important role in the Islamization of Minangkabau, 'Abdul Muhyi from Karangnunggal, West Java, Abd al-Malik bin Abdullah, alias Tok Pulau Manis, from Trengganu, and Dawud al-Rumi, who was his successor in Aceh. The first three mentioned established the

Shattariyya in West Sumatra, West Java and Trengganu respectively. Whether Dawud al-Rumi, who probably was the son of a Turkish mercenary in Aceh, was able to develop and expand the Shattariyya tradition in Aceh cannot be confirmed from historic records.

Abdurrauf died around 1693, at a time when the political power of Aceh was on its decline. The successfully enforced trade monopoly of the Dutch greatly reduced the power of the sultanate. The loss of the once dependent areas in West and East Sumatra, and of Kedah on the Malay Peninsula, was a result of this decline and accelerated further decline. Because of the weakening of Aceh's commercial and political power, its long-distance trade was near collapse. During the eighteenth century, more and more traders from India, Arabia and China avoided the Acehnese harbours. The commercial decline went hand in hand with a decline in communication with the heartlands of Islam and a decline in religious learning. The sultanate lost its position as the centre of Malay Islamic literature and mysticism to Palembang, Patani and Banjarmasin. Aceh's cosmopolitan atmosphere was replaced by a new provincialism.

This decline affected the quality of religious knowledge. *Ulama* were no longer adequately supported by the rulers; the urbane character of Kota Raja (Aceh's capital) broke down, and scholarship fell into decay. Local traditions gained greater significance in Acehnese Islam; the countryside had defeated the city. That affected the Shattariyya as well, as it had reached Aceh in the seventeenth century as an "urban order", allied to the newest intellectual developments in the Islamic world. Now, it had to fall back on the resources of folk Islam, lost its reforming power, and became part of a syncretistic tradition. The mysterious *ileumue* (or *éleumée) sale'*, the existence of which has been documented since about 1850, was one of these pantheistic developments in Acehnese Islam and the Shattariyya.

Snouck Hurgronje, who more or less regarded any form of local development in Islam as illegitimate, described the Shattariyya in the nineteenth century in Aceh as "corrupt". He writes:

> I have called this school of Qushashi [that is, the Shattariyya] corrupt for two reasons. In the first place its Indonesian adherents have been so long left to themselves that this alone is enough to account for the creeping in of all manners of impurities in the tradition. But besides this, both Javanese and Malays have made use of the universal popularity enjoyed by the name Satariah as a hallmark with which to authenticate various kinds of village philosophy to a large extent of pagan origin. We find for instance certain formulas and *tapa* (meditation) — rules which in spite of unmistakable indications of Hindu influence may be called peculiarly

> Indonesian, recommended for use as Satariah often along with salasilahs in which the names of Abdurra'uf and Ahmad Qushashi appear. (Snouck Hurgronje 1906, p. 18)

During Snouck Hurgronje's time, the Shattariyya in Aceh must have been of little importance. He reports that "adherents of a Shattarite tariqah or school of mysticism are few and far between" (Snouck Hurgronje 1906, p. 20). As mentioned before, mystical brotherhoods in Aceh played a much smaller role than in other parts of Indonesia. J. Kreemer, in his two-volume monograph about Aceh, confirmed this thirty years after Snouck Hurgronje. He writes:

> In Aceh, one hears little of mystical brotherhoods (*tarekat*). In any case they are of much less importance here than in many other areas of the archipelago. Probably this is a result of the Aceh War. The names Na'tjabandi, Sjatariah, Kadriah and others are not unknown here in Aceh, but one finds no organised brotherhoods. (Kreemer 1922–23, p. 501)

The reasons for this development are to be found in the isolation of Aceh in the middle of the nineteenth century, and in the long Aceh War, which not only cut off the region from the dynamic thrust of nineteenth century Islamization, but put an end to all organized religious life in the region. During the twentieth century, the Naqshbandiyya-Khalidiyya advanced from the great Sufi centre of Babussalam in Langkat, North Sumatra, towards South and Central Aceh, and in West Aceh, the same brotherhood got a foothold within the Aneuk Jameu (Minangkabau) population of South Aceh, especially after the establishment of the important Dayah Darussalam in Labuhan Haji. The Shattariyya receded and many observers thought that the Shattariyya, introduced by Abdurrauf, had failed to survive the changes of the last hundred years. Teungku Haji Abdullah Ujong Rimba, the former chairman of the Acehnese association of *ulama*, does not even mention the Shattariyya in his book about Islamic mysticism in Aceh (Ujong Rimba 1975).

Nevertheless, the Shattariyya is still alive in Aceh. In the course of my research, I have found a number of Shattari centres, like the *dayahs* of Seulimum and Tanah Abee, between Banda Aceh and Sigli, and the existence of a Shattariyya community in Ulee Jalang Beutong, near Meulaboh, West Aceh. In addition to these centres, there are plenty of people in Acehnese *gampongs* (villages) who feel affiliated to the Shattariyya. Soeyatno writes about a Shattariyya community in Sibreh, a village on the road between Banda Aceh and Seulimum (Soeyatno 1977, pp. 67–69).

THE SHATTARIYYA IN SEULIMUM

The Shattariyya *dayah* in Seulimum was founded in 1953 by Haji Hanafia and is a good example of a traditional *pondok pasantren*.[10] Several small dwellings, built and inhabited by the *santri* (students), are grouped around the house of the sheikh and the mosque. A few houses for the assistant teachers, classrooms and a shop (*warung*) complete the picture. Like the design of the site itself, the curriculum in Seulimum is traditional. The age of admission is between ten and twenty-five years, there are no formal classes and the length of study is unlimited. Stays of up to nine years are not unusual. For instruction, the traditional *kitab kuning* (yellow books: so called because of the colour of the paper of these old books) are used. Islamic mysticism is taught mainly with the help of the *Kitab al-Hikam* and the *Minhaj al-Abidin*; both works are of orthodox nature. The *Kitab al-Hikam* of Ibn 'Ata Allah (d. 1309), the third *khalifa* of the Shadiliyyah brotherhood, is the best known work of Sufi literature in Indonesia. It is a jewel of Arabic literature: a compendium of Sufism based on the orthodox school of al-Ghazzali. Paul Nawiya, a commentator on the *Hikam*, characterizes the *Hikam* as "a dialectic of the mystery of God who is both obscure and transparent" (Schimmel 1975, p. 252).

Abdul Malik bin Abdullah of Pulau Manis, Trengganu, made the first Malay translation of the *Hikam* in the seventeenth century (Shafie bin Abubakar 1977). His *Kitab Hikam Melayu* was probably the basis of Raymond LeRoy Archer's English translation of the *Hikam*; the core of his dissertation was titled *Muhammadan Mysticism in Sumatra* (Archer 1937). Archer used "a Sumatran manuscript", but does not tell us exactly which one it was. He described the *Hikam* as "one of the principal texts used by the teachers of Sufism in Sumatra" (Archer 1937, p. 1), which is still the case. The *Kitab al-Hikam* and its commentaries (*Sharh al-Hikam*) can be found in most *tarekat* centres. In addition, almost every night market in Sumatra and Java offers inexpensive Indonesian editions for sale.

The second book, the *Minhaj al Abidin*, is an anthology of the most important works of al-Ghazzali: the *Ihya 'Ulum Addin*, the *Kitab al-Asrar* and the *Kitab al-Qurbah*. Sheikh Daud ibn 'Abdullah al-Jawi al-Fatani selected them and translated them into Malay. Sheikh Daud Fatani, who finished his translation in AH 1240 (AD 1823) in Taif, Arabia, is considered one of the most important Malay scholars of the nineteenth century. Together with Abd al-Samad al-Palembani, he was responsible for the al-Ghazzali renaissance in the Malay world. In addition, he was a Shattari sheikh of high standing. Even at the end of the nineteenth century, many years after Daud Fatani had died, Indonesian informants still described him as the "head" of the Shattariyya

(Henny 1921, p. 816).[11] The Shattariyya *silsilah* of Sheikh Daud Abdullah corresponds to a large extent to that in Seulimum.

The Shattariyya brotherhood in Seulimum is called the Shattariyya-Khalwatiyyah. This double name, however, does not signify a fusion of the two brotherhoods — Shattariyya and Khalwatiyyah — but indicates that during the months of Ramadan and Dhu'l-hijja, the brotherhood engages in a forty-day retreat — called *khalwat* or *suluk* — that takes place in Seulimum. During these months, or rather ten days earlier, about forty members of the Shattariyya gather in order to concentrate, in complete isolation, on the existence of God. In contrast to the *suluk* of the Naqshbandiyya, where common *dzikir* exercises are prescribed, the believers in Seulimum are completely cut off from other human beings (with the exception of the sheikh) for forty days. If they have to go outside, they are expected to cover themselves completely. Historically, the *khalwat* was not a part of Shattari tradition; in Southeast Asia, it is associated with the tradition of the Naqshbandiyya. Presumably, the Shattariyya in Seulimum adopted the practice of the *khalwat* from the Naqshbandiyyah.

During my visit to Seulimum, the then presiding sheikh told me that his brotherhood has the additional name of Samadiyyah, Shattariyya Khalwatiyyah Samadiyyah. There was a brotherhood called Samadiyyah in Syria, but I do not believe that we can construct a relationship between the Syrian Samadiyyah and the *tarekat* in Seulimum.[12] I believe that the sheikh of Seulimum, perhaps as a whim, adopted the additional name from the Khalwatiyya Sammaniyya, which is widespread in South Sulawesi, and which was introduced by Bugis transmigrants to Sumatra as well. In any case, the sheikh of Seulimum could not give me a convincing explanation as to the origins of the name Shattariyya Khalwatiyya Samadiyyah; in fact, he did not even care to think about it. Surprisingly, he could not (or would not) provide information about his Shattari *silsilah* as well. However, he was certain that Abdurrauf had nothing to do with the Shattariyya in Seulimum. He was convinced that Abdurrauf had been a Naqshbandi. Still, from the little information that I was able to obtain in Seulimum and from other sources, it is possible to reconstruct the *silsilah* of the Shattariyya in Seulimum.

The present sheikh received his *ijazah* (right to teach) from Haji Hanafia, who died in 1965 at over ninety years of age. Haji Hanafia received his *ijazah* from Tuangku Haji Abdul Jalil bin Hassan of Abée Gatah — an old and important centre of Islamic knowledge in Aceh. Tuangku Abdul Jalil, who lived in Mecca for forty years, was a contemporary and friend of Tuangku Chik Tanoh Abée, also known as Sheikh Abdul Wahab Tanoh Abée, founder of the great manuscript collection of Tanoh Abée, which still exists. I was able to copy his *silsilah* in Tanoh Abée, and I assume that it is the same as that of his friend and colleague Abdul Jalil. The reconstructed *silsilah* of Seulimum may, thus, look like this:

Sheikh Seulimum
Haji Hanafia, Seulimum, Aceh
Abdul Jalil bin Hassan, Abée Gatah, Aceh
Muhammad Asat Tahir, Mecca
Muhammad Said Tahir
Mansur Badiri
Muhamat Asat Tahir
Ibrahim Tahir
Muhammad Tahir
Ibrahim al-Kurani
Ahmad al-Kushashi
(and so on, like that of Abdurrauf)

From this *silsilah*, we can conclude, first, that there was a new introduction of Shattariyya in Aceh towards the end of the nineteenth century, and second, that the Shattariyya *silsilah* that goes back to Abdurrauf and which is widespread in Southeast Asia, no longer exists in Aceh — the very land in which Abdurrauf lived and taught.

The above mentioned Shattari *silsilah* is to be found in a slightly altered form in Buntet, Cirebon, and in Bantul, Yogyakarta, as well. Incidentally, it disproves Snouck Hurgronje's assertion that the Shattariyya was no longer known in Mecca in the nineteenth century, for the spiritual genealogies of Seulimun and Tanah Abée were definitely acquired by Malay *ulama* in the Haramayn.

In addition, this *silsilah* reflects a typical development in Sufism over the last few centuries: the increasing tendency for descendants to inherit spiritual offices. Up to Sheikh Ibrahim Kurani, the succeeding masters of the *silsilah* had not been related to each other. However, from Ibrahim Kurani onwards, the office of *tarekat* sheikh was passed down within the same family. Muhammad Tahir was his son, Ibrahim Tahir, his grandson, and so on.

The Shattariyya *dayah* of Seulimum gets little attention and little respect from the Islamic intelligentsia of Aceh. The sheikh, his teachings and practices are the object of scepticism, if not rejection. Although he, as can be seen from the books he uses for the purpose of teaching is beyond any suspicion of having deviant beliefs, many aspects of his Islam are regarded as *bidah*. Urban, educated Muslims have a certain reservation about mystical thought.

The attitude of my Acehnese colleagues who took me to Seulimum was ambivalent. On the one hand, they were amused by all these (as they called it) "relics of the nineteenth century". On the other hand, they were impressed by the self-assured calmness and charisma of the sheikh. It seemed to me that in their hearts, rejection competed with yearning. The tension between literal, rational-contextual and gnostic understanding of belief are the major lines that cut across urban Acehnese Islam. Naturally, the peasants of Seulimum do not experience this ambivalence. For them, the mystical version of Islam is Islam itself, and the sheikh is their unquestionable spiritual leader.

The *santri* of the *dayah* of Seulimum come from nearby rural households. As a rule, they return there after their studies, so they regard their time in the *dayah* less as training for a subsequent profession, than as learning for life and the hereafter. *Santri* regard the state-run schools not as competing but as complementary institutions, which however are incapable of transmitting the most important part of Aceh's cultural heritage, an extensive Islamic education. The many hundreds of young people in Seulimum also demonstrate that Islamic knowledge in Aceh still represents a value, even if this kind of knowledge contributes little to preparing them for a modern, achievement-oriented society.

As a rule, the *santri* are not initiated into the brotherhood during their training. They enter the brotherhood once they have fulfilled their duties to their families, when they are about forty years old. Within the esoteric evaluation of numbers, which is widespread in Sufism, forty is the number of perfection. Muhammad had his first vision at the age of forty, forty is the numerical value of the letter "*mim*" (the first letter of the name of the Prophet Muhammad), and forty divides man from God, "because the difference between the heavenly name of the Prophet, Ahmad, and the word *ahad*, 'the One', that is, God, is only an 'm', the number forty" (Endres and Schimmel 1984, p. 265). So, at the age of forty, many former *santri* return to Seulimum to be initiated into the Shattariyya brotherhood.

Politically, the *dayah* and the *tarekat* in Seulimun were always affiliated with Persatuan Tarbiya Islam (PERTI), which now is part of the Islamic party PPP (Partai Persatuan Pembangunan).[13] PERTI was founded as a traditional Islamic party in the 1930s in West Sumatra, as a political response to modernistic Islamic movements (especially the Muhammadiyah). It was a kind of Sumatran answer to the Nahdlatul Ulama, a Javanese party of orthodox Sunni (the Ahlussunnah wal Jama'ah). In the beginning, PERTI was dominated by sheikhs from the various Sufi brotherhoods.

In Seulimum, however, people emphasized to me that political questions play little role in day-to-day matters and that they thought of themselves as neutral in respect to political parties. I have seen no election statistics from Seulimum, but there are some for the neighbouring district of Sukamakmur, where there are a number of small Shattariyya *dayah*, branches of that in Seulimum. These statistics reveal the charismatic influence of the Shattariyya sheikhs. For example, in the village of Lemtengoh, Lambaro, where the Shattariyya is present, two-thirds of the population voted for PERTI in 1971. Whereas, in the whole province of Aceh, PERTI only received 13 per cent of the votes (Soeyatno 1977, pp. 73–74). Apparently, the Shattari sheikhs are not as politically detached as they claim to be in interviews with foreigners.

To summarize: the Shattariyya in Aceh no longer exists in its original form (i.e. the *silsilah* tradition of Abdurrauf. The Shattariyya in Seulimum arrived in Aceh only at the beginning of the twentieth century and has hardly expanded during the last eighty years. It is a typical rural brotherhood, which has to some extent developed its own rituals, as the example of the introduction of the *khalwat* indicates. There are no ties to other Shattari groups (except to those of Tanah Abée). The Shattaris of Seulimum regard themselves as orthodox representatives of the Ahlussunnah wal Jama'ah and call themselves the Salafiyah (which is in contrast to the common use of the word in Indonesia, which is a synonym for a modernist Muslim). The mystical system of the seven degrees of being, Martabat Tujuh, is completely unknown in Seulimum.

THE SHATTARIYYA IN SEUNAGAN, WEST ACEH

The Shattariyya in Seunagan has up to now not found any scholarly attention. My writing has to be regarded as a first approximate look at the history and transformation of this group. It is based on published and archival material, an article in the Indonesian magazine *Editor* (12 September 1987) and on interviews I did in Meulaboh in March 2005, June 2006 and April 2007.

West and South Aceh were and are of only marginal significance for Acehnese culture. Commercially, the West Coast was of no big importance over many centuries, because of its poor harbours and narrow hinterland. Only after pepper plantations were opened there during the nineteenth century did this part of Sumatra increase in importance and draw settlers from Pidie, as well as from Minangkabau. Despite the region's economic and political underdevelopment, Islam seem to have arrived early to the West Coast, at least to its southern fringe around Singkel and Barus.

It was the area around the Meulaboh and the Seunagan River that permitted more concentrated settlement. There, the mountains recede a little from the coast and two river basins permit the cultivation of wet rice. The area around Meulaboh and Seunangan was settled about three hundred years ago by people from Minangkabau and Pidie, who displaced a small ethnic group related to the Batak and Gayo, the so-called Mantir (Langen 1888). The Minangkabau were mainly rice farmers, pepper planters and traders. The people from Pidie were gold miners, at least as long as there was gold to be found in the rivers (*Memorie van Overgave*, 1935). The opening of pepper plantations along the west coast started in the late eighteenth century, when the demand for pepper on the world market could not be met by other regions anymore. The first plantation were opened south of Meulaboh, in a region called Nagan Raya today (Drewes 1980, p. 3). At first, the harvest was taken to the pepper ports in Minangkabau, but during the nineteenth century, pepper traders, mostly Americans, started going straight to the source in West Aceh.

Seunagan is situated in one of the areas that were already open in the early nineteenth century for pepper production. Its settlers came primarily from Pidie. Seunagan also had an especially high proportion of descendants of the Prophet Muhammad, called "*Teungku Jet*" or "*Habib*". Snouck Hurgronje, however, assumed that these people were "pseudo sayyids". Unfortunately he gives us no argument that would support this statement. Still, they were and still are highly respected. All leading *ulama* of Seunagan are descended from this group. Thanks to endogamy and their religious knowledge, they have maintained their important social status up to this day.

The centre of the Shattariyya in West Aceh is the small town of Ulee Jalang, the capital of the sub-district (*kecamatan*) of Beutong, which is part of the newly established Kabupaten Nagan Raya. Here, the Shattariyya seems to have emerged from the *éleumée salé*, which attracted some attention from the Dutch at the beginning of the twentieth century. "*Éleumée salé*" can be translated as "teaching of the wanderer (on the way to God)" — a term which the Shattaris also use to describe themselves. The first reference to this "sect" I found in a letter by Snouck Hurgronje to Ignaz Goldziher. Snouck wrote on 18 October 1898 to his Hungarian friend, from Telok Semawe (Lhok Seumawe):

> On our excursions to the interior of Pidie we came across an unusual Sufi sheikh, who had many followers among the headmen and lesser folk. Some years ago, his teacher felt victim to the orthodox fanaticism of the Fuqaha. He now lives with his disciples in a fortified village, in the middle of which is the grave of that martyr of tasawwuf. Fortunately for him, public opinion has since resisted further executions *in majorem fidei gloriam* [for the greater glory of the faith]. He is the only spiritual leader who preaches against the

> jihad,[14] but he does not dare to show great enthusiasm for peace, for that would be the end of his popularity. (Snouck Hurgronje 1985, p. 223)

The martyr that Snouck Hurgronje mentions was Muhammad Sa'id, better known as Teungku Teureubue.[15] He was a charismatic teacher who drew hundreds of men and women under his spell and, as a result, aroused the mistrust of his colleagues. Teungku Teureubue was accused of heresy and executed, together with several of his followers, between 1860 and 1870. This Sufi sheikh, who was also reputed to be a master of Arabic grammar, was buried in the fortified village of his disciple Teungku Gan: Gampong Teupin Raya, Pidie (Snouck Hurgronje 1906, vol. II, pp. 13–14).

A *Nota van toelichting betreffende het Landschap Seunagan* of July 1935 erroneously reports that this "Teungku Teurabo" brought the "teaching of Salik or Sulu'" (that is the Shattariyya) to Seunagan, West Aceh, around 1870 (*Memorie van Overgave*, 1935, pp. 9–10). This could not be true, since Teunku Teureubo was, as Snouck Hurgronje reported above, killed around 1860 in Pidie. The Shattariyya was introduced to Seunagan by Habib Seunagan, a man from Peunado' in Pidie, who died in 1888.[16] According to the testimony of his enemies, he propagated an extremely eclectic doctrine and reformulated the creed as follows: "There is no God beside God and this habib is the body of the Prophet" (Snouck Hurgronje 1906, vol. II, p. 14). One of the spiritual successors of Habib Seunagan was a certain Teungku di Krueng (d. 1902) (Langen 1888, p. 467).

When Dutch troops occupied West Aceh between 1900 and 1910, they met strong resistance organized by the "*sale'-clergy*". It is said, that the son and grandson of Habib Seunagan, Teungku Padang Sale' and Teungkuh Puteh, played leading roles within the anti-colonial resistance movement. Only after their surrender in 1910 was the region subdued.

The Shattariyya or *ilmu* (*éleumée*) *sale'* again was involved in the "religious crazes" in Mandjeng (in 1916) and in upper and central Tadu (in 1922). At the time, the head of the *tarikat sale'* was Habib Muda, another grandson of Habib Seunagan. In the 1920s, the "sect", as the Shattariyya was called by the Dutch, was well entrenched in Meulaboh, Seunagan, Blang Pidie and Susoh. Its adherents were accused of meeting secretly for spectacular rituals, in which ritual sexual practices supposedly took place. The charge that adherents of the *tarekat* violated sexual norms was a common way of discrediting Sufi brotherhoods in the archipelago. We find it directed against the Ahmadiyya in Kelantan, the Shattariyya in Minangkabau, and the Khalwatiyya Sammaniyya in South Sulawesi. Certainly this charge says more about the imagination of their opponents than about the religious practices of the brotherhoods.

The Dutch colonial officials in West Aceh regarded the "sect of the teaching of Salik or Sulu'", as they called the Shattariyya Brotherhood, and as a kind of dinosaur — as a religious-historical fossil that would not survive the "civilizing" impact of colonial rule. Measured against this expectation, the Shattariyya in West Aceh survived the tremendous upheavals of the twentieth century surprisingly well. The Shattariyya today is still an important religious, social and political force in West Aceh. It has remained one of the pillars of popular Islam. Furthermore, its leadership is still in the hands of the family of Habib Seunagan, who established it in the region more than a hundred years ago. Thus, it is an example of the ability of the traditional elites to adjust to changed political and social conditions and to carry on their task of leadership in a modern context.

Habib Muda, the grandson of the founder of the Shattariyya in Seunagan, who is said to have played a role in the "religious crazes" in Mandjeng (1916) and in upper and central Tadu (1922), was to become even better known in his later years under the name of Habib Muda Mahyiddin Seunagan. For a long time, he was the unchallenged religious head and most important political figure in West Aceh. When, in the 1950s, Daud Beureu'eh and his forces rebelled against the Indonesian central government in Jakarta and wanted to establish an Islamic state in Aceh, he looked around for allies. Above all, he turned to the religious authorities of the individual regions of Aceh. With their help, he hoped to achieve the broadest possible support for his movement. Although he was successful with this strategy in the great centres of population in North Aceh, where the reform-minded *ulama* supported him, almost all of the *tarekat* leaders refused to cooperate with the rebels.

Habib Muda Mahyiddin Seunagan also denied Daud Beureu'eh his support.[17] He explained that political activities were not among the duties of a *tarekat* sheikh. Had he forgotten that he himself organized the local anti-colonial opposition in the 1920s? Certainly not. Habib Muda was simply not willing to support the policies of the modernist union of *ulama*, PUSA, which had led the insurrection. His refusal was most probably not a question of any great sympathy for the central government led by Sukarno, but represented his disdain for Islamic modernism. Even the fact, that only a few years after the fall of Sukarno, Habib Muda let himself be recruited by the Order Baru (Suharto's regime) as an important Islamic supporter, did not mean very much. Jakarta is, from the perspective of Seunagan, a place on a different planet: too far to influence everyday life in West Aceh, but too close to be totally neglected. However, for Habib Muda's grandson, Teungku Said Hasbi Daud, the distance and political space has already been bridged. He joined, as a member of GOLKAR, the Acehnese provincial parliament.[18]

Another grandson, Dr Teuku Zulkarnaini was elected Bupati of Nagan Raya in December 2006. The fact that he came to power through a democratic election shows that the traditional standing of the Habib Muda family has survived all the troubles of the last few years and is still strong and unchallenged. Interesting is the fact that Dr Zulkarnaini, who is not a religious scholar (*teungku*), has been conceded the title of *teuku* (quasi aristocrat) (*Serambi Indonesia*, 30 April 2007). The long tradition of leadership in his family in the Seunagan area have made these "psyeudo sayyids", in the words of Snouck Hurgronje, "psyeudo aristocrats".

The most important person among the Shattaris in Seunagan in recent years has not been Teungku Said Hasbi Daud, but his mother, Maknah. Maknah (her full name being Hajjiah Aja Peunawa) is a daughter of Habib Muda Seunagan. In popular imagination, she has inherited a great share of the *baraka* (spiritual power) of her father, and, by leading an exemplary life, has acquired even more of it. In the 1980s, her house was a pilgrimage site. Every day, people came to ask her for amulets or spiritual formulas to cure their sick children or to ward off other adversities.

Maknah, however, was never the official head of the Shattariyya in Seunagan. Her brother, Habib Quraisy bin Habib Muda Seunagan, held that office. As a rule, women may play an important role in "brotherhoods"; in fact, in *dzikir* practices, they are usually in the majority. However, public offices, like that of the *khalifa*, remain barred to them. Maknah, however, is proof that office and charisma are not necessarily linked: the brother has the respect of the people, while the sister has their love and their blind trust.[19]

I have, unfortunately, found no information about the *silsilah* (the spiritual and historical lines of transmission) of the Shattariyya in West Aceh. Archival material suggests that the Shattariyya in Seunagan can be traced back to the above-mentioned Teungku Teureubo. In the Dutch colonial government's *nota* of July 1935 (*Memorie van Overgave*, 1935), the Shattariyya in Seunagan was called the "teaching of Salik or Sulu'". A *salik* is a "wanderer on the mystical path", an adherent of a mystical brotherhood. The *suluk* or (*sulu'*) is the ten-, twenty- or forty-day retreat of the Sufis, which we already came across in Seulimum. The *suluk* is today an essential feature of the Shattari in Seunagan; there, it is also called the *mujahadah* (striving for inner purification) or *riadhah* (exercise of the self). The *suluk* takes place during the month of Ramadan and, optionally, during the month of the birthday of the Prophet, Rabi'ul-awwal, or during the month of the pilgrimage, Dhu'l-hijja. They attract hundreds of people, so much so that the little *meunasah* (house of prayer) of Maknah often is not large enough to accommodate all of them. The goal of these strenuous meditation exercises is, through the virtually endless, rhythmic repetition of the names of Allah, to lessen the indescribable distance between man and God. "Members of a *tarekat* have no other goal than to come closer to God. Only that. There is no other purpose," said Teungku Haji Muhammad, leader of the *suluk* meetings in Seunagan (Musthafa Helmy 1987). Certainly his statement is correct, although from the standpoint of group dynamics, the imposing experience of a forty-day retreat probably has far-reaching effects on the individuals participating. Today, the psychosocial role of the *tarekat* in village society has still lost nothing of its importance, and the charismatic leadership of the brotherhoods still exercises great attraction, in spite of the widespread existence of state and religious bureaucratic structures.

In view of the central importance of *suluk* for the Shattari in Seunagan, I am convinced that the Shattariyya in Seunagan comes from the same tradition as that in Seulimum. That means that the Shattariyya in West Aceh did not descend from the great Acehnese saint Abdurrauf, but rather represents a relatively new introduction. Probably, it was brought from Mecca through Patani to Aceh in the nineteenth century. Perhaps, Teunku Teureubo was even a student of Daud Abdullah Patani.

CONCLUSION

The short history of the Shattariyya in Aceh reflects a continuum of transformation and reinvention. The Shattariyya came to Aceh in the seventeenth century as a reform movement which was supported by the Islamic elite. Abdurrauf, one the most important Islamic scholars in the history of Malay Islam, introduced a new approach to Islamic mysticism in Aceh and beyond. The Shattariyya became a powerful instrument for the Islamization of the archipelago. However, in the course of time, the Shattariyya sank to the level of folk Islam and Abdurrauf survived in the consciousness of the Acehnese only as a miracle-working holy man, as the Sjech Kuala (the master of the river mouth, as he is thus known because his tomb lies near the mouth of the Aceh River). When, during the nineteenth century, a new, powerful wave of Islamization reached the Malay world, the Shattariyya was reintroduced into Aceh. This time, too, the Shattariyya came as reform movement, as part of the great al-Ghazzali renaissance. The Acehnese experience contradicts the prevalent opinion that the Shattariyya was a "spent bullet" by that time, displaced by the recently introduced (or re-introduced) *tarekats:* the Naqshbandiyya, Qadiriyya and Sammaniyya. Because of the colonial war in Aceh, the "new Shattariyya" could not form strong roots or develop any strength as a reform movement. By the end of the Aceh war, most Acehnese *ulama* had been killed or driven into exile. The next generation of religious leaders, who studied in Minangkabau, Kedah and the Middle East were strongly influenced by the Salafiyah — Islamic modernism. Once again, the Shattariyya slipped to the level of "Little Tradition". However, the Shattariyya took its chances and adjusted, especially after Indonesian independence, to the new situation. During the time of a authoritarian rule, some of them were integrated into the pseudo-parliamentary system of the province, and now, in the time of democracy, one of them has been elected Bupati. Others have remained the charismatic religious focus of local cultural life. The Shattariyya, who reached Aceh almost 350 years ago, has somehow survived to this day. This is, by all accounts, not a small achievement.

Notes

1. All quotations from the Qur'an are from *Der Koran* (1977), translated by Rudi Paret.
2. The social system of the Sultanate of Buton, in southeast Sulawesi, was organized along the seven categories of the mystical system of Martabat Tujuh. The lowest strata of society corresponded with first differentiation within the seven grades of being (Martabat Tujuh). The architecture of the mosques in Kelantan also drew on this mystical system.
3. In the case of Hamzah Fansuri, this supposition is based on the following two lines of poetry:
   Hamzah Fansuri sedia zahir
   Tersuci pulang pada sayyid Ábdu'l-Qadir.
   (Hamzah Fansuri, who at first followed external science, was brought by Sayyid Ábdu'l-Qadir to the pure (inner) path.)
   This by no means implies actual membership in the Qadiriyya. It would have been strange if the "monistic" Hamzah were in the orthodox Qadiriyya and the orthodox ar-Raniry in the heterodox Rifaiyya. ar-Rainiry is said to have been inducted into the Rifaiyya by Sayyid Abu hafs Úmar ibn Ábdullah Ba Syaiban.
4. See the work of Geertz (1971) and Gellner (1969).
5. These were by Isma'il Ya'kob (1975), Said Aiyub Abdullah (1979), Usman Nuris (1979), Jumat Sehat (1983), and Jamluzzaini (1995).
6. On the life of Muda Wali, see Teungku Muhibbuddin Waly (1993).
7. See the biographies of leading Acehnese *ulama* in Ali Hasjmy (1997), and the *Ensiklopedi Pemikiran Ulama Aceh* (2004). Another important influence was the *pondok pesantren* of Yan in Kedah, which had been established by Acehnese *ulama*.
8. Johns (1965) is an edited translation of this work.
9. The term "neo-Sufism" is still controversial in Islamic studies and has not yet been fully elaborated upon.

10. All information about Seulimum comes from interviews and observations made during a visit at the beginning of April 1986.
11. Henny's article is extremely confused; Snouck Hurgronje (without having read the article) understandably spoke negatively above him (Snouck Hurgronje 1957–65, p. 1465).
12. The Samadiyyah is a little-known descendant of the Qadiriyyah that goes back to Muhammad as Samadi (d. 1589), and existed mainly in Syria.
13. PERTI is divided into two factions: PERTI Asli, which belongs to the Islamic party PPP, and PERTI Murni, which is part of the government party GOLKAR. The people in Seulimun are attached to PERTI Asli.
14. This refers to the resistance of the Achenese against the Dutch.
15. Teureubue is in IX Mukum Keumangan, Pidie.
16. This is according to Kreemer (1923), p. 500.
17. Here, he went along with the Naqshbandi Sheikh Muda Wali of Labuhan Haji, Aceh Selatan, and Teungku Haji Muhammad Hasan Krueng Kaleé, a sheikh of the Haddadiyya *tarekat*. All three of them stayed loyal to the republic.
18. This and the following information is from the article by Musthafa Helmy (1987).
19. The same situation can be found at present at the Naqshbandiyya Dayah Darussalam in Labuhan Haji. There as well, it is the women who are the charismatic personalities. When we visited the place in 2005, it was basically the women who talked to us and supplied us with valuable information. The sheikh was a weak man who was unable to hold up the presumption that he was the boss of the *dayah*.

12

NIAS AND SIMEULUE

Wolfgang Marschall

A chain of islands follows the west coast of the Indonesian island of Sumatra at a distance of about one hundred kilometres. Some call this chain the Barrier Islands. It consists — from the southeast to the northwest — of Enggano Island and the Mentawai archipelago, situated south of the equator, and the islands of Nias (with Hinako to the west and the Batu Islands to its south) and Simeulue (with the Banyak Islands to its east) situated north of the equator. It is the latter two, Nias and Simeulue, and some adjacent small islands just mentioned, which were highly affected first by an earthquake and then, the tsunami on 26 December 2004, and again by an earthquake (of 8.7 on the Richter scale) on 28 March 2005. This chapter offers a summary of the social history of Nias (and Simeulue) and the cultural repertoires and attitudes of their inhabitants.

SOME SIMILARITIES, MANY DIFFERENCES

Geologically, these islands are part of the non-volcanic outer arch of the Sunda continent; they are, in general, formed of sedimentary rocks (Scholz 1983, p. 191). The soils of Nias and Simeulue are similar, podsolic soils, which in spite of high temperatures and abundant rainfall, allow mainly swidden agriculture. Beyond these few though important elements, Nias and Simeulue are quite different.

In terms of administration, Simeulue forms one *kabupaten*, and the Banyak islands, being a part of the *kabupaten* of Aceh Singkil, belong to Nanggroe Aceh Darussalam (the official name of the province of Aceh), while Nias, consisting of two *kabupaten*, belongs to the province of North Sumatra. Language-wise the inhabitants of Simeulue and Nias both speak languages and corresponding dialects that belong to the Austronesian language family. However, they differ in that the Simeulue language is closely related to Acehnese, with strong Malay influences, whereas the Nias language, with its two dominant dialects, is more closely related to languages from Sulawesi and probably Oceania. On the other hand, one of the languages of Simeulue, Sikhule, is related to Nias and is probably proof of the assumption that, in earlier, pre-Islamic times, Simeulue was inhabited by Nias-related people.

Also, in cognitive ordering and religious attitudes, people on Simeulue and people on Nias differ widely, with Simeulue being inhabited almost exclusively by Muslims, while Nias has a mainly Christian population. Before going into this in some detail, a last field of differences shall be mentioned, i.e. the history of research on Nias and Simeulue.

While there have been only a few publications on Simeulue, written mainly by linguists, literature on Nias is wide and encompassing. While there are three monumental early works on Nias by the Italian natural scientist Modigliani (1890) and the two Dutch authors Schröder (1917) and Kleiweg de Zwaan (1913–15) and also, an important early travel report by Brenner-Felsach (1998), nothing comparable can be found for Simeulue. While there is more recent anthropological literature based on fieldwork for Nias, e.g. Marschall (2002), Feldman et al. (1990), Beatty (1992), Viaro (1980), Ziegler (1985), Scarduelli (1985, 1990) and others, one looks in vain for scientific results based on field research in Simeulue. And, if there did not exist the mainly linguistic studies by Kähler (1938, 1940, 1952, 1955, 1959, 1961, 1963) on Simeulue, one would also have to look in vain for something comparable to what has been described, analysed and compiled by missionaries and physicians, working for them, on Nias, in the works of Thomas (1886), Fehr (1911), Sundermann (1905), Fries (1911) and Steinhart (1934), and in the analysis of religion by Moelder and of a religious movement by Müller (1931; cf. Müller-Krüger 1968), and more recently, in the writings of Hämmerle (1982, 1999). Nor has Simeulue social and cultural history ever given rise or added to wider anthropological comparison or theory like Nias has in the work of Heine-Geldern (1961), Birket-Smith (1946), Kunst (1939–40), Suzuki (1970), and others. And finally, nothing comprehensive has been written on or recorded of Simeulue music, whereas Kunst (1939–40) has done so for the rich music of Nias, and nothing comparable to Nias wood and stone carving has ever been detected on Simeulue.

NIAS

Settlements and Houses

The island of Nias is a hilly and very rugged country of close to 5,000 square kilometres. Due to high precipitation, rivers in their narrow valleys can swell within minutes and can destroy lives and land through floods and landslides. Before the Dutch conquered the island in the early twentieth century and forced the Niha to settle in the plains or at the foot of the mountains, settlements were built on top of hills, as can still be seen in many place names (the prefixes *hili-* and *bavö-* meaning "hill"). These settlements were often surrounded by palisades, serving mainly as shelter against attacks from other villages.

Villages appear in two forms. In the northern and central parts, houses are arranged as stray settlements, whereas the southern part of the island features houses arranged in two rows along the long sides of a paved village square. This is unique in Indonesia, as it shows traits of urban planning. In fact, villages in the south were planned after calculating how many people might live in it after it was built, before a group would split off to form another village. The number of people in a village depended on it having relatively easy access to the fields. All people on Nias lived in villages; field buildings were used only for specific agricultural reasons and seasons, and occasionally, as a place for young people to meet. That quite a number of them live in small hamlets now has to do with population growth, scarcity of land and lack of good building material. Also, coastal settlements were rare and used mainly for external trade and by some fishing families. Most Niha are afraid of the sea and try to avoid travelling by boat; thus, many local fishermen are Malays.

A village *banua* is the architectural, social, political and symbolic space for Nias, encompassing all public life in the south and most of it in the central and northern parts of the island. To let the water run off, *banua* are always built on slightly sloping ground. In the south, two prominent stairs made of often figurative stone slabs lead to the village from above and below. These stairs are indicators of the importance of the settlement since most people will remember that a slave was sacrificed and put under each stair to protect the village, and of the importance of social layers, since the upper part of anything — village court, house, landscape, humans — is the good or better part as compared to the lower. High-ranking families live in houses in the upper part of the village; the cemetery is beyond the lower stair. Usually the *bale* (the Office of Weights and Measures), housing the measures used for measuring pigs, stands in the centre of the village court. It is a modest open building, where village councils hold their meetings. In front of the houses, there may be megaliths, benches, tables, and figures of stone. Up to two thousand people live in these villages, while in the north, villages are much smaller, sometimes consisting of a few houses only. Only in southern Nias does one encounter such urban elements like a paved central way forming the *iri* (the backbone) of the village court. All adults have to walk on the *iri*, and not just when they leave the village to go to the fields, the bathing places or to other villages, but even when they are visiting people living only a couple of houses away. Thus, social control can easily be exerted. The bathing places for women and men respectively are made of dry masonry work, and the amount of settlement planning becomes apparent when one considers that villages in the south are founded only in places where two springs have their source. And, which is also singular in Indonesia, in southern Nias, village gutters drain away the rainwater from roofs.

Nias villages have astonished visitors from early on. In Idrisi's geography, from the twelfth century,[1] the dense settlement of the island and the existence of a town there are mentioned. Nias houses astonish visitors until today. They come in two types: with an oval ground plan in the north, and a rectangular ground plan in the south. These houses are built of ironwood and fit together without nails or any metal parts. They are built on huge poles and these, in turn, rest on wide stone slabs. During the frequent earthquakes, these houses just shift a little with no real damage done. In the humid climate of Nias, building material has to be solid to survive more than a couple of years. Ironwood was readily available up to World War II, when the Japanese army occupied Nias and felled almost all ironwood trees. In the 1990s, so much ironwood had regrown and to such a degree that many people started building their houses using their favourite material again. However, ironwood is on the decline again due to illegal logging.

No truly complete description of Nias houses can be given here, and so, the following brief points must suffice. Due to their extremely steep roofs and two specially hinged windows, air circulates freely through these houses, making them comfortable. The living area is divided into a front room where guests are received and where family members spend their time sitting at the open windows and looking over the village court, and the back room, which is the family room and which no one should enter unasked. Family members spend the night there, and may take their meals there. The fire place is there, and any valuables belonging to the family are stored there, usually in a wooden box. On the walls, one can occasionally see wooden ancestor figures (*adu*), which used to be in every house, but were sometimes given away or destroyed when people converted to Christianity, or were destroyed by missionaries or were sold to tourists and art dealers. These ancestor figures were regularly offered food, especially rice, to ensure good harvests. The pedestals of these figures can still be seen in many houses. The area between the piles of the house is used as a storage space for building material and is usually where the pigs are kept at night. In addition to the functional aspects of these houses, there is a strong symbolic one, in that the three levels of these houses — roof, living area, and pile area — correspond to the levels of the cosmos as conceived by the Niha people: the upper world, world of the human beings, and underworld, respectively. This strong vertical frame in the Nias world view is apparent also in how they view trees and those birds that sit at the top of trees, like the hornbill, as being closer to the upper world, while swamps, slow-running water and the sea are potential points of entry to the underworld, and no other animal is connected more closely to this than the crocodile. Their emotional distance from the sea may also have its root in this symbolism.

Elements of Nias Social Organization

This vertical frame comes even more to the fore in social organization. Nias people are organized according to *mado* (clans in patrilineal descent), which can ideally be traced back to some first being — very often to four original brothers sent down from the upper regions of the world. Nias society is not only ideologically patrilineal; it has all the characteristics of it in daily life. Women, upon marriage, go to live with their husbands, their children belong to their husbands' clan, they receive their father's clan name, and sons remain in their village, while daughters very often have to move to their husbands' villages. The ideal marriage for a man would be with his mother's brother's daughter — a so-called cross-cousin marriage. Since a man's mother should come from another clan, her brother and his daughter would also belong to this other clan. Since clans are often identical to villages, these marriages are inter-village marriages.

Out of these marriages regular marriage bonds develop, and it may well be that the often-discussed *öri* (socio-political and administrative units), of which there were more than fifty until the late nineteenth century, were mainly such marriage-conglomerates of villages than incipient state formations. More important is the regulative character of these *öri* and similar organizations: they seem to have celebrated something like the Greek *amphiktionies* (ritual meetings), during which general moral rules were made known again, including what measures were controlled, and where young people from different villages could meet or at least see each other, and during which no skirmishes or other violence was allowed. Interestingly, until today, Nias men may declare that "we marry those we fight", although there is no actual fighting any more between the clans and their villages. However, the attitude of men of different clans is always ambivalent. Men of one clan know that they need the consent of men from another clan to give them their daughters as wives, and negotiations may last for quite some time until the dowry offered is accepted and the wife will move to the man's village. On the other hand, as the father of a daughter, a man can apply many tactics to receive as much as possible for the "work force" he is giving to another clan. The "right" women may often not be available, or someone may just not have the means to ask a woman from another clan to become his wife, and thus, especially in the lower levels of society, a man may also marry a woman of the same clan under the condition that the relationship between them be farther than that of cousins of the third degree.

All these details are given not only for the interest they have as flexible elements of a complex social structure, but for their importance in structuring the life of the Nias people in the modern world. Positions in public life have to do with clans and clan names. Marriage between the clans is still considered ideal, and discussions are lively about the precedence of some clans over others and the relative and absolute value of clans. The importance of the vertical line pops up here again, since a clan, that has split off from an already existing clan, will always be reminded that it is a "younger" clan and therefore, not of the same quality. That political positions are closely linked to clans goes without saying.

There is another characteristic of Nias social structure that is so prevalent and relevant that it has to be seen as a counterpart of the clan system: social stratification. The vertical frame is obvious here. Nias society was divided into three strict layers and one additional group. The upper stratum was formed by the *si'ulu* (meaning "those from upstream" or "those from above"). They had (and have) all rights and privileges in Nias society, but were also under strong moral obligations. They formed the upper stratum in all respects. They started the agricultural circle, they organized village life, they were the ones who founded new villages, and, until two generations ago, all village heads were *si'ulu*. Only *si'ulu* were allowed to recite genealogies of more than twenty ancestral generations, only they organized jurisdiction, and only they celebrated the huge feasts of rank, where hundreds of guests were invited to luxurious meals of cooked pork and plain rice and where the *si'ulu* gave lengthy speeches and had gold ornaments made for their wives. *Si'ulu* went through a series of feasts with ever higher demands made upon them to give more. They also sought to receive a great name, a higher rank, the right to have a megalith erected for them or for someone of their choice, and to gain more and more control over the general population — the *sato* (the many).

The *sato* lived in the same type of houses as the *si'ulu*, although some of their houses might be smaller. They dressed likewise, and they followed many of the rules that the *si'ulu* were supposed to. However, the *sato* had no access to jurisdiction; they had only short genealogies, which meant that they were not allowed to speak of more than four generations of ancestors. This, of course, would prevent them from ascending to those levels close to the upper stratum, which the *si'ulu* could reach. *Sato* could only give small feasts, and could never set up megaliths. They had to step aside when a *si'ulu* passed by. *Si'ulu* created in an early but unknown period a special group out of the *sato*, whom they called the *si'ila* (those who know). This was a good strategy, since the *si'ila* were a good source of information for the *si'ulu*, and served to silence any protest by other *sato* just through their existence, and, if necessary, through their activities. *Si'ila* could acquire strong influence through their knowledge and through being good speakers during legal cases. Legal action in Nias was one of the most important social activities, not only in making a cause legally binding, but also in demonstrating who in the village belonged to the intellectual elite. Legal action was (and is) important in that, throughout the legal action, examples of good behaviour were given, moral rules were enumerated, and hints to good everyday behaviour were given. It could happen that during such sessions all the attending people were reminded that when the seashore recedes (the pre-tsunami sign), the people should run away from the shore to higher areas. Until today, no study on village law exists for Nias or any of its villages.

What happened to those who were sentenced to death? Although this was a common sentence for serious crimes, there was very often the possibility of changing the sentence to that of slavery, i.e. becoming a house slave of a *si'ulu*. These slaves were called the *savuyu* (the young ones), indicating that they needed a master to direct them. This opens a complex chapter of Nias social history and wealth. Everybody in Nias villages knows to which family and which social stratum the other villagers belong. And people will talk and gossip about someone who stems from a slave family. Male slaves, when they lived in the village, usually were forced to marry slave women to make sure that there were always a certain number of slaves "available". And if not, the *si'ulu* might organize slave raids in other parts of the island, and then, they would sell the slaves.

The gold in the wooden boxes of the Nias *si'ulu* have stemmed mainly from the sale of slaves. Iron they received for coconuts and pigs, but gold (and brass gongs) was received for slaves. Against the standard settlement pattern, some Nias people founded several coastal settlements, where slaves were sold to whoever needed them, mostly prominent Acehnese and Dutch colonists.

When the first European reports on Nias appeared, in the sixteenth century, it was clear that the Sultanate of Aceh had concentrated much of the spice trade through its port and, in addition to that, had established and controlled huge pepper plantations all along the west coast of Sumatra. For two reasons, Nias slaves were much sought after to work in these plantations. They were considered to be very strong and suitable for this work, and, since they did not follow the Islamic faith, they could be used without any objection from local Muslims. Later, from the seventeenth century on, Dutch settlers entered the arena and looked for Nias slaves to work in their gold mines in the mountain ranges of the southern part of Sumatra.

In Nias, this was literally the golden age for the *si'ulu*. Through raids or by sentencing people to slavery, the *si'ulu* received gold, which was necessary to form ornaments for their wives, to exchange for other objects, or to give as dowry. Nias *si'ulu* did not become rich and important in their society because they made people work for them (that happens still, but to a minor degree), but because they sold their own people to work for others. When the demand for slaves declined, since the plantations did not desire more slaves, and slavery was abolished, the unproductive slave-based economy of the *si'ulu* declined too.

In the meantime, however, the *si'ulu* had established a wide-ranging ideology around them, and some of them had collected huge amounts of gold, so that they could continue to survive in their position and also ask or force people to work for them. This happened regularly before celebrating the feast of rank. Someone had to find the many pigs to be slaughtered for the guests and to the honour of the feast-giver. A *si'ulu* could order a *sato* to take a young piglet and return after a given time period — usually one year — with two fat sows. Since this is not possible to achieve by just feeding the piglet, the *sato* has to take up a burden of debt to buy another pig. However, the liquidation of this debt will be very difficult.

During my first field work on Nias in 1973, the *si'ulu* showed me their empty, or almost empty, treasuries, while complaining that they did not have enough gold any more to buy bride gifts for their sons. Others did not have the money or gold to pay the dowry for their daughters. Their ceremonial expenses, as a demonstration of their wealth, helping them to receive titles and more influence, were a kind of economic bubble for the Nias *si'ulu*. Nevertheless, these families still play an extraordinary role in Nias society.

Making a Living

Alongside the extravagances of the *si'ulu* during the boom of the slave trade and probably before and after that period to a certain degree, the Nias people lived mainly on swidden agriculture. They were experts in it. Nias men would select a given plot of secondary — rarely primary — forest, cut down the undergrowth and burn it, clear the forest, and keep potential firewood and building materials. While clearing the plot, wild animals might be killed, mostly boar. Some experts would find plants used to prepare herbal medicine. Then, hill rice was sown and a whole patchwork of cultigens were planted, including sweet potatoes of many kinds, other tubers, including taro and manioc (but not yams), sugar cane, bananas, corn, and chili. The farther south one goes in Nias, the better are the yields. It is hard work to clear fields. However, the results, the combination of tasty hill rice, pork and vegetables was good.

After two years, the Nias people gave the field back to the forest. They even prepared for that by leaving an occasional tree in the new field, and by planting small trees so that the forest would grow faster. Then, they left the field fallow for ten to twelve years before clearing and cultivating it again. Earlier agricultural and anthropological studies had it that this was done since the soil was so leached that it had to regenerate. Today, most researchers are of the opinion that the main reason for the long fallow period was that weeding took so much more effort and did not offer wood suitable for cooking or construction.

In a good rotation programme in the swidden system, a given society would need about seven times as much land as would be cultivated at a given moment. This has several serious consequences. One is the development of linear societies, as they are in a better position to develop a common ground based on ancestry rather than location. Nias society is a good example of such a linear society, which, in addition, developed a tradition of inter-village fighting, even among those villages for which close relationship by marriage existed. Villagers of one village would try to "take over" land from another village. Nias stories tell of these "events" time and again. Another consequence of leaving a major part of one's land fallow was that foreign settlers could say that this was unused land. And this is what happened with planters and their plantations, which were mainly rubber plantations. Not only did the planters take as agricultural land fallow land from the villages, but possibly without knowing it, made use of a special provision in Nias land rights. Although land is considered the common property of a clan, there is a tendency towards assigning groves as private property, especially those of coconut trees. Coconut trees of the good old variety on Nias start bearing fruit at the age of twelve years. So, there is not much sense in planting coconut trees and then leaving the grove in a rotating system to be harvested by somebody else. There is a tendency in Nias villages to say that a grove is "the grove of so and so". When the planters started rubber plantations, the situation was not so different. The planters might have paid something for planting the trees, but did not, and usually could not, buy the ground that they grew on. However, they had planted the rubber trees and so it was determined that they should be granted the yields.

There were and are other reasons why Nias agriculture does not work that well any more. One is owing to Indonesian administrators' and European missionaries' insistence that the Nias people should start working wet rice fields (*sawah*). Time and again, sometimes on the flimsiest recommendations, and occasionally with some violence, the Nias people have been forced to cultivate *sawah*. The results were soon to be seen. Since most of the soil in Nias is not dense and loamy enough to support *sawah* cultivation, it has not given good, let alone better harvests. People have no time any more to work in the swidden fields with their plurality of plants. Food has become one-sided, and the *sawah* rice seeds have to be bought in at regular intervals. Fertilizer has also to be bought, and by this change, Nias peasants have become more dependent on traders and have yields of lower quality. By this process alone, Nias has become a region with poor agricultural yields. The third reason involves the wild logging that has been going on in Nias for at least the last fifteen years at high speed. Trees giving good quality wood are felled rigorously, so that people are losing building material that has just become available after the heavy losses during World War II. They are losing land to cultivate, and they are losing land through a growing number of landslides and floods.

And to this situation are added the effects of the 2004 earthquake and tsunami, which did relatively little damage. However, the effects of the earthquake of 28 March 2005 were devastating. It killed more than a thousand people and wounded many more, and damaged thousands of buildings, among them almost all those built of stone and cement and concrete, since they did not have the flexibility to withstand a quake of 8.7 on the Richter scale, but also unnumbered traditional houses, since the Nias village people did not have the time nor the building material to maintain them on a regular basis. And thus, they were left at the mercy of aid organizations.

The local government was not able to help much. The Indonesian government promised help and gave some support. However, it was mainly organizations from outside the country which helped the people to overcome the terrible situation, especially after the earthquake of 28 March 2005. Almost all roads were damaged and blocked by landslides, and almost all bridges fell down and many have still not been repaired. As the situation is changing so fast, no figures are given here. Rather, I will turn to a field which is connected closely to the people's attitudes and reactions, namely their world view and religion.

In everyday life and in festive life, Nias people are closely connected to their ancestors. The fertility of humankind, of animals and of the fields depend on the generosity of one's ancestors, and it is to them that offerings are brought. These offerings are mainly in the form of boiled rice deposited on the pedestals of the *adu* ancestor figures, which adhere to the walls of the *omo niha* (the traditional houses). Irrespective of sacrifices which may also have been made, it is these offerings that keep everyday life at the cognitive and emotional levels going. Evil spirits are feared, since one never knows what they might do, but the ancestors will be benevolent if a person behaves according to general moral expectations. That *si'ulu* are extravagant in their worship, especially in how they order craftsmen to make bigger and more exclusive sculptures of their ancestors, has not diminished the general trust of Nias people in their ancestors.

In 1832, two young Catholics went to Nias in order to proselytize. Within a few days of their arrival they died. In 1865, the Rhenish Missionary Society sent its first missionary to Nias to convert the inhabitants. Ernst Ludwig Denninger moved from Padang in West Sumatra to Gunung Sitoli, the now capital of Nias and the seat of the Dutch colonial authorities. Later during that century, missionaries visited the south of the island, which was not yet under Dutch control and whose inhabitants were considered to be very difficult to access. Missionary work was hard and during the first few decades, they were not very successful in making converts. A dramatic change started in 1916, when among the Nias people an awakening movement started, which brought many people to join the Protestant Church. During the Japanese Occupation, the Niha suffered very much. And missionary work came to a standstill, since the missionaries were expelled. After World War II, the Protestant Church came back to life on the island. In 1955, Catholic missionaries started proselytizing on Nias. They were mainly Capuchins who had been expelled from China a couple of years before. There were and are conflicts between the adherents of the two churches, to which have been added conflicts brought about by various religious sects.

Islam had a weak standing on Nias up to World War II. One of the reasons for this was that it was not a notable place for trade, and many Muslim people in Indonesia were involved in trade in some way. Another reason, for a long time, was the eminent position of pig breeding, which during the 1920s and 1930s resulted in the regular export of pigs to Singapore, where pigs were much in demand by the Chinese community. Islam, confined to coastal areas until the 1970s, became stronger mainly through the money behind it and through social work and schools run by Muslims. Now about 85 per cent of the population are Christians and about 10 per cent are Muslims. Since the Indonesian government usually prefers the building of mosques to that of churches and much financial support from Arabian countries flows to Muslim organizations in Indonesia, there is almost everywhere, and also on Nias, a permanent tension among the adherents of the different religions.

It can also be said that quite a number of the Nias people have already made use of rivalries between Christian churches. Now, some parents send their children to different religious groups for instruction; they "distribute" their children to get maximum benefits or at least, profit from each source. In the rescue operations after the tsunami and the Easter Monday earthquake, non-governmental organizations gave their support, distributed material, started building houses and began repairing roads and bridges. Given the topographic and climatic conditions, this was extremely hard work. And reconstruction did not and could not proceed as quickly as many people wished and as many helpers wanted. However, even with the large amount of help provided to restore habitats and networks, the biggest hurdle for the inhabitants still lies ahead. This problem is how to fill the needs of over 700,000 inhabitants, living on less than 5,000 square kilometres, if their livelihood cannot be returned to them. On a basic level, economic help and humanitarian support is necessary and is successful and should be continued. On an islandwide level, many more and more comprehensive efforts have to be started to help the Niha survive. As holds true for many Indonesian regions, corruption prevents much of the capital from being reinvested into rural life and into education. Jobs in commercial agriculture, the public sector and the tourism business are tempting but they offer yields only for a few people.

Since 2003, the local administration has changed so that Nias has been divided into two districts: the *kabupaten* Nias with Gunung Sitoli as its capital, and the *kabupaten* Nias Selatan (South Nias) with Teluk Dalam as its capital. Now, it will be of extreme importance to help reliable and responsible persons to take over these positions of local authority. Foreign aid will be necessary for many years to come, but it also needs local people who are willing to transform foreign help into self-help.

SIMEULUE

As mentioned in the introduction, outside knowledge about Simeulue and its inhabitants is very small and confined to the works of Kähler, with his most important booklet (1938) hardly accessible. Simeulue came under Aceh's influence very early, and today, the island can be considered a part of Aceh in social, religious and linguistic terms. Marriage patterns, be it with some local variations, follow here the patrilineal patterns of the Aceh-Islamic system. Couvade and levirate were present on Simeulue, but in this, as in most other fields, the recent mixing of Orang Aceh, Malay and Batak elements, including some earlier Nias items, is characteristic. Of houses and villages not much was left after the earthquake of 28 March 2005, as the infrastructure of the island was left almost completely in ruins. For the population, it is important to restore their infrastructure, since those who live on clove production rely on it as well as those who are fishermen — the two most important sources of income after wet rice cultivation. Dutch companies have started logging on Simeulue, and timber is still a source of income for a few. The population, being much smaller than that of Nias, is estimated to be between 32,000 and 77,000 individuals and could well survive in restored and improved surroundings. Most other elements will coincide with the situation in the areas along the west coast of Aceh.

Note

1. Cf. the edition of Idrisi (1960).

PART IV
Current Debates in Religion and Culture

13

PICTURING ACEH
Violence, Religion, and a Painter's Tale

Kenneth M. George[1]

The Acehnese have long been pictured as a thoroughly Islamic society, a people whose fervent attachment to *dar-al-Islam* (the abode of Islam) has earned their Sumatran homeland the nickname of *Serambi Mekkah* (Mecca's Verandah). For a time between 1945 and 1953, or — by another reckoning — from 1945 through 1976, the Acehnese also proved to be fervent Indonesian nationalists, playing a key role in the formation of the Republic of Indonesia. The discourses of a transcendent religion and a transcendent nation have been powerfully compelling forces in Acehnese public life, yet they could not put a check to the spread of grievance and fear or to the culture of violence and martial law that have possessed Aceh for the past fifteen years. Indonesia's calculated civic interventions — renaming the province Nanggroe Aceh Darussalam (The State of Aceh: The Abode of Peace) in 2001 and instituting *syari'ah* (Islamic) law in Aceh in 2002 — have been ineffective in soothing social wounds and bridging the troubled gap between identifications: Acehnese, Indonesian.

That gap has become visible in Indonesia's own visual culture, especially that precinct we might call "Islamic art" because of the way its practitioners conjure an Islamic aesthetic heritage and future. It is made visible in the embrace and repudiation of images, and in the ratios of abstraction and figuration seen in painting. It can be found in the split between words and images and sometimes in their virtual fusion. Its history is a history of art and violence, and is told in a painter's tale.

THE ART AND ART HISTORY OF THE LEAST WELL-MANNERED

Consider first, a passage taken from Snouck Hurgronje's classic ethnographic work, *The Acehnese* (1906). Brought to Aceh to assist the Dutch in their programme of pacification and rule, near the close of the nineteenth century, Snouck was charged with the task of assembling a political and cultural report on Sumatra's northernmost sultanate. Snouck considered the Acehnese to be "among the least well-mannered" (Snouck Hurgronje 1906, Vol. 1, p. 119) people in the Dutch East Indies, and he had this to say about their art and art history:

> On the whole we gain the impression that the artistic sense of the Acehnese is but little developed, except in the manufacture of silk fabrics, in which much taste is displayed in both colouring and in pattern. During the period of the prosperity of port-kings, constant intercourse with strangers, and the desire of those of high rank to rival other peoples in show and splendour, may have led to the temporary importation of some degree of art, but this quickly disappeared with the political degeneration which supervened. The foreign civilization which has exercised the most lasting influence on the Acehnese, namely that of Islam, is but little favourable to the awakening or development of the artistic sense. (Snouck Hurgronje 1906, Vol. 2, p. 65)

Snouck's picture of Acehnese art is consistent with the dismissive and antagonistic views expressed in his work as a whole. The passage, however, is worth a few moments' reflection. In it, we see Snouck drawing a line between the indigenous and the alien: most Acehnese art — though Snouck hardly wants to call it that — is imported, he says, and it is the stranger — most likely the Muslim stranger — who has brought it to Aceh. It is brought at a time of prosperity and global reach, and it serves the vanities and rivalries of the elite. Its moment is the sixteenth and seventeenth centuries. The subsequent era of "political degeneration" puts it into eclipse. Though Snouck looked upon the Acehnese largely as failed Muslims,[2] he suggests here that Islam — an alien civilizing force — had little capacity to stir artistic expression. He reserves his admiration for the taste shown in local silk fabrics — their colour, their pattern. Their makers are invisible and unnamed, however. He does not say so here, but these silks are usually fabricated by women, and so the passage surreptitiously conjoins the indigenous with the hands and eyes, the looms and dyes, of Aceh's mothers, daughters, sisters, and wives. Acehnese men, by implication, are artless and visibly so. Their metalwork, jewellery, and carving do not seem to count for much.[3]

Artlessness perhaps was next to boorishness for the ethnographer. What fascinates me about the passage is how closely Snouck ties the historical trajectory of Acehnese art to politics, religion and gender. Art's absence — its not being seen — relates directly to political decline, the influence of Islam, and the marginality or eclipse of women with respect to public cultural expression. At the same time, art's absence relates directly to Snouck's ethnographic vision. His report is empty of any Acehnese claims with respect to local visual culture, and he surely had a biased view regarding what counted as "art". I also wince at his remarks on Islam, which merely repeat commonly held ideas about the way Islam is indifferent or hostile to artistic work.[4] Treating Islam as a predominantly "artless" faith is but yet another political gesture aimed at subordinating and debasing this religion vis-à-vis the Christian West and its aesthetic or visual traditions.

Yet, it is not only discursive violence that haunts Snouck's account. His ethnographic report was prepared while the Dutch sought complete occupation of Aceh in the longest war of the colonial era (1873–1914). His observations followed upon atrocities and acquiescence, and it is hard to imagine how the art of the vanquished would have been as eye-catching as the unacknowledged spectacle of death and dislocation that claimed nearly an eighth of Aceh's inhabitants.[5] "No plunder here", the ethnography could be reporting. In Snouck's eyes, the vanquished were hardly an exalted people, and in most respects were already dispossessed of cultural splendour. That lack of splendour — that absence of art — foretold political and cultural defeat before the disciplined energies and vision of the Dutch.

Perhaps the art and art history of "the least well-mannered" was not so meagre as this report suggests, even in the face of colonial violence. Consider the work of images evoked in language; although certain visual arts may have languished in Aceh, a distinct and religiously impassioned imagery endured in the *Hikayat Prang Sabil* (the *Chronicles of the Holy War*). Written by *ulama* and sung by Acehnese men, the *Hikayat Prang Sabil* were versions of an epic poem that recounted the stories of those Acehnese who had martyred themselves in the forty-year struggle against the infidel Dutch.[6] Visions of paradise are central to these poems and were an inducement to young men who assembled at the *pesantren* (Muslim boarding school) and *meunasah* (a kind of dormitory and meeting hall) to martyr themselves. Paradise is radiant with gold and opal and pearls, redolent with perfume, incense, and oil of roses, and traversed by rivers of honey and paths of diamond dust. Nymphs of astonishing and incomparable beauty attend to the pleasure and desires of the martyred. (Women stand problematically with respect to the rewards of martyrdom, which the *Hikayat* pictures as a masculine pursuit.) Paradise, of course, can only be seen after death and, according to the *Hikayat*, in reward for the violence of one's martyrdom. Violent, masculine self-sacrifice of this sort initiates a gift exchange with Allah and acts as a bridge leading over the gulf between word and image. The *Hikayat Prang Sabil* — regarded as a sort of image-text — promises (men, seldom women) a sort of visuality more immediate and present than that which can be evoked by the imagistic and image-making words that must suffice in this worldly existence.

The image-text of the *Hikayat Prang Sabil* is thus a different fabric (cf. the etymology of "text"), but an Acehnese fabric nonetheless, and one Snouck does not see or grasp as visual art. Nor could he, unless Snouck held decidedly un-Western ideas about the relationship of word and image. Unlike the striking silk fabrics that caught Snouck's eye, the *Hikayat Prang Sabil* circulated in secret recitation and manuscript form, and led some of those who heard or read it to slay infidel Europeans in what the Dutch would come to call acts of *Atjehmoord* (Acehnese murder).[7] Violence threatened to spill forth from such recitations, and so they earned violent suppression from Dutch authorities. Silks were permitted to remain in the open in a pacified colonial public, while a regime-menacing image-text was withdrawn to the margins of colonial surveillance. Acehnese visual culture in the early years of the twentieth century was thus subject to the violent dialectics at work between colonizer and the colonized. I have selected Snouck Hurgronje as its principal historian, but now turn to someone else as a figure of that history's future.

ACEHNESE FIGURES

Although he was destined to become one of Indonesia's leading painters, my friend Abdul Djalil Pirous was not "born Indonesian". Rather, he was born in 1932 in the coastal town of Meulaboh, Aceh, as a colonial subject of the Dutch East Indies. In local reckoning, things got off to an auspicious start. Pirous was born at noon on Friday, March 11, of that year. The Friday noon hour is, of course, the time set aside for the weekly convocation known as *shalat Jum'at*, a time when Muslims gather together to make their obligatory midday prayers at the mosque or prayer-room and to listen to sermons. His father, Mouna Piroes Noor Muhammad (1871–1946), asked the religious teacher who boarded with the family, Fakih Nurdin, to name his infant son. And so young Pirous came into the world bearing the name Abdul Djalil Saifuddin (meaning, "son of"–"the sublime"–"the sword of the faith"). Mouna Piroes Noor Muhammad was a descendant of a Gujarati-Sumatran trading family and was given the nickname 'Piroes" because of an unusual turquoise (*pirus*) birthmark on his left arm. Many thought the birthmark a sign of spiritual significance and potency, one that set Mouna Piroes Noor Muhammad apart from others. Indeed, he was the head of the town's Asia Muka (South Asian) community, and had built a *madrasah* (religious school) and *surau* (prayer room). Djalil — as his son was called — was thus blessed, born during an auspicious moment of communal *shalat* (prayer) and *dzikir* (remembrance), and in time, taking the name derived from the potent bluish birthmark on his father's arm.

Djalil's mother, Hamidah, (1892–1957), was Acehnese, though it is not clear whether one would have used, in those days, an ethnic term like that about people or art from Aceh. Hamidah was from Meulaboh and did not trace descent beyond her natal town. She was no less pious than her outsider husband, but unlike him, Hamidah was drawn toward religious practices associated with the mystical Islamic *tarekat* — for example, reciting the twenty exalted qualities of God or the ninety-nine "beautiful names" of God (*asma Tuhan*). And unlike Mouna Piroes Noor Muhammad, who frowned on art as something that conflicted with Islam, Hamidah seems to have pursued her faith in part through artistic endeavours. When speaking to curators, art journalists, critics, and scholars, Pirous generally points to his mother Hamidah as a driving force and inspiration in his becoming an artist. As he put it, "My mother was truly an artist. My father didn't have a drop of artistic blood, but my mother had it strong." Hamidah was an adept in several of the Islamic arts. She was especially skilled in Qur'anic recitation and in storytelling, and made a practice of writing down Acehnese and Malay-language stories and poems in Arabic script. She also excelled at sewing the gold-embroidered velvets, felts, and silks used for ceremonial occasions, like weddings and circumcisions. Among these are the *kasab* (see Figure 1), whose geometric patterns Pirous would later appropriate as icons of his ethnic roots. Making a *kasab* could take a year or two of labour, sometimes more, and Hamidah was assisted by her children in preparing patterns, stretching fabric, and so on. It often fell to Djalil to mix inks and prepare varnishes, and to this day, Pirous can detail every step and technique used in preparing the *kasab*. Pirous' enchanted reverence for the artistry his mother brought to stories and fabric found its most explicit expression in a 1982 serigraph (see Figure 2) called *Sura Isra II: Homage to Mother* (*Sura Isra II: Penghormatan buat Ibunda*). It features brightly coloured vertical borders patterned directly after Acehnese ceremonial curtains called *tabir*; an image of the winged *bouraq* (the Prophet Muhammad's legendary mount); and a two-dimensional reproduction of a red and gold *kasab* made by Hamidah herself, inscribed with the Qur'anic verse revealed at Mecca and traditionally associated with the Prophet's night journey and ascension to Heaven on the *boura*q (QS 17 Bani-Isra'il, verse 1).

At first glance, it might seem that Pirous' recollections more or less recapitulate the views of Snouck Hurgronje from a century before regarding Acehnese art. Pirous' father appears a bit foreign and artless, and that artlessness coincides with a conventional Muslim piety that looks unfavourably upon the arts. His mother's artfulness, in contrast, finds expression in fabric, the Acehnese material that Snouck prized for its exceptional workings of colour and pattern. However, I want to suggest that Pirous' homage to Hamidah does not accord so fully or simply with his recollections about his artistic roots, or with Snouck's historical views on art. Let us examine that silk-screened image *Sura Isra II*, again, this time in juxtaposition with the *kasab* of Hamidah's original manufacture. The serigraph erases the gold arabesque that Hamidah embroidered into the *kasab*'s central diamond of blue and replaces it with Qur'anic calligraphy. This gesture, in my view, does two things: it defaces and replaces the visual centre of an originary, remembered, and revered object. It substitutes writing for the arabesque image, and at the same time turns writing into image — writing not just to be read, but writing at which one will contemplatively look.

Not reading but looking at the single Qur'anic verse in *Surat Isra II*, I note the way it is placed on a diamond of blue that recedes from the eye, giving the illusion of disclosed depth behind the advancing reds of the *kasab*-square. The writing is thus made to float. Even so, the floating image of Qur'anic verse is complicated by a square pane of white and dark blue at the centre of the *kasab*-shaped field, a pane that formally recuperates the arabesque square at the heart of Hamidah's embroidery. The orthographic form of "Allah" resides as an icon of divinity at the top of the blue diamond, just beneath the mathematical centre of the serigraph as a whole.

The image is that of revealed writing. What that writing signifies — when read — is the initial line of the Qur'an's story of the Prophet's night journey. It is paired with the iconic image of the *bouraq*, taken from Hamidah's oral versions of Muslim legend. The serigraph thus pictorially renders Qur'anic scripture and religious legend as linked dimensions of Aceh's Islamic visual culture. I would argue, too, that this pairing potentially draws upon the contrast of father and mother, or masculine-feminine, as well. That is, broadly held ideas about Acehnese men and their association with Qur'anic verse and *akal* (rationality) conjoin in the serigraph with ideas about Acehnese women and their association with the sensuousness of colour, pattern, and narrative (though we should keep in mind that Hamidah and many other Acehnese women did write and recite Qur'anic verse). *Sura Isra II: Homage to Mother* thus captures some of the contending oppositions in Acehnese visual culture, and potentially refigures them through the use of writing as image.

At this point, I have gotten ahead of myself in the story I wish to tell. What will suffice for now is an appreciation of the way Pirous' work may be drawn into tensions between, and hybridizations of, word and image. That work did not just take place in paintings and serigraphs, but even in one of the most personal signs of subjectivity and identity, the writing of his name in national orthography. In the mid-1950s as he was just starting formal art training at the Bandung Institute of Technology, Indonesian orthography was officially revised so that "oe" would be rendered as "u". The artist did not like the "look" of "Pirus". To suit his graphic tastes, he wrote his name as "Pirous". Had the nation not intervened, he might still be signing himself as "Piroes". Had the nation not intervened, he might be picturing Aceh rather differently than he does today, and not as an Indonesian citizen.

NATIONALISM FROM ABOVE, ISLAMIC ART FROM AFAR

Pirous was fifteen when he started to think of himself as Indonesian. It was 1945. Aceh's part in an Indonesian identity and an Indonesian national community was not easily imagined into being at the time. Pirous remembers back:

> What did independence truly mean? The only thing we knew was that we had been ruled by the Dutch, ruled by the Japanese, and that we now wanted to have our own government ... One day a plane suddenly appeared overhead dropping leaflets and I picked one up and there was the text of the declaration ... "Our independence" and so forth. "So that the people live as one" and so on. I didn't understand what it really meant. ...[8]

Dropping a people's identity papers on them from the sky may not be a particularly efficacious speech act (and makes us realize that J. L. Austin's (1962) discussion of felicity conditions in *How to Do Things with Words* does not take readers to the political heart and horizons of "Says who?"). But like they say, it is a start. At age sixteen, Pirous joined the Indonesian Student Army and put his art skills to work, making handbills and leaflets for the nationalist campaign. So commenced his affiliation with the nation. It was through art, revolutionary violence, and Bahasa Indonesia that Pirous began to shape and understand himself as an Indonesian citizen.

A decade later, Pirous was in Bandung, West Java, pursuing formal art training with Dutch cubist Ries Mulder and absorbing the latest lessons on modernism and abstraction emanating from New York. By now, he was deeply drawn into the social and cultural energies of an urban postcolonial world, and into its tensions and debates as well. Throughout this time, Indonesian nationalism provided Pirous and his colleagues with the most crucial terms for personal allegiance, for forms of collective solidarity, for reckoning cultural pasts, and for working toward cultural and political futures. Just as crucially, nationalism also established the principal terms for mediating the artist's place in a global art world.

Not long ago, while browsing in Pirous' library in Bandung, I came across a 1957 paperback copy of Henri Pirenne's *Mohammed and Charlemagne*. The bastard page is inscribed in ink and in Pirous' hand. It reads, "States are as men, they grow out of the character of men — Plato." On the title page that follows, Pirous has placed his signature in brown pencil and beneath that, the date "4/58." The inscription reads as aphorism and lesson to the artist himself, for who else other than Pirous would likely peruse this very volume, kept in his private library? I perhaps read too much into the passage, but to me its rings of a mystifying cultural nationalism as it traces the roots of the nation-state back to the ethical conduct and thought of those individuals who are its citizens. It certainly requires of us a romantic and heroic idea of the citizen if we are to give it our assent.

But such thinking was no doubt common among the artists of the early postcolonial period. Writing about another postcolonial nation — India — Geeta Kapur has portrayed the early postcolonial artist-citizen as a figure formed by two very modern and contraposed modes of political and aesthetic will: to aspire not only to a unique and innovative artistic subjectivity, but also to an identity as a representative of a people and a nation (Kapur 1996, pp. 60–69). Holding those contradictory strains together was a faith in a unified and bounded cultural location — a nation — and an "idealized notion of the artist immersed in an undivided community" (ibid., p. 60). The heroic stature of the artist, the unitary nation, and their links to the modern are normative constructs now undergoing acute interrogation. Such interrogations notwithstanding, the pull between pursuing an autonomous and unique subjectivity and serving as a representative of a people and a nation has been the principal (if normative) tension for most Indonesian artists and art critics in the post-independence period (1945–present). In short, searching for a distinctive national identity has been as crucial to locating postcolonial aesthetic projects as it has been to asserting political autonomy. To be modern, the "imagined community" aspiring to nationhood needed modern artists whose work would be emblematic of the nation.[9] At the same time, achieving a modern artistic subjectivity, and securing a place in an international art world, demanded that an artist claim a national identity and location. Being subject to a nation, then, meant acknowledging a set of imagined political and social differences that when refracted through the discourses and techniques of art production would yield a recognizable "Indonesian" art.

Those same differences and discourses would have obscured "Acehnese art" or "Acehnese visual culture" as distinct modalities and precincts of expression, and would have rendered them as "Indonesian". Pirous, for example, showed no interest in Acehnese aesthetic traditions at this time. Nor did he claim to be making, or understand himself to be making, "Acehnese" art. The idea of "Aceh" or "Acehnese-ness" did not mediate his relationship to the Indonesian nation-state, the wider world, or his art. Neither did "Islam." To the contrary, he thought of himself in rather universalist and humanist terms as an Indonesian who made "modern art". That stance was not without its problems and dangers in the late Sukarno years, when Socialist Realism and its romantic politics of visuality were in their heyday. Pirous' rejection of realism and his decision to opt instead for the elite, universalist, and bourgeois language of the abstract was interpreted by many as a rejection of the *rakyat* (the people) — and their socialist national identity. Pirous' circumstances changed abruptly and favourably following the anti-leftist massacres of 1965 and 1966 that ushered in the Suharto era. Abstraction was no longer in danger of attracting public rebuke and ridicule, and for a time, was the pre-eminent form of Indonesian painting. Pirous felt secure, and the three years following the mass violence revealed the daring and romantic reinventions of an artist who was convinced that abstraction afforded a direct and privileged inscription of one's unique painterly subjectivity.

Pirous' immersion in abstract modernism during the 1950s and 60s in some ways produced a rupture in his artistic life. The arts of his Acehnese homeland and personal past were not recognizable to him as art, but, at best, as the sort of craft or tradition from which the modernist wants to escape. What beckoned him away from this art was a glimpse of a globalizing art world, the horizons of which were largely inscribed by Euro-American institutions and ideologies. Oblivious at the time to the Orientalist hierarchies within Euro-American discourse that would dismiss Indonesian modern art as "derivative" and "inauthentic", Pirous pursued an unconstrained subjectivity, even while mimicking — in ways charted for us by Albert Memmi (1991), Ashis Nandy (1998), and Homi Bhabha (1994) — the emergent trends of the Euro-American avant-garde.

His attitude changed significantly in the winter of 1969–70 while Pirous was on an art fellowship in the United States. The painful and growing realization that Indonesia did not count for much in the galleries and museums of the West provoked a period of search and reflection that would end in an embrace of Islamic aesthetics. Visiting the New York Metropolitan Museum of Art, he experienced what he has described in published interviews as a moment of intimate self-recognition. Looking at the museum's standing collection of Islamic art — ceramic fragments, manuscripts, calligraphy, and miniatures — he saw "Aceh". From Pirous' vantage point at that moment, Acehnese art looked neither ethnic nor primitive, but civilizational and museum-class: a local Indonesian expression of something global in scale. Once familiar possibilities of expression, long ignored during his training in modernism, returned to enthral him. They reoriented his eye and his imagination, and suggested a way to express a self-conscious Indonesian-ness in his art.

ACEHNESE ISLAMIC ART IN AUTHORITARIAN TIMES

That moment of self-recognition in New York City posed a problem for Pirous: what made an object or a set of practices "Islamic", "art", and "Indonesian"? What made them "Acehnese"? What made them "modern"? Exploring these terms and coming up with solutions was not free and open-ended work, especially in the nascent and arrested art public of Suharto's Indonesia. It is true that ideas and ideologies of nation, ethnicity, religion, modernity and art are never settled matters; they are continually up for grabs. They shift and intermingle and become subject to political manoeuvre in the most open of publics. Suharto's authoritarian regime, however, placed severe constraints on artistic expression in an attempt to purge it, and the public sphere in general, of political critique and threatening oppositional discourses. To mention just one especially relevant example, Suharto personally intervened to prevent the 1991 Istiqlal Festival from being promoted as a celebration of "Islamic Art in Indonesia" (*Seni Islami di Indonesia*). Suspicious of any gesture that would place faith before nation, he insisted instead that the event be billed as a festival of "Indonesian Art Inspired by the Spirit of Islam" (*Seni Indonesia yang Bernafaskan Islam*).

How Pirous has rethought and repositioned his art over the course of five decades is the subject of a broader work I have under way. Here, I want to dwell on the picture of Aceh that we get from his artwork. To do so, I need to emphasize that from 1945 to 1970, the prevailing discourses of Indonesian nationalism and aesthetic modernism more or less trumped his Acehnese heritage and estranged him from it politically and artistically. Therefore, whatever else it might be, however else it may be conjured, Aceh was for a time a sign of dislocation for the artist: the social, political, and cultural home he had left behind. Pirous' rediscovery of "Aceh" was more than a postcolonial artist's sincere but self-mystifying and nostalgic search for lost roots. His effort to recuperate an Acehnese-ness in his art was a calculated way to assert a distinctive religious and national identity within Indonesia, the West, and the Islamic world. Pursued during a time of authoritarian rule, this project lacked overt oppositional or critical expression and resulted in a largely acclamatory art. Following the regime's collapse in 1998 and revelations of state-sponsored atrocities in Aceh, Pirous took direct steps to depict the tragedies of state and separatist violence. That effort, on the one hand, included a re-embrace of human figuration, something that Pirous had largely abandoned after 1970. On the other hand, it also involved a reworking of the word-image emblematics that he had articulated in his thirty-year exploration of Qur'anic themes and Qur'anic calligraphy. These changes, I want to argue, are materials through which we may discern a split, or a gap, in Pirous' political and aesthetic subjectivity.

It is important to see that Pirous required not only a national Indonesian identity, but also a working notion of Islamic art, as the legitimating framework for recuperating his Acehnese-ness. That is, his painterly and graphic exploration of "Aceh" was intended to show Acehnese culture as an example of a transnational and multicultural Islamic civilization. In this respect, Pirous, the postcolonial artist, is not that different from Snouck Hurgronje, the colonial ethnographer: both see Acehnese art as Islamic in character. Whereas Snouck saw little in Islam to favour "the awakening or development of the artistic sense", Pirous saw in it an enormously productive aesthetics. However, his years of formal art training had, of course, left him unacquainted with Islamic art. For the fifteen-year period between 1955 and 1970, Pirous gave little thought to Islamic art, neither missing it nor paying any attention to it. To have done so would have served him poorly, given the polemics of nationalism and modernism to which he was subject. Following his return from New York, he had to sort out for himself what Islamic art could or should be.

I do not have the space here to rehearse all the challenges Pirous faced in sorting out possible answers to this question. The fact is that Islamic art at this historical moment has become so thoroughly diversified, pluralized and contestatory, so frequently recruited for struggles against Western cultural imperialism, and so often demonized as a sin by Islamist regimes, that it was, and is, misleading to think of Islamic aesthetics as a settled matter in a world of such varied nationalisms, transnationalisms and travelling cultures. That said, Pirous adapted into his abstract modernist work two gestures or features — one ending in an absence, the other in a presence — commonly associated with Islamic visual culture: the abandonment of human figuration, and the celebration of calligraphy. The strategy of fusing calligraphy — Islam's most privileged and sacred art form — with abstraction happened to coincide with Pirous' first experiments with high-viscosity etching techniques in printmaking, and his initial explorations with acrylics and modelling paste in painting. A tension resulted: the discipline and self-surrender associated with the precincts of calligraphy and Islam met with the impulse and self-assertion associated with abstract modernism.

Unsurprisingly, discipline and self-assertion achieve different ratios in his earliest paintings, done between 1971 and 1974. These paintings featured deformations of Arabic or Arabic-like characters worked up in modelling paste and acrylics. All bore titles that referred to inscribed objects of considerable antiquity — plaques, pillars, tombstones and manuscripts — or to textual genres or styles of writing. A good example is *White Writing* (*Tulisan Putih*, 1974; see Figure 3) in which characters are deformed beyond legibility — a style that Pirous today calls "expressive calligraphy" (*kaligrafi ekspressif*). Differences between legible and illegible Arabic may have been lost on Western or non-Muslim viewers, who generally are unable to read Arabic and can only see such writing as image. For many Indonesians, however, *White Writing* was a disturbing deformation of sacred orthography, and indeed the painting drew criticism from Muslim clerics. By 1975, Pirous moved closer to what we might call a "Qur'anic aesthetic". For his calligraphic works of 1975 and after, Qur'anic verses enjoy special focus; orthographic clarity, wholeness, immutability, and an emphasis on moral reflection and vision usually prevail over self-expression. Untethered self-expression gives way to a contemplative and harmonious abstract iconography aimed at illuminating Qur'anic passages that appear in the paintings. *And God the Utmost* (*Dan Dia Yang Maha Segala*, 1978) is a good example of this (see Figure 4). This is a small canvas done in acrylics, modelling paste, and gold leaf. Symmetries and triangular forms surround a turquoise (*pirus*) field, in which is inscribed the 189th verse of QS 3 Al-'Imran, which reads, "For God's is the kingdom of the heavens and earth, and God's is the power over all things." *The Night Journey* (*Perjalanan Malam*, 1976) is another example, this one quoting several verses from the QS 17 Bani-Isra'il (verses 1, 12–14, 16, and 35–37) — the same *sura* that would appear so prominently in *Homage to Mother* six years later. Here, the iconography and symmetries of weathered plates or tablets evoke the material culture of Aceh, where the earliest Islamic inscriptions appear on segmented tombstones called *nisan*.

It was 1981 before Pirous produced a work of art that made explicit reference to Aceh in its title or in its iconographies. The occasion was the Twelfth National Qur'anic Reading Competition (*Musabaqah Tilwatil Qur'an*, or MTQ), held in June 1981 in the city of Banda Aceh, for which Pirous served as one of the organizers. His most demanding task for the MTQ was staging a massive display of calligraphy rendered with electric lights for ceremonies attended by President Suharto. However, his efforts also included organizing and curating an innovative exhibition of calligraphic paintings, prints, photographs and carvings.[10] It was here that Pirous exhibited three stunning paintings and a silk screened homage to Aceh — the first of his works to make visual reference to Aceh. All three paintings measured one by one-and-a-half metres, and were made from canvas, panels, etched copper and acrylics. The three paintings together constituted a series, *The Wall of Aceh I, II, and III* (*Dinding Aceh I, II, and III,* 1981). The first work consists of six etched plates bearing twenty-three of God's beautiful names, and borders patterned after Acehnese fabric design. The second features a large copper plate shaped and etched in the fashion of an Acehnese *nisan*, or tombstone; on it was etched the QS 96 Al-'Alaq, verses 1–15, generally regarded as the first *sura* revealed to the Prophet Muhammad, and thus having a special place for Muslims of any background. Two vertical curtain-like panels frame the copper etching. The last painting includes the QS 114 An-Nas, the recitation of which is considered to be a talisman for warding off evil.[11]

The serigraph, meanwhile, is called *Prayer XII/Homage to Tanöh Abée* (*Doa XII/Penghormatan Kepada Tanöh Abée*, 1981; see Figure 5), which refers to the site of a famous Muslim library and *pesantren* founded by the revered historical figure, Teungku Tanöh Abée. The library is the pride of Aceh and holds hundreds of religious and historical manuscripts dating back to the seventeenth century. Calligraphy abounds in this silkscreen print — some from the Qur'an; some from fragments of Acehnese and Malay manuscripts; and even some in the form of seals, such as the one in the lower left that bears the painter's name. The print, in its entirety, presents a landscape of sorts, with sky, clouds, sunlight, hills and mountains, sea, and earth — perhaps suggesting that Aceh is "grounded" in Muslim manuscript culture. Above and below are recognizable Qur'anic passages — "God's is the power over all things" (a fragment of QS 3 Al-Imran, verse 29), and QS 5 Al-Ma'idah, verse 74: "Why do they not turn to God and ask His forgiveness? God is forgiving and kind." The text fragments forming hills and mountains in the centre of the print are in Arabic and in Jawi, that is, in Malay and Acehnese written in Arabic orthography (the dominant form of writing in Aceh until the twentieth century).

The politics behind this exhibit need comment and prefigure opportunities and crises to come. As early as 1953, many Acehnese had grown disenchanted with the erosion of their political autonomy and Indonesia's failure to become an Islamic nation-state. A rebellion led by Daud Beureu'eh began that year and continued until 1961, when an agreement was reached with Jakarta. Fifteen years later, in reaction to what its leaders perceived as Javanese neo-colonialism in the guise of the nation-state, GAM — the Movement for a Free Aceh (Gerakan Acheh Merdeka) — launched another separatist rebellion. This one has persisted until today. Staging the national Qur'anic recitation contest in Banda Aceh in June of 1981 was not a coincidence. It has to be seen as an effort on the part of the central government to use religious and cultural events as a means of quelling separatist sentiment and power. In particular, the festival served as a vehicle for the government to co-opt and neutralize Islam and the local *ulama*, drawing the religious leadership away from separatist leanings and into the national fold.[12]

Pirous has never acknowledged or admitted to me that he was recruited for political goals such as these, or that his Indonesian nationalist outlook and identity might represent the sort of political subjectivity the central government would like to instil in all Acehnese.[13] The opportunity to exhibit in Aceh was no doubt an inducement to making the works he did, when he did. In fact, the artist is, in my experience, shrewd enough to have knowingly used the central government to advance his own aesthetic project. The point I wish to make here is that Pirous' exploration of Islamic, Acehnese and Indonesian art could not be worked out within the precincts of aesthetics alone. It required, first, a nationalist political imagination as described by Geeta Kapur, noted above, and second, a public venue in which to exhibit. The project unfolded in a politically circumstanced art world in which the authoritarian nation-state figured as a powerful patron and censor (George 1998, pp. 693–713; 1997, pp. 599–634). Pirous' art would never have appeared in an Acehnese exhibit hall had the Suharto regime construed any separatist sentiment in its iconographies and visual representations.

The Qur'anic passages in the works shown in Banda Aceh are familiar to most Muslims, and are to be read, of course. At the same time, the inscriptions are to be taken in whole, as part of the work's visual totality. They are simultaneously word and image, and in ways that challenge ideologies of pictorial and linguistic signs in the non-Muslim West.[14] One of the passages, however, betrays a political stance unforeseen and unremarked upon by the festival's government sponsors. It is the one situated at the foot of *Prayer XII/Homage to Tanöh Abée*: "Why do they not turn to God and ask His forgiveness? God is forgiving and kind." I asked Pirous about this passage, whose tone seems so curious in a work meant to pay homage to his homeland:

> The passage from *Sura* 5 was for all Indonesians. The shock of modernization in Indonesia's development began to include several kinds of secular deviations and distractions, ones that were increasingly colliding with the faith. But the passage was also intended especially for the people of Aceh, whose character was being ruined ... because of modern urban values. The direction of society and economy, a la Jakarta, was increasingly ... in collision with local tradition and faith. [The] passage from *Sura* 5 is a reprimand, an admonition.[15]

Here is a critique; one conjured from the oppositional space of Islam. Both Indonesian and Acehnese Muslims appear out of touch with their religious roots and teachings, and Pirous is urging them to return to a more pious, observant way of life. Yet, the threat to Islam, to Aceh and to the nation as a whole, according to the artist, stems from Jakarta — a complaint not unfamiliar to supporters of GAM.

LATE AUTHORITARIAN OCCUPATIONS

Throughout the 1980s, the Suharto regime recognized that the oppositional potential of Islam was too threatening to be left unpoliced and unchecked. By 1985, the central government successfully pressured Islamic political parties and organizations into adopting *Pancasila*, the state ideology, as the basis of their activities. Having choked the political aspirations of Islamic groups, the regime quickly began to establish itself as the central patron for Islamic values and culture. Suharto went on the *haj* (pilgrimage to Mecca), state funds were dispensed for Islamic schools and *da'wah* (missionary and religious outreach), and highly placed bureaucrats formed ICMI (Ikatan Cendekiawan Muslim se-Indonesia), the Indonesian Association of Muslim Intellectuals. In Aceh, the central government had succeeded in putting into place a leadership that owed allegiance to Jakarta. When the separatist movement re-emerged in the late 1980s with increased spark, Indonesia unleashed a deadly programme of counterinsurgency and military terror (Kell 1995; Robinson 2001, pp. 213–42; Siegel 1998).

Pirous never again exhibited in Aceh, but continued to explore what he calls the "visual language" of Aceh. In some respects, this exploration resulted in a visual meta-language — an art about art — especially in the way modernist and Islamic visual idioms are used to depict the visual language of Aceh. Overall, this project led to an iconographic "folklorization" and "essentialization" of Acehnese aesthetics. In Pirous' version of Acehnese aesthetics, authenticity resides in old textual materials written in Arabic orthography and in the artful objects he associates with his mother, Hamidah: *tabir*-curtains, *kasab*-embroidery, and *tilampandak*-patterns. This very selection of materials renders Acehnese art as anonymous and shared, empty of difference, debate and contradiction, and expressive of Islamic aesthetic principles. A heterodox and hybrid Aceh, perhaps best personified by Pirous' Gujarati-Sumatran father, is left artless and out of the picture.

Pirous put this sort of approach to work in organizing the national Istiqlal Festivals of 1991 and 1995 for government sponsors (George 1998). By showcasing regional arts that would reveal the spirit and cultural impact of Islam throughout Indonesia, Pirous and his colleagues made a bold moral and civic claim on the cultural heritage and future of the nation-state: the nation had its roots in an Islamic multiculturalism (*tamadun*) and in this, owed more to Aceh, Sumatra and other Melayu regions than to the Hindu-Buddhist traditions of Java and Bali. This claim, and the visual logic used to support it, are most clear in Pirous' immense collaborative and public artwork, the *Al-Qur'an Mushaf Istiqlal — The National Independence Illuminated Qur'an*. Completed in 1995, during the opening ceremonies of the second Istiqlal Festival, and in celebration of Indonesia's fiftieth year of independence, the *Al-Qur'an Mushaf Istiqlal* was an icon of the country's national Muslim *ummat* (community) viewed as "united and peaceful in its ethnic plurality" (Mahmud Buchari 1994, p. 6). Carving Indonesia into over forty Muslim cultural regions, Pirous and his team of graphic artists and computer-assisted design specialists borrowed freely from the country's folk arts and came up with border illuminations representing each cultural area. Aceh was divided into several regions and had designs on roughly eighty pages of the finished text, including the prologue, *al-Fatihah*, and the closing of the Qur'an, *Sura* 114.

In the end, the *mushaf* project was a form of acclamatory art, both for the nation and for Islam. Its appeal to constituent folk aesthetic and manuscript traditions in conjuring a multicultural nationalism and a multicultural Islam, it seems to me, leans heavily on a Herderian notion of culture. As both Seyla Benhabib (2002, pp. 3–4) and Terence Turner (1993, pp. 411–29) have pointed out, the epistemic premises behind such appeals give a faulty and reductionist picture of cultural life: the emblematic iconographies to which they have given rise presume a congruence, homogeneity, conformity and force that seldom obtain in social life. They also pose a trap for political and artistic subjectivity, especially when the image of a unified polity is brought into question by asymmetries of power and violence.

PICTURING THE ACEHNESE TRAGEDY

The fall of Suharto in May 1998 was followed soon after by public disclosure of state-sponsored atrocities in Aceh. It is ironic that Pirous was born in the waning years of the *Prang Sabil* and *Atjehmoord*, only to live to see a different war in his homeland: this time between Indonesian compatriots. For someone of such creativity, good will and national pride, this tragedy was very hard to bear. He expressed his anguish and anger most clearly in a public speech he delivered in Bandung in August of that year, around the time state military operations were temporarily suspended in Aceh:

> With every day it is increasingly clear that the dead did no wrong, did not get a proper burial, and were killed without reason. And now it is in the open. This didn't happen just in Aceh, but throughout Indonesia, it happened everywhere.[16]

Earlier that day, he showed me the first of the paintings he would make having to do with the atrocities in Aceh (see Figure 6). It was called, *Once There Was a Holy War in Aceh: Homage to the Intrepid Hero Teuku Oemar, 1854–1899* (*Suatu Waktu Ada Prang Sabil di Aceh: Penghormatan Kepada Pahlawan yang Gagah Berani Teuku Oemar, 1854–1899*). There, as the visual focus of this lurid painting, was the figure of Teuku Oemar, a martyr from the Dutch-Acehnese War. His figure is surrounded by excerpts from the *Hikayat Prang Sabil* and other related poems. The raised, red Arabic characters about him are Acehnese and quote the *Oath of the Holy War* (*Sumpah Prang Sabil*). The oath reads: "Rather than die in the home of your wife, better to be slain by the infidel's weapon. Rather than die on a pillow, better to be sprawled as a martyr in the front lines." Pirous appeared to shudder when he finished reading it to me in Indonesian.[17]

Pirous had abandoned human figuration years before, during his early embrace of Islamic aesthetics. When I pressed him about his willingness to include figurative elements in this painting, he explained:

> In an atmosphere like this, themes in art tell stories of turmoil. … Because of that, figurative forms that are realistic rather than abstract have become important. They are a very common language for telling stories. … I look at the army, I look at the people in GAM. They can't think, they can only see. Because of that, a picture is worth a thousand words.[18]

In his reply, Pirous depicts his painting as narrative: it tells stories. The character of the violence that needs to be narrated is such that it demands "realism" in figurative form. Vision is key to the agents of violence, just as it is to the artist who looks at them from afar. Seeing is understanding, and the realistic figure is regarded as a transparent window on a violent world. What figures do we see in this work? There is a likeness of Teuku Oemar bearing a weapon, splatters and gashes of red that we may see as blood, the oath in written form and in the colour of blood, and fragments of the *Hikayat Prang Sabil*, written in Arabic orthography but unreadable to those who do not know Acehnese; Pirous himself has difficulty reading the fragments and does not understand them.[19] Unlike the Qur'anic passages often found in his paintings, the *Hikayat* passages here are cut and placed on the work's surface in a way that would thwart a "grammatical" reading of the *Hikayat* narrative.

An ideology in which figurative images are said to have special purchase on reality is recruited for a portrayal of recurrent violence. Here, figuration plays a part in a visual allegory in which the violence of present-day Aceh is understood through historical reference to the Acehnese anticolonial *jihad* of the late nineteenth and early twentieth centuries. The painting summons the Indonesian national hero, Teuku Oemar, from the dead and reclaims him as Acehnese, as the honoured figure of local resistance to all colonialism, be it Dutch or Indonesian.[20] Icons from Hamidah's Aceh are absent in this work. Instead, we see icons from a culture of violence that Pirous has long left out of his artwork. Missing, too, is Qur'anic calligraphy: the very image of Islam. Calligraphy remains, but in place of Qur'anic verse, we have the Acehnese *Oath of the Holy War*. The exhortative verse of the Qur'an is regarded as Truth by Muslims, and would call upon the reader to submit to Allah, something we saw in *Prayer XII/Homage to Tanöh Abée*. In *Once There Was a Holy War in Aceh*, by contrast, the *Oath of the Holy War* calls upon readers to resist, but the religiosity of that call is largely left out of the picture. Islam does not figure strongly here, and indeed, the painting does not conform easily with any aesthetic that Pirous has deemed "Islamic".

For Pirous, it seems, the visual culture of violence in Aceh cannot or should not be rendered "Islamic". That violence is the very antithesis of the peace and harmony he has sought in his faith. He does not want the current conflict to become a *jihad*, he tells me, for holy wars are never quenched by amplified violence. Other paintings in what he has come to call his *Acehnese Series* seem more anguished than the homage to the fallen hero, Teuku Oemar. In them, we see the human figure brought back as an anonymous ghost or corpse. Take for example, *A Face Buried with No Name* (*Wajah Terkubur Tanpa Nama,* 2000), or *They Who are Buried Without Names* (*Mereka yang Terkubur Tanpa Nama*, 2001; see Figure 7), or *The Heads II: They No Longer Know What to Dream* (*Kepala-Kepala II: Mereka Sudah Tak Tahu Bermimpi Apa*, 1999). These are paintings that lead one to grieve and grow angry, or so Pirous would have it. Yet, identification with the murdered threatens to turn into vows for vengeance. The *Chronicle of the Holy War* has to be kept bound and sealed as in *The Restraining of the Chronicle of the Holy War II* (*Pemasungan Kitab Prang Sabil II*, 1999; see Figure 8). Paradise does not await those seeking vengeance. This is not a holy war. It is the nation splitting apart, unhealed by common faith.

Pirous' paintings make visible his troubled national self and remind us that an individual does not have a singular and univocal political self, but a hybrid one constituted through conflicting narratives and images of affiliation, allegiance and betrayal.[21] As James Siegel has remarked, there was for the longest time "no contradiction between being Acehnese and being Indonesian" (Siegel 2000, p. 366). However, the "and" in "being Acehnese *and* being Indonesian" is now a conjunction far more fraught and uncertain than it has been in the past. The fracture, I should insist, takes place in distinct locations, not in some abstract conceptual realm. For the time being, Pirous has located himself rather squarely in the space of the Indonesian nation-state, and so the culture of violence in Aceh is seen and depicted by him from the precincts of Indonesian visual culture. One reason for saying so is that Pirous has not exhibited his *Acehnese Series* beyond Bandung and Jakarta. In fact, the *Acehnese Series* was placed in the gallery hall that served as entry to Pirous' recent retrospective show in Jakarta's Galeri Nasional. Although these works some day may be seen by separatist Acehnese in Aceh, Pirous has made sure that they have come to the attention of Indonesia's gallery-going elite. In exhibiting and talking about this series as he has, Pirous seems intent on displaying his outrage and anguish before an Indonesian art public, rather than before an Acehnese one, where such display might incite violence.

There is one more abstract image I want to discuss; one that I will place in counterpoint to the *Acehnese Series*. Begun in October 1999 as a sketch entitled *Has That Light Already Shone Down from Above?* (*Telah Turunkah Cahaya Itu?*), it eventually made its way into paint and onto canvas in early 2002 as *The Fate of a People is in Their Own Hands* (*Nasib Suatu Kaum Terletak di Tangannya Sendiri*; see Figure 9). It features two Qur'anic passages. The first is from QS 13 Al-Ra'd, verse 11: "Verily God does not change the state of a people till they change themselves. When God intends misfortune for a people no one can avert it, and no savior will they have apart from Him." The second is from QS 2 Al-Baqarah, verse 153: "O you who believe seek courage in fortitude and prayer, for God is with those who are patient and persevere." The title of the image in its life as a sketch invites us to see the steeply pitched diagonal of colour that splits the surface of the painting as a shaft of light. That same gesture formally separates the two Qur'anic verses. Pirous has been a bit of a wag about this painting, in that he has refrained from clearing up its ambiguous politics. I frankly saw the painting as a potential incitement to Acehnese separatist sentiment — "take matters into your own hands and persevere" — and told him so. "Well, you see what you want to see," he replied. A few short weeks later, this painting was taken to Jakarta for inclusion in Pirous' retrospective show and displayed apart from the *Acehnese Series* on walls and panels displaying his abstract calligraphic work. I was not surprised by the move, for it seemed to me that the painting's Quranic passages and its title (see Figure 10) show a kinship with the nationalist inscription Pirous placed on the bastard page of *Mohammed and Charlemagne* forty-four years earlier. Both regard a people's outward state — especially that manifest in a polity — as a product of their spiritual character and interior virtue. "Who are your people?" I once asked Pirous. He rejoined without a moment's pause, "Why the Indonesian people!"[22]

CONCLUSION

Picturing Aceh as tragedy, I want to suggest, requires a vantage point and a visual culture *outside* of a location marked or claimed as "Aceh". Picturing Aceh as outrage places us *within* its suffering and wounds. Pirous' artistic recuperation of Aceh, until 1998, served the transcendent discourses of nationalism, Islam and abstraction. As state-sponsored atrocities came into public view — and with traumatic effects for Indonesian visual culture — Pirous suffered a betrayal. The goodness of the nation-state was never guaranteed by the character of its artist-citizens, or by their piety and faith. Pirous is not trying to make the Acehnese see what they already see too well. His appeal is Indonesian. He is trying to make Indonesians see, recognize and acknowledge their nation-state's self-wounding and self-negating culture of violence, even at the risk of inciting separatist hostilities should his images make their way to Aceh.

Pirous' *Acehnese Series* makes visible the ghosts and secret recitations of the colonial era and allows them to haunt the present. Teuku Oemar and the *Hikayat Prang Sabil* are pried loose from national history, summoned onto his canvasses, and turned back against the contemporary nation-state. What is it about resurrecting the Acehnese past and exhuming the nameless dead from Aceh's mass graves that calls for "realism"? What gives the conventions of realism special purchase on suffering and pain? The visual language Pirous once contrived for things Acehnese, grounded as it was in an exceedingly formalist visual philology, offered no images for that pain. In that sense, it was well suited to the political quiescence of the New Order regime.

The return of realism announces a politics and a visuality that Pirous left unformulated in his earlier explorations of Islamic aesthetics. However,

I should caution against pitting that realism against the transcendentalism of his abstract work in too sharp a fashion. We need to bear in mind that Pirous has long been a Qur'anic realist, in that his Qur'anic paintings demand orthographic precision in making visible a divine and immutable text. So long as the Qur'an is in this world in a way no less real than the deaths of the innocent in Aceh, it is impossible for the politics of word and image, of orthographic and human figures, to remain a strictly iconological issue. For Indonesians in particular, the ideological struggles over word and image will make visible the problem of citizenship, its tragedies, and its sometimes violent effects.

Notes

"Picturing Aceh: Violence, Religion, and a Painter's Tale" originally appeared in *Spirited Politics: Religion and Public Life in Contemporary Southeast Asia*, edited by Andrew C. Willford and Kenneth M. George (Ithaca, NY: Cornell Southeast Asia Program, 2005). It is reprinted here with permission.

1. I wish to thank the Aga Khan Trust for Culture, the Social Science Research Council, and the Wenner-Gren Foundation for their support as I pursued the field research that led to this paper. A fellowship from the John Simon Guggenheim Foundation and one from the Vilas Associates Fellowship Program at the University of Wisconsin-Madison gave me time to write it. I thank, as well, my three institutional sponsors in Indonesia: Yayasan Festival Istiqlal (the Istiqlal Festival Foundation); FSRD-ITB (Fakultas Seni Rupa dan Desain di Institut Teknologi Bandung; the Department of Fine Arts and Design at the Bandung Institute of Technology); and LIPI (Lembaga Ilmu Pengetahuan Indonesia; the Indonesian Institute of Science). My deepest, warmest and most abundant thanks of course go to A. D. Pirous, Erna Garnasih Pirous, and their family for their years of patience, interest, conversation and hospitality. It was a pleasure to give this paper in seminars at the Department of Anthropology at Cornell University, and at the Centre for Southeast Asian Studies, Northern Illinois University. I thank my hosts and colleagues in these venues for their critical response. Last, and not least, Andrew Willford and James Siegel deserve special mention for their discerning comments and criticisms about this work. I am grateful for their encouragement and interest.
2. See Siegel (1979), p. 14.
3. Acehnese men were also prominent in several genres of dance. I thank A. D. Pirous for this observation and his reminder about the role of men in carving, jewelry and metalwork.
4. Muslim religious authorities, it is true, have not always looked upon the arts with favour. To presume an intrinsic or widespread antipathy toward art among them is a mistake, however, and dismisses prospects for a cultural and historical understanding of art production and reception in the Islamic world.

5. See Reid (1969); Siegel (1979).
6. For an introduction to the cultural politics of reading the Hikayat Prang Sabil, see Siegel (1979), pp. 229–65.
7. The Acehnese had a different term for the incidents: *poh kaphe* (killing the infidel).
8. Interview with the author, 22 March 1994.
9. I borrow the term from Benedict Anderson (1991).
10. The exhibition and the accompanying competition in Qur'anic calligraphy were so successful that they became part of the standard programme at subsequent MTQ competitions.
11. Pirous no longer has complete documentation about *The Wall of Aceh III*. I have yet to see the painting or a reproduction of it.
12. Cf. Kell (1995); Siegel (2000), pp. 336–39.
13. After reading the penultimate draft of this paper, Pirous remarked that organizers in Aceh were eager to have a turn at hosting the 1981 MTQ so that Aceh could outshine other provinces in running the competition. It is important not to discount the civic and religious prestige that comes with outdoing rivals in "show and splendor" (to use Snouck Hurgronje's phrase) as a "local" motivation for holding the event in Aceh. Nonetheless, Pirous went on to acknowledge that, "At the same time, the national MTQ succeeded in erasing political wounds such as the one Aceh made in opposing Jakarta since 1953, or — in the case of the 1983 MTQ in Padang — the one in West Sumatra that came as a result of the PRRI [Pemerintah Revolusioner Republik Indonesia; the Revolutionary Government of the Indonesian Republic; 1958–1961] revolt." Personal email communication with the author, 6 November 2003.
14. For a superb discussion on ideologies of the image, see Mitchell (1986) and (1994).
15. Interview with the author, 13 March 2001.
16. Excerpt from a talk on art and oppression delivered at an evening ceremony in memory of Dharsono, Bandung, 22 August 1998.
17. For an anecdote about how an Acehnese *ulama* would shiver upon hearing anything about the Prang Sabil, see Snouck Hurgronje, "Eene onbezonnen vraag" (1924, vol. 4, Part 1, p. 1). This passage is also quoted and translated in Siegel (2000), p. 81.
18. Interview with the author, 15 March 2001.
19. That is, Pirous is not well versed in how to apply phonemic values in Acehnese to Arabic orthography.
20. Compare this local reclamation of Teuku Oemar from national precincts to the Kodinese reclamation of their hero, Wono Kaka, from Jakarta. See Hoskins (1987), pp. 605–22.
21. Cf. Aretxaga (2002); Benhabib (2002), pp. 15–16; Narayan (1993), pp. 671–86.
22. Interview with the author, 13 March 2001.

1. A *kasab* designed and embroidered by Hamidah in 1941.
Source: Courtesy of A. D. Pirous.

2. *Sura Isra II: Homage to Mother* (A. D. Pirous, 1982; 80 × 54 cm, serigraph).
Source: Courtesy of the artist.

3. *White Writing* (A. D. Pirous, 1972; 100 × 180 cm, marble paste, acrylic on canvas).
Source: Courtesy of the artist.

4. *And God the Utmost* (A. D. Pirous, 1978; 30 × 30 cm, marble paste, gold, acrylic on canvas).
Source: Courtesy of the artist.

5. *Prayer XII/Homage to Tanöh Abée* (A. D. Pirous, 1981; 84 × 56 cm, serigraph).
Source: Courtesy of the artist.

6. *Once There was a Holy War in Aceh: Homage to the Intrepid Hero Teuku Oemar, 1854–1899* (A. D. Pirous, 1998; 145 × 150 cm, mixed media on canvas).
Source: Courtesy of the artist.

7. *They Who are Buried without Names* (A. D. Pirous, 2001; 122 × 122 cm, marble paste, sand, acrylic on canvas).
Source: Courtesy of the artist.

8. Detail from *The Restraining of the Chronicle of the Holy War, II* (A. D. Pirous, 1999; 72 × 77 cm, mixed media on canvas).
Source: Courtesy of the artist. Photograph by the author, 2002.

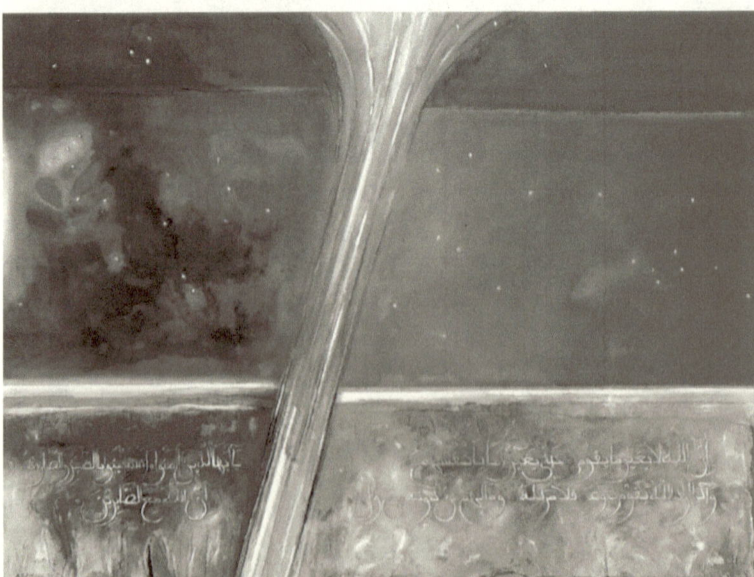

9. *A People's Fate is in Their Own Hands* (A. D. Pirous, 2002; 140 × 190 cm, marble paste, gold, acrylic on canvas).
Source: Courtesy of the artist.

10. In his own hand(s): Putting the title and signature on the reverse of the canvas.
Source: Photograph by the author, 2002.

14

APPLYING ISLAMIC LAW (*SYARI'AT*) IN ACEH
A Perspective from Within

Hasan Basri[1]

> ...Islam is not concerned with only one of the many departments of human life, it covers all the departments; it covers life as a whole lived according to the will of God. It is an all embracing system, a complete code of life, bearing on and including every phase of human activity and every aspect of human conduct. All its laws, social, political, and other are religious laws. They all tend to realization of the one and same ideal, viz., obedience to God and to His laws (Umaruddin 1996, p. 307).

The implementation of Islamic law (*shari'a*) in Nanggroe Aceh Darussalam still evokes discussion among experts. These debates began after the Law of the Republic of Indonesia Number 44 of 1999 regarding the Special Status of the Province of Aceh and Law Number 18 of 2001 regarding the Special Autonomy of the Special Region of Aceh, which formed the basis for the creation of Islamic Courts in Nanggroe Aceh Darussalam.[2] Apart from this, Nanggroe Aceh Darussalam comprises, geographically, part of the united nation of the Republic of Indonesia and is, hence, required to apply its laws in accord with national law or law that follows national structures. Nevertheless, in reality this region has its own legal system that differs from that in other regions of Indonesia. This difference has thus put in motion the dualism of law in one nation that has led to discrimination within the legal system between one region and another. This difference is suspected of causing a "domino effect" or a simultaneous influence in other regions to the degree that others prioritize the application of a similar legal system, that is, Islamic law.

Following this, with the ratification of the Law of the Republic of Indonesia Number 44 of 1999 regarding the administration of the Special Region of Aceh, which was clarified by the Provincial Decree (Peraturan Daerah) of the Special Region of Aceh Number 5 of 2000 regarding the Application of Islamic Law in Nanggroe Aceh Darussalam and Legislation Number 18 of 2001 regarding the special autonomy of Nanggroe Aceh Darussalam, the region of Aceh, which had previously had a distinction between religion, *adat* law, and norms without specific legislation, now came with authority and certainty under the jurisdiction of a specific composition of law. Nevertheless, there will still be problems based on how to administer civil law with respect to criminal law in Nanggroe Aceh Darussalam in the future within the framework of pre-existing law, including national law. This assumption naturally requires more in-depth study in order to position the application of Islamic law in the structure of national law.

Considering this, the law that exists in order to move forward sound Islamic principles in the areas of family and social life more widely, at the very least requires three fundamental supports: first, the strength of doctrine; second, the realization of morality; and third, the application of *shari'a* (Islamic law). This aspect of doctrine and morality is more important on the side of inculcating and deepening meanings previously established. For the time being, *shari'a* impacts more on the side of actual application and its real impact in everyday life. This having been said, the external as well as the internal influences represent two conditions, which reinforce each other in the cultivation of humanity that is balanced and complete ("the perfected human being").[3]

From a juridical perspective, the application of Islamic *shari'a* law in Nanggroe Aceh Daarussalam represents the first time in any location, since national independence, that there has been a territory under the Indonesian legal system that has applied a system of law that differs in relation to the general system of law that is in effect nation-wide. Whereas, from an historical perspective, the people of Aceh were already accustomed to Islamic law, which has existed in Aceh for hundreds of years and which formed an inseparable aspect of their identity. In addition to that, the Constitution of 1945 contains fragmentary paragraphs that represent an opening for the insertion of legal norms that, in both qualitative and quantitative terms, can fulfil the needs of the people of Indonesia. These needs are open to the addition of religious values to the national system of civil law, and at the same time serves as a mechanism for the appearance of a national system of (religious) law in the future (Hartono Mardjono 1997, p. 28).

Paragraph 29 of the Constitution of 1945, for example, states that (1) the nation is founded on the principle of the Unity of God ("Ketuhanan Yang Maha Esa"), and (2) the nation guarantees the freedom of every citizen to adhere to his or her religion and to worship in accord with that system of belief. The assurance of paragraph 29, sentence 1 that emphasizes the principle of the "Unity of God" has three fundamental senses of meaning. These are, first, that the government may not form laws or policy that conflict with the fundamental belief in one God. Second, the government is required to form a legal system and to enact policies that reinforce belief in the one God. And, third, the government is required to form a system of law that forbids anyone from obstructing the goals of religion (ibid., p. 28).

The word "guarantee", as is written in the second sentence of paragraph 29, conveys the sense that this is imperative. This means that the nation is required to undertake active efforts so that each citizen may embrace religion and worship according to his or her respective religion. The activity of the government in this regard aims to assure citizens of their freedom of choice as to which religion he or she wishes to embrace. In addition, it assures citizens that they may practise their religion according to the faith to which they subscribe. Of course, the activity of the government not only aims to address what could be considered to be strictly internal matters within a religion. The freedom of each citizen of the nation to choose his or her religion has so far only been applied in a way that is less serious. With this, what has become a major issue is the assurance of the nation for the freedom of each citizen to practice religion according to the respective faith which he or she confesses to follow (ibid., p. 29).

The proposition that was offered by Hartono Mardjono emphasizes even more the possibility of the introduction of Islamic law in a formal manner into the system of national law or the administration of governmental affairs. However, it cannot be denied that Pancasila and the Constitution of 1945 must remain the foundation of the nation and must be upheld by all the people. Viewed from this perspective, it is all the more the case that it cannot be assured that Islamic law can be applied in an effective manner within the system of national government. This ineffectiveness is rooted in the arrangement of law as it is currently applied throughout every stratum of society, based in Pancasila and the Constitution of 1945, whereas Islamic law or the law of other religions is the realization of historical and demographic aspects of communities within Indonesian society.

As is well known, there are three systems of law that are in effect in Indonesian society. These are Western law (*hukum Barat*), customary law (*hukum Adat*), and Islamic law (*hukum Islam*). However, whereas these three types of law have not known a harmonious place of intersection, the colonial powers were concerned with the mismatch between the three types of law, such as the clash of *adat* law and religious law. Because these three types of law have been in effect for the people of Indonesia — all the more since the era of Dutch imperialism — these three spheres of law have been in constant conflict and collision.[4]

In connection with Western law, there exist several law codes, taking the form of civil law, penal law, commercial law and procedural law for civil and penal cases. Each volume of codification, which is still used until today, diverges all the more in application from the material that preceded it. Even more ironic is that, until the present day, Indonesia has not yet had a single theory of law that is in accord with native culture and civilization; the legal theory that has been in effect until now is a remnant of Dutch colonialism. The legal system has been subject to various changes based on individual views from legal experts, including those taken from other countries as well as those considered to have originated in regional custom.[5] Up until now, there has not yet been the confidence among legal specialists to do away entirely with these old theories and to replace them with new thinking in order to make them more appropriate and relevant to the conditions of Indonesian society today.

There is even law that in actuality has no basis in Indonesian cultures themselves, but was founded by the Dutch legal specialist, van Vollenhoven. The Indonesian people only know that this law was developed in an academic fashion by experts in law, to fulfil a need to codify *hukum adat* (customary law). It is already well known that *adat* law varies a great deal and that it has been influenced by the many ethnic groups that exist within this country. Nevertheless, in specific cases, *adat* law may play an important role in the cessation of conflict between individuals and groups within society. In contrast, national civil law, in specific cases, cannot solve problems such as these. The potential of the law to develop further in order to match the present conditions of society and to evidence distinctively Indonesian characteristics is extremely significant. Therefore, *adat* law may be seen to be the solution to this problem.

Islamic law is a system that is based on Islamic teachings. Islamic law has greatly influenced the law as it is applied throughout much of Indonesia. Among the factors behind this is that approximately 83 per cent of the Indonesian population of 203 million adhere to the religion of Islam. In addition to this, the Islamic faith differs from other religions, which confine themselves to the connection of human beings to God. In contrast, Islam is a religion that is concerned with both the details of human life in this world and the appropriate relations of humanity to God, while it also determines the appropriate relations among human beings both in this world and in accord with its law and principles.

In a more detailed way, Daud Ali[6] has explained that the system of Indonesian law, as a result of historical developments, has a social character. He says this because, up until now, the Republic of Indonesia has applied several legal systems, and each of which has possessed its own characteristics and distinctive arrangement — these being the system of *adat*, Western law, and Islamic law. These three legal systems were first applied in Indonesia at different times. *Adat* law has been in effect for a long time as an informal, customary practice, whereas as a formal system of law, it was only applied in the twentieth century. Western law has been known in Indonesia since 1902. However, Islamic law has existed since Islam was first known and accepted officially among the people of Indonesia, from the seventh to the thirteenth centuries. These three systems of law are recognizable by their arrangement of rulings and statues, grounding within the population, and development in legal theory and practice.

During the process of the Islamization of the islands of Indonesia, that was carried out by traders by way of commerce and inter-marriage, the role of Islamic law has been very great. This can be seen by the fact that if a Muslim trader wanted to marry an indigenous woman, for example, that woman entered Islam beforehand so that the wedding could take place following Islamic law. After Islam took root among the people, the role played by traders was replaced by religious scholars who became teachers and originators of Islamic systems of law. Thus, Islamic law was followed and promoted by adherents of the Islamic religion in regional kingdoms such as those of Aceh Darussalam, Demak, Jepara, Tubam, Gresik, Ampel and Mataram. This is evidenced by the work of chroniclers of the era, such as Sajinatul Hukum.[7] In the kingdom of Aceh, among the religious scholars who played a role at that time were Nuruddin ar-Raniry (1658), Syamsuddin as-Sumatrani (1661), and Abdurrauf al-Singkili (1691). A later work dealing with the organization of criminal and penal law, *Safinatul Hukkam fi Takhlish al- Khashsham*, was written by Jalaluddin at-Tarusani. This work was written on the special commission of Sultan Alaiddin Johansyah (1735–60) (Rusidi Ali Muhammad 2003, pp. 48–49).

In the course of Indonesian legal politics, the word "*syari'at*" emerged as late as 1945, when the Preparatory Committee for the Independence of

Indonesia (Panitia Persiapan Kemerdekaan Indonesia, PPKI) offered the Jakarta Charter (Piagam Jakarta) as the basis for the Republic of Indonesia, which contained, among other phrases, the following: "A state based on the belief in God with the obligation to apply the syari'at law of Islam for all its adherents." Unfortunately, this very piously Islamic phrase, after a long debate within the circle of this nation's founders, had to be eliminated from the Jakarta Charter, which then became the prologue to Indonesia's 1945 Constitution (Pembukaan UUD 1945).

In 1955, the words "*syari'at* Islam" echoed again in the parliament during sessions on a new constitution (*Konstituante*), when pro and contra attitudes led to an intense debate on reinstituting the Jakarta Charter as the basis for the nation. Consequently, for yet a second time, the words "*syari'at* Islam" were removed from the constitution, mainly because President Soekarno had produced the 5 July 1959 Decree, which had essentially removed the 1950 Temporary Constitution (UUD Sementara 1950) and replaced it with the 1945 Constitution (UUD 1945). Since that 5 July 1959 Decree, the words "*syari'at* Islam" have spread fear throughout the broader society, particularly among civil servants.[8]

Because of this, it is not surprising that many Islamic religious figures (*tokoh Islam*) regretted their previous agreement to erase the seven crucial words from the abovementioned phrase contained in the Jakarta Charter. Apart from that, they (the *tokoh Islam*) were also disappointed with the government's position and policies concerning these antipathetic attitudes towards *syari'at* Islam. Although truly not as loudly as in the 1950s, the words "*syari'at* Islam" did echo again in the Senayan Parlement Building, when the People's Council Assembly of the Republic of Indonesia (Majelis Permusyawaratan Rakyat Republic Indonesia, MPR, RI) held their Annual Plenary Meeting in 2000. However, once more the desire to apply *syari'at* Islam completely and comprehensively failed as it was only supported by two fractions, namely the United Development Party (Partai Persatuan Pembangungan, PPP) and the Moon and Star Party (Partai Bulan Bintang) (Muhammad Amin Suma 2004, pp. xvii–xviii). It has to be stated that they did not garner enough votes to bring about a decision. Nevertheless, still they accepted and respected the majority vote wholeheartedly. That is, in brief, the history of Islamic law in Indonesia.

As far as Nanggroe Aceh Darussalam is concerned, it can be said that *syari'at* Islam in that region, as mentioned above, existed as soon as Islam arrived.[9] Throughout their long history, the population of Nanggroe Aceh Darussalam has always highly respected Islamic teachings, been firm in enacting their religious duties, and faithfully practised *syari'at* Islam. The various sultans of Aceh Darussalam, throughout their long reign, carried out the *fatwa* (legal opinion) issued by the *ulama* in the realization of Islamic law until the arrival of Dutch colonial rule in 1873, which tried to suppress Acehnese adherence to Islamic law (Rusidi Ali Muhammad 2003, p. 327).

Therefore, it can be said that the implementation of *syari'at* Islam in Nanggroe Aceh Darussalam is nothing new, nor is it only reserved to Aceh. In fact, in the past, Islamic communities in Java, Banten, Cirebon and other regions thoroughly applied Islamic law as a system through which they ordered their lives. Observed from the perspective of legal history, it was principally Islamic law that, early on, already had deep roots in the Muslim societies of Indonesia.

It also has to be noted that the implementation of *syari'at* Islam in Nanggroe Aceh Darussalam within the context of national law and the framework of the constitution cannot be separated from the long and protracted conflict that took place in the region. In fact, the social and political conflict within Acehnese society has been taking place for a long time, and it began with the uprising led by Daud Beureu'eh on 21 September 1953[10] and further continued with Hasan di Tiro's actions from 4 December 1976 until today.[11] In dealing with the prolonged conflict, the Indonesian central government has searched for a solution, and one way to resolve this conflict has been to bring to realization certain demands of the Acehnese people, namely for *syari'at* Islam to be implemented within specific limits, in the context of national law.

In order to implement *syari'at* Islam, two national laws were born, namely Law of the Republic of Indonesia Number 44 of 1999, concerning the Special Implementation of the Province of Aceh, and Law of the Republic of Indonesia Number 18 of 2001, concerning Aceh's Special Autonomy. There was also Regional Regulation (Peraturan Daerah, PerDa) Number 5 of 2000 regarding the Implementation of *Syari'at* Islam, and two *Qanun* (common law, e.g. administrative law), respectively *Qanun* Number 10 of 2002 covering *Syari'at* Islam Courts and Number 11 of 2002 covering the Implementation/Application of Islam in the Fields of *Akidah* (creed; article of faith), *Ibadah* (ritual) and *Syi'ar* (promoting the greatness of Allah). With these regulations in place, the green light for the implementation of *syari'at* Islam in Aceh was given.

External interest was now focused on that region, as observers from the outside waited for the time when *syari'at* Islam would be applied through a *kaffah* approach, i.e. in totality. If indeed the Acehnese truly wished to uphold the law of Allah, what would the applied format be? Further, how was one to position *syari'at* Islam within the framework of national law? Were the Acehenese prepared to apply *syari'at* Islam in real life, or was the wish for *syari'at* merely a temporary desire that would dim and extinguish overtime? Many more such questions arose once the green light for the implementation of *syari'at* Islam in Aceh was given. At the same time, its reverbations were felt and its spirit spread to other regions.

At Syarif Hidayatullah State Islamic University (UIN Syarif Hidayatullah Jakarta), for instance, a public discussion was held on 16 April 2003 on the topic "Prospek Mahkamah Syar'iyah di Nanggroe Aceh Darussalam" (Prospects for the Syar'iyah Court in Nanggroe Aceh Darussalam). Similar questions to those posed above emerged suddenly during this discussion. There sounded as if there was a lack of confidence — an uncertainty — in both the ability of the Regional Government (Pemerintah Daerah, PemDa) and Acehnese society to make use of and bring to fruition the opportunity given them by the Central Government. The questions that arose, particularly in dealing with the establishment of the Syar'iyah Court (Mahkamah Syar'iyah) on 1 Muharram 1424 AH,[13] were among others: have all the problems arising from the demands of the Acehnese been resolved, will it (the Mahkamah Syar'iyah) persist amidst uncertainty about its implementation on the ground, does this "special" court still need to be further "socialized", and is there sufficient local expertise for its implementation?

SYAR'IYAH COURTS (MAHKAMAH SYAR'IAH): DUTIES AND AUTHORITY

Assessing the impact of the presence of the Mahkamah Syar'iyah, in an article in *Buletin Cipta* entitled "A Sharp Controversy Surrounds Syar'iyah Courts", Salim Ruhana put forward several questions.

Firstly, what is its, as he terms it (in English), "wider mandate", or broader authority, i.e. how does it handle Islamic civil and criminal issues. In such cases, it is fitting to inquire as to how far the Syar'iyah Court is legally prepared, both in material and in formal dimensions. This includes the readiness of its judicial apparatus, which clearly in this case must thoroughly and completely comprehend *jinayat*,[14] for instance. If not, it is possible that precocious haste in enacting a law will turn counter-productive and even destroy the good image of that same law.

Secondly, if the Mahkamah Syar'iyah will take over responsibilities from both the Religious Courts (PA) and the normal State Courts (PN), what will its function be in relation to the higher authority of the PTUN Court and the Military Courts? After all, in Indonesia, there are four judicial bodies, based on Law Number 17 of 1970. So, what is the legal basis for "unifying" the authorities of the PA and PN under the umbrella of this Syar'iyah Court?

Is one Regional Regulation (PerDa), whose strength stands weak within the hierarchy of Indonesia's laws, sufficient as a legal basis for this action? Imagine, the police, in accordance with existing laws, must hand over their cases to the State Courts, that will then be confronted with orders formulated in a *Qanun* (being of the same legal status as Regional Regulations), which might instruct the police apparatus to transfer cases over to the Mahkamah Syar'iyah. Certainly, Regional Regulations, despite being national laws, will have a lower status.

Thirdly, an assumption could be that already existing Indonesian law has taken on the character of civil law that is "bottom-up", i.e. laws are forged out of the existence of certain phenomena within society. With *syari'at* law to be tested and tried by the Mahkamah Syar'iyah, clearly, this character might take on a "top-down" aspect. Alternatively, *syari'at* law could be seen as existing separately, being implemented on the lives of society.

And fourthly, there are several elements that count as exceptions within the Law for Regional Autonomy, amongst them religious affairs. If the Syar'iyah Courts in Nanggroe Aceh Darussalam (NAD) implement Islamic law, does this not constitute regional autonomy for religious matters in general? Will this situation, if tolerated by the government for the sake of dispelling Acehnese rebellion, not in turn become a precedent for other regions challenged with a similar state of affairs — namely the formalization of Islamic law — such as Pamekasan, Sumenep, Gresik, Malang, Sulawesi Selatan, Cianjur, Banten, Garut, Tasikmalaya, and many others? Or perhaps other provinces where the majority is non-Muslim may chose to institute their own religions?

What Salim Ruhana examines is in reality an important concern for the government. And Ruhana's concerns regarding the overlapping duties and mandates of the Syar'iyah Courts have been previously addressed through Qanun NAD Number 10 of 2002. What still needs further study is the practised form of the implementation. It is important to note that the implementation of *syari'at* Islam in Aceh is not the sole avenue to conflict resolution, nor is it the only way for the government to fulfil the hopes and wishes of the people. After all, without any formal regulations or laws, aspects of Islamic law have already long been in effect in Aceh, and *syari'at* Islam will never be a burden for those who have sincere faith in Allah and his Prophet since implementing *syari'at* Islam should be a mere consequence of one's faith. If national law could be characterized as civil law and "bottom-up", then, it could be considered to be quite distinct from *syari'at*. National law is the product of human beings, whereas *syari'at* is the product of Allah and certainly, the law of Allah should stand above everything else. Hence, it is quite natural that the Islamic community should choose the law of Allah to order their lives. In effect, law that was created by human beings is not seen to necessarily guarantee safety or justice, particularly if the supremacy of the law is not respected as deserved. Consequently, law breaking will occur ubiquitously. On the other hand, the law of Allah is seen to guarantee safety and justice. Whoever transgresses these laws, aside from receiving earthly punishment, will be punished at the end of days. Clearly, it is Allah who more fully comprehends the life of human beings. Thus, He created a law that is compatible with the baser instincts of humans. This is one of the clear advantages of *syari'at* Islam.

Thus, many questions that require considerable thought will arise. And, clearly, more than just a brief moment is required to answer those questions. Or perhaps such issues cannot be answered at all.

An avenue for resolution to the conflict between the government of the Republic of Indonesia and the Free Aceh Movement (GAM) was the signing of the peace agreement, the Helsinki Memorandum of Understanding, on 15 August 2005. Likewise, with the institution of *syari'at* Islam, tackling philosophical questions that demand difficult answers is not what is most important; rather, it is the willingness and sincerity with which it is embraced in everyday life. When *syari'at* Islam is carried out with devotion, consistently and with consequence by the followers of Islam, it will follow that the scepticism regarding its implementation will disappear.

Among the duties and responsibilities of the Syar'iyah Court, or Mahkamah Syar'iyah, are to inspect, to decide upon and to resolve issues at the first level of the judiciary system in the fields of *ahwal al-syakhsiyah* (civil law),[15] *mu'amalah* (communal exchanges)[16] and *jinayah* (criminal law). In addition to that, the Mahkamah Syar'iyah has the duty and authority to analyse and deliberate upon issues stipulated under its mandate at the second level of the judiciary system, as well as to judge and sentence at the first and final levels, and to settle conflicts amongst the Mahkamah Syar'iyah in Nanggroe Aceh Darussalam.

SYARI'AT ISLAM AS LIVING LAW

In fact, if we think through it carefully, after deliberating all the pros and cons, we might agree with Mutammimul Ula (1994) that "...the development of national law must have Islamic Law as its core inspiration, complemented by *adat* law to give local input as well as by Western law in order to benefit from advanced technologies and other elements of 'earlier developed' civilizations, primarily concerning practical issues." (Mutammimul Ula 1994, pp. 20–21) Islamic law thus is seen as "mainstream", whereas *adat* law and Western law are seen as complementary.

Furthermore, Mutammimul Ula states that this assertion is based on a number of sound reasons. One of these is the consensus among legal experts that an ideal law must fulfil certain requirements: first, philosophical aspects (an orientation towards and a vision for justice); second, juridical aspects (an orientation towards and a vision for legal certainty); and third, sociological aspects (an orientation towards social benefits and effects).

Philosophically, *syari'at* Islam possesses forms of justice that are suited to the nature of human beings. Juridically, *ijtihad* (legal reasoning) matters aside, Islamic law embodies a value system that most meticulously orders human life, from the individual and the family all the way to the whole of society. And sociologically, it is appropriate as the majority of the Indonesian people have chosen Islam as their religion. Moreover, during the course of the nation's history, Islamic law has developed into a "living law" within society. As a result, the formal application of Islamic law is not new nor does it feel foreign.

THE APPLICATION OF SYARI'AT ISLAM: TYPOLOGY AND CHARACTERISTICS

Lately, the general religious atmosphere of the Islamic community has been pointing more and more to the demand of implementing *syari'at* across all aspects of life. This phenomenon can be seen in the growth and development of *syi'ar Islam* (Islamic texts and/or compositions) and in the increasingly intensifying Islamic spirit among the Muslim community in various levels. The attention to build and develop religious institutions, likewise, indicates how well integrated within public life Islam is. The Islamophobia attitude, which oftentimes was a source of fear, is now gradually eroding. Islamic symbols are more and more transparent in many places. Similarly, Islamic themes that previously were rarely heard in official forums are no longer a rare occurrence these days. Also signs and billboards with Islamic logos and messages can be found throughout university campuses. Even bureaucrats and political party leads are no longer ambivalent about using Islamic terms in their political speeches and addresses.

Another aspect is the steadily increasing number of mosques, although their quality might still be questionable, throughout Indonesia. It seems that the motivation for building such mosques has become a characteristic of the Muslim society in this country. Unfortunately, the people establishing such mosques rarely have thoughts about how to establish lasting sources of income for these mosques. In addition, the popularity of various forms of study of the Qur'an, great religious conventions for important sermons (*tabligh akbar*), and the announcement of religious activities through print and electronic media further point to the momentum. A highly interesting trend is the increasing inclination of parents to send their children for education to Islamic boarding schools (*pesantren*), general religious schools or schools affiliated with a *madrasah*. This underscores a rapid transformation compared with previous years.

In addition, books and magazines about Islam; art exhibitions with Islamic nuances; the "Islamization of educational institutions", by setting up a dichotomous system of education, for instance the former State Islamic Institutes (Institut Agama Islam Negeri, IAIN) which are now becoming State Islamic Universities (Universitas Islam Negeri, UIN) — all indicates that an Islamic spirit is now on the rise. In a similar vein, the establishment of the Amil Zakat National Body (Badan Amil Zakat Nasional, BAZNAS) and the Amil Zakat Foundation (Lembaga Amil Zakat, LAZ); the management of donated assets and estates of deceased people (*dana wakaf*), *hibah* (donation), and *infaq* (maintenance); and the strict management of *hajj*, highlight the serious attention to the teachings of Islam on the part of the Government.

Other phenomena include year-to-year increases of *hajj* pilgrims, surpassing even the set quotas. These phenomena signify that the Islamic spirit of the Islamic community need not be questioned again. Evidently, the image of Islam being marginalized has been eradicated. In certain cases, it even serves as a model for the broader society. However, it cannot be denied that the emergence of Muslim extremist groups and terrorist acts at regional, national and even international levels in various Muslim areas denigrated the positive image of Islam in the eyes of the world.

Based on the facts described above, the diversity of the Islamic community in Aceh in particular and in Indonesia in general can be classified into five types: nominalistic, symbolic, ritualistic, legalistic, and holistic.

The Nominalistic Type

This type is generally referred to as nominal Islam or Islam by name only (in everyday terms it is known as "Islam KTP" ("ID Card Muslim"). The individual's faith in Islam is the result of his ancestor's decision to embrace Islam. This kind of Islam is characterized by the existence of *syahadat primordial*,[17] *khitan* (circumcision), marriage, and death handled in the tradition of Islam. Praying at the mosque is carried out once or twice a year only, on the days of Idul Fitri[18] and Idul Adha.[19] People who practise nominal Islam emphasize more on the local traditions rather than on the pure traditions of Islam.

The Symbolic Type

Under this type of Islam, aside from having the characteristics found in the first type, proof of Islamic piety is marked by symbols highlighting the person's identity. For instance, his clothing tends to be Arabicized, as well as wearing a *selempang, peci haji,*[20] and carrying *tasbih* beads in hand or having it inside his car. The Qur'an is for mere display. In addition, an increase in religious activities can be noted. These are expressed through dutiful attendance of the weekly Friday prayers (*shalat Jum'at*), participation in activities during the main celebratory days of Islam, *kenduri,* as well as partaking in mass congregations in open fields to perform *istighatsash akbar,* mass prayers, *zikir akbar* (repetitive chant praising the greatness of Allah), membership/support of Islamic-oriented political parties, and so forth. This form of Islam stresses formality or external appearances over substance.

The Ritualistic Type

In addition to possessing the characteristics of the two above types — with several exceptions or excluding unnecessary issues — this type is diligent in praying five times a day (*shalat fardhu lima waktu*), and performing *shalat sunat* (non-obligatory prayer) *rawatib* and other *shalat sunat.* The ritualistic type also enjoys reading the Qur'an, fasting during Ramadhan and for *sunat*[21] occasions, carries out *i'tikaf,*[22] saves according to the rules of Islamic banking (*zakat mal*), donates money according to *zakat fithrah,*[23] prays individually in the *zikir*[24] way, prays with *khusyu'* (humility), carries out *qurban 'aqiqah,*[25] fulfils *nadzar* (vow), and saves for the *hajj.* This model of Islam merges formality with substance. Islam is not only limited to external appearances, but also its teachings are carried out consistently and with consequence.

The Legalistic Type

Aside from possessing the characteristics of the above three types, under the legalistic type, Islamic teachings tend be carried out in a broader level, or they even reach the sphere of the official political system. The strict and devoted application of Islamic Law must obtain official legal authority, primarily in relation with the practice of *mu'amalah,* for instance economic activities, the carrying out of *zakat, wakaf* (charitable trust), *hibah,* inheritance, marriage laws, and so forth. In particular cases the timeliness for implementing this kind of teachings will be highly determined by governmental legalization. This factor, for example, is seen in the importance given to the Office of Religious Affairs (Kantor Urusan Agama, or KUA) for notarizing the donation of land for religious purposes (*wakaf or hibah*), for the fulfilment of *zakat*, especially for civil servants through the bureaucracy within which they are embedded, and for marriage ceremonies that are held in the presence of employees from the Office of Religious Affairs. This importance also extends to the determination of the beginning of Ramadhan, and its days of celebration are determined in a similar fashion.

The Holistic Type

This type surpasses the previous four. This fifth type is also referred to as the Ideal Islamic Type; or, according to proper Qur'an terminology it is called *Islam kaffah*. This means that an individual practises Islamic teachings completely across all aspects of life in line with the mission and core values of Islam that are universal in character. At this level, Islamic teachings are inextricable from all aspects of life at the individual, household, community, and governmental levels. Further, this type of Muslim sees himself grounded in the Qur'anic verse that orders the faithful to practise *syari'at* in a *kaffah* manner (al-Baqarah: 208). Islam is understood as an *Ilahiyah*[26] system; not as a system of *Jahiliyah*.[27] This is required in the Qur'an: *Is it Jahiliyah law that they search for; and which law is better than the law of Allah for those who are firm in their faith?* (al-Maidah 5:50). This type, it seems, has yet to reach full realization in the everyday lives of Islam's followers.

THE IMPLEMENTATION OF SYARI'AT IN ACEH: ITS INITIAL FORMAT

Looking at the typologies and characteristics in the practice of Islam described above, the implementation of the Islamic doctrine across all facets of life, in effect, is not as simple as the discourse that has developed to date would suggest. This concerns particularly the extremely essential matter, *syari'at*. To date, we are preoccupied with *fiqhiyyah*[28] matters, which tend to confuse people; and with specific arrangements that invite splits (*iftiraq* or secession) within the Islamic community. Clearly, *fiqh* (jurisprudence) and *syari'at* differ. *Syari'at* (or Islamic Law) are rules from Allah and His Prophet that are characterized as general and objective with reference to the Qur'an and the Sunnah. On the other hand, *fiqh* are subjective understandings of *syari'at*. Thus, *fiqh* give rise to a variety of understandings, while *syari'at* in principle integrates the spectrum of differing interpretations, precisely because it has clearly defined references, namely the Qur'an and Sunnah. In short, it can be stated that *syari'at* are *Ilahi* (theological) teachings that touch upon heaven;

whereas, *fiqh* are teachings that are attached to the ground. Thus, our task is to figure out how to translate *syari'at Ilahiyah-samawiyah* to *lughat insaniyah-ardhiyah* that is applicable.

It is important to note that the implementation of *syari'at Islam* will not be successful without the participation of all sides. Apart from academics, the nobility (*umara*), the clergy (*ulama*), the pious people from the Islamic boarding schools (*santri*), also the traditional *adat* leaders and the representatives of the society at large all have a great responsibility for the success or failure of the implementation of *syari'at Islam* in Aceh. Furthermore, the existence of Syar'iah Courts that follow exactly their duties is the most important key to the success of the implementation of Allah's law in Aceh.

Lastly, it is important to give full responsibility or autonomy, without any intervention from "outside", to the Syar'iah Courts, so that they can deliberate among themselves their decisions to implement *syari'at Islam.* Without that, the Law about the Special Autonomy and the Islamic decretes (*Qanun*) of Nanggroe Aceh Darussalam about the implementation of *syari'at Islam* will become documents of history; and will be in future only part of the collective memory of the generations to come in Aceh. We and many other Muslim communities in other regions who are committed to Islam are hoping that Aceh will become an example for the implementation of *syari'at Islam.* We do not wish that the "green light" for its implementation will be extinguished along the way until it is finally in place. Possibly, *syari'at Islam* will be able to unite and bring peace to the human beings, and at the same time it will preserve the peace agreement that has been achieved. The possibility of implementing *syari'at Islam* needs to be addressed with wisdom, fairness, and deep sincerity. If not, then the "bell of failure" will ring once more, and the people of Aceh will fall into yet another disappointing fiasco.

THE CANING SENTENCE: INITIAL PHENOMENA IN THE APPLICATION OF ISLAMIC LAW

Caning (*cambuk*) is also known as *sebat* or *dera.* In Arabic, it is commonly referred to as *jald*, which stems from the word *jalada*, meaning to strike/hit the skin or beat with a cane made of leather. Thus, such punishment is felt strongly on the skin, although its intention is to shame and prevent people from engaging in wrongdoings rather than to hurt them. Based on various narratives, people sentenced with flogging were not asked to unclothe themselves; instead, they were asked to plan on wearing thick clothing that were resistant to lashes. Imam al-Syafi'i and Iman Ahmad both stated that those sentenced to caning must wear undergarments, either a single or double layer. One narrative explains that during caning, different parts of the body are to be hit so as to avoid causing wounds in a specific area. Care must be taken to avoid striking the face or reproductive organs.

Corporal punishment: Pros and Cons

Fiqh jinayat[29] bears a contradiction within itself. Legal structures were created to protect human beings from various problems, losses, bankruptcy, suffering, and misery. However, criminal law in actuality regulates misery and pain that are handed out to human beings, namely, those who break the law.

In the realm of Islamic Law, there is a wide range of legal stipulations, and they clearly are in the form of suffering and misery towards offenders committing such acts as adultery (*zina*), stealing, murder, and false allegations. In the Qur'an, adulterers are subject to caning or flogging. However, according to the *hadith*,[30] *zina* is divided into two categories: *muhshan* and *ghairu muhshan*. *Muhshan* refers to adultery, whereas *ghairu muhshan* to extramarital sexual intercourse. Stoning or *rajam* (stoning to death) punishes adulterers. Unmarried *zina* offenders are caned a maximum of a hundred times; the couple involved is separated and not allowed to meet for a period of one year. All of the above is enforced according to the official prescriptions in Qur'anic texts as well as in the *hadith* of the Prophet.

Pertaining to this issue, pro and contra perspectives have emerged within Muslim scholarly circles: Is it true that stoning and *rajam*, as a prescription punishment exists within Islam? Is not such punishment found in the Jewish traditions of punishment? Why did Islam reinstitute its application? Hence the opinion emerged that the punishment of stoning that was applied during the time of the Prophet was against actors of *zina* from the Jewish community; precisely because Islam prescribed Jews and Christians to follow the official laws written in their respective holy texts. Further, a debate has emerged concerning *syari'at* punishment against non-Muslim transgressors. *Jumhur ulama* have stated that the punishment applies to all transgressors, Muslims and non-Muslims alike; nonetheless, there are those of the opinion that *had*[31] punishment should be applied in line with Islamic Law.

Within modern legal theory, discussions have arisen regarding the principles of the territory and the person (*asas teritorial* and *asas personal*). Yet, the usual practice is that the principle of the person applies in civil law, whereas the principle of the territory operates within criminal law. This means that in criminal law the jurisdiction is based on a specific territory. Whoever transgresses the rules of criminal law in that territory is subject to the legal stipulations that apply within that region.

ISLAMIC LAW: INTERPRETATION AND CONTEXTUALIZATION

The abovementioned debate demonstrates that Islamic Law is open to a wide range of interpretations. It seems that the Prophet himself had engaged in his own interpretations of Islamic Law when he applied the stoning (or *rajam*) sentence to Muslims who committed adultery. This interpretation was based on the fact that the Qur'an itself does not mention that kind of punishment. Perhaps the Prophet took inspiration from the Jewish tradition, which used *rajam* as punishment, to the point that he integrated it into the Islamic tradition; and then it was applied specifically to married *zina* offenders. The reasoning might have been that such category of offenders should be given a heavier punishment.

The punishment for stealing can perhaps be utilized as a more concrete example. It is stated in the Qur'an that a robber, regardless whether a woman or a man, will have her/his hand cut off. No further clarification is given, for instance, regarding the amount stolen, the situational context when stealing, and so forth. Hence, there were Muslim scholars, such as al-Hasan and the Zahiri group, who were of the opinion that every act of thievery or robbery — regardless of form or quantity — must be punished with the corporal punishment of hand-cutting. This differs from the perspectives of the *jumhur ulama* (religious leaders and scholars) who believe that certain conditions do exist that modify cases that might lead to the amputation of the hand in case a person steals. These *ulama* based their argument on the Prophet's *hadith*, which states: "the hand of a thief that receives amputation as punishment has *nisab*,[32] or a clear limit."

During the times of Khalifah Umar bin al-Khattab it is recorded that a thief was not amputated since he had stolen out of hunger. It seems that Umar understood that this individual stole not because he was a bad person, but because he needed to fulfil his basic economic needs. Thus, this person was "truly" in a state of "emergency" (*darurat*). In this case, Umar undertook an interpretation of the law that hitherto had not been attempted. Umar's approach demonstrates his genius in understanding the spirit of Islamic law. At the very basic level, punishment exists in order to subdue criminality. Thus, if a crime is committed unintentionally (or *semu*) or it is not meant to hurt (*menzalimi*) others or because it was forced, then, it is case-based or *kasuistik*. Umar concluded that theft or robbery, if committed under extenuating circumstances (i.e. poverty, or dire economic need), then it could be forgiven. Even if subject to punishment, the sentence should be reduced.

The above examples depict the flexibility of Islamic Law throughout history as practised by the Prophet himself and his friends and followers. Apparently, such law can be interpreted according to cultural, social, and psychological developments of a society in a particular time and place. There is no rigidity in interpreting *syari'at* precisely because Islam aims for the prosperity of its followers and to foster *kemaslahatan-kemaslahatan* for their own safety and well-being in this world and beyond (*akhirat*). All the more if it is noted that the sentences are given and effected with extreme care. Umar once stated that it was preferable to err on the side of no punishment rather than give the incorrect or inappropriate sentence. For instance, the requirement of four witnesses to determine the sentence for adultery offenders can be said is nearly impossible in the context of our times. As result, there is no wrong in re-discussing this matter more thoroughly with the spirit of law embraced by society today.

THE IMPLEMENTATION OF CANING PUNISHMENT IN ACEH: DISCRIMINATORY?

A historical incident took place in Bireuen district on 24 June 2005 with the implementation of Islamic law by the caning of twenty-seven gamblers. However, one of them was able to evade punishment as she/he was willing to pay a fine of Rp25 million. This meant that twenty-six were punished. On the first day, only fifteen public floggings took place. The individuals had been declared ready for caning, following medical examinations. The remaining eleven persons would be caned on another day. After the individuals were noted to be in good health, the floggings were carried out in the backyard of the Agung Bireuen Mosque, Aceh Utara.[33]

They were sentenced with caning as they were caught gambling. Their actions had violated *Qanun* No. 13/2003 on *Syari'at Islam* in Aceh. The Syariah Court in Bireuen handed down their caning sentence publicly. The defendants wore similar clothing, specifically, knee-length white robes or *jubah*. The cane used was made of rattan 1 metre long with a diameter of 0.75 cm.

Apart from gambling, other misdeeds subject to flogging in Aceh include *khalwat* or *mesum* (indecent acts between a woman and a man) and *khamar* (alcohol consumption). Those who do not attend Friday prayers (*shalat Jum'at*) at the mosque three consecutive times are at risk of caning. During the month of Ramadan, adults found to be not fasting are subject to public flogging. Caning also applies to persons proven to have disseminated deviant teachings or ideologies. According to the *Qanun*, flogging may be substituted with imprisonment or fines. Those who are able to pay fines will be exempted from corporal punishment. Caning is therefore being implemented in a discriminatory manner. This means that it only affects the lower strata or grass roots levels, while those in the upper strata (e.g. bureaucrats or the wealthy) who commit one of the three violations mentioned will certainly opt to pay fines rather than being flogged or incarcerated.

As a result, the implementation of law is uneven. In other words, application is not fair and is partial to the wealthy and powerful. Various opinions have emerged within Acehnese society, questioning why caning only applies to the poor and disempowered. If Islamic law were applied appropriately, officials would not allow waivers in those cases. At the least, one could learn from Khalifah Umar bin Khattab's case, who caned his own child in public because he/she had committed *mesum*. Or from Prophet Muhammad who was going to cut his daughter's hand, if it was proven that she had committed theft.

Such is the early shape of the application of *syari'at Islam* in Aceh. Nonetheless, there is a section of society who is dissatisfied with such implementation of Islamic law; in any case, sentencing and punishment has already taken place. For those who have experienced it, what remains is to engage in deep thought, as caning does not only bring shame to oneself but also to one's family. Essentially, the application of Islam is to educate society and not to violate a regulation for the safety and well-being of all.

CONCLUSION

Despite the fact that the implementation of *syari'at* in Aceh is determined within legislation (*undang-undang*) and rules (*Qanun*), it has not yet been applied in a comprehensive manner to the system of life of the Acehnese. It appears that the implementation of Islamic law was merely a government strategy to appease those who fought during the conflict in Aceh. Consequently, the application of Islamic law did not receive complete support from the regional government. In fact, strong support came precisely from the lower strata of society. To date, only Bireun District has been strictly serious in applying Islamic law as mandated by the *Qanun* of Nanggroe Aceh Darussalam. Such case notwithstanding, it is still limited in regard of types of criminality and punishment. Oddly, the implementation of *syari'at Islam* has been limited to the surface level affecting only the lower classes, while the political elite and government officials have not been touched at all. Perhaps this is the reason why the bearers of authority have not been interested in applying Islamic law. To them, *syari'at* is merely political jargon to decrease the restlessness of a society that yearns for the glory of the past; a time when *syari'at Islam* was applied effectively in the social and political lives of the Acehnese. It is conceivable that the powerful are concerned that if Islamic law is effective, they will be impeded in transgressing and misusing their authority.

The implementation of Islamic law is only one aspect in the process of resolving the conflict in Aceh, which requires a comprehensive approach. As a result, a resolution to the conflict will not be reached merely by applying *syari'at Islam*, particularly if the process is not supported by other factors such as justice and economic development for the prosperity of the people. The implementation of Islamic law will promote effectiveness in establishing law and order within society, because legal regulations have been derived from religious teachings which have merged in the collective consciousness of the people. Abiding by the law is viewed as part of being religiously faithful.

The application of Islamic law fulfils one of the aspirations of Acehnese people, namely a need to protect their identity. Islam represents an Acehnese identity that has been shaped through a long historical process. The people of Aceh themselves have made demands for the implementation of *syari'at* since early stages of the independence. According to some, this *syari'at Islam* fostered the nationalist spirit of the Acehnese to defend the territory of this archipelago. If this necessity were ignored, conflict between Aceh and the central government would take place. When the central government finally fulfilled the aspirations of the Acehnese at a time when the conflict had already taken place, its meaning was different, namely not wholeheartedly, and thus suspicions would arise.

The cruelties and atrocities that happen in a society where law enforcement is weak, imply dangers that are much greater and much more destructive. Almost every day in several print media there are reports about murders, abuse, thefts and so on. But almost all of these crimes seem to happen without any sufficient judicial persecution. As a consequence, there are also news that people are lynched by a crowd just because somebody loudly accused them of being thieves. Sometimes these lynched people are even put ablaze by the crowd. However, if investigated carefully, one would have found that these lynched people are often innocent. In such cases, obviously a punishment that is bound to a clear legal foundation is very much needed in order to prevent a much greater damage.

Notes

1. Translated from Indonesian by Anna Gade and Mercedes Chavez. Arabic terms translated by Karin Hoerner.
2. This name is based on the Law of the Republic of Indonesia Number 18 of 2001 regarding the designation of the Special Region of Aceh Province (Provinsi Daerah Istimewa Aceh) as the Province of Nanggroe Aceh Darussalam (NAD).
3. Cf. Rusjdi Ali Muhammad (2003), p. 6.

4. Cf. Bustanul Arifin (1996), p. 70.
5. Ibid., p. 72.
6. Cf. Daud Ali (2001), pp. 58–59.
7. Ibid.
8. For a more detailed discussion on this, see Muhammad Amin Suma (2004), pp. xvii–xviii.
9. Regarding the history of Islam's introduction into Aceh, read Ali Hasjmy (1993). In truth, Islam had been already introduced into Indonesia, especially Aceh, in the first century *hijriyah*, or the seventh century AD, directly from Arabia. Nevertheless, according to Western historicans, Islam only arrived in Indonesia in the twelfth century AD. For further details, also read Ismail Suny (1980).
10. This uprising, which was a tragedy for the Acehnese people, is generally called the "incident of bloodshed" (*peristiwa berdarah*). It took place in the period when Ali Sastroamidjojo was prime minister. The official name for this incident is the "Uprising of Daud Beureueh". For further information on the uprising led by Daud Beureu'eh, see M. Nur El Ibrahimy (2001).
11. The Hasan di Tiro movement is usually referred to as Free Aceh (Aceh Merdeka), and was originally known as the Free Aceh Movement (Gerakan Aceh Merdeka, GAM). This movement embodies the people's resistance towards the central government of the Republic of Indonesia, and demands that Aceh becomes a free (read, independent) nation, that can stand on its own without the interference from the central government. For further information, see M. Isa Sulaiman (2000).
12. The opposite of *mu'amalah* (communal exchanges).
13. A date in the Muslim calendar, the first day of the first month of the year 1424 after the Prophet's Hijra (emigration to Medina).
14. Plural of *jinayah* (criminal law).
15. Concerning personal status.
16. The opposite of *ibadah*, e.g. buying and selling.
17. *Syahadat* is a declaration of faith. A person must recite the *syahadat* to convert to Islam, namely: "I testify that there is no god but Allah and I testify that Muhammad is the Messenger of Allah" <www.islamcan.com/dictionary>. (Note by M. Chavez).
18. Festival of Breaking the Fast (after Ramadan, begins on 1 Shawal).
19. Sacrificial Feast (10 Dhul-Hijja).
20. *Peci* is a black cap worn by men of the Islamic faith.
21. Practice of the Prophet or recommended practice.
22. Retreat in a mosque for several days.
23. Obligatory donation of food at the end of Ramadan.
24. Formulaic repetitive recitation, Muslim "litany".
25. Sacrifice on the 7th day of the birth of a child.
26. Fem. form of *ilahi*.
27. Ignorance, unbelief.

28. Derived from *fiqh*: matters concerning jurisprudence.
29. Jurisprudence of major crimes, criminal law.
30. Tradition of sayings and actions of the Prophet.
31. Punishment, or crimes mentioned in the Quran, e.g. *zina*.
32. Literally: proportional.
33. From "Caning The Ones Who Don't Pay (and Civilians)" ["*Mencambuk yang Tak Bayar (dan Sipil)*"], *Aceh Kita* Magazine, Edition 018/Year II/July/2005, pp. 6–8.

15

READING THE TSUNAMI AND THE HELSINKI ACCORD
"Letters to the editor" of *Serambi Indonesia*, Banda Aceh

Arndt Graf[1]

Nearly eight months after the catastrophic tsunami of 26 December 2004, the Helsinki peace accord between the Indonesian government and Gerakan Aceh Merdeka (GAM) was signed on 15 August 2005. Underlying both events (natural and political) is the tragic loss of human life coupled with the hope for a peaceful and prosperous future for Aceh. My question in this chapter is how experiences of these life-changing events are addressed and articulated in Acehnese public opinion. As a case study, I analyse the online edition of the "letters to the editor" column "*Droe Keu Droe*" ("From heart to heart")[2] of Banda Aceh's leading newspaper *Serambi Indonesia*, from the month of August 2005.[3] This online edition is of particular significance during this politically decisive month as it represents an important link to the debates at home for all those Acehnese living abroad, be they supporters of GAM or not.

As Hogan (2006, p. 63) has pointed out, the genre of "letters to the editor" (henceforth: LEs) deserves attention not so much because it accurately represents "people's voice" (*vox populi*), as certain earlier research suggests (for example, Brown 1976). Published LEs are typically shortened by the journal's redaction, which can considerably alter the letter's intended message and tone. In addition, contributed letters must undergo a selection process carried out by the journalists in charge. Thus, such letters generally represent, to a certain extent, the agenda of the publishing journal, which is informed by its own in-house as well as more general power relations. At the same time, LEs are generally written by laymen who often try to advance their own personal interests in order to influence public opinion. In this sense, LEs can be seen as interesting opinion pieces that render visible some of the (vested) interests of the micro level of civil society.

This proves even more relevant in terms of the highly contentious political situation in Aceh in which the LEs of *Serambi Indonesia* constitute one of the very rare opportunities for individual members of society to gain access to wider public attention. Such letters, then, can be seen as a forum for promoting, disseminating and debating values and issues within officially tolerated limits. At the same time, LEs are quite relevant at the grassroots level of Acehnese public opinion — possibly, but not necessarily, linked to greater debates and discourses otherwise dominated by powerful institutions such as the state, the (post) guerrilla movement, or religious elites.

In terms of research methodology of this case study, it is important to note here that in August 2005 the terrible experience of the tsunami still played a nearly ubiquitous role in Acehnese public opinion. For example, tsunami victims who lost members of their families during the catastrophe write a number of LEs in the sample. Their trauma sets central ethical parameters for my research questions and the degree of criticality with which I analyse the texts generated by these letter writers. I will therefore focus on a more descriptive synthesis of the textual strategies and issues as these are put forward and addressed by the letter writers themselves (hereafter contributors).

REGIONAL ORIGINS OF THE LETTER WRITERS

In general, LEs constitute a textual genre through which individual interests and agendas are put forward. The purpose is often to mobilize public opinion for a particular cause and/or to exert pressure on other parties with vested interests in the issue. In order to render such an intervention in public discourse acceptable to a wider audience, the contributor often embeds his concerns within references to cultural values, convictions, and other social and cultural tropes commonly held among his target audience.

In this light, it is important that in many LEs of *Serambi Indonesia*, the contributor introduces himself or herself explicitly as being a member of a particular local or regional community (*warga masyarakat*). As such, the letter therefore can be read not only as an individual's voice, but also often as representative of a larger interpretive community. The newspaper *Serambi Indonesia* enhances this regional identification in at least two ways. Firstly, LEs are published in a column with the Acehnese name *Droe keu droe*. As Acehnese remains the dominant language of the province as opposed to the national language of Bahasa Indonesia, publishing a letter in this regionally "addressed" column gives the contributor a specific regional legitimacy. Secondly, *Serambi Indonesia* typically discloses the contributor's name and regional origin by village (*kampung* or *desa*), town (*kota*), regency (*kabupaten*), etc. Other identity markers, such as profession (student, fishermen, etc.), or institutional and political (PAN, PDI-P) affiliation, are rarely given. Gender markers play no particular role, possibly because it is assumed that most letter writers are men. Clearly, the imagined community constructed and/or reflected by this redaction policy of *Serambi Indonesia* emphasizes the regional aspect.

The majority of contributors reside in the capital city of the province of Nanggroe Aceh Darussalam, Banda Aceh. Thirty-two out of the forty-six letters in the sample are from inhabitants of the capital (69.6 per cent). Three (6.5 per cent) come from the neighbouring regency (*kabupaten*) of Aceh Besar, while only one letter each from the regencies of Pidie, Bireuen, Lhokseumawe, Aceh Utara, Aceh Barat Daya (Abdya), and Aceh Selatan. The remaining eleven regencies of Aceh are not represented among those who contributed letters during the month of August 2005. In addition, a letter was by a resident of the province of Lampung at the Southern tip of Sumatra, one from the Indonesian Students' Organization (PPI) of Great Britain, London, and one from a writer living in Gold Coast, Australia. This suggests that, at least during the period under consideration, the published "voices from the people" in *Serambi Indonesia* are almost exclusively those from the capital, and that only nine of Aceh's regencies are represented.

THE TSUNAMI

In the LEs of *Serambi Indonesia* of August 2005, the topics of the tsunami catastrophe of December 2004 as well as of the subsequent earthquake of March 2005 are present in almost all letters. However, in only a few of these do their contributors describe damages incurred in their neighbourhood, or request more assistance.[4] Apparently, eight months after the tsunami, immediate relief efforts were no longer the most urgent topic for most of the letter writers. Rather, several letters discuss problems related to these relief efforts, such as the garbage left behind by NGOs.[5] Frequently, the local government is urged to do more, for instance, in preventing fishermen from further damaging the remaining dikes.[6]

This kind of critical appeal to the local government is not limited to tsunami-related issues; rather it seems to be part of the genre's tradition. The letters of the month of August 2005 are also critical of other environmental issues endemic to the area, such as illegal trash dumping next to a mosque,[7] forest fires that are not handled effectively,[8] or roads in the state of disrepair.[9] In most of these letters, the local government is portrayed as not doing enough for the population. One letter, however, contributed by a member of a team of experts (*tim ahli*) from the Provincial Governor's office of Aceh Nanggroe Darussalam, responds to such concerns by explaining the sometimes quite complicated legal context responsible for possible delays. In this case, the problem is due to the delay in obtaining an official permit by a local airline.[10] In the post-tsunami situation, private companies are also scrutinized through public opinion. Some company spokespersons use the forum of LEs in their attempts to improve their public image.[11]

While the issue of the immediate impact of the tsunami seems to have been replaced in many cases with concerns over subsequent relief and reconstruction efforts, the experience of the tsunami has apparently become part of a more general cultural framework. It now serves as a frequent point of common reference for various members of the Acehnese society. The most direct examples are those in which the tsunami trauma even serves to position and identify the writer's person within the first sentence:

> I am one of so many victims of the tsunami (*saya adalah satu dari sekian korban tsunami*).[12]

However, such a personal experience is then often transformed into or embedded within a collective experience that serves as the principal point of reference in broaching other issues of common interest:

> The tragedy of the tsunami of 26 December 2004 we have all experienced together...
> (*tragedi tsunami 26 Desember 2004 telah kita rasakan bersama*...).[13]

The status of victim of the tsunami, or, as it is more often represented, as a member of a (village) community that suffered collectively under the tsunami, is frequently invoked in such a way that establishes the contributor's opinion as indisputable authority:

> Why don't you think clearly about what I am suggesting as I am a member of the community that were victims of the tsunami in the village of Lampulo
> (*Coba Bapak pikirkan secara jernih pendapat saya selaku masyarakat yang pernah mengalami korban tsunami di Desa Lampulo*...).[14]

In general, it thus can be assumed that the LEs of August 2005 represent a short phase in what is arguably a much longer process within which individual traumatic experience is reformulated collectively; in turn, increasingly acquiring formulaic qualities. It would seem that such formulae of the tsunami trauma are generally accompanied by other typified identity markers, such as those specific to the regional interpretive community (Aceh, regency, village) and/or strong religious framings of the event.

ISLAMIC PERSPECTIVES

While Aceh is known for its particularly strong Islamic identity, it is apparent through many letters that the construction and further development of that identity is carried out through a broad discourse where multivalent positions and perspectives necessarily play a role. One such position interprets the tsunami as Allah's punishment:

> There are still heavy traces in the thoughts of the people from Padang Bakau Pesisir, Labuhan Haji Aceh Selatan of just how terrible the tsunami catastrophe was, which was given by Allah the Almighty...
> (*masih membekas di pikiran masyarakat Padang Bakau Pesisir, Labuhan Haji Aceh Selatan, betapa dahsyatnya bencana alam tsunami diberi Allah SWT...*).[15]

This assumed punishment handed down by Allah is then often associated with immoral behaviour before and after the tsunami. A typical passage relates the following in which the writer entreats his fellow citizens of Aceh to cease their immoral behaviour, in order to avoid Allah's punishment in the future:

> This is why we ask our brothers and sisters to become conscious of what happened, to get back to the path of Allah the Almighty. Let the first catastrophe be enough that Allah has given us, and let us not ask for a second punishment of that kind. Let us think of all our faults. Truly Allah knows everything what you have done. Because Allah brings judgment to all regardless of who committs the sin, we all share in it.
> (*Oleh karena itu kami mohon kepada saudara-saudari marilah kita sadari apa yang telah terjadi, marilah kembali ke jalan Allah SWT, cukupkanlah musibah yang telah Allah berikan ini dan jangan lagi meminta adzab Allah yang kedua kalinya. Marilah kita renungkan kesalahan diri masing-masing. Sesungguhnya Allah mengetahui apa yang telah kamu kerjakan. Karena Allah memberikan bala tidak memilih siapa pelakunya, semua kita rasakan...*)[16]

In general, many letters employ a prayer-like style invoking Allah's blessing, for instance concerning the peace process.[17] Other elements of religious reference in the LEs include the asking for Allah's blessing and guidance for fellow citizens, such as in the following letter:

> Hopefully they are blessed with insight by Allah so that their heart is open and that they receive guidance by Allah the Almighty
> (*mudah-mudahan mereka diberikan nur oleh Allah SWT agar hati mereka dibuka dan diberikan petunjuk oleh Allah SWT...*).[18]

It is typical that such letters end with a long formula of a traditional word of thanks from the writer to the reading community:

> So it is our hope that you please fulfill the wishes of the community of Dewantara, especially of the village of Paloh Lada so that the world of our education, particularly in Aceh Utara, may soon emerge from neglect. Thank you very much, daily *Serambi Indonesia* for publishing this text. May Allah the Almighty give blessing to all of us. Amen.
> (*Demikianlah harapan kami kepada Bapak agar sudi kiranya memenuhi keinginan masyarakat Dewantara khususnya Desa Paloh Lada, agar dunia pendidikan kita khususnysa Aceh Utara segera bangkit dari ketinggalan. Terima kasih kepada Harian Serambi Indonesia yang telah memuat tulisan ini semoga Allah SWT memberi berkah kepada kita semua. Amin...*).[19]

Apart from such formulaic religious evocations, a group of seven letters explicitly intend to defend Islam and Islamic values. Each of these letters raises the problem of public immorality: pointing to issues of prostitution, illegitimate sexual relations in general, and of unmarried couples in particular who are seen together in public or who are seen touching one another.[20] Concerning such issues, the contributors demand more enforcement in implementing *Syari'ah* law, citing for instance the "sweeping" that occurred in the district of Bireuen as a positive example.[21] In this context, the local government and the *Wilayatul Hisbah* (WH) or *Syariah* Police are also strongly urged to act against perceived negative Western influence in the local schools.[22] Similarly, the WH are mandated to increase surveillance of Western NGOs, which, allegedly acting as human relief organizations, are suspected by the letter writers and perhaps their local communities of an agenda of illegal Christian missionizing in these areas.[23]

In general, the LEs demonstrate thus both a customary piety informing religious formulae, as well as a strong religious undertone in how the tsunami is interpreted. This latter element at times bears almost apocalyptic dimensions; reminding of the Last Judgment not as an ultimate possibility, but rather as an immediate experience. Such letters need to be taken seriously as voices from important parts of the society since they most probably reveal a strong current in post-tsunami Acehnese culture.

ELITE POLITICS

Marks of identification used by letter writers such as members of a local community, tsunami victims, and/or true believers are often paired with allusions to class identity, particularly the poor. Implicit in this self-characterization is also a construction of an alienated "elite" class who neither understands nor sympathizes with the real needs of the people:

> It is necessary that you the politicians know that for us the proletarian (poor) community…
> (*Perlu Bapak-Bapak politisi ketahui, bagi kami masyarakat proletar (miskin)…*).[24]

This critical undertone colours much of twelve of the sample LEs that deal with official politics. Seven letters relate specifically to aspects of the 15 August Helsinki agreement, including the agreed upon local elections. A general concern of this sub-group of letters is the potential for manipulation of the elections by local elites for their own agendas.[25] Others voice concern over the possible high cost of the elections that would take away desperately needed aid for tsunami victims. One tsunami victim even suggests a postponement of these elections since relief efforts concerning food, housing, work, and education are, in his opinion, more urgent.[26] Finally, one letter in this sub-sample implicitly refers to the traditional role students have played in national and local politics in the past by suggesting that students supervise the upcoming elections.[27]

Professional politicians also use the LEs as an opportunity to promote their views. A primary example is that contributed by Ade Darmawan, a politician from the PDI-P party who accuses his own regional party's leadership of being hypocritical and its actions morally unsound.[28] In another such letter, H Slamat SM, Bandar Lampung criticizes the PDI-P national leader, Megawati Sukarnoputri, for her stand against establishing local parties. Generally, it can be assumed that the published reactions in the LEs regarding the proposed local elections are representative at least of some of the sentiments of the general populace in Aceh. As such, it should be underlined that most letters express a deep-seated distrust of political machinations on both the regional and national levels, most especially the actions of the political parties.

This distrust and disillusionment is also visible in the sub-group of letters related to inefficiencies of local bureaucracy. Three letters deal with such aspects in greater detail. Representative is, for instance, Mukhlisuddin's letter from Kuta Alaman, Banda Aceh, entitled "*Wahai Pak Pejabat*" ("Have pity,

Mr. Bureaucrat"). In it, the writer morally admonishes the state officials for not caring enough about the tsunami victims, about how they live, whether in provisional barracks or not. Mukhlisuddin associates this lack of compassion at the level of government with the spectre of corruption. While Mukhlisuddin utilizes a sermon-like rhetoric, Akhiruddin Mahjuddin, the coordinator of an anti-corruption NGO, employs a style revealing an academic training. In his letter, Mahjuddin lists a series of points and programmes where he suspects post-tsunami relief efforts to have been corrupted, and he requests those politically responsible to submit a detailed account of transactions and budgets related to these relief programmes. A similar tone comes across in a letter pertaining to the state-funded radio stations *Visi* and *Asyifa* that had stopped broadcasting. Its contributor, Anwarsyah from Banda Aceh, raises the question of potentially wasted public funds, and of illegal behaviour of state authorities because the radio subventions have never, according to him, been declared properly in the provincial budget.[29]

A third sub-group of the letters dealing with specific aspects of official politics and government concerns interregional problems in Aceh. The first of two letters in this sub-group suggests redrawing the boundaries of a district (*kecamatan*) in Southern Aceh (Aceh Selatan), the second requests more post-tsunami support for reconstruction in Simeulue. In both cases, the letters address government issues that in the post-New Order environment are no longer exclusively the matter of appointed elites. They also reveal how issues that touch upon the foundations of the regional constitutional framework, such as inner-provincial borders, are being discussed freely and openly in a more democratic Indonesia. If one would want to put it positively one could state that these LEs thus demonstrate how much progress the democratic process in Indonesia has made at the grassroot level since the late 1990s, and especially in the politically sensitive region of Aceh.

ISSUES OF EDUCATION

In the sample of forty-six LEs, the largest group (fourteen letters or 30.4 per cent) deals with issues of education and student affairs. It is not clear whether this heavy emphasis on education reflects a particular policy of *Serambi Indonesia* or whether it is representative of most letters that were sent to the redaction. In any case, it seems that the topic of education is strongly associated with hopes of a better future for Aceh, despite pessimism about individual problems discussed in many of these letters.

Six of the letters in the education sample concern the relationship between education and politics, especially at the district and provincial levels.

Three of these letters aim at influencing regional budgets in order to hire more teachers and to obtain higher salaries for teachers,[30] to build a student hostel for a particular district,[31] or to devote more of the budget for (higher) education in general.[32] Another two letters explicitly attack circumstances of individual school projects at the local/regional level, again suggesting that corruption may play a role. The cases mentioned concern the building of a private school on previously common land[33] and the personal role of the regency head (*bupati*) in the alleged corruption of funds set aside for another school project.[34] In the latter case, however, party politics might play a role since the letter writer identifies himself as the head of the opposition party PAN[35] of that district.

Issues of student finances, such as tuition fees and stipends, are the explicit topic of three letters. They reveal the different aspects of stipend programmes. There is, to begin with, the letter of the President of the Organization of Indonesian Students in England (PPI) announcing a scholarship programme for students from Aceh financed through the solidarity of Indonesian students abroad.[36] In line with these relief efforts is the letter by the Head of Public Relations of Universitas Syiah Kuala, stating that this university had decided not to ask for tuition fees from students who had lost both parents in the tsunami.[37] Yet, there is also another letter, by a student representative involved in the administration of a scholarship programme, who reveals administrative problems within the city administration of Lokseumawe of being responsible for the non-release of funding.

In general, the role of students is portrayed in very positive tones, as being helpful and idealistic. However, this is countered in at least one letter by an opinion that students of contemporary Aceh have lost their moral and religious roots and have already become too Westernized. The hope of this particular letter writer is that the regional government intervene more in the moral and religious education of students.[38] The general public picture of idealistic and high-minded students is also challenged by three LEs that deal specifically with the practice of and the proposed end to hazing at Universitas Syiah Kuala and other universities in Aceh. The letter by Irfanul Hadi, student representative at Universitas Syiah Kuala, triggered this debate. He declares his support for the rector's decision of that same university to abolish widespread hazing, especially since such student practices might pose yet another psychological pressure for the traumatized victims of the tsunami.[39] This view is challenged by another student contributor, Muhsin, who accuses existing student representatives of not being democratically elected and, therefore, of having no legitimate right to speak "in the name of the students" on this issue. According to Muhsin, except for a few exaggerations, there has been no excessive hazing; hence these rites of orientation should not be abolished.[40] Two days later, Irwansyah, also a student from Universitas Syiah Kuala, criticizes Muhsin's opinion by defending the democratic legitimacy of the student representatives as well as the rector's decision.[41] The dispute that took place through the LEs might well have continued after August 2005. Nonetheless, it shows the lively, highly critical, controversial, and at the same time democratic debate on such matters carried out in a widely read public forum. In comparison with practices of repression and intimidation of public opinion during the New Order, it seems remarkable the extent to which questions of democratic legitimacy and decision-making processes are now openly scrutinized. This is also visible in the last letter in this group concerning education/student affairs, namely that of a student from the State Islamic Institute (IAIN) Banda Aceh. He attacks the rector of that IAIN directly for allegedly not preventing the police from arresting several students after a quarrel.[42] Again, the direct, personal and highly critical tone of that public letter is astonishing, especially if compared with the modes of normative communication enforced under the New Order.

CONCLUSION

The LEs of the journal *Serambi Indonesia*, Banda Aceh, during August 2005, were written in the same month as the signing of the Helsinki peace accord. The devastating tsunami remains an almost ubiquitous theme on a number of levels. While needs for more immediate relief efforts remain the primary topic of letters from particular villages, eight months after the catastrophe such direct concerns are not (or no longer) the main topic. Rather, it seems that fundamental to the traumatic experience of the tsunami has been an altered notion of identity, both that of the individual and community. The individual and communal experience has been expressively reformulated, building upon and reshuffling already existing tropes. The result is a type of formulaic summary of the trauma that then can be evoked in extended or shorthand versions.

Related to such formulaic markers for such an experience, often essentialized as victimization through the catastrophe, are in many cases tropes evoking a particular regional Islamic identity. Often, such LEs conclude with religious formulae (like *amien*) specific to the genres of sermons and prayers. Although Aceh was known for its particular Islamic identity prior to the tsunami, some of the textual evidence suggests that experiences of and living through the tsunami might have intensified these traits. In some letters, the tsunami itself is interpreted as Allah's punishment; prompting one contributor to warn of potentially similar apocalyptic judgments if un-Islamic behaviour in Aceh is allowed to continue. This then serves as an important reason to call for a much stricter implementation of Islamic law.

Since the published LEs of *Serambi Indonesia* represent the choice of the redaction, it is not clear the degree to which the published contributions realistically represent actual public opinion in Aceh. This is not only the case for the letters with religious overtones and/or messages. It also pertains to those discussing education issues, which is one of the most frequent topics in the sample. Here, higher education and student affairs play a particularly important role. It is amazing to see how critical many of these letters are, directly attacking authority figures such as university rectors or senior students serving in administrative functions.

This highly critical attitude towards "elites" of any kind is also apparent in many letters on political issues. "Selfish and corrupt politicians" are here often characterized as antagonistic to the "poor, but honest people". In many letters, the sole source of help for the victimized population appears to be idealistic students and/or a "return" to true religious values.

Notes

1. I would like to thank Amanda Rath for helping me with the English of this paper, as well as for her comments. All remaining errors are of course my responsibility.
2. The meaning of *Droe Keu Droe* can loosely be translated as "From heart to heart", its literal translation being something like "From us to us". I would like to thank Hasan Basri for helping me with this translation.
3. The sample of the 46 "LE" in the online edition of *Serambi Indonesia* was accessed in August/September 2005 <www.serambinews.com>.
4. Cf. for example the letter of 2 August 2005, by Munawar Hasan from Jalan T Hasan Dek, Brawe, Banda Aceh.
5. 1 August 2005, letter by Rusli from Lambaroskep, Kuta Alam, Banda Aceh.
6. 7 August 2005, letter by Rusli Hs from Dusun Inti Jaya, Lambaro Skep, Kuta Alam, Banda Aceh.
7. 15 August, letter by Muhammad S from Ulee Kareng, Banda Aceh.
8. 18 August 2005, letter by Rusli Hs from Kuta Alam, Banda Aceh.
9. 22 August 2005, letter from Asih Lestari from Kuta Alam, Banda Aceh.
10. 19 August 2005, letter by Drs HS Soetarji M, Wakil Koordinator, Tim Ahli, Pemda NAD.
11. 8 August 2005, letter by Tom Ehrhart.
12. 1 August 2005, letter by Akmal Abzal Manggeng from Simpang Surabaya, Luengbata, Banda Aceh.
13. 1 August 2005, letter by Rusli, Lambaroskep, Kuta Alam, Banda Aceh.

14. 1 August 2005, letter by Rusli, Lambaroskep, Kuta Alam, Banda Aceh.
15. 10 August 2005, letter by Drs Abdurrani Msc from Aceh Selatan.
16. 8 August 2005, letter by Azhari UA, Syiah Kuala, Banda Aceh.
17. 13 August 2005, letter from Hadi Iskandar Sofyan, student of the Faculty of Law, Universitas Malikussaleh.
18. 13 August 2005, letter by Hadi Iskandar Sofyan, student of Universitas Malikussaleh.
19. 3 August 2005, letter by Nurlina Kusma, Dusun Teungoh Paloh Lada, Dewantara, Aceh Utara.
20. Letters from Malik Ridwan from Syiah Kuala, Banda Aceh (3 August 2005), Tgk Yusuf Al-Qardhawi El-Idrissi from Kabupaten Bireuen (7 August 2005), Azhari UA from Syiah Kuala, Banda Aceh (8 August 2005), Irzal from Tanjung Selamat, Darussalam, Aceh Besar (8 August 2005), Hasballah Djamaluddin from Kuta Alam, Banda Aceh (22 August 2005), Surya Ibrahim from Kuta Alam, Banda Aceh (22 August 2005), and M Ali from Kota Langsa, Aceh Timor (30 August 2005).
21. 7 August 2005, letter from Tgk Yusuf Al-Qardhawi El-Idrissi from Bireuen.
22. 8 August 2005, letter from Irzal from Tanjung Selamat, Darussalam, Aceh Besar.
23. 28 August 2005, letter from Fitri Yuliana from Krueng Barona Jaya, Aceh Besar.
24. 1 August 2005, letter by Akmal Abzal Manggeng from Simpang Surabaya, Luengbata, Banda Aceh.
25. 7 August 2005, letter from Subdi SR, student of IAIN Banda Aceh.
26. 1 August 2005, letter from Akmal Abzal Manggeng, Simpang Surabaya, Luengbata, Banda Aceh.
27. 3 August 2005, letter from Banta Diman, Jalan Tgk Chick Dipineung, Syiah Kuala, Banda Aceh.
28. 9 August 2005, letter from Ade Darmawan.
29. Letter from 2 August 2005, by Anwarsyah from Jln Kartika Bandarbaru, Kuta Alam, Banda Aceh.
30. 15 August 2005, letter from Taufiq Abdullah from Pidie.
31. 25 August 2005, letter from Saifullah, district of Nagan Raya.
32. 25 August 2005, letter from Maimun, Syiah Kuala, Banda Aceh.
33. 3 August 2005, letter from Nurlina Kusma, Dusun Teungoh Paloh Lada, Dewantara, Aceh Utara.
34. 18 August 2005, letter from Sumitro Candra, Blangpidie, Kabupaten Abdya.
35. PAN = Partai Amanat Nasional, party founded by Amien Rais in the era of reformation, with a programme that is very critical of corruption and social injustice.
36. 10 August 2005, letter from Suyanto Mahdiputra, President of PPI-England.
37. 20 August 2005, letter from Dr. Rusli Yusuf MPd, Universitas Syiah Kuala, Banda Aceh.

38. 8 August 2005, letter from Irzal, Tanjung Selamat, Darussalam, Aceh Besar.
39. 14 August 2005, letter from Irfanul Hadi, student representative at Universitas Syiah Kuala, Banda Aceh.
40. 23 August 2005, letter from Muhsin, student of Universitas Syiah Kuala, Banda Aceh.
41. 25 August 2005, letter from Irwansyah, student representative of Universitas Syiah Kuala, Banda Aceh.
42. 18 August 2005, letter from Salamuddin, Darussalam, Banda Aceh, student of the IAIN Banda Aceh.

16

RAISING FUNDS, LIFTING SPIRITS
Intersections of Music and Humanitarian Aid in Tsunami Relief Efforts

Bethany J. Collier

This chapter explores some musical responses to the devastating earthquake and tsunami that struck Aceh in December 2004, and offers snapshots of the ways that music has been used both to help survivors overcome the trauma of the disaster and to raise money for victims and rebuilding efforts. The integral place of traditional music in these efforts allows for simultaneous examination of relief-oriented musical activity and exploration of selected traditional Acehnese instruments and performance forms.[1] This basic overview of the interactions between well-established and newly-developing artistic expressions in Aceh, then, becomes a lens through which the significance of artistic forms, more generally, can be better viewed.

HISTORICAL CONTEXTS FOR MUSIC-MAKING

The bulk of scholarly writing on music in Indonesia focuses on the gamelan traditions of Bali and Central Java. Ethnomusicologists who work in other areas of Indonesia have long bemoaned the lack of attention paid to the artistic practices and performers from the geographic regions of their studies.[2] Ethnomusicologist Margaret J. Kartomi was the first scholar to publish an English-language study of music and dance in Aceh, and she remains one of the few ethnomusicologists working in this area.

According to Kartomi, Acehnese writers and performers identify three kinds of producers of musical sound: the "instruments of material culture", the "animate human voice", and the "human body moving while producing percussive sound" (Kartomi 2005, pp. 27–28). Those sound-producers that belong in the "instruments of material culture" category are further classified by the way the instrument produces sound, whether by being beaten (*peh*), blown (*yub*), or bowed (*geusok*) (Kartomi 2005, pp. 30–32).

While there is a tendency in much musicological scholarship to categorize musical instruments and artistic forms according to historical period, it is more useful, in this case, to examine commonalities among kinds of performance contexts and genres. A historical categorization for artistic forms in Aceh might classify instruments based on their emergence or prominence in the pre-Islamic, Islamic, colonial, national independence, or post-colonial resistance periods, as briefly outlined below. A genre- or context-based approach might group instruments and forms, as ethnomusicologist Marc Perlman suggests, into such categories as devotional choral singing in single-sex groups; laments at funerals, weddings, or by spirit mediums; percussion-based ensembles; flutes, whether played solo or as accompaniment to singing; and music for entertainment (Perlman 2001). This second kind of classification system allows for better consideration of instruments that appear across historical periods, whether or not their functions change over time. Also, as Kartomi suggests, this latter approach is more attentive to the ways that Acehnese musicians and dancers conceive of and categorize their musical instruments.

Historians estimate that the arrival and development of Islam in Aceh likely occurred over a period of several hundred years, beginning at the end of the thirteenth century. There is evidence that animist and Hindu-Buddhist practices were prominent at that time (Kartomi 1998, pp. 600–601), but as Islamic brotherhoods began to play a larger role in local communities, the use of musical instruments associated with those animist-Hindu practices fell out of use. During the period of Dutch colonial rule, the high-class, land-owning *uleebalang* regularly clashed with *ulama* (religious leaders) regarding many matters, including religion and the arts. In post-colonial times, the Indonesian national government began to sponsor festivals and encourage both the continued practice of existing traditional arts and the development of new dance and music forms (Kartomi 2005, pp. 33–34).

The Islamic injunction that musical instruments are not essential for the fostering of religious experience has likely affected the development of musical systems and practices in Aceh. The prominence of such a highly developed system of body percussion and the importance of frame drums and religious chanting in traditional Acehnese performance support this claim, which is now commonly accepted among ethnomusicologists and historians. There remains a general disapproval of dance and music forms in Aceh that have their roots in Hindu-Buddhist or animistic practices. While performance of such forms may become permissible if preceded by appropriate Islamic prayers or rituals, instruments and dances that are believed to originate from Sumatra's pre-Islamic period or that are perceived to have developed as a result of modern influences from the Western world still do not receive wide acceptance among contemporary Aceh's more conservative practitioners of the Islamic faith. Despite these common sentiments, however, traces of animist and Hindu-Buddhist influences are still apparent in many music and dance forms in Aceh, and the popular music market continues to grow.

FACING DISASTER: THE MUSICAL COMMUNITY RESPONDS

Performing artists and music industry officials in Indonesia responded swiftly to the devastating earthquake and tsunami of December 2004. Through various efforts — the production and sales of benefit recordings, the writing of new, commemorative songs, the integration of elements of traditional culture into popular music, and the sponsoring of, production of, or performance in relief aid concerts — the Indonesian musical community focused attention on the disaster in Aceh and contributed billions of rupiah to relief efforts.[3]

In a fund-raising event sponsored by Masyarakat Peduli Indonesia (MPI, or Citizens Caring for Indonesia) held at Jakarta's Hard Rock Café on 6 January 2005, Indonesian popular musician Iwan Fals performed three songs that he had written in response to the tsunami and its devastation in Aceh and North Sumatra.[4] Written on 28 December 2004, Fals' "Saat Minggu Masih Pagi" was auctioned off to businessman/artist Setiawan Djodi and singer/band-leader Meta. The winning bidders paid Rp85 million for the song, the largest sum of money offered for any of the items auctioned that evening (Ati 2005).

Three days later, on 9 January 2005, over 300 artists gathered on Jakarta's Pantai Karnaval (Carnival Beach) to perform for thousands of fans in a spectacular day-long "humanitarian concert" (*konser kemanusiaan*), themed "Care about Aceh and North Sumatra" ("*Peduli Aceh-Sumut*"). This twelve-hour event, also sponsored by MPI, presented a wide range of musical offerings, including heavy metal, pop, rock, jazz, and *dangdut*. With ticket prices set at an affordable Rp10,000, thousands of attendees present, and half of the admission sales marked for donation,[5] MPI presented Palang Merah Indonesia (PMI, the Indonesian Red Cross) with a contribution of approximately Rp4 billion in cash and goods for refugees.[6]

The following month, Indonesian rock group Slank joined forces with Iwan Fals for a three-month, twenty-seven city concert tour, "Unite in Peace: Solidarity for Aceh" ("*Bersatu dalam Damai: Solidaritas untuk Aceh*").[7] During the first concert of this A Mild Live tour, Fals sang his three new songs, including "Harapan Tak Boleh Mati" ("Hope May Not Die"), which he wrote just six days after the tsunami hit, inspired by the story of a small crab that survived the disaster by clinging to a mattress (Hazmirullah and "PR" 2005; Ati 2005). Contributions from this first concert alone, held at Bandung's Nusantara Fairground IPTN on 9 February 2005, totalled Rp110 million (Hazmirullah and "PR" 2005). At the end of the concert tour, Fals and Slank donated Rp1.4 billion and Rp2.9 billion, respectively, to the Provincial Library of Nanggroe Aceh Darussalam. The funds were designated for the repair and reconstruction of the library building and for the replacement of many of the library's furnishings and books ("IRN" 2005).

The Indonesian jazz community also joined forces to present a series of six benefit concerts, entitled *Konser Kemanusiaan: Jazz untuk Aceh* ("Humanitarian Concert: Jazz for Aceh"). For each of these concerts, all musicians, technicians, sound and lighting equipment rental agencies, and performance venues donated their services, ensuring that operating and production costs were minimal. While admission to the concerts was free, relief funds were raised by making a wide variety of merchandise available for audience members' purchase. Items for sale included compact discs donated by their featured artists, and jazz-themed posters, drawings, and paintings. Additionally, songs were auctioned off to the highest bidders and donation boxes were placed around the concert venues and circulated during the performances. Each evening's performance in the series featured a jam session from within which one song was dedicated, explicitly and spontaneously, as the evening's "Tribute to Aceh" (Arif Budiman and Wartajazz.com, 2005).

The first concert of this five-week tour, held at Jakarta's Graha Bakti Budaya on 22 January 2005, brought together Indonesia's leading jazz musicians and several special guest performers.[9] An important part of these artists' contribution was the musical language that many of them chose to use in response to the tragedy. By inserting elements from traditional Acehnese performing arts and invoking aspects of Islamic religious practice in their performances of both classic jazz standards and contemporary jazz compositions, the performers gave tribute to survivors and casualties of the tsunami in a particularly evocative way.

Pianist Tjut Nyak Deviana Daudsjah, for example, played a jazz arrangement of the Acehnese folk song "Bungong Jeumpa" ("The Jeumpa Flower") with the Tjindo Quintet, who inserted *saman* movements into their performance (Arif Kusbandono, Nana and Wartajazz 2005).

Saman is a well-known traditional performing art from the Gayo region of Aceh. According to M. Junus Melalatoa (2001, pp. 6–8), the form is nearly non-existent in Gayo Lut, but has developed significantly among the people of Gayo Luwes. While the historical roots of *saman* are unclear, there is some evidence that the art form developed from *ratib*, a form of chanting practised in Sufi brotherhoods during the eighteenth and nineteenth centuries (Perlman 2001). This all-male song and movement-based form is popularly referred to as the "dance of a thousand hands", for the song is performed without instrumental accompaniment, relying instead on the men's gesturing, hand clapping, finger snapping, and thigh or chest slapping for rhythmic accompaniment. A competitive form, the contemporary practice of *saman* consists of around fifteen men kneeling closely together, singing romantic, religious, or entertaining texts while performing hand gestures and head and body motions. The complex vocabulary of hand motions consists of over 130 different documented gestures, with new sequences constantly being composed. A similar dance form, called *meuseukat*, is performed by women (H. Smith 1997, p. 57).

That evening's performance by popular Indonesian band Krakatau, known for its stylistic fusion of jazz, light rock, pop, and Indonesian traditional music genres, featured three artists in addition to the band's usual personnel. Two vocalists, Marzuki, an artist from Aceh, and Iskandar, a Gayo performer who sang with *didong*-style vocal ornamentation, appeared with the group, and musician Alex played the well-known, distinctive *serunai* (Arif Kusbandono, Nana and Wartajazz 2005).

Didong is a competitive game that combines physical movement, vocal music, and poetry. Two opposing clubs, called *ulu* or *kelop* (Junus Melalatoa 2001, p. 2), are each made up of thirty to forty men sitting in a circle. The group's leader is called the *ceh*, and he is responsible for (often spontaneously) composing creative poetic lyrics and singing them to a melody of his own composition (Thatawy, Kilang and Darulaman 1998, p. vi). There are usually two or three *ceh* in each group. The most prominent one, the *ceh utama*, usually has the best voice, and he is supported by one or two helpers. The remaining members of the group accompany the *ceh* with variations of body movements and clapping, adding rhythm to the melody. The only instruments used in *didong* are small pillows or cushions, called *kampas*, which each member hits rhythmically to accompany the singing (Junus Melalatoa 2001, p. 11). One or two of these members lead the others, giving signals with claps or body motions (ibid., pp. 16–17).

The *ceh*'s voice must be melodious (*merdu, ling temas*), and he must have a complete knowledge of the community's traditional practices (*adat-istiadat*) in order to compose interesting, relevant, and effective lyrics (ibid., pp. 11–13). The themes contained in the lyrics usually align with happenings in the area or with well-known historical events (ibid., p. 31). Today, *didong* is usually performed for weddings or other large celebrations in all-night contests (Thantawy, Kilang and Darulaman 1998, p. vi). While *didong* is found in all three Gayo regions — Gayo Lut, Gayo Luwes, and Gayo Serbejadi — the form has developed to a greater extent among the people of Gayo Lut than in the other groups (Junus Melalatoa 2001, pp. 5–6).

The *seurune kalee* is perhaps the most well-known, identifiably Acehnese musical instrument. Crafted from aged hardwood (most often from a jackfruit tree), this double-reeded wind instrument is characterized by its piercing, reedy tone and microtonal style of elaboration. The technique of circular breathing allows for the performer to realize long melodies with extensive ornamentation. Description of the *seurune kalee*'s sound as "dynamic" and "heroic" (Firdaus Borhan and Idris Z.Z., eds., 1986/87, p. 81) reflects well the Acehnese characterization of the instrument as stereotypically masculine (Kartomi 2005, pp. 42–43). The *seurune kalee* is prominent in Aceh proper, especially around the city of Banda Aceh (Kartomi 1998). In other areas of Sumatra, and in Vietnam and Malaysia, similarly constructed instruments with the same name are also ubiquitous, although the spelling of the instrument's name may differ: *sarunai, sarune, sarunei,* or *serune*, for example, are alternate versions (Kartomi, Moore, and Nguyen 1984).

Other performances that evening also included sonic references to Acehnese musical and religious practices. The group Groovology began their performance of Stevie Wonder's "Superstition" with the standard, respectful greeting, *saleum pembuka.* The Culture Music Factory performed a medley of Chick Corea's "Crystal Silence" and Duke Ellington's "Caravan", during which vocalist Nita recited *istighfar*, an Islamic appeal for forgiveness and expression of remorse. The piano-drum duo formed specifically for this concert, featuring Dwiki Dharmawan and Budhy Haryono, was joined by singer Nyak Ina "Ubiet" Raseuki, who performed with an explicitly Acehnese vocal style (Arif Kusbandono, Nana and Wartajazz 2005).

In addition to the staging of large concert events and the writing and release of new songs, complete benefit albums were released in the first months following the tsunami disaster as a means to fund relief efforts. Produced by Musica Studios, in conjunction with the Sampoerna Foundation and the Guruh Soekarnoputra Foundation, the benefit album "Dari Hati untuk Aceh"

("From the Heart for Aceh" or "To Aceh, From the Heart") was released on 22 February 2005. According to the album's initiator, Guruh Sukarnoputra, proceeds from the album's sales (Rp5,000 per cassette and Rp10,000 per compact disc) will be donated to help restore Aceh's archives and establish an art and culture centre in the region.

The album features two selections of poetry, read by Sinetron star Tamara Bleszynski, and nine songs, seven of which are older songs performed by long-established Indonesian musicians.[10] Each of these seven songs had been used as accompanying music to news briefs and short televised informational clips in the weeks following the tsunami. Hearing the same songs again, even when the news briefs they once accompanied are no longer being broadcast, can evoke feelings in listeners similar to those that they experienced at the time of the disaster. The thematic association, then, of this compilation of musical selections with the tragedy both commemorates the event and provides a material contribution to productive rebuilding efforts.[11]

One song on the album, "Aceh/Ayah", is a remake of Rinto Harahap's famous 1970s hit, "Ayah" ("Father"). While "Ayah" was not used in the mass media in the same way as the seven other older songs featured on "Dari Hati untuk Aceh", its inclusion on the album is poignant. Originally a child's mournful plea to see his beloved father (*ayah*) again, this song was remade lyrically, to reflect the situation in Aceh, and musically, to adapt to current trends and tastes in contemporary Indonesian music.

The lyrics of the original refrain were changed only by the substitution of the word "Aceh" for the original "Ayah".[12]

*Untuk **ayah** tercinta*	For my beloved **father**
Aku ingin bernyanyi	I want to sing
Walau air mata di pipiku	Even with tears on my cheek
***Ayah**, dengarkanlah*	**Father**, listen please
Aku ingin berjumpa	I want to visit you
Walau hanya dalam mimpi	Even only in [my] dreams
*Untuk **Aceh** tercinta*	For my beloved **Aceh**
Aku ingin bernyanyi	I want to sing
Walau air mata di pipiku	Even with tears on my cheek
***Aceh**, dengarkanlah*	**Aceh**, listen please
Aku ingin berjumpa	I want to visit you
Walau hanya dalam mimpi	Even only in [my] dreams

The phenomenally popular group Peterpan was responsible for preparing and performing the song's new arrangement.[13] Updated both in thematic focus and musical sound, the new version of Harahap's 1970s hit is one of the two songs on "Dari Hati untuk Aceh" that is performed by young musicians, and is still the subject of much discussion in Internet chat rooms and on young adults' weblogs (blogs).

An earlier benefit album, "Kita untuk Mereka" ("Us for Them"), features fifty-eight singers, many of whom are established musicians in the Indonesian musical community and others who are relatively new to the scene. The recording features twelve songs, and includes the voices of stars from the wildly popular reality shows "Indonesian Idol" and "Akademi Fantasi Indosiar" ("Indosiar Fantasy Academy").[14]

Indonesian R&B star Glenn Fredly composed and named the title song for "Kita untuk Mereka", which was released by Sony and BMG on 24 January 2005. After Fredly wrote the title track's lyrics, arranger Erwin Gutawa orchestrated the song, adding traces of world and pop music influences to the underlying orchestral layers. The voice of Acehnese singer Ubiet opens and closes the song, ornamenting a brief, but evocative vocal phrase.[15] Each verse showcases solo lines by individual or pairs of singers, then the group of fifty-eight joins together in the chorus-style refrain.[16] Proceeds from sales of the album were promised to the Indonesian Red Cross, whose head Mar'ie Muhammad commented, "Honestly, I have never seen such strong social solidarity as in this moment…"[17]

IMMEDIATE AND CONSTANT: THE HUMANITARIAN AID COMMUNITY RESPONDS

Relief organizations and the humanitarian aid community also responded quickly and decisively to the crisis in Aceh and North Sumatra. Realizing the important role that traditional and artistic practices play in the lives of many of those affected by the disaster, the cultural unit of the United Nations Educational, Scientific, and Cultural Organization (UNESCO) carried out a "Rapid Appraisal on Socio-Cultural Conditions[s] in Nangroe Aceh Darussalam". In this April 2005 assessment, UNESCO Indonesia stated that approximately 500 artists were reported missing or deceased as a result of the earthquake and tsunami.[18]

The report identifies a series of different activities that are considered effective ways for dealing with the kind of deep trauma experienced by survivors, especially children, including drawing, reading poetry, dancing, singing, watching movies, and religious study activities (*pengajian*, *tilawat*, and *zikir*). Recognizing the integration of dance and music in Acehnese performing arts, and the importance of physical activity for those experiencing depression and trauma, the UNESCO cultural unit sought to build an emotional and spiritual recovery programme based on traditional artistic practices.[19]

Following this appraisal of the situation in Aceh, UNESCO teamed with the Sacred Bridge Foundation (Yayasan Titian Budaya) to implement a programme they named "Rising Above the Tsunami, Phase I" (RAT I). This three-month programme was designed to train local artists to visit and help young tsunami survivors. Artists visited surviving children in two refugee camps and temporary shelters in order to teach them songs and dances, intending to provide therapeutic activity for and to pass on traditional cultural practices to the displaced, traumatized children. For the artists, too, this programme provided an opportunity for them to continue filling their roles as teachers and transmitters of cultural knowledge. After seeing the success of RAT I, the Office for the Coordination of Humanitarian Affairs (OCHA) contributed funds to finance a second phase of the same programme. "Rising Above the Tsunami, Phase II" (RAT II) was an expanded version of RAT I, with artists visiting and teaching in four camps over the course of four months.[20]

In coordination with the Sacred Bridge Foundation and the Indonesian Department of Culture and Tourism, UNESCO then sponsored "Rising Above the Tsunami: A Transmission of Acehnese Cultural Heritage" in May 2006. This event, held at the Ministry of Culture and Tourism's Sapta Pesona Building in Jakarta, aimed to "share experiences and lessons learnt during the UNESCO Cultural and Psychotherapeutic Healing Programme, conducted in Nanggroe Aceh Darussalam..., as well as to raise awareness on [*sic*] the importance of culture in any sustainable development efforts, especially in the context of post-disaster situations."[21] Forty-six tsunami survivors were brought to Jakarta for the evening-long programme, which featured the survivors in a stage demonstration of the RAT I and RAT II methods. Thirty-two of the forty-six individuals who were brought from North Sumatra were young tsunami survivors, children living in camps or temporary shelters, and another two were barracks coordinators. Eight programme instructors and four of the traditional artists who had visited and taught the children in the programme also participated in the evening's showcase.

Two of the four invited artists were prominent *seudati* masters Syeh Lah Bangguna and Syeh Lah Geunta, who demonstrated their art and the teaching approaches they used for the RAT programmes.

> The martial male song and dance form *seudati* combines choreography of body motions with song, hand clapping, finger snapping, and rhythmic slapping of the body. The men stand in circular or linear formation, accompanying their song leaders, who sing religiously-themed or historical-/political-inspired texts, with quick percussive body movements. Similar versions of this art form performed by girls are called *seudati inong*, *laweut*, and *pho* (Kartomi 1998, p. 604).[22]

The third Acehnese performer was well-known dancer and teacher Marzuki Hasan, who demonstrated *saman* and other traditional dance forms. He was joined by musician Ismail Sarong, the fourth invited master artist, who demonstrated both the *seurune kalee* and the *rapa'i* (UNESCO Indonesia, "Press Release", 2006).

Identified by Kartomi (1998, p. 604) as "by far the most important instrument" in Aceh, the *rapa'i* is a frame drum that is used to accompany devotional singing, dance, and praise. The medium-sized *rapa'i daboih* can be found in all areas of Aceh, and is used to accompany the worship form *daboih*. The smaller *rapa'i peulot* (or *geurimphang*) is found primarily in Pidie, and the largest *rapa'i Pase* (or *rapa'i urok*) is dominant in North Aceh (Kartomi 1998, p. 604). The *rapa'i* frame is made from hardwood or, sometimes, from the wood of a jackfruit tree. The drum's membrane is usually a stretched goatskin, but the skin of a certain kind of monkey, called *himbe* in Acehnese, can also be used (Firdaus Burhan and Idris Z.Z., eds., 1986/87, p. 69).

Other relief organizations have also recognized the valuable role that the arts can play in helping disaster victims recover from their traumatic experiences. The American and Indonesian Red Cross organizations worked together in several coastal villages to coordinate a series of community-based activities, designed to encourage survivors to gather together again in enjoyable social contexts. As one of the activities, children were given the opportunity to sing traditional songs, and to compose and perform songs about the tsunami in a small performance for adults from their villages (American Red Cross, n.d.).

Humanitarian aid organization Mercy Corps organized a two-day cultural festival in Banda Aceh. Attended by between 5,000 and 6,000 people, the event offered various music performances, traditional Acehnese dance stagings, movie screenings, and a photo exhibition. John Brownlee, the Social Revitalization programme manager for Mercy Corps' unit in Banda Aceh explained the aims of this festival. "Since the tsunami, there has been a lot of talk about trauma healing and psycho social [sic] interventions for survivors.... The basic concept of the Heritage Fair is to allow cultural and artistic expression and celebrate Acehnese traditions and culture, while also remembering what happened and at the same time carrying on." (Bakhat, n.d.).

For many Heritage Fair attendees, the highlight of the event was a free evening concert by popular Acehnese musician Rafly and his band, Kande.[23] In the first weeks following the earthquake and tsunami in Aceh, several of Rafly's hit songs were used as background music to accompany informational clips shown on private Indonesian television stations. These brief airings, showing photographs of the region and its people, provided visual and sonic reminders of the disaster, reminding television viewers throughout the archipelago of their social and moral obligation to help the people of Aceh.[24]

Also in the aftermath of the tsunami, Rafly has been touring camps for internally displaced persons (IDPs), singing new versions of older Acehnese songs and encouraging survivors to maintain a sense of hope. Mixing religious messages with music and singing to crowds in the refugee camps, Rafly's performances allow the children and adults in his audience to experience familiar, culturally-associated musical sounds. These sonic reminders, he hopes, evoke memories and help his listeners to move, slowly, through their grief. Quoted in *Time Asia*, Rafly explains that "when we are children, our mothers sing to us in Acehnese. We hear this music from when we are born... We cannot dwell in trauma for too long. We must think of our future. We must pray to God. We must recite the Quran. Then we will find the answers."[25]

In 2005, Indonesian filmmaker Alex Sihar produced a fifteen-minute film, "Ubat Até Allah Allah, Ubat Sösah Pëyasan Beuna" documenting Rafly and his band Kande's work bringing music and healing to children and adults living in camps for IDPs.[26] The film's title (which translates as "Prayers for Allah Are the Medicine for the Troubled Heart, Comforting Songs Are the Medicine for Grieving Souls"[27]) is an old Acehnese expression that Rafly has adopted for use as an entry point into both his humanitarian and performing efforts (Agnes Aristiarini 2005).

Rafly's popularity and musical success are not limited to the boundaries of refugee camps. Although his lyrics are in Acehnese, and are therefore not understandable to non-Acehnese-speaking Indonesians, his musical and vocal styles have become popular throughout much of the Indonesian archipelago. A brief glance at weblogs and chat lists shows fans from across Indonesia praising his music and its message, scrambling to find translations of his lyrics, and struggling to obtain his recordings for purchase. On one website, a lucky fan using the screen name "amirsodikin" advises another distressed fan about where she might locate a copy of Rafly's popular song "Seulanga".

> Post-tsunami, finding [recordings of] Rafli's songs certainly is difficult, especially in Banda Aceh. The only alternative place to find that song ["Seulanga"] is in Lhokseumawe, but at this point, the bigger the store selling VCDs is, the emptier it'll be. I actually got Rafli's VCD from a street vendor, and it's even an original, for only 20,000 rupiah [...] There are also some that have been made into MP3s (most likely illegal ones). It's possible that there are some in Medan, you just have to look. In Jakarta, I'm not sure that there are.... Happy hunting...[28]

Another Rafly fan, a non-Acehnese concert-goer, wrote in her blog about the accessibility of his music to an ethnically-mixed, multi-generational audience.

> Not everyone understood Rafly's lyrics, but everyone reacted, emotions excited, joining in singing. The audience was so diverse, beginning with the villagers who flooded Calang beach, where the performance was held, to volunteers from NGOs the world over who also attended. It was so obvious that they all enjoyed the musical treat... (Putireno Baiak, n.d.).[29]

In addition to their appearances in refugee camps where their aid to victims is primarily emotional and spiritual, Rafly and Kande have performed in benefit concerts in order to raise funds for victims and rebuilding efforts. One such performance event, organized and staged in March 2005 by the Acehkita Foundation, reached for the attention of a high-class, international audience. The evening's programme was widely publicized, in both the Indonesian and English languages, as a charity fund raiser. Tickets for this elite benefit concert and dinner event were priced at Rp250,000 per person, a cost that would be prohibitive for many of Rafly's ordinary fans. One hundred paying guests attended the event, including the head of the Italian Cultural Centre and Dutch, Danish, and Swiss ambassadors. Rafly (vocals) and Kande (made up of an electric bassist, two electric guitarists, and a drummer) were joined by three prominent artists with national reputations (Dwiki Dharmawan and Didi on keyboards and Tjut Nyak "Ubiet" Raseuki on vocals).[30] Fifteen children also appeared on stage as a chorus for one of the evening's selections, and several performers of traditional Acehnese musical instruments — four *rapa'i* players, one *seurune kalee* performer, and one *geundrang* player — played along throughout the night (Ati 2005).

> The *geundrang* is a large, double-headed drum that is played with either a stick or the performer's hands. The body of this important drum is made from the wood of a jackfruit tree, and its heads are made either from goatskin or very thin cowhide. Geundrang are usually played in pairs, and often form an ensemble with the *seurune kalee*. In contemporary Aceh, this *geundrang* pair-*seurune kalee* ensemble often accompanies sung poetry and celebratory or traditional dances.[31]

Using his profound success to improve his political leverage, Rafly has travelled to Jakarta as an unofficial spokesperson in the hopes of refining the prevalent image of Aceh and the Acehnese people that has, by and large, been created and fortified by non-Acehnese (Maria Hartaningsih 2005).

MOVING ON

Music and elements of musical behaviour are known to play an important part in identity formation and memory. Artists and mental health experts have long been aware that music is capable of effecting a positive change in traumatized patients, and the blending of traditional instruments and musical techniques into popular music has been common in Indonesia and other parts of the world for decades. Operating as sonic markers of an experience or a cultural group, for example, specific sounds can evoke associations for an individual listener or an entire community.

The urgency and severity of circumstances in the regions affected by the December 2004 earthquake and tsunami demanded an immediate response from the Indonesian government, from local and regional associations, and from international organizations. In the face of a disaster of such profound proportions, relief workers and aid organizations used the skills, resources, and compassion available to them, assisting the physical, emotional, and spiritual needs of hundreds of thousands of displaced persons. At the same time, Indonesian musicians summoned their creative energies —performing concerts, producing commemorative albums, writing new songs, and combining new sounds with traditional instruments — to respond with consideration, resourcefulness, and much-needed financial contributions. As rebuilding and recovery continue even now, the results of these efforts by humanitarian aid, artistic, and many other communities become increasingly tangible in post-tsunami Aceh.

Notes

1. While the limitations of this article permit for description of only a few, selected traditional musical instruments and dance and music forms, more comprehensive studies are available. In the English language, see Kartomi (2005, pp. 25–57). In the Indonesian language, see Z.H. Idris et al. (1993); and Firdaus Burhan and Idris Z.Z., eds. (1986/87). For a concise overview of Sumatra's cultural history, see other contributions in this volume, and Kartomi (1998) in the *Garland Encyclopedia*. A significant portion of the Garland volume is devoted to the history, politics, and cultural and musical practices of the Indonesian archipelago.
2. See, as a recent example of this, Sutton (2002), and Sean Williams' review commentary, printed on the volume's back cover.

3. See examples in Eri Anugerah (2005); Ukon Ahmad Furqon (2005); and r/a (2006).
4. Commonly called Indonesia's "Ballad King" (*Raja Balada*), Iwan Fals is often considered the Bob Dylan of Indonesian popular music. He is well-known for his politically-concerned, socially-motivated songs, like his 1980s "Ethiophia," which describes the malnourished, starving population of Ethiopia.
5. "Konser 318 Artis Untuk Aceh." *Pikiran Rakyat* (10 January 2005). Accessed online at <http://www.pikiran-rakyat.com/cetak/2005/0105/10/0107.htm>.
6. "Masyarakat Peduli Indonesia Serahkan Bantuan Rp4 Milyar Bagi Aceh." *Gatra* (1 February 2005). Accessed online at <http://www.indonesia-ottawa.org/information/ details.php?type=news&id=500>.
7. First formed as primarily a cover band in 1983, the Indonesian rock group Slank has released eleven original albums and their popularity continues to rise, especially among young listeners. Their official website is <http://www.slank.com>.
8. For another report on this same concert, see the article "Iwan Fals-Slank Bersatu Demi Aceh". *Republika Online* (13 February 2005). Accessed online at <http://www.republika.co.id/koran_detail.asp?id=187260&katid=103 &katid1=&kat_id2=>.
9. The remaining five concerts were staged in Yogyakarta, Bandung, Kuta (Bali), Batam, and Medan.
10. RRI-online. (n.d.). "Release: Dari hati untuk Aceh". Accessed online at <http://www.rri-online.com/modules.php?name=Music&op=album_baru_resensi&id=15>.
11. Mediaindo, "'Dari Hati untuk Aceh: Upaya Ikut Membangun Kembali Aceh", 27 February 2005. Accessed online at <http://www.mediaindo.co.id/resensi/details.asp?id=46>.
12. Refrain from "Ayah", written by Rinto Harahap and made popular by The Mercy's.
13. The six member pop-rock band Peterpan from Bandung was formed in 2000. The group has become wildly popular since they start playing alternative rock covers in Bandung clubs and cafes, releasing two original albums, "Taman Langit" ("Sky Garden") in 2003 and "Bintang di Surga" ("Star in Heaven") in 2004. Peterpan's official website is <www.peterpanband.com>.
14. Astaga!com, "Album Kita untuk Mereka: Solidaritas Musisi Tanah Air untuk Aceh dan Sumut", 26 January 2005. Accessed online at <http://astaga.com/musik/index.php?cat=126&id=94290>.
15. Ibid.
16. The assembling of this kind of "all-star" line-up for performance of the album's title song is reminiscent of the 1985 USA for Africa production and recording of "We Are the World."
17. Astaga!com, "Album Kita untuk Mereka". The original quote reads, "Sejujurnya,

saya tidak pernah melihat solidaritas sosial yang begitu kuat seperti saat ini…" Translation by the author.

18. UNESCO Indonesia, "Rapid Appraisal on Socio-Cultural Condition in Nangroe Aceh Darussalam", 18 May 2005. Accessed online at <http://www.unesco.or.id/activities/culture/completed/248.php>.
19. Ibid.
20. UNESCO Indonesia, "Press Release: Rising Above the Tsunami: A Transmission of Acehnese Cultural Heritage", 12 May 2006. Accessed online at <http://www.unesco.or.id/ activities/culture/286.php>.
21. "Acehnese Cultural Event, 9 May 2006, Jakarta, Indonesia", 26 April 2006. Accessed online at <http://www.unesco.or.id/events/285.php>.
22. Iwan Dzulvan Amir, one of Kartomi's Ph.D. students at Monash University, produced the first ever documentary film on *seudati* in 2005. The seventy-eight-minute film, "Seudati: Percakapan dengan Seniman" ("Seudati: Conversations with Artists"), features footage of live *seudati* performance and conversations with *seudati* supporters and performers. In Indonesian and Acehnese languages with English subtitles, the film is based on Amir's 2004 fieldwork in Aceh. See <http://www.arts.monash.edu/mai/newsletters05/news181005.txt>.
23. Originally from Singkil, South Sumatra, Rafly's musical and personal style has dramatically changed from his 1980s rock star image. Reportedly, after praying in a mosque one day he felt an urge to become more devout, an impulse that is reflected in his present musical style, characterized by the fusion of traditional and popular musics. See this account in "Aceh Pop Star Tours Tsunami Camps", 3 May 2005. Accessed online at <http://news.bbc.co.uk/1/hi/world/asia-pacific/4497753.stm>. The article "Rafly 'Kande' Digaet Dwiki Dharmawan", available at <http://kompas.com/gayahidup/news/0503/15/163918.htm>, also discusses this change in musical style.
24. "Rafly, "Penyanyi Aceh yang Berpacu dengan Maut Saat Tsunami, Bersama Wali Kota yang Kemudian Tewas", in *Padang Ekspres*, 27 January 2005. Accessed online at <http://www.padangekspres.com>.
25. Rafly, quoted in Marshall (2005).
26. Ubat Até Allah-Allah Ubat Sosah Pëyasan Beuna" (n.d.). Accessed online at <http://www.konfiden.or.id/pages/pro_ubatate.php>; and "Film Screening: 3 Indonesian Documentaries" (n.d.). Accessed online at <http://www.asianheritagemonth.net/ Calendar%20of%20Events%202,2006.htm>. A second short film, produced by Indonesian filmmaker Syaiful Halim in 2005, depicts a small number of stories from the tsunami, focusing in particular on one victim's story. While attention in this film, "Atjeh Lon Sayang" (My Beloved Aceh), is not focused on Rafly in the same way that it is in Sihar's film, a portion of the documentary centres around local artists' efforts to help children using prayer and song. See "Film Screening". Translation of Halim's title is taken from this online posting.
27. "Film Screening". Title translation above is taken from this online notice.

28. "Posting subject: Re: Terjemahan lagu aceh Seulanga", reply by user amirsodikin. Accessed online at <http://jurnalisme.org/Forums/viewtopic/t=46/postdays=0/postorder=asc /start=0.html>. The original posting reads: "Pascatsunami tentu saja cari lagu-lagu rafli susah, apalagi di Banda Aceh. Satu-satunya alternatif cari lagu itu di Lhokseumawe, tapi justru di toko-toko besar yang jualan VCD akhir-akhir ini malah kosong. Saya dapat vcd rafli justru di kaki lima, tapi original kok, harganya cuman Rp 20.000 [...] Ada juga yang sudah di MP3-kan (dugaan kuat ilegal). Di Medan kemungkinan juga ada, cuman harus nyari dulu. Di jakarta, aku gak yakin kalo ada.... Selamat berburu..." Translation by the author. The difficulties encountered while trying to obtain these recordings are certainly compounded by recent, more stringent enforcement of regulations on pirated CDs, VCDs, and DVDs in Indonesia.
29. The original Indonesian reads: "Tak semua orang mengerti lirik-lirik lagu Rafly, tapi semua orang bereaksi, tergugah emosinya serta ikutan bernyanyi. Penonton sangat beragam, mulai dari masyarakat desa yang membanjiri tepi pantai Calang dimana pentas digelar, juga para relawan dari berbagai NGO seluruh dunia. Nampak sekali mereka semua menikmati musik yang disuguhkan..." Translation by the author.
30. Dharmawan, a member of Krakatau, and Rafly had performed together earlier in the year, when Dharmawan travelled to Banda Aceh to visit and entertain refugees in IDP camps with Rafly.
31. See Firdaus Burhan and Idris Z.Z., eds. (1986/87), p. 55; and Kartomi (2005), pp. 36–37.

17

GOD SPEAKS THROUGH NATURAL DISASTERS, BUT WHAT DOES HE SAY?
Islamic Interpretations in Indonesian Tsunami Poetry

Edwin Wieringa

AN ACT OF GOD

In the literatures of the Indonesian seafaring peoples, the sea quite naturally belongs since time immemorial to the most familiar tropes used by poets and storytellers. Their maritime metaphorical field is vast and can evoke a wide variety of possible meanings and connotations, presenting "the sea" in a dazzling array of different perspectives. In older texts the sea is mostly associated with positive elements, and it seems that this tendency has even intensified in modern Indonesian poetry. Ever since the 1930s, Indonesian poets writing in the national language like to employ the sea as a prominent metaphor to denote beckoning freedom (Goenawan Mohamad 2002). To them the sea is an adventurous place of boundless infinity, offering unexpected vistas. In a country, in which the term for "fatherland, native land" is expressed as the collocation *tanah air* or "land-sea", the sea forms an integral part of the national territory. That the sea not only constitutes the nation, but the national identity as well is, for example, aptly phrased by the poet Isma Sawitri, born in 1940 in Langsa (Aceh), in a proud appeal to her compatriots which she made in 1964:

We are the sea, the mighty vessels
From the Arafura Sea to the Sunda Strait and the Malacca Strait
Such was the history of the people in its glorious era
Before Sultan Agung and the monopoly of armed trading ships

We are the sea, before cloves and nutmeg
We are the sea, after oil and steel
The boats so sweet, the ships mightier
Look straight at the sea, the open sea[1]

Understandably, Indonesian tsunami poetry, which was composed en masse immediately after the tragic event, could not be modelled on enthusiastic evocations of the sea that have become so characteristic of contemporary Indonesian literature. The gruesome side of nature that the real sea had suddenly and dramatically shown to mankind on 26 December 2004 was a ghastly aspect, which hitherto had not kindled the imagination of Indonesia's guild of literary craftsmen. What sort of poem can you write to encompass such a destructive seismic sea wave?

On the worldwide web one can easily find many examples of tsunami poetry from all over the world. They are typically the emotional outpourings of engaged people, and in this occasional poetry the social function overwhelmingly dominates over literary quality. Confining myself to Indonesia only, it is absolutely impossible to give a survey of that what has been produced so far. Newspapers have reported of numerous poetry events in many major cities. In the capital Jakarta alone several "engaged poetry platforms" (*panggung puisi peduli*) were staged (see, for example, Ruslan 2005). Half a year after the disaster, four anthologies of tsunami poetry were already for sale in Indonesian bookshops: *Duka Atjeh Duka Bersama* (The Misery of Aceh is Our Misery), *8.9 Skala Richter Lalu Tsunami* (8.9 on the Richter Scale and then the Tsunami), *Duka Aceh Luka Kita* (The Misery of Aceh is Our Wound), and *Aceh.* Islamic scholars, too, have actively contributed to the tsunami discourse. Best-selling titles include *Tsunami: Tanda Kekuasaan Allah* (Tsunami: A Sign of God's Power), *Tsunami dan Keajaibannya* (Tsunami and its Miracle), and *Tsunami Aceh: Adzab atau Bencana?* (The Acehnese Tsunami: Punishment or Disaster?).

My intention in this contribution is to look into some Indonesian poetic utterances about the tsunami, focusing on two collections: firstly, poems by Acehnese writers of local renown which were published in the anthology *Ziarah Ombak* (Pilgrimage to the Waves) and, secondly, poems composed by literary unknowns who as non-Acehnese "bystanders from afar" posted their thoughts and feelings about the disaster on the Internet. The tenor of the poetic voices of both groups is in tune with those of the contemporaneous letter writers discussed in Chapter 15 by Arndt Graf, that is, strongly religious. The preoccupation with religion and morals has long had roots in Indonesian literary discourse, but in the case of tsunami poetry it is undoubtedly closely connected to the popular view, shared by Acehnese and non-Acehnese alike, of Aceh as a staunchly Muslim region. Why was the "Veranda of Mecca", as Aceh is famously known, hit so hard?

Was this an example of God's hand at work? Across the battered shores, dozens of mosques had defied the onslaught, which reinforced the popular view that the disaster was an unmistakable message from God. Aerial photographs taken immediately after the event showed "Houses of God" as the sole surviving buildings in entirely devastated areas.[2] About this "miracle" Ida N. Chazanah devoted a poem entitled "Thoughts about the tsunami catastrophe" (*Renungan bencana tsunami*):

> O God…
> What are these signs?
> You have destroyed everything
> Completely pulverized!
> Apart from Your Mosques![3]

Of course, theological responses in the wake of natural catastrophes are not specific for Aceh or Indonesia. Following the tsunami tragedy, mourning people of all faiths across a wide arc of South and Southeast Asia have speculated about the deeper meaning of the sudden cataclysm that struck them, looking to their faith to make some sense out of it. In an article in the American weekly *Newsweek* on how different religious groups have dealt with the tsunami, the journalist Kenneth Woodward (2005) wrote: "Little wonder that from Sumatra to Madagascar, innumerable voices cry out to God. The miracle, if there is one, may be that so many still believe".

The latter remark betrays a way of thinking that is perhaps typical for many inhabitants of the secular Western world. But for what reason should a calamity have a faith-undermining quality? In the course of human history, undeserved suffering has proved to be a fact of life for zillions of people around the globe, again and again. Undeniably the tsunami caused wide-scale human misery, but the problem of evil in the presence of God long predates the fatal day of 26 December 2004. There is no need to delve into the intricate question of theodicy here. Opinions on this issue not only widely differ between but also within the various religions and, as Niven (1913, p. 324) once concluded, "every proposed solution either leaves the old question" — *si deus bonus, unde malum?* — "unanswered or raises new ones". For example, in the history of Islamic theology the question of how the sufferings of little children can be in harmony with God's justice has brought forward a variety of opinion, giving rise to elaborate discussions on the question of God's will.

The composers of Indonesian (Islamic) tsunami poetry, however, as a rule appear to be untutored in refined theological reasoning. For them, as for most common believers, the orthodox Islamic answer to the question of predestination that everything that happens is the product of the divine decree is apparently sufficient.[4] As all that happens is God's doing, natural phenomena, such as earthquakes, floods, volcanic eruptions or droughts, are necessarily interpreted as signs of His mercy and compassion. Even the devastating tsunami, therefore, must have some hidden, positive purpose. On an individual level, the idea of divine testing and the patience it requires offers solace to believers who have to cope with personal losses. As Akbar S. Ahmed, professor of Islamic Studies at American University, Washington, put it, the decisive question confronting those who have lost a child or a spouse in the tragedy is: "Will you lose your faith or will you continue to believe?" Ahmed argues that the view of God putting mankind on trial is a comfort, providing "an in-built psychological cushion which allows Muslims to absorb a tragedy of this scale" (Woodward 2005). Needless to say perhaps, it also effectively prevents asking any other worrying questions.

PILGRIMAGE TO THE WAVES

One of the most intriguing examples of Indonesian tsunami literature is the anthology *Pilgrimage to the Waves* (*Ziarah Ombak*), because it contains hundreds of poems from about forty Acehnese writers who have had first-hand experience with the tsunami. It also features tsunami poetry by a few well-known non-Acehnese "outsiders": the Indonesian writers Rendra, Taufiq Ismail, and Amien Wangsitalaja, while neighbouring Malaysia is represented by A. Samad Said, Raja Ahmad Aminullah and Siti Zainon Ismail. This book was published in 2005 by LAPENA (Lembaga Penulis Aceh or Institute of Acehnese Writers) and edited by D. Kemalawati and Sulaiman Tripa.

Mohd Harun al Rasyid (born in Laweueng, Pidie Aceh, in 1966), a prolific writer and literary critic, has dedicated a very appreciative article-length review of it, entitled "The Optimism of the Acehnese and Cross-Cultural Empathy" (*Optimisme orang Aceh dan empati lintas kultural*).[5] In facing the tsunami catastrophe, Harun points to what he calls "the very strong cultural tenacity" of Acehnese culture that is imbued with Islamic values. Islam forbids the Acehnese to be pessimistic or hopeless, and he quotes several Acehnese tsunami poems that are suffused with "positive" religious interpretations, testifying an unshakable trust in God and unabashed optimism. Harun approvingly quotes Sukran Daudy's poem "I haven't lost God" (*Aku tidak kehilangan Tuhan*), in which the first-person narrator has lost all that he loved, but to live without God would mean to be truly lost:

My mother is gone
My father is gone
My children are gone
My grandparents are gone
My beloved is gone
My family is gone

I search in the mess
Human beings are gone
Tears are gone too
The address of my house is gone
I stay in loss
My crying is gone

I am lost for words
I wade through loss
But I haven't lost God[6]

Harun himself has also contributed to "Pilgrimage to the Waves" and in "I am asking You" (*Aku Bertanya Pada-Mu*) he initially wants to protest against God, but finally realizes that mankind is God's property, and resigning himself to his fate he asks God to turn his sad feelings into a string of prayer beads (*tasbih*) and his restlessness into a prayer mat (*sajadah*), concluding with the lines:

God the Master Designer
I am asking You
Because I am aware of owning You[7]

Fikar W. Edi, a prolific poet and journalist of *Serambi Indonesia*, asks God in "Aceh's Pain" (*Nyeri Aceh*) to let the suffering function as a mirror from which deeper insight can be gained:

And to us, o God
Give us strength

To bear the pain
To turn it into a mirror
From which we derive wisdom[8]

Fikar does not look upon the tsunami as a divine curse, and neither does Nurdin F. Joes who believes it was a test from God. In the opening strophe of the rather long poem "You never hate" (*Engkau tak pernah membenci*) he writes:

My beloved Lord
You never hate
But only test
To what extent we stand suffering
To what extent we accept

In his last strophe this poet then, almost triumphantly, declares:

God the forgiver
We still can stand suffering
We have been able to accept
We still implore your warning tests[9]

Wina SW still feels confident in the power of God's love although we may perhaps not directly see it. In the final strophe of her poem "If You will forgive me" (*Kalau Kau Mau Memaafkanku*) she states:

I believe that this is a sign of His love
For us
An eternal love wrapped in secrets, which can never
Be grasped[10]

In her "Bouquet of Flowers" (*Bunga Setaman*) Rosni Idham expresses the feeling that the bereaved may find comfort in the idea that the victims have gone to heaven:

My flowers, oh there…
At His side you blossom
Peacefully in His loving embrace
Wholeheartedly we let you go
Farewell my flowers
At heaven's gate we meet[11]

The imagery of "flowers" suggests that the people, who have been killed, have entered heaven as "martyrs" (*syahid*); in common parlance "flowers of the nation" refers to the fallen heroes of the nation, those killed in battle. The renowned poet Taufiq Ismail (born in Bukittinggi in 1935) is harping on the same idea in his poem "Reading the Signs" (*Membaca Tanda-Tanda*). Whereas Rosni Idham metaphorically referred to the victims as martyrs, Taufiq is more direct, unambiguously speaking of "thousands of martyr troops" (*barisan ribuan syuhada*) who are escorted by angels to paradise:

> And the Acehnese babies are running quickly to heaven's gate
> There they are waiting for their parents who are sad on earth
> "Don't be so sad, father and mother, follow your children
> At the main entrance of the garden of paradise your children are waiting."[12]

As anyone familiar with older Malay literature readily knows, the idea of the deceased beloved who is gone before his or her time and is waiting at heaven's gate is a conventional image. Practically every Indonesian schoolchild has heard the famous lines

> Pluck a spray of cypress for me
> Should I meet an early fate;
> And if you should die before me,
> Wait for me at Heaven's Gate[13]

It is tempting to provide more quotes from "Pilgrimage to the Waves", but I think that the thematic elements in this work have become sufficiently clear by now. Incidentally, many of the contributors to this anthology have also written in another collection of tsunami poetry in the same year 2005, viz. the bundle "Speechless Song" (*Lagu Kelu*), in which the editors Doel CP Allisah and Nani HS assembled the works of forty Acehnese poets on 280 pages. The gist of this publication appears to be identical. The motto on the cover conveys the same moral:

> God has given His lesson
> So let's stop being sad
> Let's work and pray
> Setting out for a secure Aceh[14]

Whatever one may think of the contents, the poems quoted above at least show that its composers could demonstrate certain penmanship skills.

Note, for example, the use of repetition in Daudy's "I haven't lost God" or the epigrammatic turn at the end of Harun's "I am asking You" with the unexpected final statement "Because I am aware of owning You".[15]

CYBERSASTRA'S POETRY FOR ACEH

If, however, we turn our attention to tsunami poetry by literary unknowns, we will observe that aesthetic qualities hardly play a role, and that the religious message is predominant, more often than not couched in the form of prayers or sermonettes. My main source is *Cybersastra* <http://www.cybersastra.net>, a well-known website for Indonesian belles-lettres, which in January 2005 placed about a dozen poems on the Internet in the category "poems for Aceh". In a disclaimer *Cybersastra* stated that the poems were "expressions of sadness and empathy dealing with the tsunami disaster in Aceh and North Sumatra".[16]

Cybersastra claims to be open for everyone who can read and write, a fact, which has solicited sharp criticism from literary critics: what about quality when literary selection criteria are not applied? Repeatedly critics have caustically remarked that most authors who published their work on the Internet did so, because they knew it would never appear in the print media (Maier 2004, p. 502). The question, however, is whether in this case the literary quality is all-important. In a disclaimer *Cybersastra* declared about the tsunami poems: "Forget about the question of quality now, because empathy has a right to be expressed".[17] But is "empathy" really the appropriate word here? The first poem posted is by a certain Rita Achdris:

Catastrophe
— to the tsunami victims

From the south to the southeast
Tears are flooding
Thousands of lives disappear
Bowing my head I call You
(why weren't we clever enough to read Your signs?)[18]

All I read is that the author ascribes divine intent to the natural disaster, but in spite of the poem's dedication I fail to detect a trace of empathy with the tsunami victims. The same author also asks for introspection in the poem *tsunami*, which consists only of two lines:

When Moses parted the sea
Were we the pharaoh's followers?[19]

What does this mean? The Qur'an (8:54) declares, in Arberry's translation (Arberry 1983, p. 175),

> Like Pharaoh's folk, and the people before him,
> Who cried lies to the signs of their Lord,
> So We destroyed them of their sins,
> And we drowned the folk of Pharaoh; and
> All were evildoers.

Probably Rita Achdris meant to pose a rhetorical question, and perhaps she wanted to warn "us Muslims" to repent and stop denying the signs or revelations of the Lord, but what about the people seized by the seismic waves: were they, like Pharaoh's folk, unbelievers, too?

That the tsunami provides a terrifying lesson for "us Muslims" who have been spared is more clearly expressed in the rather long poem *Tsunami 2004* by Rudi Suryadi who writes that he composed his poem in Plaza Kuningan, Jakarta, on 27 December 2004 at 14:21. Contrasting the tragedy in Aceh to his own comfortable situation, he prays to God:

> Thank you God
> You have hit me on the back to remind me of You
> But why are there so many victims to admonish us[20]

It is undisputed in this kind of poetry that the tsunami should be seen as an act of God. Ramli Abdul Rahman from Malaysia, whose poem was also posted online by *Cybersastra*, asked "Who is it that plans a natural disaster?" (*Siapa yang merencana bencana alam?*). He mocked politicians who declared that they were concerned about the "natural disaster", thus obliterating God's role. To Him alone, Ramli sternly reminded his readers, belongs all that is in the heavens and the earth.

God's omnipotence is an oft-repeated refrain. Sudaryono Achmad from Purwokerto (Central Java) wrote in his *Tsunami*:

> Not more than a brief moment
> All kind of people
> Don't know where to go
> That's the way it is
> One sign
> Of His power
> What's there to compare with it...[21]

A poet called Mega Vristian from Hong Kong first gives a description of nature's devastation in *Tsunami*, concluding with the lines

It is the Lord who has the power
We are weak and powerless[22]

Someone named Djenar praises the Acehnese people who have suffered so much since Indonesia's Independence. This person combines the themes of martyrdom and God's test:

To be born in Aceh is a disaster
To be born in Aceh is a curse
But the Acehnese people are mighty proud and die there
God is Great
By God, the Acehnese people are already used to tests[23]

Djenar closes with a well-known Acehnese proverbial saying, often used by the jihadis in the colonial Aceh War:

Live in honour!
Die as a martyr!
Greetings.[24]

In the rather long, sermonizing poem "Is the Lord cruel, because he sent the tsunami?" (*Kejamkah Tuhan sebab mengirim tsunami?*) by Subagyo, an uncompromising tone is used. Although in my view no tsunami poem of *Cybersastra* can be said to promote much empathy with the victims, Subagyo (probably hailing from Java) is perhaps the least emotional type among *Cybersastra*'s new poets, as the following lines may show:

It is already clear that the Lord who is worshipped
and on whom mankind has turned its back
or made fun of
has openly pulverized the lives
of thousands of people and their environments
Is the Lord cruel?
If we only look upon suffering as suffering
the Lord is the Most Cruel
But what if we consider the heat of the fire as needed for purifying the bits of gold that are mixed with clay, then what do we know about what the Lord wants?[25]

The purifying motif is Subagyo's comfort for the victims who have been gathered by the Lord, now living closely and happily in God's company:

> We hope that the disaster that struck our brethren
> will be a way to reach true happiness[26]

WHO'S TO BLAME?

Readers who come from another cultural tradition may feel nonplussed about the self-assured, "positive" decoding of God's message as displayed in the poems that we have discussed so far. In all fairness, it should be pointed out that other, much more nuanced, voices may also be heard from within the Indonesian Muslim community which in academic, densely footnoted prose address the question of evil befalling the people of God.[27] The poets, however, give the impression of speaking from the heart, expressing what seems to be the *vox populi*.

A foreign observer can hardly escape the conclusion that for these Indonesian Muslims the disaster, in a perverse way, was apparently a blessing in disguise: God mercifully gave a warning to the faithful who received another chance to better their sinful ways, whereas the seized Islamic victims immediately entered heaven as happy martyrs. Another stunning conclusion that they can come to is that in the twenty-first century the doctrine of philosophical optimism still has its adherents. For those who have grown up with Voltaire's 1758 satire, *Candide ou l'Optimiste* (Candide or the Optimist) the tsunami poems quoted in this article must be baffling. Hadn't this Enlightenment thinker already long ago exposed the "fallacy" of exactly this mode of optimism that "all is for the best in this best of all possible worlds"?

Yet, however banal this may sound, it is important to realize that the tsunami poems were not composed for the literary satisfaction of foreign connoisseurs. Possible criticism, I think, must be tempered by the recognition that in the case of the poets who contributed to *Pilgrimage to the Waves*, the majority were not armchair philosophers who easily expounded abstract notions of optimism which have little bearing on real life. Most of these writers have lost their nearest dearest kin. Mohd. Harun al Rasyid who praised the optimistic tone of the poetry bundle has himself lost his wife and children as well as all his possessions. The writings of the Acehnese authors who are victims themselves express thoughts and feelings that the intended readers — the Acehnese tsunami victims — can relate to, and according to Harun, the intended reading public finds the works most rewarding.

Journalists have reported that, as one reporter put it, in Aceh "in angry waves, the devout see an angry God" (Cody 2005). A few weeks after the tsunami disaster, a Bahasa Indonesia teacher at a Junior High School in Meulaboh, hoping perhaps that poetry could provide a form of psychotherapy, asked the students to write a poem on the catastrophe. A fifteen-year-old Acehnese girl called Cut Nurfajria recited her poem "Our Prayer" (*Doa Kami*), dedicating the work to her many friends who had become a victim of the tragedy, reading:

Our prayer

O God
You are the Compassionate, the Merciful
We are weak and powerless servants
Don't you bring us any more ordeals
Don't you scatter any more suffering
Because we know this is our own fault

O God
You have brought us an ordeal
We do not want to see the crying of our brothers and sisters again

O God
Please forgive us our mistakes
Only you we implore
And only you we ask
Amen, o Lord of Mankind[28]

This tsunami poem, which is cast in the characteristic form of a prayer, addresses such familiar themes as God's Omnipotence, the Lord-servant relation, God's test of loyalty, and the sinfulness of humanity. In a version of *Pop Idol* organized by the American and Indonesian Red Cross in a camp near Banda Aceh to cheer up survivors, the winner was a twelve-year-old girl whose song equally had the theme of the tsunami being God's punishment for sin. Her father, who died in the wave, would have approved, she said (Meo 2005*a*, 2005*b*).

There are psychological explanations for why theories of Divine Intent are so seductive. Psychologists who study conspiracy theories argue that such beliefs meet a basic human need: in order to become understandable, a major incident needs to have a major cause behind it. In that sense, the idea that there is a controlling force orchestrating global events is comforting (cf. Grossman 2006). Although reliable opinion polls do not exist, the information provided in newspapers seems to suggest that the conviction of the tsunami as an act of God is widespread in Aceh and the rest of Indonesia.[29] This is not a fringe phenomenon, but a mainstream political reality, being a specific form of communal mourning.

God's will, however, is interpreted in different ways. Local imams emphasized that the disaster should be a lesson to more closely observe the tenets of Islam. Drawing personal conclusions for themselves, some people indeed said they planned to be more observant (Cody 2005). Others explained that the provincial rebellion had offended the Almighty, because it was a conflict of Muslims vs. Muslims. Dino F. Umahuk, a human rights activist and journalist (born in Capalulu, North Moluccas, in 1974), who regularly posts his poems on literary websites, touched upon this political topic in his sarcastic poem "Prayer of a Soldier after the Tsunami":

> Lord
> Why did you strike us with this flood
> Even though Noah is not here
> Why did your anger strike us
> Even though we are engrossed in sins
> Even though we are passionately oppressing our brethren
> And you did not order us to make a single ship
> But only hundreds of tanks and trucks[30]

Some hardliners, however, harbouring their own Muslim political agenda, scapegoat women for the disaster. Pointing to the fact that more women and children had been killed by the tsunami than men, they asserted that the tsunami was caused by women's sin, insisting that Acehnese women should strictly conform to Islamic law to avoid another disaster. One year on, the U.N. special envoy for tsunami recovery reported that "[i]t is common in Aceh to find banners on the side of roads sponsored by conservative Ulama saying: "Disaster has happened, so women cover yourselves up".[31]

Emboldened by the widely shared belief that the disaster was heaven-sent to punish non-practising Muslims, the Wilayatul Hisbah, a *shari'a* police force patterned after the Saudi Arabian "Mutaween" or moral enforcers, is said to be gaining power.[32] The will to enforce *shari'a* seems to have increased due to people's fear of another tsunami (Meo 2005*a*, 2005*b*). Poor women are the prime targets of the "vice and virtue patrol". As Mardiyah Chamim, an Indonesian journalist, writing about her experiences with the application of *shari'a*, describes:

> Many Acehnese were demanding Wilayatul Hisbah (WH, the religious police) should redouble their effort to supervise people applying syariah. Everyone who was considered to [be] acting against the law must be punished without mercy. Gambling, adultery, stealing have to be eliminated. Whipping

> shows in front of public which [had] already taken place many times in cases of gambling and adultery has to be done more often. "We need strong action. God already punished us. We don't want other tsunami," that kind of comments frequently appears in newspapers and posters.[33]

To be sure, the rigorous actions of the religious police are not uncontroversial amongst the populace. "There's a wide gulf between the popularity of Islamic law in principle and the unpopularity of how it's being enforced", says Sidney Jones, Crisis Group Southeast Asia Project Director. "But for many", she adds, "that may be beside the point: the real issue is whether man's law or God's will prevail".[34]

A LINE OF DISASTERS: WILL IT EVER END?

The significance of a traumatic event like the tsunami changes with the passage of time. Since the December 2004 tsunami, few months have gone by without landslides, earthquakes, volcanic eruptions or floods in the archipelago. The Indonesian Council of Ulama (Majelis Ulama Indonesia or MUI) has sought to dispel the popular view that the disasters are somehow a curse or punishment by God. "They were all trials and tests that we should bear with fortitude and patience", MUI deputy chairman Din Syamsuddin told the press in July 2006, immediately after a tsunami had brought death and destruction in Pangandaran, West Java, killing a few hundred people.[35] This Islamic scholar, who leads the thirty million modernist organization *Muhammadiyah*, called on the people to do some "introspection" on what they had done before the series of natural disasters.[36]

As we have seen, the Aceh-related tsunami discourse has been very religious in nature, emphasizing the question of ethnic identity and Islam. More recently, in the Central Javanese province of Yogyakarta a Javanese folk theory has gained popularity, which declares that it was no coincidence that nature has hit the most "arabized" areas so hard. The underlying criticism is: did these proud, "pure" Muslims convert to Islam or to an alien ethnicity? The unruly sea was furthermore interpreted as a warning by the "Queen of the South" (*Ratu Kidul*), the powerful spirit-queen of Javanese mythology who rules the Indian Ocean, immediately south of Yogyakarta. She was angered by Indonesia's controversial "anti-pornography and porno-action law" that would criminalize, among other things, the exposure of naked shoulders, so characteristic of the nymph queen.[37]

In this age of faith-driven certainties, Indonesians mull a line of disasters that have hit the nation within a short period of time. One certainty amongst the uncertainties is that Indonesia's geographical position will remain a near-constant source of misery for its inhabitants. The archipelago, poetically often described as islands draped around the equator like a girdle of emerald, is located on the Pacific "Ring of Fire", where continental plates meet causing seismic and volcanic activity. That naturally means a greater, if unpredictable, probability for disasters than in the rest of God's creation.

Notes

1. Last two quatrains of her poem *Pantai Utara* ('North Coast'), first published in 1964. The Indonesian text reads: laut adalah kita, perahu-perahu berkuasa / dari Arafura, selat Sunda, selat Malaka / demikian sejarah bangsa dalam masa jaya / sebelum Sultan Agung dan monopoli kapal dagang bersenjata // laut adalah kita, sebelum cengkeh dan pala / laut adalah kita, sesudah minyak dan baja / perahu-perahu begitu manis, kapal-kapal lebih perkasa / luruskan pandang ke laut, laut yang terbuka //. As quoted in Suryadi AG (1989), pp. 103–104 who has drawn a sympathetic portrait of the "forgotten" poet Isma Sawitri.
2. See, for example, <http://www.islamcan.com/miracles/indonesia.shtml>. Note that all cited Internet sources were last accessed on 21 September 2006.
3. Ya Allah… / tanda-tanda apakah ini? / semua kau hancurkan / luluh lantak tak berkeping! / Kecuali Masjid-Mu! As quoted in Tjahyadi (2005). The poem appeared in the anthology *Duka Atjeh Duka Bersama* (Dewan Kesenian Jawa Timur & Logung Pustaka, 2005).
4. Mohd Harun al Rasyid's statement that the majority of the Acehnese cling to the belief that "anything that happens, will surely happen in its allotted time" (*segala sesuatu yang terjadi, memang akan terjadi pada saatnya*) should also be seen against this same unreflective background, <http://www.rumahykp.org.my/aktiviti2005ykp11.html>.
5. It can be found on <http://www.rumahykp.org.my/aktiviti2005ykp11.html>.
6. Ibuku hilang / Bapakku hilang / Anakku hilang / Kakek nenekku hilang / Kekasihku hilang / Keluargaku hilang // Aku mencari dari gelimpangan / Manusia telah hilang / Air mata juga hilang / Alamat rumahku hilang / Aku tinggal di kehilangan / Tangisku hilang // Aku kehilangan kata-kata / Aku melangkahi kehilangan / Tetapi aku tidak kehilangan Tuhan //, <http://www.rumahykp.org.my/aktiviti2005ykp11.html>.
7. Tuhan Yang Maha Perencana / Aku bertanya pada-Mu / Karena aku sadar memiliki-Mu //, <http://www.rumahykp.org.my/aktiviti2005ykp11.html>.
8. Dan kepada kami, ya Allah / berilah kekuatan / menanggungkan perih ini / menjadikannya cermin / tempat kami memungut hikmah //, <http://www.rumahykp.org.my /aktiviti2005ykp11.html>.
9. Tuhanku kekasih / Engkau tak pernah membenci / kecuali menguji / sejauhmana kami bersabar / sejauhmana kami merela / Tuhan yang pemaaf / kami masih dapat bersabar / kami telah dapat merela / kami masih meminta uji tegur-Mu //, <http://www.rumahykp. org.my/aktiviti2005ykp11.html>.

10. Aku percaya, ini adalah tanda cinta-Nya / buat kita / cinta abadi berbalut rahasia yang tak pernah / mampu tercerna //, <http://www.rumahykp.org.my/aktiviti2005ykp11.html>.
11. Bunga-bungaku, wahai… / Di sisi-Nya engkau adalah kesuma / Damailah dalam pelukan kasih-Nya / Ikhlas kami melepas / Selamat jalan bunga-bungaku / Di gapura syurga kita bertemu //, <http://www.rumahykp.org.my/aktiviti2005ykp11.html>. A more literal translation of the second line would be "At His side you are flowers", which would sound bland in English. In Indonesian the poet plays here upon the word *kesuma* in its double meaning of "flower" and "flower of a country's youth; the fallen heroes of a nation".
12. Dan bayi-bayi Aceh itu berlari-larian lincah ke gerbangnya / Di sana mereka tunggu orangtua mereka yang sedih di dunia / "Jangan sedih begitu, ayah dan ibu, susul·anakmu / Di pintu agung Taman Firdaus anakmu menunggu." <http://www.rumahykp.org.my/aktiviti2005ykp 11.html>.
13. Kalau tuan jalan dahulu / carikan sahaya daun kemboja / kalau tuan mati dahulu / nantikan sahaya di pintu sorga // The kemboja with its frangipani flowers is associated, like the cypress in Western cultures, with graveyards. Text and translation in Wilkinson (1959, p. 550).
14. Allah telah memberikan pelajaran-Nya / Maka berhentilah berduka / Marilah bekerja dan berdoa / Menuju Aceh sejahtera /, as quoted by Agnusi AH (2005).
15. For the importance of repetition in Malay literature, see the seminal work of Sweeney 1987.
16. Inilah sebagian ungkapan kepedihan dan empati atas bencana Tsunami di Aceh dan Sumatera Utara, <http://www.cybersastra.net/modules.php?name=News&file=print&sid=4263>.
17. Lupakan dulu soal kualitas, karena empati mempunyai hak untuk diungkapkan, <http://www.cybersastra.net/modules.php?name=News&file=print&sid=4263>.
18. Bencana 7 — kepada korban tsunami / dari selatan ke tenggara / air mata meluap / ribuan nyawa menguap / tertunduk kuseru Engkau / (kenapa kami tak juga pintar membaca isyaratMu? //, <http://www.cybersastra.net/modules.php?name=News&file=print&sid=4263>.
19. Ketika musa membelah laut / adakah kami pengikut fir'aun? Quoted in Puisi-Puisi untuk Atjeh (1).
20. Terima kasih Tuhan / Engkau telah memukul punggungku untuk mengingatMu / Tapi mengapa begitu banyak korban untuk menegur kami /, <http://www.cybersastra.net/modules. php?name=News&file=print&sid=4263>.
21. Sekejap saja / manusia-manusia / tak tahu harus kemana [sic] / begitulah / satu pertanda / tentang kuasaNya / Adakah yang bias menandinginya…, <http://www.cybersastra.net/ modules.php?name=News&file=print&sid=4263>.
22. Tuhan ada berkuasa / kita lemah tak berdaya //, <http://www.cybersastra.net/modules. php?name=News&file=print&sid=4263>.
23. lahir di aceh adalah sebuah musibah! /lahir di Aceh adalah sebuah kutukan!

/ tapi rakyat aceh bangga besar dan mati disana / allahuakbar / demi tuhan rakyat aceh sudah terbiasa dengan ujian /, <http://www.cybersastra.net/modules.php?name=News&file=print&sid=4263>.

24. udep sare! / mate syahid! Saleum., <http://www.cybersastra.net/modules.php?name=News&file=print&sid=4263>.
25. Sudah jelas Tuhan yang disembah / dan yang dipantati manusia / atau yang dibuat bahan tertawaan / telah terang-terangan meluluh-lantakkan kehidupan / ribuan manusia dan lingkungannya / Kejamkah Tuhan? / Kalau saja kita menggagap derita sebagai derita / maka Tuhan Maha Kejam / Tapi seumpama kita menganggap panas api diperlukan untuk memurnikan emas-emas yang bercampur lempung maka kita pun tak tahu apa yang dimaui Tuhan /, <http://www.cybersastra.net/modules.php?name=News&file=print&sid=4263>.
26. Kita berharap bencana yang menimpa saudara kita / sebagai jalan untuk meraih kebahagian sejati /, <http://www.cybersastra.net/modules.php?name=News&file=print&sid =4263>.
27. See, for example, the lengthy and learned articles in the national daily *Kompas* by the liberal Muslim activist Novriantoni (2005) or by Haidir Bagir (2005), the general director of the well-known Muslim publishing house Mizan in Bandung.
28. Ya Allah / Engkau maha pengasih dan maha penyayang / Kami selaku hamba yang lemah dan tak berdaya / Jangan engkau berikan cobaan ini lagi / Jangan engkau taburkan derita ini lagi / Karena kami tahu ini kesalahan kami / Ya Allah / Engkau memberi kami cobaan / Kami tak ingin lagi melihat tangisan saudara-saudara kami / Tangisan adik-adik kami / Ya Allah / Engkau mau memaafkan kesalahan kami / Hanya kepadamu kami memohon / Dan hanya kepada mu kami meminta / Amin Ya Rabbal Alamin. As quoted in Ardiansyah (2005).
29. For comparison's sake: according to a poll conducted in January 2005, one in four Americans believed the tsunami was an act of God, while half of Malaysian respondents attributed the disaster to God, <http://www.gmi-mr.com/gmipoll/release.php?p=20050119>.
30. Tuhan / Mengapa air bah itu kau timpakan kepada kami / Padahal di sini tak ada Nuh / Mengapa murka kau timpakan kepada kami / Padahal kami sedang terlena dalam dosa / Padahal kami sedang asyik menindas saudara-saudara kami / Dan tak satupun perahu yang Kau suruh kami buat / Selain beratus-ratus tank, dan truk /, <http://www.ceritanet.com/91doa.htm>. This edition of *ceritanet* is dated 26 January 2005.
31. The report of the U.N. Office of the special envoy for tsunami recovery, entitled "Peace after the Waters? Aceh: One year after the tsunami", can be found at <www.globalexchange.org/countries/asia/indonesia/AcehReport.pdf>.
32. Wilayatul Hisbah could loosely be translated as "vice and virtue force". This inspectorate, set up in 2001, is charged with the exercise of "censorship", that is making sure that conduct in the public realm confirms to Islamic criteria, detecting offences and punishing offenders. For a discussion of *hisba*, which

in Islamic thought belongs to the duty of "commanding right and forbidding wrong", see Michael Cook (2006), p. 676, index under *hisba.*

33. As quoted in "The trouble with Syariah", <http://www.indonesiamatters.com/258/the-trouble-with-syariah/>.
34. As quoted in the press release "Islamic law and criminal Justice in Aceh" of the International Crisis Group, <http://www.crisisgroup.org/home/index.cfm?l=1&id=4295&m=1>.
35. News report "Successive disasters not punishment nor curse on Indonesia: ulema", dated 18 July 2006, <http://www.antara.co.id/en/seenws/?id=16568>.
36. Ibidem.
37. See, for example, Buchsteiner (2006) or "An anthropologist's report from Yogyakarta, Indonesia" by Noel B. Salazar, <http://www.museum.upenn.edu/new/research/blogs/earthquake_ entries.shtml>.

GLOSSARY

Bethany J. Collier, Karin Hörner, Saiful Machdi, and Edwin Wieringa

Since so far there is no general standardization of the spelling of Acehnese terms, this book, mainly written by foreigners, does not attempt to establish such a standardized system of orthography. Rather, in the following, several variants are given, as they appear in the texts of the contributors to this volume. In contrast, for Indonesian terms, the variants established as standard Indonesian by the Pusat Bahasa in Jakarta are the ones followed in this book.

ABK, Anak Buah Kapal	boat crew
Angkatan Bersenjata Republik Indonesia, ABRI	Armed Forces of Indonesia
'aqiqah	sacrifice on the 7th day of the birth of a child
'Idul Adha	Sacrifical Feast (10 Dhul-Hijja)
'Idul Fithri	Festival of Breaking the Fast (after Ramadhan, begins on 1 Shawwal)
1 Muharram 1424H	date in Muslim calendar: the first day of the first month of the year 1424 after the Prophet's Hijra (emigration to Medina)
Aceh Barat	West Aceh
Aceh Besar	Greater Aceh
Aceh Selatan	South Aceh
Aceh Tengah	Central Aceh
Aceh Tenggara	Southeast Aceh
Aceh Timur	East Aceh

Aceh Utara	North Aceh
adat bak po teumeuruhom, hukum bak Syiah Kuala	proverb, literally: "Customary Law is dictated by Wise Lady Teumeuruhom, Islamic Law is dicatated by the famous *ulama* from Syiah Kuala"
adil	just
ahwal al-syakhsiyah	personal status in civil law
akhirat	Hereafter World
Akidah	creed, article of faith
al-Qur'an	Koran
Angkatan Pemuda Indonesia (API)	Indonesian Youth Forces
Aoki	the judicial official of the Japanese occupation forces in Aceh
asoe lhok	native of a region (village, *mukim*, etc.)
Atjeh-moord	literally: "Aceh murder", surprise tactics of stabbing Dutch soldiers during the Aceh War
Badan Keinsyafan Rakyat (BKR)	People's Awareness Agency
Badan Pemuda Indonesia (BPI)	Indonesian Youth Agency, later renamed Pemuda Republik Indonesia (Indonesian Republic's Youth, PRI)
bahar	a measure of weight in Malaya. The value of a *bahar* varied from place to place but remained fairly constant throughout the Peninsula at between 360–370 lbs. per bahar.
bawar	ceremonial dagger
BPA (Persatuan Bekas Pejuang Islam Aceh)	Association of Former Acehnese Islamic Fighters
bupati	district leader(s)
cheumuelo	threshing harvested rice by stamping on it to separate rice from its straws
CMI	Crisis Managament Initiative
daerah istimewa	special region
Daerah Operasi Militer (DOM)	military operation area
dana wakaf	management of donated assets and estates of deceased people
dayah	form of informal education, indigenously very Acehnese and community-based. It is similar to, but not the same as, *pesantren* known in other parts of Indonesia
Dayah Manyang	traditional Islamic boarding schools, seen as equal to university.

DPR (Dewan Perwakilan Rakyat)	parliament
fatwa	legal opinion
fiqh	jurisprudence
fiqh jinayat	jurisprudence of major crimes, criminal law
fiqhiyyah	derived from *fiqh*: matters concerning jurisprudence
gadai	to put a collateral to borrow money or other form of capital
gala	Acehnese form of mortgage
gampong, kampung	village
Gerakan Aceh Merdeka, GAM	Free Aceh Movement
geumeuklèh	woman considered independent of her parents
ghairu muhshan	being not *muhshan*
Giyugun	volunteer forces which were not part of the Japanese army, but auxiliary forces which were intended to resist an Allied invasion as guerrillas (in Java known as *Peta*)
GoI	Government of Indonesia
GOLKAR (Golongan Karya)	literally: "Functional Groups" (= pro-government organization taking part in elections)
habib	those who claim to be descendants of the Prophet Muhammad. They come from Mecca, Medinah, and Yemen and are extraordinarily respected in the eyes of the Acehnese people. Usually they are called by the technical term *Sayid*
had	punishment, or crimes mentioned in the Koran, e.g. *zina*
hadih maja	collection of Acehnese wise words/proverbs, from old institutions
hadith, hadits	tradition of sayings and actions of the Prophet
haji	Pilgrim to Mecca
Heiho	the indigenous auxiliary defence forces which were part of the Japanese army
hibah	donation
hôkôhai	Japanese-created Aceh-wide unitary organization for all local citizens
i'tikaf	retreat in a mosque for several days
ibadah	ritual, opposite of *mu'amalah*

iftiraq	secession, division
ijtihad	legal method of reasoning
Ilahi	theological
Ilahiyah	fem. form of *ilahi*
imeum	imam
Imum Mukim	prayer leader of a *mukim*
infaq	maintenance
Iskandar Muda, Iskandar Mudah	Acehnese Sultan, reigned 1607–36
istighatsash akbar	mass congregations in an open field
jahiliyah	ignorance, unbelief
jaroe bak langai, mata u pasai	proverb, literally: "hands hold the plough, eyes point toward the market"
jeungki	rice-pounder
jinayah	(criminal law)
jinayat	pl. of *jinayah*
Johor, Johore	state on the Malay peninsula
jumhur ulama	religious leaders and scholars
kabupaten	regency, district
kadhi	judges dealing with Muslim affairs
Kadhi Mukim	judge at the level of the *mukim*
kaffah	totality
KB, Keluarga Berencana	family planning
kerajaan	the entire Kingdom referred to in the name Kerajaan Aceh Darussalam. It is led by a king with the title of *Sultan Imam Malikul Adil* [the Sultan Imam Angel of Justice] who is helped by a judge who is styled *Qhadi Malikul Adil* [the Judge Angel of Justice]
keuchik, keuchi	village head
keujruen-blang	village caretaker for wet rice plantation affairs
khalwat	retreat, seclusion
khamar	alcohol consumption
khitan	circumcision
khusyu'	humility
KNIL	the colonial army of the Dutch
KOPASSUS (Komando Pasukan Strategis Khusus)	Strategic Command of Special Forces
KOSTRAD (Komando Strategis Angkatan Darat)	Strategic Army Command
kota	city
keris, kris	dagger

laksamana	admiral
Lembaga Amil Zakat, LAZ	Amil Zakat Foundation
lhok	literally: "shore-line", its geographical area is not necessarily according to boundaries of government administration
madrasah	college
Mahkamah Syar'iyah or syari'at	Syari'ah Court
merantau	expected behaviour of men to leave their families and go to another village, province or island in order to earn money
meunasah	praying hall
Muhammadiyah	modernist religious movement in Indonesia
meunyoe taleung panjang, meunyoe ta lingka paneuk	proverb, literally: "laid down it is long, circled it is short"
minyeuk panyot	literally: "lamp oil", monetary honorarium for *imum meunasah*, so small that it is considered to be enough only to buy lamp oil
MPR (Majelis Permusyawaratan Rakyat)	the highest Indonesian state assembly
mu'amalah	communal exchanges, opposite of *ibadah*, e.g. buying and selling
mugee	originally, fish buyer (collector) who then sells the fish to people of the area far away from the coastal region. Now, *mugee* can be a buyer (collector) of any products
muhshan	personal status of being chaste
MUI (Majelis Ulama Indonesia)	Ulama Council of Indonesia
mukim	group of villages form a *mukim*
nadzar	vow
nanggroe	usually called an *Ulee Balang* district, consists of between three and eight *mukim*. Within its borders, a *nanggroe* has a special autonomous status.
Nanggroe Aceh Darussalam	State of Aceh, Abode of Peace
Negara Kesatuan Republik Indonesia	Unitary State of Indonesia
nisab	proportional
njang po rumoh	idiomatic term for wife as "the one who owns the house"
orangkaya	elite (literally: wealthy people)
Orde Baru	New Order
otonomi daerah	regional autonomy

panglima glee	mountain affairs caretaker
panglima laot	coastal region caretaker for fishing and sea-related affairs
pangulee' hareukat meugoe	proverb, literally: "farming is the primary source of livelihood"
pawang pukat	the caretaker of *tarek pukat* fishing activities
pawang uteun	woods' affairs caretaker
PDI, Partai Demokrasi Indonesia	Indonesian Democratic Party
peci haji	black cap worn by men of the Islamic faith
Persatuan Ulama Seluruh Aceh	All-Aceh Ulama Association
pesantren	Islamic boarding schools
PESINDO (Pemuda Sosialis Indonesia)	Indonesian Socialist Youth
petua seuneubok	the elders of a settlement (village)
PPI (Pelabuhan Pendaratan Ikan)	fishing port
PPP (Partai Persatuan Pembangunan)	United Development Party
PRI (Pemuda Republik Indonesia)	Indonesian Republic's Youth
PTP (PT Perkebunan)	state-owned plantation and forestry company
PUSA (Persatuan Ulama Seluruh Aceh)	All-Aceh Ulama Association
Qanun	common law, e.g. administrative law
rajam	stoning to death
Ramadhan	ninth month of the Muslim calendar
reusam	everyday customs
sagoe	federation of several *nanggroe*. A sagoe is led by a military commander, called the *Panglima Sagoe* or, in Acehnese, the *Pang Sangoe*.
shalat fardhu lima waktu	praying five times a day
shalat Jum'at	weekly Friday prayers
shalat sunat	supererogatory prayer
shalat sunat rawatib	non-obligatory prayer
shari'a	set of rules and laws according to Islam
sinetron	short-form for *sinema elektronik* = soap opera produced by TV stations
Sultanah	female Sultan
Sumatera Utara	North Sumatra
sunat or *sunnah*	practice of the Prophet, recommended practice
syahadat primordial	a declaration of faith. A person must recite the *syahadat* to convert to Islam, namely:

	"I testify that there is no god but Allah and I testify that Muhammad is the Messenger of Allah."
syahbanda, syabander	caretaker of a seaport
syaria, syari'at, Syar'iyah, etc.	*sharia* = religious law, religion
Syi'ar Islam	Islamic texts and/or compositions
tabligh	kind of public speeches which are held from time to time in the mosques or related places
tabligh akbar	great religious conventions for important sermons
tarek pukat	literally: pulling a seine-net. A form of fishery activity where people work together to pull the net for a share of income
tasbih	Muslim prayer beads
TKR (Tentara Keamanan Rakyat)	People's Safety Army (the official Acehnese army after 1945)
Teuku	nobility who the Sultan has entrusted with unconditional power over the districts
teumupoh/awak teumarek	the puller of seine-net, consisting of members of the local community
teungku	religious authority
Teungku Imum or Imum Meunasah	prayer leader of a village (*meunasah*)
TNI (Tentara Nasional Indonesia)	Indonesian military
toke	a (wealthy) merchant, usually used for Chinese merchants, but now also used to call anybody who owns a shop or a store
toke bangku	a person who sells the fish caught by boat fishermen or *pukat* fishermen
TPR (Tentara Perjuangan Rakyat)	People's Struggle Army
Tuha Lapan	literally: "Eight Members", extended village council
Tuha Peut	literally "Four Members", four elderly chosen among villagers to be consulted in village affairs
ulama	religious scholars
Ulama, ulamma	Islamic scholars and leaders (singular: *alim*)
Uleebalang, Ulee Balang	Nobility and district chiefs
uleu beu matee', ranteng bek patah	proverb, literally: "killing a snake without breaking tree-branches"
umara	"emirs"
umma	community of believers in Islam

uroe peukan	the remote market day, where and when mobile merchants and local producers meet the buyers on certain day of the week at certain market, permanent or, mostly, temporary one. A certain area *uroe peukan* is uniquely identified with a certain day, for example, Saturday is an *uroe peukan* of area X. Then people will know that every Saturday, in the area will be a market
ureueng baroh	people of the coast
ureueng tunong	people of the hinterland
wakaf	charitable trust
wazir	advisor
zakat	the obligatory alms tax which belongs to the five pillars of Islam
zakat fithrah	obligatory donation of food at the end of Ramadhan
zakat mal	saves according to the rules of Islamic banking
zat ngon sifeuet	substance and its characteristics
zikir	formulaic repetitive recitation, Muslim "litany"
zikir akbar	*zikir* of "Allahu akbar"
zina	extramarital sex, adultery

BIBLIOGRAPHY

Archival Sources and Unpublished Documents

Ahtisaari, M. 7 February 2005. "Letter to Mr Malik Mahmoud". Crisis Management Initiative, Helsinki.

Algemeene Rijksarchief [A.R.A.], 's-Gravenhage:
  Ministerie van Koloniën [Kol.]
  Ministerie van Buitenlandse Zaken [B.Z.]
  Vereenigde Oostindische Comagnie [VOC]

MoU 2005. "Memorandum of Understanding between the Government of the Republic of Indonesia and the Free Aceh Movement, 17 July 2005".

Public Record Office, London. CO 273 — Correspondence from the Straits Settlements.

Adat Aceh, transcribed by Teungku Anzib Lamnyong, from Manuscript India Office Library, pp. 52–65 (1976).

"Voyage Made by Jacob Janssen de Roy to Borneo and Atcheen, 1691. Completed in 1698 in Batavia at the order of William van Oudtshoorn, Governor-General of Netherlands East Indies. Translated from Dutch into English in 1816". India Office, MSS Eur/Mack (1822/5).

TNI. "Daftar nominatif personel Batalyon Kavaleri 11/Serbu". Unpublished paper, Tentara Nasional Indonesia Angkatan Darat, Komando Daerah Militer Iskandar Muda, Banda Aceh, 2005*a*.

TNI. "Nomor N A M A PANGKAT N R P JABATAN / KESATUAN T M T KET, URT BAG /CORPS LAMABARU, TENTARA NASIONAL INDONESIA ANGKATAN DARAT Lampiran Surat Pangdam IM KOMANDO DAERAH MILITER ISKANDAR MUDA Nomor R // VIII / 2005, August 2005. 2005*b*.

General Internet Sources and The Media

Astaga!com
Kompas
Mediaindo
Neue Zürcher Zeitung (NZZ)
Padang Ekspres
Pikiran Rakyat
Republika Online
RRI-Online
Serambi Indonesia
United Press International (UPI)

http://web.amnesty.org/library
www.lestariheritage.net/aceh/
www.serambinews.com
http://www.slank.com.
www.peterpanband.com
http://www.arts.monash.edu/mai/newsletters05/news181005.txt.

Printed Literature

All personal names and work titles are listed according to the bibliographic rules of the respective language. For Indonesian/Malay names, for instance, the names are given according to the current bibliographic rules in Malaysia (i.e. "Abdul Karim Jakobi", instead of the Western-style "Jakobi, Abdul Karim").

ADB. See Asia Development Bank.

Abdul Karim Jakobi. *Aceh daerah modal. Long march ke Medan area*. Jakarta: Yayasan "Seulawah RO-001", 1992.

———. *Aceh dalam perang mempertahankan proklamasi kemerdekaan 1945–1949 dan peranan Teuku Hamid Azwar sebagai pejuang*. Jakarta: Gramedia Pustaka Utama & Yayasan "Seulawah RO-001", 1998.

Abdurrahman Wahid. "Elites' xenophobia." <www.gusdur.net/ english/index.php?option=com_content&task=view&id=680&itemid=40>. Accessed 11 February 2005.

Agnes Aristiarini. "Membangkitkan kembali semangat yang tersisa ..." <http://www.kompas.com/kompas-cetak/0502/17/humaniora/ 1564873.htm>. Accessed 17 February 2005.

Agnusi AH. "Lagu kelu 40 penyair Aceh: sebuah rekaman batin dan imbas luka tsunami". *Waspada Online*, <http://www.waspada.co.id/serba_serbi/features/artikel.php?article_id=70688>. Accessed 19 December 2005.

Agussabti. *Kajian Seuneubok sebagai sistem pengelolaan kawasan berbasis adat. Penelitian dasar atas biaya DIKTI*. Jakarta: Departemen Pendidikan Nasional, 2004.

Ali Fachry. "Aceh baru, politik baru". *Zaman baru Aceh*, 3 June 1989. p. 17.

Ali Hasjmy. *Peranan Islam dalam Perang Aceh dan perjuangan kemerdekaan Indonesia.* Jakarta: Bulan Bintang, 1976.

———. *59 tahun Aceh merdeka di bawah pemerintahan ratu*. Jakarta: Bulan Bintang, 1977*a*.

———. *Apa sebab rakyat Aceh sanggup berperang puluhan tahun melawan agresi Belanda.* Jakarta: Bulan Bintang, 1977*b*.

———. *Bunga rampai revolusi dari tanah Aceh.* Jakarta: Bulan Bintang, 1978.

———. *Jembatan Selat Melaka.* Banda Aceh: Pusat Informasi Sejarah dan Kebudayaan Islam, Perpustakaan dan Museum Yayasan Pendidikan Ali Hasjmi, 1997.

———, ed. *Sejarah masuk dan berkembangnya Islam di Indonesia. Kumpulan prasaran pada seminar di Aceh.* 1st ed. Jakarta: Beune, 1981. Bandung: PT. Alma'arif, 1993.

———, ed. *Ulama Aceh. Mujahid pejuang kemerdekaan dan pembangunamadun bangsa.* Banda Aceh: Perpustakaan dan Museum, Yayasan Pendidikan Ali Hasjmy, 1997.

——— et al., eds. *Aceh Membangun.* Banda Aceh: [s.n.], 1995.

Ali Muhammad, Rusjdi. *Revitalisasi Syari'at Islam di Aceh: Problem, solusi dan implementasi*, edited by Hasan Basri. Jakarta: Logos dan Ar-Raniry Press, 2003.

Ali Said; Wenefrida D.; Widyanti. "The Impact of Economic Crisis on Poverty and Inequality in Indonesia". Paper presented at the Symposium on Poverty Analysis and Data Initiative, Manila, April 2001.

Alisjahbana, Armida S. "Does Indonesia have the balance right in natural resource revenue-sharing?". In *The Politics and Economics of Indonesia's Natural Resources*, edited by Budy P. Resosudarmo, pp. 109–24. Singapore: Institute of Southeast Asian Studies, 2005.

American Red Cross. "One Year Report: Helping Reestablish Community Traditions". <http://www.redcross.org/sponsors/irf/1yrtsustewrep commhealth.asp>, n.d.

Amirul Hadi. *Islam and State in Sumatra: A Study of Seventeenth-Century Aceh.* Islamic history and civilization, no. 48. Leiden: Brill, 2004.

Ananta, Aris and Lee Poh Onn, eds. *Aceh: A New Dawn.* Singapore: Institute of Southeast Asian Studies, 2007.

Andaya, Leonard Y. "'A Very Good-Natured but Awe-Inspiring Government.' The Reign of a Successful Queen in Seventeenth-Century Aceh". In *Hof en handel. Aziatische vorsten en de VOC 1620–1720: opgedragen aan Jurrien van Goor*, edited by Elsbeth Locher-Scholten and Peter Rietbergen, pp. 59–84. Verhandelingen van het Koninklijk Instituut voor Taal-, Land- en Volkenkunde. Leiden: KITLV, 2004.

Anderson, Benedict R. O'G. *Imagined Communities. Reflections on the Origin and Spread of Nationalism.* Rev. and extended ed. London and New York: Verso, 1991.

Arberry, Arthur J. *The Koran Interpreted.* Reprint. Oxford: Oxford University Press, 1983.

Archer, LeRoy R. "Muhammadan Mysticism in Sumatra". *Journal of the Malayan Branch of the Royal Asiatic Society* 15, II (September 1937): i–ii, 1–126.

Aretxaga, Begoña. "Before the Law: The Narrative of the Unconscious in Basque Political Violence". Unpublished manuscript presented at the workshop on "The Poetics of Violence", School of American Research, Santa Fe, May 2002.

Arief Budiman and Wartajazz.com. "Jazz untuk Aceh Bali: Nonton gratis sambil beramal". <http://www.wartajazz.com/news/news 270105.html>. Accessed 27 January 2005.

Arif Kusbandono, Nana, and Wartajazz, "Laporan dari konser kemanusiaan". <http://www.wartjazz.com/news/news240105.html>. Accessed 24 January 2005.

Ariffadillah. "The Recent Situation in Aceh after the Joint Understanding on a Humanitarian Pause for Aceh". In *Violence in Indonesia*, edited by Ingrid Wessel and Georgia Wimhöfer, pp. 317–34. Hamburg: Abera, 2001.

Arnold, Thomas Walker. *The Caliphate.* Oxford: Clarendon Press, 1924.

Arskal Salim. "'Shari'a from Below' in Aceh (1930s–1960s): Islamic Identity and the Right to Self-Determination with Comparative Reference to the Moro Islamic Liberation Front (MILF)". *Indonesia and the Malay World* 32, no. 92 (2004): 80–99.

Asia Development Bank (ADB). "News Release: Indonesian Economy Forecast to Pick Up Speed over Next Three Years, Despite Tsunami". 6 April 2005.

ASNLF. "Declaration of Independence of Acheh — Sumatra. Acheh, Sumatra, December 4, 1976." <http://acehnet.tripod.com/declare.htm>. Accessed 4 July 2007.

Aspinall, Edward. "Sovereignty, the Successor State, and Universal Human Rights: History and the International Structuring of Acehnese Nationalism". *Indonesia* 73 (2002): 1–24.

———. "Modernity, History, and Ethnicity. Indonesian and Acehnese Nationalism in Conflict". In *Autonomy and Disintegration in Indonesia*, edited by Damien Kingsbury and Harry Aveling, pp. 128–47. New York: RoutledgeCurzon, 2003.

———. *The Helsinki Agreement. A More Promising Basis for Peace in Aceh?* Policy Studies, no. 20. Washington, D.C.: East-West Center, 2005.

Aspinall, Edward and Harold Crouch. *The Aceh Peace Process: Why it Failed.* (Policy Studies, no. 1. Washington, D.C.: East-West Center Washington, 2003.

Aspinall, Edward and Greg Fealy. "Introduction: Decentralisation, Democratisation and the Rise of the Local". In *Local Power and Politics in Indonesia*, edited by Edward Aspinall and Greg Fealy, pp. 1–14. Singapore: Institute of Southeast Asian Studies, 2003.

Astaga!com. "Album kita untuk mereka: Solidaritas musisi Tanah Air untuk Aceh dan Sumut.". <http://astaga.com/musik/ index.php?cat=126&id=94290>. Accessed 26 January 2005.

Ati. "Iwan Fals: Lagu Rp85 juta untuk korban tsunami". *Kompas*, 6 January 2005. Accessed online at <http://www.kompas.com/gayahidup/news/0501/06/212704.htm>.

Attir, Mustafa O., Burkart Holzner, and Zdenek Suda, eds. *Sosiologi modernisasi: talaah kritis tentang teori, riset dan realitas*. Yogakarta: Tiara Wacana, 1981. Indonesian translation of *Directions of Change. Modernization Theory, Research, and Realities*, edited by Attir, Mustafa, Burkart Holzner, and Zdenek Suda. Boulder, Colorado: Westview Press, 1981.

Austin, Jane Langshaw. *How to Do Things with Words*. Cambridge: Harvard University Press, 1962.

Azyumardi Azra. *Jaringan ulama: Timur Tengah dan kepulauan Nusantara abad XVII dan XVIII: Melacak akar-akar pembaruan pemikiran Islam di Indonesia*. Bandung: Mizan, 1994.

———. *The Origins of Islamic Reformism in Southeast Asia: Networks of Malay-Indonesian and Middle Eastern 'Ulama' in the Seventeenth and Eighteenth Centuries*. Crows Nest, NSW, Australia: Asian Studies Association of Australia in association with Allen & Unwin; Honolulu: University of Hawai'i Press, 2004.

———. *Jaringan ulama: Timur Tengah dan kepulauan Nusantara abad XVII & XVIII: akar pembaruan Islam Indonesia*. Rev. ed. Jakarta: Kencana, 2004.

Bachtiar Effendy. "Some Notes on the Congeniality of Islam and Civil Society in Indonesia". Paper presented to the 6th Asian-European Editors Forum, organized by Konrad Adenauer Stiftung, Singapore, 29 August 2005. Online resource, <http://www.kas.de/db_files/dokumente/7_dokument_dok_pdf_8035_2.pdf>. Accessed 4 July 2007.

Badan Pusat Statistik dan Badan Perencanaan Pembangunan Daerah: *Aceh dalam Angka*. Nanggroe Aceh Darussalam: Badan Pusat Statistik dan Badan Perencanaan Pembangunan Daerah, 2003.

Badruzzaman Ismail. *Mesjid dan adat Meunasah sebagai sumber energi budaya Aceh*. Banda Aceh: Majelis Pendidikan Daerah, 2002.

Bagir Haidar. "Membincang keadilan Tuhan (teodise) dalam bencana tsunami di Aceh". *Kompas*, 2 February 2005. Available online at <http://www.kompas.com/kompas-cetak/0502/02/Bentara/1530661.htm>.

Bakhat, Shirine. "Restoring the Acehnese Spirit". N.d. Accessed online at <http://indonesia.mercycorps.org/index.php?option=com_content&task=view&id=43&Itemid=38&lang=en>. Republished in Indonesian as "Pameran Pusaka di Banda Aceh- 4 dan 5 Juni 2005". N.d. Accessed online at <http://aceh.mercycorps.org/index.php? option=com_content&task=view&id=58&Itemid=77&lang=id>.

Bakker, Hans J. I. "The Acehnese War and the Creation of the Netherlands East Indies State". In *Great Powers and Little Wars: The Limits of Power*, edited by A. Hamish Ion and Elizabeth Jane Errington, pp. 54–82. Westport, Connecticut: Praeger, 1993.

Barakat, Sultan, ed. *After the Conflict. Reconstruction and Development in the Aftermath of War.* International Library of War Studies, no. 1. London and New York: I.B. Tauris, 2005.

Beatty, Andrew. *Society and exchange in Nias.* Oxford: Clarendon Press; New York: Oxford University Press, 1992.

Beaulieu, Augustine de. "The Expedition of Commodore Beaulieu to the East Indies ...". In *Navigantium atque itinerantium bibliotheca. Or, a Complete Collection of Voyages and Travels,* edited by John Harris, pp. 717–49. Revised ed. 2 vols. London: Woodward etc., 1744.

Beets, K. Th. *Memorie van overgave van de afdeeling Gajo- en Alaslanden.* Amsterdam: Koninklijk Instituut voor de Tropen, 1933.

Benda, Harry J. *The Crescent and the Rising Sun. Indonesian Islam under the Japanese Occupation, 1942–1945.* Dordrecht: Foris, 1983.

———. "Christiaan Snouck Hurgronje and the Foundations of Dutch Islamic Policy in Indonesia". In *Readings on Islam in Southeast Asia,* edited by Ahmad Ibrahim, Sharon Siddique; Yasmin Hussain. Singapore: Institute of Southeast Asian Studies, 1985.

Benhabib, Seyla. *The Claims of Culture: Equality and Diversity in the Global Era.* Princeton, NJ: Princeton University Press, 2002.

Bernhard, Fernand. *A travers Sumatra. De Batavia à Atjeh.* Paris: Boulevard Saint Germain, 1904.

Bertrand, Jacques. *Nationalism and Ethnic Conflict in Indonesia.* Cambridge Asia-Pacific Studies. Cambridge: Cambridge University Press, 2004.

Bhabha, Homi K. *The Location of Culture.* London and New York: Routledge, 1994.

Birket-Smith, Kaj. *Kulturens veje.* Kopenhagen: Jespersen og Pios, 1941/2. [German transl. *Geschichte der Kultur. Eine allgemeine Ethnologie.* Zürich: Orell Füssli, 1946; English transl. *The Paths of Culture. A General Ethnology.* Madison: University of Wisconsin Press, 1965.]

Boland, Bernard Johan. *The Struggle of Islam in Modern Indonesia.* 2nd rev. ed. (1st ed. 1971). Verhandelingen van het Koninklijk Instituut voor Taal-, Land- en Volkenkunde; no. 59. The Hague: Nijhoff, 1982.

Booth, Anne. *The Indonesian Economy in the Nineteenth and Twentieth Centuries. A History of Missed Opportunities.* Basingstoke: Macmillan Press; New York: St. Martin's Press, 1998.

———. "Indonesia: Will Decentralisation Lead to Disintegration?". Paper presented at the EUROSEAS Conference, 6–8 September 2001, London.

———. "The Changing Importance of Off-Farm Income for Agricultural Households in Indonesia". In *The Indonesian Rural Economy. Mobility, Work, and Enterprise,* edited by Thomas R. Leinbach. Singapore: Institute of Southeast Asian Studies, 2004.

Bowen, John R. "The Transformation of an Indonesian Property System. Adat, Islam, and Social Change in the Gayo Highlands". *American Ethnologist* 15, no. 2 (1988): 274–93.

———. "Poetic Duels and Political Change in the Gayo Highlands of Sumatra". *American Anthropologist* 91, no. 1 (March 1989): 25–40.

———. *Sumatran Politics and Poetry. Gayo History, 1900–1989*. New Haven: Yale University Press, 1991*a*.

———. "Return to Sender. A Muslim Discourse of Sorcery in a Relatively Egalitarian Society. The Gayo of Northern Sumatra". In *Understanding Witchcraft and Sorcery in Southeast Asia*, edited by C.W. Watson and Roy Ellen, pp. 179–90. Honolulu: University of Hawai'i Press, 1991*b*.

———. "On Scriptural Essentialism and Ritual Variation. Muslim Sacrifice in Sumatra and Morocco". *American Ethnologist* 19, no. 4 (1992): 656–71.

———. *Muslims Through Discourse*: *Religion and Ritual in Gayo Society*. Princeton, NJ: Princeton University Press, 1993.

———. "Neo-Patrimonialism and National Integration in Indonesia. The Case of Aceh". In *The State and Ethnic Politics in Southeast Asia*, edited by David Brown, pp. 112–57. London: Routledge, 1996.

———. "Modern Intentions. Reshaping Subjectivities in an Indonesian Muslim Society". In *Islam in an Era of Nation-States*: *Politics and Religious Renewal in an Indonesian Muslim Society*, edited by Robert W. Hefner and Patricia Horvatich, pp. 157–82. Honolulu: University of Hawai'i Press, 1997.

———. *Islam, Law and Equality in Indonesia*: *An Anthropology of Public Reasoning*. Cambridge: Cambridge University Press, 2003.

Bowrey, Thomas. *A Geographical Account of Countries Round the Bay of Bengal, 1669 to 1679*, edited by R. C. Temple. Works issued by the Hakluyt Society, 2nd series, no. 12. Cambridge: Hakluyt Society, 1905.

Boxer, Charles. "A Note of Portuguese Reactions to the Revival of the Red Sea Spice Trade and the Rise of Aceh, 1540–1600". *Journal of Southeast Asian History* X, no. 3 (1969): 415–28.

Braginsky, Vladimir. "The Science of Women and the Jewel: The Synthesis of Tantrism and Sufism in a Corpus of Mystical Texts from Aceh". *Indonesia and the Malay World* 32, no. 93 (2004): 141–75.

———. "Stucture, Date and Sources of Hikayat Aceh Revisited. The Problem of Mughal-Malay Literature". *Bijdragen tot de Taal-, Land- en Volkenkunde* 162, no. 4 (2006): 441–67.

Brakel, Lode F. "State and Statecraft in 17th century Aceh". In *Pre-colonial state systems in Southeast Asia: The Malay Peninsular, Sumatra, Bali-Lombok, South Celebes*, edited by Anthony Reid and Lance Castles, pp. 55–66. Monographs of the Malaysian Branch of the Royal Asiatic Society, no. 6. Kuala Lumpur: Malaysian Branch, Royal Asiatic Society, 1975.

Brass, Paul R. *Ethnicity and Nationalism. Theory and Comparison*. New Delhi; Newbury Park; California: Sage Publications, 1991.

Brenner-Felsach, Joachim Freiherr v. *Eine Reise nach Nias: unveröffentlichte Manuskripte aus dem Museum für Völkerkunde in Wien*, edited by R. Mittersakschmöller. Wien: Böhlau, 1998.

Broersma, R. *Atjeh als land voor handel en bedrijf.* Utrecht: Cohen, 1925.

Brown, R.U. "Letters to the editor". *Editor and Publisher* 109 (25 September 1976): 68.

Buchsteiner, Jochen. "Die Rache der schulterfreien Meeresgöttin: Wie sich die Javaner die rätselhafte Häufung indonesischer Naturkatastrophen erklären". *Frankfurter Allgemeine Zeitung*, 5 September 2006.

Budy B. Resosudarmo. "Introduction". In *The Politics and Economics of Indonesia's Natural Resources*, edited by Budy P. Resosudarmo. Singapore: Institute of Southeast Asian Studies, 2005.

———, ed. *The Politics and Economics of Indonesia's Natural Resources*. Singapore: Institute of Southeast Asian Studies, 2005.

Buendía, Rizal G. *Ethnicity and Sub-Nationalist Independence Movements in the Philippines and Indonesia: Implications for Regional Security*. Manila: De La Salle University Press, 2002.

Bukhari Daud. "Writing and reciting in Aceh. Perspectives on language and literature in Aceh". Unpublished Ph.D. dissertation, Department of Linguistics and Applied Linguistics, University of Melbourne, 1997.

———. *Kamus Basa Aceh = Kamus Bahasa Aceh = Acehnese-Indonesian-English: Thesaurus*. Pacific Linguistics, Series C, no. 151. Canberra: Research School of Pacific and Asian Studies, Australian National University, 1999.

Burke, Adam. "Current Society and Politics in Aceh. Key Trends, Local Figures, and other Issues". 2005. Online resource, <www.humanitarianinfo.org/sumatra/reliefrecovery/cross/docs/ DFID-CurrentSocialPoliticalContextAceh-210705.pdf>. Accessed 4 July 2007.

Busthanul Arifin. *Pelembagaan hukum Islam di Indonesia: Akar, sejarah, hambatan dan prospeknya*. Jakarta: Gema Insani Press, 1996.

Cheah Boon Kheng. "Power Behind the Throne: The Role of the Queens and Court Ladies in Malay History". *Journal of the Malaysian Branch of the Royal Asiatic Society* LXVI, Part 1, no. 1 (1993): 1–21.

Chijs, J.A. van der et al., eds. *Dagh-Register gehouden int Casteel Batavia vant passerende daer ter plaetse als over geheel Nederlandts-India. Anno 1641–42*. 's-Gravenhage: M. Nijhoff, Batavia: G. Kolff & Co., 1887–1928.

Christie, Clive J. *A Modern History of Southeast Asia. Decolonization, Nationalism, and Separatism*. London and New York: Tauris Academic Studies, 1996.

Clauss, Wolfgang. *Nelken und der Clan der Händler: Agrarproduktion und Handel auf der Insel Simeulue (West Aceh, Indonesien)*. Working Paper, no. 108. Bielefeld: University of Bielefeld, Faculty of Sociology, Sociology of Development Research Centre, 1988.

———. "Clove Traders and Peasants in Simeulue, Aceh". In *The Moral Economy of Trade. Ethnicity and Developing Markets*, edited by Hans-Dieter Evers and Heiko Schrader, pp. 88–84. London: Routledge, 1994.

CMI (Crisis Management Initiative). "Agenda for the Second Meeting between the Government of Indonesia and the Free Aceh Movement 21–23 February 2005". Helsinki, 21–23 February 2005*a*.

———. "Working Paper on Aceh Monitoring Mission (AMM)". Helsinki, 13 May 2005*b*.

Cody, Edward. "In Angry Waves, the Devout Sea an Angry God". *Washington Post*, 5 January 2005. Available online at <http://www.washingtonpost.com/wp-dyn/articles/A48407-2005Jan4.html>.

Cook, Michael. *Commanding Right and Forbidding Wrong in Islamic Thought*. Cambridge: Cambridge University Press, 2006.

Cribb, Robert. "Independence for Java? New National Projects for an Old Empire". In *Indonesia Today: Challenges of History*, edited by Grayson Lloyd and Shannon Smith, pp. 298–310. Singapore: Institute of Southeast Asian Studies, 2001.

Crouch, Harold. "Wiranto and Habibie: Military-Civilian Relations since May 1998". In *Reformasi. Crisis and Change in Indonesia*, edited by Arief Budiman, Barbara Hatley, and Damien Kingsbury, pp. 127–48. Clayton: Monash Asia Institute, 1999.

CS (Civil Society). "Position Statement of the Acheh Civil Society at the conclusion of the GAM-Acheh Civil Society meeting of 23 and 24 May 2005". Saltsjöbaden, 24 May 2005.

Dampier, William. *Voyages and Discoveries*. London: Argonaut Press, 1931.

Damsté, H. T.: "Memoires van een Atjehsen balling". In *Letterkunde van de Indische Archipel. Oorspronkelijke vertalingen*, edited by Jan Gonda. Amsterdam: Elsevier, Amsterdam, 1947.

Daud Ali. "Peluang penerapan hukum Islam dalam perspektif normatif dan sosio-politis". *Majalah Akses* I, no. 1 (2001): 58–59.

Davies, Matthew N. *Indonesia's War over Aceh. Last Stand on Mecca's Porch*. London and New York: Routledge, 2006.

Dawood, Dayan and Sjafrizal. "Aceh: The LNG Boom and Enclave Development". In *Unity and Diversity: Regional Economic Development in Indonesia since 1970*, edited by Hal Hill, pp. 107–24. Singapore: Oxford University Press, 1989.

de Klerck, E.S. *De Atjeh-oorlog*. 's-Gravenhage: Nijhoff, 1912.

de Soto, Hernando. *The Mystery of Capital. Why Capitalism Triumphs in the West and Fails Everywhere Else*. New York: Basic Books, 2000. New ed. Black Swan, 2001.

Dedy Ardiansyah. "Sepenggal puisi untuk teman". 31 January 2005. Posted on <http://acehupdate.degromiest.nl/archives/001887.php>.

Der Koran. Translated by Rudi Paret. Reprint. Stuttgart: Kohlhammer, 1979.

Drewes, G.W.J. *Two Acehnese Poems; Hikayat Ranto and Hikayat Teungku di Meuké*. The Hague: Nijhoff, 1980.

Duka Atjeh Duka Bersama. Jakarta: Dewan Kesenian Jawa Timur and Logung Pustaka, 2005.

Durie, Mark. *A Grammar of Acehnese on the Basis of a Dialect of North Aceh*. Verhandelingen van het Koninklijk Instituut voor de Taal-, Land- en Volkenkunde, no. 112. Dordrecht and Cinnaminson: Foris, 1985.

Eaton, Richard Maxwell. *Sufis of Bijapur, 1300–1700: Social Roles of Sufis in Medieval India*. Princeton: Princeton University Press, 1978.

Eaton, Richard M. *The Sufis of Bijapur 1300–1700: Social Roles of Sufis in medieval India*. Princeton: Princeton University Press, 1976.

EL. "Musica luncurkan 'Dari hati Untuk Aceh'". 21 February 2005. Accessed online at <http://www.gatra.com/artikel.php?id=53276>.

Emmerson, Donald K. "Understanding the New Order: Bureaucratic Pluralism in Indonesia". *Asian Survey* 23, no. 11 (1983): 47–66.

Encyclopaedia of Islam. New edition. Vol. 5. Leiden: Brill, 1960–.

Endres, Franz Carl and Annemarie Schimmel. *Das Mysterium der Zahl. Zahlensymbolik im Kulturvergleich*. Diederichs Gelbe Reihe, 52. Köln: Diederichs, 1984.

Ensiklopedi pemikiran ulama Aceh. Tim penulis IAIN ar-Raniry. Banda Aceh: Ar- Raniry Press, 2004.

Eri Anugerah. "Upaya ikut membangun kembali Aceh". *Media Indonesia Online*, 27 February 2005, <http://www.mediaindo.co.id/resensi/details.asp?id=46>.

Eriksen, Thomas H. *Ethnicity and Nationalism. Anthropological Perspectives*. London and Boulder, Colorado: Pluto Press, 1993.

Ernst, Carl W. "Persecution and Circumspection in Shattari Sufism". In *Islamic Mysticm Contested*, edited by Frederik de Jong and Bernd Radtke. Leiden: Brill, 1999.

EU. "Aceh Monitoring Mission (AMM) — Selected Key Principles For Initial Agreement And For Inclusion In Concept Of Operations". Working paper. European Union, 12 July 2005.

Fadjri Alihar. "Singkil: ein Zuwanderungs- und Kolonisationsraum in Süd-Aceh, Nord-Sumatra, Indonesien". Ph.D. dissertation, University of Kassel, 1996.

Fakultas Hukum Universitas Syiah Kuala. *Inventarisasi Hukum Adat dan Adat di Provinsi Aceh Darussalam*. In cooperation with the Government of the Province of Nanggroe Aceh Darussalam. Banda Aceh: Fakultas Hukum Universitas Syiah Kuala, 2001.

Farrington, Anthony. "Negotiations at Aceh in 1684: An Unpublished English Document". *Indonesia and the Malay World* 27, no. 77 (1999): 19–33.

Fehr, F.A. *Drei Christenfrauen: Lebensbilder aus Nias*. Rheinische Missionsschriften, 44. Barmen: Missionshaus der Rheinischen Mission, 1911.

Feldman, J. A. et al., eds. *Nias. Tribal Treasures. Cosmic Reflections in Stone, Wood and Gold*. Delft: Volkenkundig Museum Nusantara, 1990.

Firdaus Burhan and Idris Z. Z., eds. *Ensiklopedi musik dan tari daerah Propinsi Daerah Istimewa Aceh*. Banda Aceh: Departemen Pendidikan dan Kebudayaan, Pusat Penelitian Sejarah dan Budaya, Proyek Inventarisasi dan Dokumentasi Kebudayaan Daerah, 1986/1987.

Fischer, Hendrik Willem. *Atjeh-, Gajo- und Alasländer. Sumatra I*. Katalog des ethnographischen Reichsmuseums, 6. Leiden: Brill, 1912.

Forum Asia. "Neither Wolf, nor Lamb. Embracing Civil Society in the Aceh Conflict". Bangkok, 2004.

Freitag, Ulrike. "Der Orientalist und der Mufti: Kulturkontakt im Mekka des 19. Jahrhunderts". *Die Welt des Islams* 43, no. 1 (2003): 37–60.

Fries, E. *Nias: amoeata hoelo nono Niha*. Ombolata: Zendingsdrukkery, 1911.

Geertz, Clifford. *Islam Observed: Religious Development in Morocco and Indonesia.* Chicago: University of Chicago Press, 1971.

Gellner, Ernst. *Saints of the Atlas.* Chicago: University of Chicago Press, 1969.

———. *Muslim Society.* Cambridge and New York: Cambridge University Press, 1981.

George, Kenneth. "Designs on Indonesia's Muslim Communities". *Journal of Asian Studies* 57, no. 3 (1998): 693–713.

———. "Some Things that Have Happened to 'The Sun After September 1965': Politics and the Interpretation of an Indonesian Painting". *Comparative Studies in Society and History* 39, no. 4 (October 1997): 599–634.

Gibb, H.A.R. and C. Beckingham. *The Travels of Ibn Battuta A.D. 1325–1354.* Transl., with revisions and notes from the Arabic text edited by C. Defrémery and B.R. Sanguinetti. Vol. IV: The transl. compl. with annot. by C.F. Beckingham. Works issued by the Hakluyt Society, 2nd series, 110, 117, 141, 178, 190. Cambridge: Cambridge University Press; London: Hakluyt Society, 1994.

Gobée, Emile and Cornelis Adriaanse, eds. *Ambtelijke adviezen van C. Snouck Hurgronje, 1889–1936.* 2 vols. Rijks geschiedkundige publicatiën, 33, 34. Kleine serie. 's-Gravenhage: Nijhoff, 1957–59.

Goenawan Mohamad. "Forgetting: Poetry and the Nation, a Motif in Indonesian Literary Modernism after 1945". In *Clearing a space. Postcolonial readings of modern Indonesian literature*, edited by Keith Foulcher and Tony Day, pp. 183–211. Leiden: KITLV Press, 2002.

GoI. "Statement in Response to GAM Proposal". 23 May 2006.

Gorjão, Paulo. "Abdurrahman Wahid's Presidency: What Went Wrong?". In *Governance in Indonesia: Challenges Facing the Megawati Presidency*, edited by Hadi Soesastro, Anthony Smith, and Han Mui Ling, pp. 13–43. Singapore: Institute for Southeast Asian Studies, 2003.

Graf, Arndt. *Indonesische Medienrhetorik. Eine methodologische Fallstudie anhand der Kommentarkolumne "Catatan Pinggir" von Goenawan Mohamad.* Veröffentlichungen des Seminars für Indonesische und Südseesprachen der Universität Hamburg, 22. Berlin: Reimer, 1998

Grossman, Lev. "Why the 9/11 conspiracies won't go away". *Time*, 11 September 2006.

Hämmerle, Johannes Maria. *Nias. Land der Menschen. Ein Beitrag aus Zentral-Nias.* Münster: Missionsprokur der Kapuziner, 1982.

Hämmerle, Johannes Maria. *Nias: eine eigene Welt. Sagen, Mythen, Überlieferungen.* Collectanea Instituti Anthropos, vol. 43. Sankt Augustin: Academia, 1999.

Hall, D.G.E. *A History of South-East Asia.* London: Macmillan, 1981.

Hambly, Gavin, ed. *Women in the Medieval Islamic World: Power, Patronage, and Piety.* New York: St. Martin's Press, 1998.

Harker, Bruce. "Usindo Open Forum. Aceh: Rebuilding the Economy". *Washington*, 25 January 2005. Accessed on 6 July 2006 <http://www.usindo.org/Briefs/2005/Aceh%20Tsunami%20-%20Bruce%20Harker%201-25-05.htm>.

Harper, R.W.E. and Harry Miller. *Singapore Mutiny*. Singapore and New York: Oxford University Press, 1984.

Hartono Mardjono. *Menegakkan syariat Islam dalam konteks keindonesiaan: proses penerapan nilai-nilai Islam dalam aspek hukum, politik, dan lembaga negara*. Bandung: Mizan, 1997.

Hasan Basry, M. *Kamus Indonesia — Aceh*. Jakarta: Yayasan Cakra Daru, 1994.

Hasan di Tiro. *The Price of Freedom: The Unfinished Day of Tengku Hasan di Tiro. Part 1*. National Liberation Front of Acheh Sumatra. Markham: The Open Press, 1984.

Hasbi Amiruddin, M. "The Response of the Ulama Dayah to the Modernization of Islamic Law in Aceh". M.A. thesis, McGill University, 1994. Published by University Microfilms, Ann Arbor, 1996. Republished as *The Response of the Ulama Dayah to the Modernization of Islamic Law in Aceh*. Bangi: Penerbit Universiti Kebangsaan Malaysia, 2005. Indonesian translation published as *Ulama Dayah: pengawal agama Masyarakat Aceh*. Lkohseumawe: Yayasan Nadiya, 2003.

Hazmirullah and "PR". "Raja Balada itu terfokus pada lagu kemanusiaan". *Pikiran Rakyat*, 11 February 2005. Accessed online at <http://www.pikiran-rakyat.com/cetak/2005/0205/11/0305.htm>.

Hedman, Eva-Lotta. "Back to the Barracks: Relokasi Pengungsi in Post-Tsunami Aceh". *Indonesia* 80 (2005): 1–19.

Heeres, J.E., ed. "Corpus Diplomaticum Neerlando-Indicum. Vol. 1. 1596–1650". *Bijdragen tot de Taal,- Land- en Volkenkunde van Nederlandsch-Indië* 57, 87, 91, 93, 96 (1907–1938).

Heiduk, Felix. *Der Aceh-Konflikt und seine Auswirkungen auf die Stabilität Indonesiens und Südostasiens. Alter Konflikt im neuen Indonesien*. Berlin: Stiftung Wissenschaft und Politik, 2004 (SWP-Studie, S 2004,5). Online resource <http://www.swp-berlin.org/common/get_document.php?asset_id=1104>. Accessed 4 July 2007.

Heine-Geldern, Robert. "Survivance de motifs de l'ancien art bouddhique de l'Inde dans l'île de Nias". In *Artibus Asiae: Felicitation Volume Presented to Professor George Cœdès on the Occasion of his Seventy-Fifth Birthday* 24, nos. 3–4 (1961): 299–306.

Henny, C. "Stille Kracht". *Indische Gids* 43, no. 2 (1921): 808–919.

Herbst, Anja. *Das Konfliktfeld Aceh im Rahmen der Dezentralisierungspolitik in Indonesien*. Südostasien Working Papers, 26. Berlin: Institut für Asien- und Afrikawissenschaften, Seminar für Südostasien-Studien, 2004.

Heri Ruslan. "Sajak-sajak peduli korban tsunami". *Republika*, 13 February 2005. Available online at <http://www.republika.co.id/koran_detail.asp?id=187277&kat_id=306&kat_id1=&kat_id2=>.

Hoesein Djajadiningrat. "Critisch overzicht van de in Maleische werken vervatte gegevens over de geschiedenis van het Sultanaat van Atjeh". *Bijdragen tot de Taal, Land- en Volkenkunde van Nederlandsch Indië*, 65 (1911): 135–265.

Hogan, J. "Letters to the Editor in the 'War on Terror': A Cross-National Study". *Mass Communication & Society* 9, no. 1 (2006): 63–83.

Honna, Jun. *Military Politics and Democratization in Indonesia*. RoutledgeCurzon Research on Southeast Asia; no. 4. London: RoutledgeCurzon, 2003.

Horowitz, Donald L. "The Cracked Foundations of the Right to Secede". *Journal of Democracy* 2 (2003): 5–17.

Hoskins, Janet. "The Headhunter as Hero: Local Traditions and Their Reinterpretation in National History". *American Ethnologist* 14, no. 4 (1987): 605–22.

Huntington, Samuel. *The Third Wave. Democratization in the Late Twentieth Century*. Norman: University of Oklahoma Press, 1991.

Ibrahim Alfian. *Mata Uang Emas Kerajaan-Kerajaan di Aceh*. Banda Aceh: Proyek Rehabilitasi dan Perluasan Museum Daerah Istimewa Aceh, 1979.

———. "The Ulama in Acehnese Society". In *Readings on Islam in Southeast Asia*, edited by Ahmad Ibrahim, Sharon Siddique, and Yasmin Hussain. Singapore: Institute of Southeast Asian Studies, 1985.

———. *Sastra perang. Sebuah pembicaraan mengenai hikayat perang sabil*. Jakarta: Balai Pustaka, 1992.

———. "Ratu Nur-Ilah". In *Wanita Utama Nusantara Dalam Lintasan Sejarah*, edited by Ismail Sofyan, M. Hasan Basri, and Ibrahim Alfian. Jakarta: Jakarta Agung Offset, 1994*a*.

———. "Ratu Nahrasiyah". In *Wanita utama Nusantara dalam lintasan sejarah*, edited by Ismail Sofyan, M. Hasan Basri, and Ibrahim Alfian. Jakarta: Jakarta Agung Offset, 1994*b*.

Ibrahimi, M. Nur El. *Peranan Tgk. Muhammad Daud Beureu-eh dalam pergolakan Aceh: manager Aceh daerah modal tergolong penyelamat Republik Indonesia, mengapa akhirnya naik ke gunung?* Rev. ed. Jakarta: Media Da'wah, 2001.

Idris, Z.H. et al. *Peralatan hiburan dan kesenian tradisional Propinsi Daerah Istimewa Aceh*. Jakarta: Departemen Pendidikan dan Kebudayaan, Direktorat Jendral Kebudayaan, Direktorat Sejarah dan Nilai Tradisional, Proyek Penelitian Pengkajian dan Pembinaan Nilai-Nilai Budaya, 1993.

Idrisi (Abū 'Abd Allāh Muhammad b. Muhammad al- Idrīsī). *India and the Neighbouring Territories in the Kitāb nuzhat al-mushtāq fī'khtirāq al-'Āfāq al-Sharif al-Idrīsī; a Transl. with Commentary of the Passages Relating to India, Pakistan, Ceylon, Parts of Afghanistan, and the Andaman, Nicobar, and Maldive Islands [etc.]*, edited by S. Maqbul Ahmad. Uitgaven van de Stichting De Goeje; 20. Leiden: Brill, 1960.

Iljas Sutan Pamenan. *Rentjong Atjeh ditangan Wanita: Zaman pemerintahan radja-radja puteri di Atjeh, 1641–1699*. Jakarta: DJ Waringin, 1959.

Indra Tjahyadi. "Puisi, ekspresi dan kesadaran kolektif personal". *Suara Karya*, 31 July 2005. Available online at <http://suarakarya-online.com/news.html?id=117155>.

"IRN". "Perpustakaan NAD Selesai Diperbaiki dari Hasil Konser Iwan Fals-Slank". *Kompas*, 29 September 2005. Accessed at <http://www.kompas.com/kompas-cetak/0509/ 29/utama/2087254.htm>. Republished on the Indonesian National Library's web-based archive, at <http://www.pnri.go.id/uploaded_files/homepage_folders/highlight/ tsunami_aceh/berita_perkembangan/index.htm>.

Isa Sulaiman, M. *Aceh merdeka: Ideologi, kepemimpinan, dan gerakan.* Jakarta: Pustaka Al-Kautsar, 2000.

Isa Suleiman. *Les Ulèebalang, les Ulémas et les enseignants de madrasah: la lutte pour le pouvoir local en Aceh de 1942 à 1951.* Ph.D. dissertation. Paris: EHEES, 1985.

T. Iskandar, ed. *Bustan Us-Salatin.* Kuala Lumpur: Dewan Bahasa dan Pustaka, 1966.

Ismail Suny. *Bunga Rampai tentang Aceh.* Jakarta: Bhratara Karya Aksara, 1980.

Isma'il Ya'kob. "Thariqat Naqshbandiyah di Daerah Istimewa Aceh". Unpublished M.A. thesis, IAIN Ar Raniry, Banda Aceh, 1975.

Ito, Takeshi. "The World of the Adat Aceh: A Historical Study of the Sultanate of Aceh". Ph.D. dissertation, Australian National University, 1984.

Iwabuchi, Akifumi. *The People of the Alas Valley. A Study of an Ethnic Group of Northern Sumatra.* Oxford: Clarendon Press; New York: Oxford University Press, 1994.

Jacobs, Julius K. *Het familie- en kampongleven op Groot-Atjeh: eene bijdrage tot de ethnographie van Noord-Sumatra.* Leiden: Brill, 1894.

Jamluzzaini. "Pengamalan Thariqat Naqsyabandiyah di abad moderen". Unpublished M.A. thesis, IAIN Ar Raniry, Banda Aceh, 1995:

Jayawardena, Chandra. "Women and Kinship in Acheh Besar, Northern Sumatra". *Ethnology* 16, no. 1 (January 1977*a*): 21–38.

———. "Achehnese Marriage Customs". *Indonesia* 23 (April 1977*b*): 157–74.

Jelani Harun. "Bustan al-Salatin, 'The Garden of Kings': A Universal History and Adab Work from Seventeenth-Century Aceh". *Indonesia and the Malay World* 32, no. 92 (2004): 21–52.

Johns, A.H. "Daka'k al Huruf by `Abd al-Ra'uf of Singkel". *Journal of the Royal Asiatic Society* 55–73 (1955): 139–58.

———. "The Role of Sufism in the Spread of Islam to Malaya and Indonesia". *Journal of the Pakistan Historical Society* 9 (1961): 143–61.

———. "Friends in Grace: Ibrahim al-Kurani and `Abd al-Ra'uf al-Singkeli". In *Spectrum: Essays Presented to Sutan Takdir Alisjahbana on his 70th Birthday*, edited by S. Udin, pp. 469–85. Jakarta: Dian Rakyat, 1978.

———, ed. *The Gift Addressed to the Spirit of the Prophet.* Canberra: Australian National University, 1965.

Jones, Leon. *The Security Disturbances in Aceh during 1990.* Working Papers, Centre of Southeast asian Studies, no. 104. Clayton: Monah University, 1997.

Jongejans, J. *Land en volk van Atjeh.* Baarn: Hollandia Drukkerij, 1939.

Jumat Sehat. "Tarekat dalam masyarakat Kecamatan Lawe Aöas di Aceh Tenggara". Unpublished M.A. thesis, IAIN Ar-Raniry, Banda Aceh, 1985.

Junus Melalatoa, M. *Didong: Pentas Kreativitas Gayo.* Seri Tradisi Lisan Nusantara. Jakarta: Yayasan Asosiasi Tradisi Lisan dan Yayasan Obor Indonesia, Yayasan Sains Estetika dan Teknologi, 2001.

Juwana, Hikmahanto. "Assessing Indonesia's Human Rights Practice Post-Soeharto: 1998–2003". *Indonesian Quarterly* 32, no. 1 (2004): 50–85.

Kähler, Hans. *Beiträge zur Ethnologie der Insel Simalur (Simeuloeë)*. Batavia: Lux, 1938.

———. *Sichule-Texte*. Batavia: Koninklijk Bataviaasch Genootschap van Kunsten en Wetenschappen, 1940.

———. *Die Insel der schönen Si Melu; Indonesische Dämonengeschichten, Märchen und Sagen aus Simalur, auf einer Forschungsreise aufgenommen und in Auswahl herausgegeben*. Eisenach: Röth, 1952.

———. *Die Sichule-Sprache auf der Insel Simalur an der Westküste von Sumatra*. Berlin: Reimer, 1955.

———. *Vergleichendes Wörterverzeichnis der Sichule-Sprache auf der Insel Simalur an der Westküste von Sumatra*. Berlin: Reimer, 1959.

———. *Simalur-deutsches Wörterbuch mit deutsch-simaluresischem Wörterverzeichnis*. Berlin: Reimer, 1961.

———. *Texte von der Insel Simalur*. Berlin: Reimer, 1963.

Kapur, Geeta. "Dismantling the Norm". In *Traditions/Tensions: Contemporary Art in Asia*, edited by Apinan Poshyananda, pp. 60–69. New York: Asia Society, 1996.

Kartomi, Margaret J. "Music and Dance in Aceh: A Preliminary Survey". *Indonesia Circle* 24 (March 1981): 15–28.

——— "Sumatra". In *The Garland Encyclopedia of World Music. Vol. 4: Southeast Asia*, edited by Terry E. Miller and Sean Williams, pp. 598–629. New York: Garland Publishing, 1998.

———. "On Metaphor and Analogy in the Concepts and Classification of Musical Instruments in Aceh". *Yearbook for Traditional Music* 37 (2005): 25–57.

Kartomi, Margaret J., Lyn Moore and Nguyen Thuyet Phong (with Jack Percival Baker Dobbs). "Sarunai". In *New Grove Dictionary of Music and Musicians*, p. 302. 1984.

Kathirithamby-Wells, Jeyamalar. "Acehnese Control Over West Sumatra up to the Treaty of Painan, 1663". *Journal of Southeast Asian History* 10, no. 3 (1969): 453–79.

Kato, Tsuyoshi. *Matriliny and migration. Evolving Minangkabau traditions in Indonesia*. London: Cornell University Press, 1982.

Kell, Tim. *The Roots of Acehnese Rebellion, 1989–1992*. Cornell Modern Indonesia Project, no. 74. Ithaca: Cornell Modern Indonesia Project, 1995.

Kemper, Barbara. *Mediation in Intrastate Conflicts: the Contribution of Track-Two Mediation Activities to Prevent Violence in the Aceh Conflict*. (INEF-Report, 88). Duisburg: Institut für Entwicklung und Frieden, 2007.

Kennedy, Raymond. *The Ethnology of the Greater Sunda Islands*. New Haven: Yale University, 1935.

Khalid M.Hussain, ed. *Taj Us-Salatin*. 2nd ed. (1st ed. 1966). Kuala Lumpur: Dewan Bahasa dan Pustaka, 1992.

Kingsbury, Damien. *Power Politics and the Indonesian Military*. London: RoutledgeCourzon, 2003.

Kingsbury. "Assessment of the State of the CMI Aceh Peace Talks at the Conclusion of Round IV, Helsinki". Unpublished manuscript, 1 June 2005.

Kleiweg de Zwaan, Johannes Pieter. *Die Insel Nias*. 3 vols. Der Haag: Nijhoff, 1913–15.

Koloniaal Verslag. 's-Gravenhage: Algemeene Landsdrukkerij, 1868–1924.

Kratz, Ernst Ulrich. *Peringatan sejarah negeri Johor: eine malaiische Quelle zur Geschichte Johors im 18. Jahrhundert*. Veröffentlichungen des Ostasiatischen Seminars der Johann-Wolfgang-Goethe-Universität Frankfurt, A, 3. Wiesbaden: Harrassowitz, 1973.

Kraus, Werner. *Islamische mystische Bruderschaften im heutigen Indonesien*. Hamburg: Institut für Asienkunde, 1990.

———. "Die Zeichen lesend. Islamische Interpretationen und Reaktionen auf den Tsunami in Aceh". *Internationales Asienforum* 37, nos. 3–4 (2006): 239–64.

Kreemer, J. *Atjeh. Algemeen samenvattend overzicht van land en volk van Atjèh en onderhoorigheden*. Leiden: Brill, 1922–23.

Kunst, Jacob. *Music in Nias*. Archives internationales d'ethnographie; 38, 1–3. Leiden: Brill, 1939–40.

Kuwajima, Sho. *First World War and Asia: Indian Mutiny in Singapore (1915)*. Osaka: Osaka University of Foreign Studies, 1988.

Kyodo. "Top Indonesian Leaders Met Secretly with GAM adviser". 28 March 2005.

Laffan, Michael F. *Islamic Nationhood and Colonial Indonesia: The Umma below the Winds*. London and New York: RoutledgeCurzon, 2003.

Lawrence, Bruce B. "Islam in India. The Function of Institutional Sufism in the Islamization of Rajasthan, Gujarat and Kashmir". *Contributions to Asian Studies* 17 (1982): 27–43.

LeBar, Frank M. *Ethnic Groups of Insular Southeast Asia*. 2 vols. New Haven: Human Relations Area Files Press Press, 1972–75.

Lee Kam Hing. *The Sultanate of Aceh — Relations with the British, 1760–1824*. South-East Asian historical monographs. Kuala Lumpur: Oxford University Press, 1995.

Lekkerkerker, Cornelis. *Land en Volk van Sumatra*. Leiden: Brill, 1916.

Lev, Daniel S. "Yap Thiam Hien and Aceh". *Indonesia* 82 (2006): 97–133.

Lily Zakiyah Munir, ed. *Memposisikan kodrat. Perempuan dan perubahan dalam perspektif Islam*. Bandung: Mizan, 1999.

Linus Suryadi AG. "Isma Sawitri: Penyair wanita Indonesia yang selalu luput". In *Di balik sejumlah nama; sebuah tinjauan puisi-puisi Indonesia modern*, edited by Linus Suryadi AG. Gadjah Mada University Press, Yogyakarta, 1989.

Locher-Scholten, Elsbeth. *Sumatraans sultanaat en koloniale staat: De relatie Djambi — Batavia (1830–1907) en het Nederlandse imperialisme*. Verhandelingen van het Koninklijk Instituut voor Taal-, Land- en Volkenkunde; 161. Leiden: KITLV uitgeverij, 1994.

Loeb, Edwin M. *Sumatra. Its History and People.* Wiener Beiträge zur Kulturgeschichte und Linguistik; 3. Wien: Verlag des Instituts für Völkerkunde der Universität, 1935. New ed. Kuala Lumpur: Oxford University Press, 1972.

Lombard, Denys. *Le sultanat d'Atjeh au temps d'Iskandar Muda, 1607–1636.* Paris: Ecole française d'Extrême-Orient, 1967. Indonesian version: *Kerajaan Aceh. Zaman Sultan Iskandar Muda (1607–1636).* Jakarta: Forum Jakarta Paris, Ecole française d'Extrême-Orient; Kepustakaan Populer Gramedia, 2006.

Lukman Thaib. *Acheh's Case: A Historical Study of the National Movement for the Independence of Acheh-Sumatra.* Kuala Lumpur: University of Malaya Press, 2002.

Mahmud Buchari. *Al-Qur'an Mushaf Istiqlal Indonesia.* Jakarta: Yayasan Festival Istiqlal, 1994.

Mahmud Bangkaru. *A Hand Book to Aceh 1998.* Banda Aceh: CV. Kharisma Putra Utama, 1997.

Maier, Hendrik M. J. *We are Playing Relatives. A Survey of Malay Writing.* Leiden: KITLV Press, 2004.

Majalah Aceh Kita. "Mencambuk yang tak bayar (dan sipil)". Edisi 018, II, July 2005.

Maria Hartaningsih. "Rafli, daya hidup yang tidak pudar". 28 January 2005. Accessed online at <http://www.kompas.com/kompas-cetak/0501/28/naper/1525748.htm>.

Markham, Albert Hastings, ed. *The Voyages and Works of John Davis: the Navigator.* 2 vols. London: Hakluyt Society, 1880.

Marschall, Wolfgang. *Der Berg des Herrn der Erde. Alte Ordnung und Kulturkonflikt in einem indonesischen Dorf.* München: Deutscher Taschenbuch Verlag, 1976.

———. "On Some Basic Traditions in Nusantara Cultures". In *Time Past, Time Present, Time Future. Essays in Honour of P.E. de Josselin de Jong*, edited by D. Moyer and H. Claessen, pp. 69–77. Verhandelingen van het Koninklijk Instituut voor Taal-, Land- en Volkenkunde, 131. Dordrecht: Foris, 1988.

———. "Social Stratification and Slavery on Nias and its Reflection in Oral History". *Indonesia and the Malay World* 30, no. 88 (2002): 309–18.

Marsden, William. *History of Sumatra: Containing an Account of the Government, Laws, Customs, and Manners of the Native Inhabitantss, with a Description of the Natural Productions, and Relation of the Ancient Political State of that Island.* 3rd ed. (1st ed. 1783). London: Longman, 1811.

———. *The History of Sumatra.* 3rd ed. Reprint. Singapore: Oxford University Press, 1986.

Marshall, Andrew. "Healing Hands". *Time Asia,* Monday, 28 March 2005. Accessed online at <http://www.time.com/time/asia/magazine/printout/0,13675,501050404-1042515,00.html>.

Martinkus, John. *Indonesia's Secret War in Aceh.* Milsons Point, New South Wales; New York: Random House Australia, 2004.

Maxwell, John, ed. *The Malay-Islamic World of Sumatra. Studies in Polities and Culture.* Melbourne: Monash University, 1982.

McCarthy, John Fitzgerald. *The Fourth Circle. A Political Ecology of Sumatra's Rainforest Frontier.* East-West Center Series of Political Issues in Asia and the Pacific. Stanford, California: Stanford University Press, 2006.

McCulloch, Lesley. "Business as Usual: Until Gus Dur Can Bring Military Business Activities under Control, They Won't Go, Back to the Barracks'." *Inside Indonesia* 63 (Jul–Sep 2000): 13–14.

———. "Greed: the Silent Force of Conflict in Aceh". In *Violence in Between: Conflict and Security in Archipelagic Southeast Asia*, edited by Damien Kingsbury, pp. 203–30. Clayton, Australia: Monash Asia Institute; Singapore: Institute of Southeast Asian Studies, 2005.

McGibbon R. *Secessionist Challenges in Aceh and Papua: Is Special Autonomy the Solution?* (Policy Studies, no. 10). Washington, D.C.: East-West Center Washington, 2004.

Mediaindo. "Dari hati untuk Aceh: Upaya ikut membangun kembali Aceh". 27 February 2005. Accessed online at <http://www.mediaindo.co.id/resensi/details.asp?id=46>.

Memmi, Albert. *The Colonizer and the Colonized.* Expanded ed. Boston: Beacon Press, 1991 [1957].

Meo, Nick. "Tsunami was God's revenge for your Wicked Ways, Women Told". *The Times*, 22 December 2005*a*. Available online at <http://www.timesonline.co.uk/article/0,,25689-1952823,00.html>.

———. "After Tsunami, Islamic Religious Police Gain Power in Aceh". *San Francisco Chronicle*, 25 December 2005*b*. Available online at <http://www.sfgate.com/cgi-bin/article.cgi?f=/c/a/2005/12/25/MNGCEGD8KC1.DTL>.

Mernissi, Fatima. *The Forgotten Queens of Islam* [Sultanes oubliées]. Transl. Mary Jo Lakeland. Minneapolis: University of Minnesota Press, 1993.

Meyers Lexikon. Leipzig: Bibliographisches Institut, 1928.

Missbach, Antje. *Freiheitskämpfer oder Geschäftemacher? Der bewaffnete Kampf der Gerakan Aceh Merdeka (GAM) unter Berücksichtigung klassischer und neuer Guerillatheorien.* Berlin: Logos, 2005.

Mitchell, W. J. T. *Iconology. Image, Text, Ideology.* Chicago: University of Chicago Press, 1986.

———. *Picture Theory. Essays on Verbal and Visual Representation.* Chicago: University of Chicago Press, 1994.

Modigliani, Elio. *Un viaggio a Nías.* Milano: Fratelli Treves, 1890.

Mohammad Said. *Atjeh sepandjang abad.* Medan: Pengarang Sendiri, 1961.

Morris, Eric Eugene. *Islam and Politics in Aceh. A Study of Center-Periphery Relations in Indonesia.* Ann Arbor: Cornell University, 1983.

———. "Aceh. Social Revolution and the Islamic Vision". In *Regional Dynamics of the Indonesian Revolution. Unity from Diversity*, edited by Audrey R. Kahin, pp. 82–110. Honolulu: University of Hawai'i Press, 1985.

Müller, Th. *Die große Reue auf Nias. Geschichte und Gestalt einer Erweckungsbewegung auf dem Missionsfeld.* Gütersloh: Bertelsmann, 1931.

Müller-Krüger, Theodor. *Der Protestantismus in Indonesien. Geschichte und Gestalt.* Stuttgart: Evangelisches Verlagswerk, 1968.

Muhammad Amin Suma. "Revitalisasi Syari'at Islam di Indonesia antara peluang dan tantangan (suatu pengantar)". In *Aiyub Ahmad, Fiqh Lelang dalam Perspektif Hukum Islam dan Hukum Positif,* edited by Hasan Basri. Jakarta: Kiswah, 2004.

Muhammad Haji Salleh, ed. *Sulalat al-Salatin ya'ni perteturun segala raja-raja.* Kuala Lumpur: Yayasan Karyawan dan Dewan Bahasa dan Pustaka, 1997.

Muhammad Hakim Nyak Pha. *Parenté (Keurabat) et relations sociales à Aceh Besar (Nord de Sumatra).* Ph.D. dissertation. Paris: EHEES, 1985.

Muhibbuddin Waly, Teungku. *Ayah Kami: Maulana Syeikh Haji Muhammad Waly al-Khalidy.* Kuala Lumpur: International Islamic University, 1993.

Mukti Ali. *Alam pikiran Islam modern di Indonesia.* Jakarta: Tintamas, 1964.

Musthafa Helmy. "Aceh. Jalan pintas menuju Tuhan". *Editor,* 12 September 1987, pp. 43–49.

Mutammimul Ula. *Prospek penerapan Syariat Islam di Indonesia.* Jakarta: Pustaka Tarbiyatuna, 1994.

Mystical Illustrations from the Teachings of Shaikh Ahmad al-Qusyasyi. A Facsimile Edition on Paper and CD-ROM of a Manuscript from Aceh (Cod. Or. 2222) in the Library of Leiden, edited by Adrianus Petrus Gerardus Janson, Roger Gérard Tol, and Januarius Justus Witkam. Manuscripta Indonesica, Vol. 5. Leiden: Indonesian-Netherlands Cooperation in Islamic Studies (INIS), 1995.

Naimur Rahman Farooqi. "Mughal-Ottoman Relations: A Study of Political and Diplomatic Relations between Mughal India and the Ottoman Empire, 1556–1748". Ph.D. dissertation, University of Wisconsin, 1986.

Nandy, Ashis. *Exiled at Home.* New Delhi: Oxford University Press, 1998.

Narayan, Kirin. "How Native is a 'Native Anthropologist'?". *American Anthropologist* 95 (1993): 671–86.

Nazamuddin. *Studi pemetaan ekonomi NAD pascabencana gempa dan tsunami.* Lembaga Pengkajian Ekonomi dan Sosial (LPES) Fakultas Ekonomi Universitas Syiah Kuala Darussalam Banda Aceh. Medan, 2005.

Nazamuddin, Putri Bintusy Syathi, Miksalmina, Miftachhuddin. "Industri perikanan di Provinsi Nanggroe Aceh Darussalam: Kondisi sebelum dan sesudah tsunami". Unpublished manuscript, 2005.

Nazaruddin Sjamsuddin. *The Republican Revolt: A Study of the Acehnese Rebellion.* Singapore: Institute of Southeast Asian Studies, 1985.

Niven, W.D. "Good and Evil". In *Encyclopaedia of Religion and Ethics,* edited by James Hastings. Vol. VI, pp. 318a–26a. Edinburgh: T. & T. Clark; New York: Charles Scribner's Sons, 1913.

Nizami, K.A. "The Shattari Saints and their Attitude towards the State". *Medieval India Quarterly* I (1950): 56–70.

"Nota van toelichting betreffende het Landschap Seunagan". (Signature of the *controleur* illegible), *Memorie van Overgave*, Collection of the Algemeen Rijksarchief Den Haag, 1935.

Novriantoni. "Tuhan pasca-tsunami". *Kompas*, 14 January 2005. Available online at <http://www.kompas.com/kompas-cetak/0501/14/opini/1499211.htm>.

Nur El Ibrahimi, M. *Peranan Tgk. M. Daud Beureu-eh dalam pergolakan Aceh: manager Aceh daerah modal tergolong penyelamat Republik Indonesia, mengapa akhirnya naik ke gunung?* Jakarta: Media Da'wah, 2001.

OCHA and HIC Situation Reports, May 2005.

O'Rourke, Kevin. *Reformasi: the Struggle for Power in Post-Soeharto Indonesia*. Crows Nest, NSW: Allen & Unwin, 2002.

Otterspeer, Willem. "The Ethical Imperative". In *Leiden Oriental Connections, 1850–1940*, edited by Willem Otterspeer. Leiden and New York: E.J. Brill, 1989.

Pandy, Chhandasi. "Private Authority and Disaster Relief: the Cases of Post-Tsunami Aceh and Nias". *Critical Asian Studies* 38, no. 2 (2005): 298–308.

Panggabean, Martin. "War in Aceh, its Economic Impact". Institute of Southeast Asian Studies website, Singapore, 20 May 2003*a*. Accessible online at <http://www.iseas.edu.sg/viewpoint/mpmay03.pdf>.

———. *Straits Times*, 20 May 2003*b*.

Pedersen, Johannes. *The Scientific Work of Snouck Hurgronje*. Leiden: E. J. Brill, 1957.

Peletz, Michael. "Neither Reasonable nor Responsible. Contrasting Representations of Masculinity in a Malay Society". In *Bewitching Women, Pious Men. Gender and Body Politics in Southeast Asia*, edited by Aihwa Ong and Michael Peletz, pp. 76–123. Berkeley: University of California Press, 1995.

Penth, Hans. *Hikajat Atjeh. Die Erzählung von der Abkunft und den Jugendjahren des Sultan Iskandar Muda von Atjeh (Sumatra).* Veröffentlichungen des Ostasiatischen Seminars der Johann-Wolfgang-Goethe-Universität Frankfurt, Main, 2.Wiesbaden: Harrassowitz, 1969.

Perlman, Marc. "Indonesia VII: Sumatra". In *New Grove Dictionary of Music and Musicians,* pp. 344–51. 2nd ed. Oxford: Oxford University Press, 2001.

Pfeiffer, Wolfgang M. "Konflikte, psychoreaktive und psychosomatische Störungen auf Nias". *Sociologus* 27, no. 1 (1977): 1–35.

Pittioni, Richard. *Die Steingeräte von Lho' Seumawe, Kreis Atjeh, Nord-Sumatra: zur Formenkunde der 'Hoabinhian' in Südost-Asien.* Denkschriften der Österreichischen Akademie der Wissenschaften, Philosophisch-Historische Klasse, 132. Wien: Verlag der Österreichischen Akademie der Wissenschaften, 1978.

Pusat Penelitian Ilmu-Ilmu Sosial dan Budaya (PPISB) Universitas Syiah Kuala. *Inventarisasi kelembagaan adat di Kabupaten Aceh Besar.* In cooperation with the Regional Planning Board (Bappeda), Kabupaten Aceh Besar. Banda Aceh: 2001*a*.

———. *Penelitian hukum adat dan pengkajian adat istiadat yang masih eksis di*

Kabupaten Aceh Besar. In cooperation with the Regional Planning Board (Bappeda), Kabupaten Aceh Besar. Banda Aceh: 2001*b*.

Putireno Baiak. "Catatan perjalanan: Festival budaya & alam Aceh". [N.d.] Accessed online at <http://www.ebloggy.com/blog.php?username=Putirenobaiak&id=1&start=12>.

r/a. "Krakatau dan Rafly hentak blang Padang". *Serambi Indonesia*, 6 April 2006 <http://www.serambinews.com/index.php?aksi= bacaberita&beritaid=16353&rubrik=2&topik=32>.

Rabasa, Angel and John Haseman. *The Military and Democracy in Indonesia. Challenges, Politics, and Power.* Santa Monica: Rand, 2003.

Reenen, Joke van. *Central Pillars of the House. Sisters, Wives, and Mothers in a Rural Community in Minangkabau, West Sumatra.* Leiden: CNWS, 1996.

Reid, Anthony. *The Contest for North Sumatra. Atjeh, the Netherlands and Britain, 1858–1898.* Kuala Lumpur: University of Malaya Press; London: Oxford University Press, 1969.

———. "The Affair of the Tjumbok traitors". *Review of Indonesian and Malaysian Affairs* 4/5 (1971): 29–65.

———. "Trade and the Problem of Royal Power in Aceh: Three Stages: c.1550–1700". In *Pre-Colonial State Systems in Southeast Asia: The Malay Peninsula, Sumatra, Bali-Lombok, South Celebes*, edited by Anthony Reid and Lance Castles, pp. 45–55. Monographs of the Malaysian Branch of the Royal Asiatic Society, no. 6. Kuala Lumpur: Malaysian Branch, Royal Asiatic Society, 1975.

———. *The Blood of the People. Revolution and the End of Traditional Rule in Northern Sumatra.* Oxford: Oxford University Press, 1979.

———. "Female Roles in Pre-Colonial Southeast Asia". *Modern Asian Studies* 22, Part 3 (July 1988): 629–45.

———. *Southeast Asia in the Age of Commerce, 1450–1680. Vol. II: Expansion and Crisis.* New Haven: Yale University Press, 1993.

———. *War, Peace and the Burden of History in Aceh.* Working Papers Series No. 1. Asia Research Institute, National University of Singapore, 2003. Accessible online at <www.ari.nus.edu.sg/docs/wps/wps03_001.pdf>.

———. *An Indonesian Frontier: Acehnese and other Histories of Sumatra.* Singapore: University of Singapore Press, 2005.

———. "Aceh's View of its Place in the World, 1500–1873". In *Verandah of Violence: the Historical Background of the Aceh Problem,* edited by Anthony Reid. Singapore: Singapore University Press, 2006.

Reid, Anthony and Takeshi Ito. "From Harbour Autocracies to 'Feudal' Diffusion in Seventeenth Century Indonesia: The Case of Aceh". In *Feudalism: Comparative Studies,* edited by Edmund Leach, S. N. Mukherjee and John Ward, pp. 197–213. Sydney: Pathfinder Press, 1985.

Reid, Anthony, ed. *Witnesses to Sumatra: A Travellers' Anthology.* Kuala Lumpur: Oxford University Press, 1995.

Reuters. "Jakarta to Reject Key Aceh Rebel Demand: Minister". Jakarta, 18 May 2005.

Richardson, John E., and Bob Franklin. "Letters of Intent: Election Campaigning and Orchestrated Public debate in Local Newspapers' Letters to the Editor". *Political Communication* 21 (2004): 459–78.

Ricklefs, Merle Calvin. *A History of Modern Indonesia since c. 1300.* 2nd ed. (1st ed. 1981). Basingstoke: Macmillan Press, 1993.

Riddell, Peter G. "Breaking the Hamzah Fansuri Barrier: Other Windows into Sumatran Islam in the Late Sixteenth Century". *Indonesia and the Malay World* 32, no. 93 (2004): 125–40.

Rizal Sukma. "Aceh in Post-Suharto Indonesia. Protracted Conflict amid Democratization". In *Autonomy and Disintegration in Indonesia*, edited by Damien Kingsbury and Harry Aveling, pp. 148–56. New York: RoutledgeCurzon, 2003.

Robertson, Roland. *Globalization. Social Theory and Global Culture.* London and Newbury Park, California: Sage, 1992.

Robinson Geoffrey. "'Rawan' is as 'Rawan' Does: The Origins of Disorder in New Order Aceh". *Indonesia* 66 (October 1998): 127–56 (Reprint as "Rawan is as Rawan Does: the Origins of Disorder in New Order Aceh". In *Violence and the State in Suharto's Indonesia*, edited by Benedict R. O'G Anderson, pp. 213–42. Ithaca, NY: Cornell University, Southeast Asia Program Publications, 2001).

Robison, Richard. *Indonesia. The Rise of Capital.* Asian Studies Association of Australia, 1986.

Röll, Werner. "Gescheiterte Ansiedlungsversuche von Toba-Batak-Kkeinbauern in Singkil, Süd-Aceh, Indonesien". *Giessener Beiträge zur Entwicklungsforschung* I, no. 21 (1994): 1–21.

Ross, M.L. "The Political Economy of the Resource Curse". *World Politics* 51 (1999): 297–322.

Ross, Michael L. "Resources and Rebellion in Aceh, Indonesia. World Bank Report on the 'Economies of political Violence'." University of California, Department of Political Science, Los Angeles, 2003. Unpublished paper at <www.polisci.ucla.edu/faculty/ross/ResourcesRebellion.pdf>.

Rusdi Sufi. "Sultanah Safiatuddin Syah". In *Wanita utama Nusantara dalam lintasan sejarah*, edited by Ismail Sofyan, M. Hasan Basri, and Ibrahim Alfian, p. 57. Jakarta: Jakarta Agung Offset, 1994.

Rusjdi Ali Muhammad. *Revitalisasi Syari'at Islam di Aceh: Problem, Solusi dan Implementasi*, edited by Hasan Basri. Jakarta: Logos and Ar-Raniry Press, 2003.

Said Aiyub Abdullah. "Tariqat Naqsyabandiyah. Studi khusus penghahayatan dan pengaruhnya terhadap masyarakat Lueng Ie Kecamatan Ingin Jaya". Unpublished Master thesis, IAIN Ar-Raniry, Banda Aceh: 1979.

Salmon, Claudine. "La séricicultture à Sumatra Nord: de l'histoire à la légende de Job". *Archipel* 70 (2005): 239–69.

Sanday, Peggy R. *Women at the Center. Life in a Modern Matriarchy.* London: Cornell University Press, 2002.

Sareen, T.R., ed. *Secret Documents on the Singapore Mutiny 1915*. New Delhi: Mounto Publishing House, 1995.

Scarduelli, Pietro. "Le système des échanges matrimoniaux à Nias". *L'homme. Revue française d'anthropologie* 25, no. 94 (avril-juin 1985): 97–116.

———. "Accumulating of heads, distribution of food: the image of power in Nias". *Bijdragen tot de Taal-, Land- en Volkenkunde* 146, no. 4 (1990): 448–62.

Schimmel. Annemarie. *Mystical Dimensions of Islam*. Chapel Hill: University of North Carolina Press, 1975.

———. *Islam in the Indian Subcontinent*. Leiden, Köln: Brill, 1980.

Scholz, Ulrich. *The Natural Regions of Sumatra and Their Agricultural Production Pattern: a Regional Analysis*. Bogor, West Java: Ministry of Agriculture, Republic of Indonesia, Agency for Agricultural Research and Development, Central Research Institute for Food Crops, 1983.

Schröder, Engelbertus Eliza Willem Gerads. *Nias. Ethnographische, geographische en historische aanteekeningen en studiën*. 2 vols. Leiden: Brill, 1917.

Schröter, Susanne. "Balancing Modernity and Tradition: Ngada Rituals as a Space of Action". In *The Nature and Function of Rituals*, edited by Ruth-Inge Heinze, pp. 131–50. Westport: Greenwood Publishing Group, 1999.

———. "Creating Space, Time and Society: The Annual Cycle of the People of Langa in Eastern Indonesia". *Anthropos* 96 (2000): 463–83.

———. "Parenté, herméneutique et notions des genres. Les facettes du pouvoir sexué chez les Ngada d'Indonésie orientale". In *Une maison sans fille est une maison morte. La personne et le genre en sociétés matrilinéaires et/ou uxorilocales*, edited by Claude-Nicole Mathieu. Paris: Éditions de l'Herne, 2006.

———. "Red Cocks and Black Hen. Gendered Symbolism and Social Practice in the Ngada Highlands". *Bijdragen tot de Taal-, Land- en Volkenkunde* 161, nos. 2/3 (2005): 318–49.

Schuck, Christoph. *Der indonesische Demokratisierungsprozess: Politischer Neubeginn und historische Kontinuität*. Baden-Baden: Nomos, 2003.

Schulten, C. M. "Tactics of the Dutch Colonial Army in the Netherlands East Indies". *Revue Internationale d'Histoire Militaire* 70 (1988): 59–698.

Schulze, Kirsten E. "The Free Aceh Movement (GAM). Anatomy of a Separatist Organization". Washington, D.C.: East-West Center Washington. Online Resource <www.eastwestcenter.org/stored/pdfs/PS002.pdf>. Accessed 22 February 2004.

Schulze, Kirsten E. "Gerakan Aceh Merdeka: Freedom Fighters or Terrorists?". In *Aceh under Martial Law. Conflict, Violence and Displacement*, edited by Eva-Lotta Hedman, pp. 29–45. RSC Working Paper No. 24. Oxford: Department of International Development, University of Oxford, 2005.

Seda, Frans. "Petroleum Paradox: The Politics of Oil and Gas". In *The Politics and Economics of Indonesia's Natural Resources*, edited by Budy P. Resosudarmo, pp. 179–90. Singapore: Institute of Southeast Asian Studies, 2005.

Shafie bin Abu Bakar. "Institusi Sheikh Abdul Malik bin Abdullah dan kitab-kitab padanya". Master thesis, Universiti Kebangsaan Malaysia, Bangi, 2007.

Shari M. "Giving Peace a Chance in Aceh". *Business Week Online*, 30 December 2002.

Sher Banu A L Khan. "A Glimpse of the Invisible: Queens and Ladies of the Court as Seen through the Eyes of the Malay Chronicles". Unpublished manuscript. 1999.

———. *Ties that Unbind: The Botched Aceh-VOC Alliance in the Conquest of Melaka.* Forthcoming.

Siboro, T. "Deadlock Looms in Aceh Peace Talks: Widodo". *Jakarta Post*, 14 July 2005.

Siapno, Jacqueline Aquino. *Gender, Islam, Nationalism and the State in Aceh. The Paradox of Power, Co-operation and Resistance.* London: RoutledgeCurzon, 2002.

Siegel, James T. *The Rope of God.* Berkeley, Los Angeles: University of California Press, 1969. New ed. Ann Arbor: University of Michigan Press, 2000.

———. *Shadow and Sound: The Historical Thought of a Sumatran People.* Chicago: University of Chicago Press, 1979.

———. *A New Criminal Type in Jakarta. Counter-Revolution Today.* Durham, NC: Duke University Press, 1998.

———. "Peduli Aceh". *Indonesia* 79 (2005): 165–67.

———. "The Curse of the Photograph: Atjeh, 1901". *Indonesia* 80 (October 2005): 21–37.

SIIA. "Rebuilding Aceh: Reflections, Prospects and Challenges". SIIA Network Seminar, Singapore, 10 May 2005.

Singarimbun, Ngasup. "Surat pembaca sebagai informasi arus balik". In *Bunga rampai sistem pers Indonesia*, edited by T. Atmadi, pp. 214–20. Jakarta: Pantja Simpati, 1985.

Siti Hawa Salleh. *Bustan al-Salatin.* 2nd ed. (1st ed. 1966). Kuala Lumpur: Dewan Bahasa dan Pustaka, 1992.

Siti Musdah Mulia. *Muslimah reformis. Perempuan pembaru keagamaan.* Bandung: Mizan, 2005.

Smit, C., ed. *Bescheiden betreffende de buiten landse politiek van Nederland*, Period 3, Vol. II. The Hague: Nijhoff, 1957.

Smith, Holly S. *Aceh: Art and Culture.* Images of Asia Series. Kuala Lumpur and New York: Oxford University Press, 1997.

Smith, Vincent Arthur. *The Oxford History of India.* 3rd ed. Oxford: Clarendon Press, 1958.

Snouck Hurgronje, Christiaan. "Een Mekkaansch Gezantschap naar Atjeh in 1683". *Bijdragen Taal- land en-Volken kunde* 1, no. 37 (1888): 545–54.

———. *Het Gaj land en zijne bewoners.* Batavia: Landsdrukkerij, 1903.

———. *The Achehnese.* 2 vols. Transl. A. W. S. O'Sullivan. Leiden: E. J. Brill, 1906.

———. *The Holy War "Made in Germany".* Trans. J. E. Gillet. New York: Putnam's Sons, 1915.

———. *Verspreide geschriften. Vol. III.* Bonn/Leipzig: Kurt Schroeder Verlag, 1923.

———. *Verspreide geschriften.* Vol IV.1 & IV.2. Bonn/Leipzig: Kurt Schroeder Verlag, 1924*a*&*b*.

———. *Ambtelijke Adviezen van C. Snouck Hurgronje, 1889–1936.* Published by Emile Gobée and Cornelis Adriaanse. Rijks geschiedkundige publicatiën. Kleine serie; 33–35. 's-Gravenhage: Nijhoff, 1957–65.

———. *Scholarship and Friendship in Early Islamwissenschaft. The Letters of C. Snouck Hurgronje to I. Goldziher* ..." Published by P. SJ. van Koningsveld: Leiden, 1985.

Soewarno. "Tanggungjawab pidana atas surat pembaca kepada redaksi". In *Bunga rampai sistem pers Indonesia,* edited by T. Atmadi, pp. 226–31. Jakarta: Pantja Simpati, 1985.

Soeyatno. "Sejarah sosial masyarakat pedesaan Sibreh, Aceh Besar". In *Segi-segi sosial budaya masyarakat Aceh,* edited by Ibrahim Alfian, pp. 51–77. Jakarta: LP3ES, 1977.

Soravia, Guilio. "The Current State of Gayo Language". In *Cultures and Societes of North Sumatra,* edited by Rainer Carle, pp. 449–56. Veröffentlichungen des Seminars für Indonesische und Südseesprachen der Universität Hamburg, 19. Berlin: Reimer, 1987.

Steinhart, Willem Leonhard. "Niassche teksten, met Nederlandsche vert. en aant". *Tijdschrift voor Indische Taal-, Land- en Volkenkunde* 74 (1934), afl. 2 (dl. I), afl. 3-4 (dl. II).

Stivens, Maila. *Matriliny and Modernity. Sexual Politics and Social Change in Rural Malaysia.* St. Leonards, NSW: Allen & Unwin, 1996.

Stutterheim, W. F. "A Malay *Sha'ir* in Old Sumatran Characters of 1380 A.D.". *Acta Orientalia* 14 (1936): 268–79.

Sugihen, Bahrein Tuhumale. *Socio-Cultural and Attitudinal Change in the Modernization Process. A Study of Acehnese Society in Transition.* Ann Arbor: The Louisiana State University, 1982.

Sulistiyanto, P. "Whither Aceh?". *Third World Quarterly* 3 (2001): 437–53.

Sukma, Rizal. "Secessionist Challenge in Aceh: Problems and Prospects". In *Governance in Indonesia: Challenges Facing the Megawati Presidency,* edited by Hadi Soesastro, Anthony L. Smith, and Han Mui Ling, pp. 165–81. Singapore: Institute of Southeast Asian Studies, 2003.

———. "Security Operations in Aceh. Goals, Consequences and Lessons". Washington, D.C.: East-West-Center. <http://www.eastwestcenter.org/fileadmin/stored/pdfs/PS003.pdf>. Accessed 19 July 2007.

Sundermann, H. *Niassisch-Deutsches Wörterbuch.* [Batavia]: Bataviaasch Genootschap van Kunsten en Wetenschappen; Moers: J.W. Spaarmann, 1905.

Suraiya Kamaruzzaman. "Women and Syariah in Aceh". *Inside Indonesia* 79 (2004): 9–11.

———. "Women's Position, Role and Rights in Aceh. Women under Armed Conflict, under Syariah Law and after Tsunami". Online available at <www.susanne-schroeter.de/pdf/suraiya.ppt>, 2005.

Susilo Bambang Yudhoyono. "Opening Remarks by the President of the Republic of

Indonesia". Sixth Asian-European Editors Forum organized by Konrad Adenauer Stiftung, 29 August 2005.

Sutton, Richard Anderson. *Calling Back the Spirit. Music, Dance, and Cultural Politics in Lowland South Sulawesi.* Oxford and New York: Oxford University Press, 2002.

Suzuki, Peter T. "Niasans of the Batu Islands, Indonesia: A Known but Neglected People and Culture". *Bulletin of the International Committee on Urgent Anthropological and Ethnological Research* 12 (1970): 61–69.

Sweeney, Amin. *A Full Hearing. Orality and Literacy in the Malay World.* Berkeley: University of California Press, 1987.

Syarifudin Tippe. *Aceh di persimpangan jalan.* Jakarta: Pustaka Cidesindo, 2000.

Székely-Lulolfs, Madelon H. *Tjoet Nja Din: de geschiedenis van een Athehse vorstin.* Amsterdam: Moussault's Uitgeverij, 1948.

Szymkowiak, André. "Lernen aus der Katastrophe. Anfälligkeit und Wiederaufbau in Aceh". *Praxis Geographie* 35, no. 4 (2005): 44–47.

Tan Ngak Yong, C. "Talking about a Devolution: a Study of Center-Periphery Relations in Indonesia: The Case of Nanggroe Aceh Darussalam". Ph.D. dissertation, National University of Singapore, 2002.

Tanner, Nancy. "Matrifocality in Indonesia, Africa and among Black-Americans". In *Woman, Culture, and Society,* edited by Michelle Z. Rosaldo and Louise Lamphere, pp. 129–66. Stanford: Stanford University Press, 1974.

Tarling, Nicholas. *Piracy and Politics in the Malay World. A Study of British Imperialism in Nineteenth-Century South-East Asia.* Melbourne, Canberra: F. W. Cheshire, 1963.

Taufik Abdullah, ed. *Agama dan perubahan sosial.* Jakarta: Rajawali, 1983.

Thantawy R, Zulkifli S. Kilang, and AR Darulaman. *Lagu-lagu daerah Gayo-Aceh ciptaan Ceh Lakkiki.* Jakarta: Pamator, 1998.

Thomas, J.W. *Die Südniasser. Drei Jahre in Südnias [Allerlei Notizen von Nord- und Südnias].* [s.l.], 1886.

Tideman, Jan. *Djambi.* Mededeling / Koninklijk Instituut voor de Tropen, 42; Serie samenvattende overzichten van gewestelijke gegevens, 1. Amsterdam: Koninklijke Vereeniging "Koloniaalinstituut", 1938.

Tim Penulis. *Akar konflik manusia.* Banda Aceh: Ar-Raniry Press, 2003.

tn-63. "Album 'Dari hati untuk Aceh': kumpulkan dana untuk budaya Aceh". 22 February 2005. Accessed online at <http://www.suaramerdeka.com/harian/0502/22/bud4.htm>.

Todaro, Michael P. *Economic Development.* 5th ed. New York: Longman, 1994.

Turner, Terence. "Anthropology and Multiculturalism: What is Anthropology that Multiculturalists Should be Mindful of It". *Cultural Anthropology* 8, no. 4 (1993): 411–29.

Ujong Rimba, Haji Abdullah. *Ilmu Tharikat dan Hakikat.* Banda Aceh: [s.n.], 1975.

Ukon Ahmad Furqon. "Menguntai kemungkinan perkembangan musik tahun 2005:

Era meredupnya popularitas 'Reality Show?'". *Pikiran Rakyat*, 9 January 2005 <http://www. pikiran-rakyat.com/cetak/2005/0105/09/09.htm>.

Umaruddin. *The Ethical Philosophy of al-Ghazali*. New Delhi: Adam Publishers and Distributors, 1996.

UNESCO Indonesia. "Press Release: Rising Above the Tsunami: A Transmission of Acehnese Cultural Heritage". 12 May 2006. Accessed online at <http://www. unesco.or.id/ activities/culture/286.php>.

———. "Acehnese Cultural Event, 9 May 2006, Jakarta, Indonesia". 26 April 2006. Accessed online at <http://www.unesco.or.id/events/285.php>.

———. "Rapid Appraisal on Socio-Cultural Condition in Nangroe Aceh Darussalam". 18 May 2005. Accessed online at <http://www.unesco.or.id/activities/culture /completed/248.php>.

U.S. Department of State. "Country Report on Human Rights Practices 2004 — Indonesia". Released by the Bureau of Democracy, Human Rights, and Labor, at <http://www.state.gov/g/drl/rls/hrrpt/2004/41643.htm> (28 February 2005).

Usman Nuris. "Tharekat dalam masyarakat kecamatan Sawang Aceh Selatan". Unpublished Master thesis, IAIN Ar-Raniry, Banda Aceh, 1979.

van Bruinessen, Martin. *Tarekat Naqsyabandiyah di Indonesia: survei historis, geografis dan sosiologis*. Bandung: Mizan, 1992.

———. *Kitab kuning, pesantren dan tarekat*. Bandung: Mizan, 1995.

van den Broek, Palmer. W. F. *Aanvullende memorie betreffende de onderafdeeling Gajo Loeös*. Amsterdam: Koninklijk Instituut voor de Tropen, 1936.

van Dijk, Cornelis. *Rebellion under the banner of Islam: The Darul Islam in Indonesia*. The Hague: Nijhoff, 1981 (Verhandelingen van het Koninklijk Instituut voor Taal-, Land- en Volkenkunde; 94).

van Eijbergen, G.J. "Atjeh 'up-to-date'". *Tijdschrift voor het Binnenlandsch Bestuur* 46 (1914): 1–53.

van Koningsveld, Pieter Sjoerd. *Orientalism and Islam. The Letters of C. Snouck Hurgronje to Th. Nöldeke from the Tübingen University*. (Abdoel Ghaffaar; 1). Leiden: Rijksuniversiteit Leiden, 1985.

van Langen, Karel Frederik Hendrik. "Atjeh's Westkust met daarbij behoorende kaart". *Tijdschrift van het Nederlandsch Aardrijkskundig Genootschap*, Tweede Serie, Deel V (1888): 45–61.

Van Leur, J.C. *Indonesian Trade and Society: Essays in Asian Social and Economic History*. Selected Studies on Indonesia, no. 1. The Hague: van Hoeve, 1955.

van Niel, Robert. "Christiaan Snouck Hurgronje — In Memory of the Centennial of his Birth". *Journal of Asian Studies* 16 (1956/7): 591–94.

Van't Veer, Paul. *De Atjeh-oorloog*. Amsterdam: De Arbeiderspers, 1969.

Veth, P.J. "Vrouwenregeeringen in den Indischen archipel". *Tijdschrift voor Nederlandsch-Indie*, Derde Serie, 4de Jaargang I (1870): 354–69.

Viaro, Alain M. *Urbanisme et architecture traditionnels du sud de l'île de Nias*. Human settlements and socia-cultural environment; 21. UNESCO (s.l.), 1980.

Vogt, Rüdiger. *Gegenkulturelle Schreibweisen über Sexualität. Textstrukturen und soziale Praxis in Leserbriefen*. Wiesbaden: Deutscher Universitäts-Verlag.

Voll, John. "Muhammad Hayya al-Sindi and Muhammad ibn 'Abd al Wahhab: An Analyses of an Intellectual Group in Eighteenth Century Madina". *Bulletin of the School of Oriental and African Studies* 38, no. 1 (1975): 32–39.

Volz, Wilhelm. *Nord-Sumatra: Bericht über eine im Auftrage der Humboldt-Stiftung der Königlich-Preussischen Akademie der Wissenschaften zu Berlin in den Jahren 1904–1906 ausgeführte Forschungsreise*. 2 vols. Berlin: Reimer, 1909–12.

Voorhoeve, Petrus. *Critical Survey of Studies on the Languages of Sumatra*. Bibliographical series/Koninklijk Instituut voor Taal-, Land- en Volkenkunde, no. 1. The Hague: Nijhoff, 1955.

Voorhoeve, Petrus, ed. *Catalogue of Acehnese Manuscripts in the Library of Leiden University and other Collections outside Aceh*. Codices manuscripti/Bibliotheca Universitatis Leidensis, no. 24. Leiden: Leiden University Library, 1994.

Wensick, Arent Jan. *The Muslim Creed: Its Genesis and Historical Development*. Oriental Books Reprint Corporation, New Delhi, 1979 (originally published by University Press, Cambridge, 1932).

Wertheim, W. F. "Counter-Insurgency Research at the Turn of the Century. Snouck Hurgronje and the Acheh War". *Sociologische Gids* 19 (1972): 320–28.

Wilkinson, R.J. *An Abridged Malay-English dictionary* (Romanised). 8th ed. London: Macmillan; New York: St Martin's Press, 1961.

Wiryono, S. "The Aceh Conflict: The Long Road to Peace". *Indonesian Quarterly* 31, no. 3 (2003): 268–80.

Woltring, J., ed. *Bescheiden betreffende de Buitenlandse Politiek van Nederland, 1848–1919. Tweede periode, 1871–1898*. 's-Gravenhage: Nijhoff, 1962, 1, p. 612.

Woodward, Kenneth L. "Countless Souls Cry out to God". *Newsweek*, 3 January 2005, available online at <http://www.msnbc.msn.com/id/6777635/site/newsweek/print/1/displaymode/1098>.

World Bank. *Social Capital, Household Welfare and Poverty in Indonesia*. Written by Christiaan Grootaert. Washington, D.C.: World Bank, Social Development Department.

Yusny, Saby. "Islam and Social Change. The Role of the Ulama in Acehnese Society". Ph.D. thesis, Temple University, Philadelphia, 1995. Published as *Islam and Social Change. The Role of the Ulama in Acehnese Society*. Bangi: Penerbit Universiti Kebangsaan Malaysia, 2005.

———. "The Ulama in Aceh: A Brief Historical Survey". *Studia Islamika* 9, no. 1 (2001): 1–54.

Zentgraaff, Henri Carel. *Atjeh*. Batavia: Koninklijke Drukkerij "De Unie", 1938.

Ziegler, Arlette. "Pratiques festives et mégalithisme dans le centre de Nias". *Bulletin annuel, Musée et Institut d'Ethnographie de la ville de Genève* 18 (1985): 53–75.

INDEX

www.ingramcontent.com/pod-product-compliance
Lightning Source LLC
LaVergne TN
LVHW090301210926
848480LV00001B/97
9789814279123